EDWARD BOND

Plays: 7

Olly's Prison

Coffee

The Crime of the Twenty-First Century

The Swing

Derek

Fables and Stories

introduced by the author

Methuen Drama

METHUEN CONTEMPORARY DRAMATISTS

Published by Methuen 2003

1 3 5 7 9 10 8 6 4 2

First published in 2003 by
Methuen Publishing Limited,
215 Vauxhall Bridge Road,
London SW1V 1EJ

Introduction and collection copyright © Edward Bond 2003

Olly's Prison first published in Great Britain in 1993 by Methuen Drama,
Notes on the Imagination and *Coffee* first published in 1995 by Methuen Drama,
The Crime of the Twenty-First Century and *The Site* first published in 1999 by
Methuen Drama. *The Swing* first published as part of *A-A-America!* & *Stone*
in 1976 by Eyre Methuen Ltd, *Derek* first published by Methuen London Ltd
in 1983. *Fables and Stories* (except *A Man in Ruins*) published as part of
Summer and Fables by Methuen London Ltd in 1983; *The Dragon, The Boy Who
Threw Bread on the Water, The Boy Who Tried to Reform the Thief,
The Good Traveller, The Cheat* and *The Fly* first published by John Calder in
New Writing and Writers 19; *Service* first published in *Fireweed*.
Introduction *The Cap* copyright © by Edward Bond, 2003

Methuen Publishing Limited Reg. No. 3543167

A CIP catalogue record for this book is available from the British Library.

ISBN 0 413 77174 1

Typeset by MATS, Southend-on-Sea, Essex
Printed and bound in Great Britain by
Cox and Wyman Ltd, Reading, Berkshire

Caution

Edward Bond

Plays: 7

Olly's Prison, Coffee, The Crime of the Twenty-First Century, The Swing, Derek, Fables and Stories

Olly's Prison: An ordinary city flat. Evening. A man tries to talk to his daughter. Slowly their world turns to tragedy . . .

Coffee: A young man alone in a room. A stranger enters. Together they journey into a dark forest . . .

The Crime of the Twenty-First Century: A woman lives in a vast desert of white rubble. A tiny group of people come to seek a hiding place but instead are exposed to the fundamental questions of human drama.

Also included in this volume are *The Swing, Derek* and *Fables and Stories*.

Edward Bond was born and educated in London. His plays include *The Pope's Wedding* (Royal Court Theatre, London, 1962), *Saved* (Royal Court, 1965), *Early Morning* (Royal Court, 1968), *Lear* (Royal Court, 1971), *The Sea* (Royal Court, 1973), *The Fool* (Royal Court, 1975), are Derek *The Woman* (National Theatre, 1978), *Restoration* (Royal Court, 1981), *Summer* (National Theatre, 1982), *The War Plays* (RSC at the Barbican Pit, 1985), *In the Company of Men* (Paris, 1992; RSC at the Barbican Pit, 1996), *Tuesday* (BBC Schools TV, 1993) *At the Inland Sea* (toured by Big Brum Theatre-in-Education, 1995), *Coffee* (Rational Theatre Company, Cardiff and London, 1996; Paris, 2000), *Eleven Vests* (Birmingham, 1997), *The Crime of the Twenty-First Century* (Paris, 2001), *The Children* (Classworks, Cambridge, 2000) and *Have I None* (Birmingham, 2000); also *Olly's Prison* (BBC2 Television, 1993 first staged Berliner Ensemble 1984), and *Chair* (BBC Radio 4, 2000 first staged Paris 2003), *Existence* (BBC Radio 4, 2001 first staged Paris, 2002). His *Theatre Poems and Songs* were published in 1978 and *Poems 1978-1985* in 1987. *Selections from the Notebooks of Edward Bond* (*Volumes One and Two*) were published in 2000–1.

Contents

vi Contents

Edward Bond: A Chronology

PLAY	*First performance*
The Pope's Wedding	9.12.1962
Saved	3.11.1965
A Chaste Maid in Cheapside (*adaptation*)	13.1.1966
The Three Sisters (*translation*)	18.4.1967
Early Morning	31.3.1968
Narrow Road to the Deep North	24.6.1968
Black Mass (*part of* Sharpeville Sequence)	22.3.1970
Passion	11.4.1971
Lear	29.9.1971
The Sea	22.5.1973
Bingo: Scenes of money and death	14.11.1973
Spring Awakening (*translation*)	28.5.1974
The Fool: Scenes of bread and love	18.11.1975
Stone	8.6.1976
We Come to the River	12.7.1976
The White Devil (*adaptation*)	12.7.1976
Grandma Faust (*part one of* A-A-America!)	25.10.1976
The Swing (*part two of* A-A-America!)	22.11.1976
The Bundle: New Narrow Road to the Deep North	13.1.1978
The Woman	10.8.1978

The Cap

Notes on Drama, the Self and Society

1 Young people have no political memory. Fifty years ago social strata were obvious to children. You wore the uniform of your class. The existence of elites could not be ignored. They were chosen by birth. Attitudes to them ranged from submission to resistance. Prestige retained its privileges. Lower classes could penetrate the elite power barrier but not the elite culture barrier. That could be penetrated only by a second or third generation.

2 Working class consciousness understood political power but not cultural power. It created an alternative working class culture. This had to do with survival – emotional, psychological. It was ghettoising and self-repressive. It could combine prudery with prurience, sentimentality with vindictiveness. Working class culture was not able to understand itself. Culture must be a structure of meanings of the world which also understands itself as part of those meanings: it must itself be the means of interrogating and understanding itself. Otherwise it reifies a static or catastrophic interpretation of the world and is sterile. A culture which is a means of survival is not a culture of change. Ultimately, as situations inevitably change it is repressive and destructive.

3 Power loses its prestige and hegemonic mystique as it loses its privacy. We live in a culturally open society. The elite power barrier is broken. The elite culture is assumed to be empty. This is because it was sustained more by power than self-understanding. Ultimately it was not creative. Its practice was of necessity material but its understanding was transcendental. Both cultures – working class and elite – had become unprogressive because they could no longer use themselves to understand themselves in a way which logically related them to social structure and the natural world. In this they were like human consciousness, which historically does not understand itself. If it did consciousness would become culture. Life would be based on a structure of skills and practices and not, as it is now, on a structure made unstable by inconsistent meanings that are both emancipating and repressive.

4   There are three negative solutions to this lack of self-understanding:

a)   Violence. Authority forcefully imposes its organisational requirements.

b)   Transcendentalism. Really this is the 'ownership of Nothingness'. Historically social authority owned Nothingness and gave it its meaning and used it as the source of meaning. All transcendentalism is madness, either clinical madness, which renders the mad incapable of social living, or social madness which enables the personally sane to live in unjust society.

c)   Somnambulism – the philosophy that culture develops without perspicacious thought, that it is only when we arrive that we know where we have been going, that material reality manufactures humanness and that humanness does not create itself. Transcendentalism is really a form of *vulgar* materialism, with human consciousness replaced by cosmic iron vapourisings (which are inscribed in Nothingness).

5   As these solutions are negative they cannot describe the future except abstractly (good, bad, scientific, irrational) or metaphorically (heaven, where angels have wings and God has a garden but is also the landlord of hell). These explanations are not extrapolations from the present but static projections of it. A culture must also be a mark of what we do not *yet* know. Then how can it interpret itself without misinterpreting human relations to the social and natural worlds? In the past it was not necessary to answer this question because authoritarian violence and transcendentalism (the ownership of Nothingness) could regulate (and through ideology, integrate) the dislocations between culture and natural reality, and because the individual was seen as an 'element in society' but society was not seen as a 'presence in the individual' – the latter role was assigned to Nothingness: the individual's essence was a soul, or the mystical participation in the tribe or (later) patria or race. The individual was to maintain society not change it. The mind was the reflection of Ideology and so the site of violence.

6   The ownership of Nothingness

Whoever owns Nothingness owns the individual by means of social madness: that is, the individual is possessed by Nothingness, or rather by the violent phantoms that make power real. (The clinically mad are owned, possessed by their madness. At least this gives them a certain innocence and security – they are not required to vote or become soldiers and may be spared some legal punishments – and though their existential anguish is more immediate, it may be less severe: the history of society shows that in the end the sane suffer more than the insane. If we were clear sighted enough and free to act only selfishly, no doubt we would all choose to go mad in the clinical not the respectable, good-citizenship sense.) The human mind is total and holistic. For the hand to perform complex skills the thumb is opposable. In order to relate to the 'infinite' vicissitudes and chances of existence the mind is self-reflexive. It is free within material limits – it cannot escape from the presence, awareness, of space and time, for instance. Mystical experiences are corruptions of reality not transcendences of it. But otherwise mind is infinite in its reflexivity. This is the site of imagination – and the self is a creation of imagination: otherwise it could not relate to Nothingness. All the phenomena which are said to be extracted from Nothingness are so multifarious and mutable that, although Empires may be built on them, they are like iron that may rust overnight. This is the instability inherent in ideology and social madness. Because of the mind's reflexivity I may ask what is unseen round the corner. This is an act of reason which invokes imagination. And so I *must* ask what is beyond the world revealed by the categories of the mind. *Must*

because it is a corner in consciousness. This is the site of
Nothingness. It becomes a social site because I cannot 'go
round this corner'. I need the authoritative report of those
who may. But Nothingness is also in me. And so society enters
into me through Nothingness just as it does through the skills
and practices in which I take part in objective reality. Society
is schizophrenic: it says I am 'here' but also 'round the corner'
– and the significance of this is revealed in the popular saying
'round the bend'. Ideology asserts what is round the corner –
what is in Nothingness – and this is the origin of social
madness. Beyond reality there is *nothing*, but society turns this
into the prestigious and potent *Nothingness*. Really there are no
corners in the universe. And if God happened to live in a flat
down the road society would have to create a God beyond
God. Nothingness is an infinity but it has 'presences' in human
reality which the cognitive categories do not delimit: such as
night, darkness, death – and so birth – chaos, madness, the
uncanny, the supernatural. And there are places which
Nothingness seems to shadow: prisons, the scenes of crime,
titanic nature (the awesome, the absence of social description)
– and in fact many of these places are the sites of events which
have their ideological cause in Nothingness: the sites of
massacres, battles and individual despair. In an obvious sense
the site of Nothingness is the site of everything, and so
whoever owns Nothingness owns everything: the state (or if
you like, culture) owns God and 'the world is the Lord's and
the fulness thereof'. If the mind tries to imagine Nothingness it
axiomatically imagines a place and time to put it in: a place at
which Lucretius's spear-thrower may aim. Common sense
imagines there must be a place for the universe to be in and a
beginning and end of time which (uncommonsensically) are in
time and so must be in Nothingness (or Nothingness must be
in time) . . . That is why authority always prescribes
Nothingness as the 'site' of eternity and infinity: which is a way
of shutting the door on questioning sceptics.

   Suppose that fifty thousand years ago I famished in a
drought. I must grow food. My skill at making and using a hoe
does not help me because the earth is dust: and *dearth* is the
shadow of death, which is the realm of Nothingness. To seek to

persuade Nothingness to send rain I sacrifice my child to it –
the child is all of value I have left. Next I *need* priests or
shamans who understand and can commune with
Nothingness. Now as well as a practical administering
authority I need sacerdotal authority. Nothingness becomes
the site of ideology, the way in which society is owned. On this
level, to own society you must own the world. The power of
Nothingness is awesome, it has killed hecatombs and done it
without its owners soiling their hands.

7   Nothingness is the site of imagination

We are not determined by a soul. Or by genes, except within
narrow physical limits. Genes may give me blue eyes, cause
my early death and in a society which has alcohol make me an
alcoholic. Even then, genes are causal epigenetically – it is the
random combination of genes and their possessor's social
experience which may be determinant. The self is an infinity –
it *is* its openness to possibility. It is a gap – which is the site of
imagination, just as Nothingness is the site of Someness. And
therefore imagination is a reality and in the material world,
not in the transcendental. It is a reality co-existent, co-equal,
with physical reality. A chair exists for a cat physically, but for
a human it must exist physically *and* with a meaning –
ultimately the meaning which is given to Nothingness. Isn't
the meaning of a chair that I can sit in it? The chair belongs to
the class of chairs and relates to a cultural series: electric chair,
throne, hot seat, grandmother's chair, parlour, cottage,
hostage-tied-in-chair, Van Gogh's chair – the chair relates to
wider social meanings. Ultimately these are the meanings
given to Nothingness, and I am part of this meaning. There
are clear differences between these two 'realities' and so the
point seems incoherent, like talking of two centres to a circle.
But in humanness neither reality exists without the other and
each affects the other. Ultimately the physical world is the
cause of that which passes in the 'gap' world, the site of
imagination is the *effect*. But this is not always immediately so,
and in ideology the time-lag may be long. The social and
psychological world are riven by practical and cultural
tensions. We have to reject all forms of natural determinism,

except within the banality of our physical limitations: but even a giant is a dwarf when he meets a colossus. Genetic determination is simply the counter-image of the transcendental. Authority takes Nothingness as the site of determination. For example, on Judgement Day God decides what we are, have been and will be; or Nothingness is the site on which the evil we do in our present life turns us into a snake or dog in our next life; or Nothingness is the mystical site of my country, which determines my treachery or faith. I might not feel guilt at massacring the innocent. Nothingness may determine that it is my patriotic duty to massacre them. If I starve in an unjust society should I feel guilt if I steal food? Should I feel guilt because the law (ideologically founded in Nothingness) finds me guilty? The two guilts may have nothing in common.

   Nothingness is the site of imagination and also of Someness. There cannot be anything in imagination which is not first in Someness. The two share the same entities but imagination combines them in new ways to create new meanings. Nothingness's infinity (like the mind's) makes it protean and infinitely adaptable. Because Nothingness can be inhabited only by the imagination, Nothingness also shares in creativity. Creativity cannot be completely erased from imagination, because imagination creates the self which is the site of human creativity. All human value comes from the imagination. The natural world is too impoverished and inert to bear the burden of human value. I practically work so that I can practically live – but what do I live for? For humans all things have some meaning beyond practicality. In humanness – that is, for humans – all things pass through the sieve of Nothingness to find their meanings. In ideology this process is ultimately bad, in imagination it is potentially good. Anything might be an evidence of God, a fragment of my *patria*, a sacred object, an heirloom, a remembrance and so on. This means that they are all objects in my imagination. If I have a scarf that belonged to my dead parent, it might seem obvious that I attach sentimental value to it. It is not obvious. The value is in me and I cathect the object with it. But surely I am attached to this child *because* it is mine? But if I sacrifice the child for my country or faith? What if a mother kills her child? Must a woman first imagine *motherhood* before she loves her child? Is this on the boundary of determinism, does the neonate signal dependency to adults? Even that – if genetic – must be recreated in imagination. And if something is in imagination it is in – floats on – Nothingness, and so is vulnerable to ideological changes in Nothingness. I sacrifice my child to my country *because* the child is precious to me? We are entangled between the two realities and this causes the torments of the struggle to be human. You can see, already, the purpose of drama – it is created by imagination to save itself from the power of Nothingness and release itself into the freedom of its own creativity.

8 If imagination (which is the origin of humanness) is not determined, is it arbitrary – 'imaginary' in the conventional misunderstanding? Imagination is logical. Its logic has two parts.

a) It must relate us to our practical life and enable us economically and technologically to sustain our life in society. But why don't we just murder our competitors? Why don't the strong take what they can and the weak give what they must? Are we restrained by fear? No, because:

b) Imagination expresses human value. It is easy to understand how imagination expresses some of reality's meanings, for instance that I fear a snake in imagination as well as in reality. But how is imagination the site of not just the *desire* for justice but – when related to a) the site of the *need* for it? These notes are intended to explain not just how the relation between a) and b) concerns drama – but also how drama expresses b). And how, because of that, though the *desire* is psychological, the *need* is ontological. This means that drama is the logic of humanness.

9 <u>Imagination is a form of materialism</u>
We see and practise all things in two realities: physical reality and imagination. They always interrelate. Practical meanings come from the first reality, human value comes only from the second. The site (but not the source) of human meanings (that is, practical meaning combined with value) is Nothingness.

Nothingness has a twofold presence in human reality: as
ideology and in the intrusion of the negative (mortality,
vulnerability, chance and their attenuation in the
psychological symbols of night, darkness, the uncanny and
so forth) into everyday practical reality. For this reason, the
functioning mind must have a 'theory of the Tragic', just as
it must have a 'theory of other minds'. Humanness is the
integration of the two realities – the skills of living in the
physical world and the creativity that comes from the second
world. Imagination is not the site of an 'essence of goodness',
or a 'soul', because the meanings in imagination are
designated by the relations between the two worlds and the
effective meanings in imagination may be corrupted by
ideology. Society mediates the relationship between the two
worlds, and hitherto society is unjust and limited in reason.
In materialism, the difference between the interactions of
physical objects and human behaviour lies in imagination.
Because of the mind's infinity and because we are in society,
we relate to the physical world (even its practicality) through
imagination. The point is: because imagination's site is
Nothingness, humanness is potential freedom. Our situation
does not have the genetic determination of biology but the
logical creativity of imagination.

10   The logic of imagination

If in the past people were to survive with an optimistic ethos,
imagination had to sufficiently meet the requirements given in
paragraph 8a) and b). 8b) is immensely complicated. For
instance, 'to live' might mean 'to die'. Nothingness defined
even death by creating immortality – and you might gain this
by martyrdom *pro patria*. Human behaviour is either
determined or dialectical, as when choices are made of various
ends. The *logic of the situation* is this: as technological (tools,
machines, scientific knowledge) relations to the natural world
changed, so the organisation of society (as part of the natural
world) changed – and so ideology, the lived meaning and ends
of society, changed. The *logic of imagination* is this: it interpreted
the world according to the changed situation. Unlike
Agamemnon I do not have to kill my daughter to influence a

goddess. As machines become more efficient I do not need slaves. The ancient slave was a human-donkey without obligations. The medieval serf had obligations (founded in faith) to his feudal lord. So imagination becomes progressively more human: which means, to recognise the humanness of others. But ideology is not logical, it tries to write the propositions of reason on paper which heaves and chops like the sea: what it writes comes out in distortions. This is because its determining concern is performance. In unjust society this means misinterpreting the consequences (in imagination and so behaviour) of injustice – performance is then synonymous with maintaining injustice. All ideology is dark. It is easy for technologically advanced societies to be irrational – to designate 'sub-humans', or 'the uncultured', or the genetically retardative. Social injustice is ideologically justified in this way. There is a gap between the possible and actual. There is a gap between the situation and the ideological interpretation of it. If we were the products of *vulgar* materialism this would not be so, as we became technologically more efficient we would automatically have become more human. We may not – as the enlightenment fades we could decline into barbarism. It is not enough for drama to know that this is so, it must know why it is so. The site of drama is not the 'what', it is always the 'why'.

11   Ideology rationalises the human situation, but it is the source of the irrational. Its irrationality derives from the abuse of Nothingness. Nothingness is the ground of our freedom, but natural disasters, epidemics, crime, economic fluctuations – such things create fear which in unjust societies leads to personal and social panic and breakdown. These compound themselves and lead to deeper corruption of the imagination, to the apathy, despair, rage and vengeance of social madness. And in the end ideology gathers this laxity and rigidity into the madness of fascism.

12   Practicality (as described at 8a) above) is determined. This brings with it a creative 'determination', i.e. that of which creativity must take account. Creativity itself is not determined (ultimately it seeks only the world home). Is the individual free? Only within two restraints:

a)   The limits to understanding imposed by ideology. A soldier 'willingly' fighting in World War One does not do so freely even if he fights with the same conviction that corporal Hitler did. The soldier's world is misdescribed by ideology. Even if he fights he may do so without conviction – ideology will have been embodied in the attitudes and behaviour of other soldiers and of civilians. Ideology's pressure will be tangible. Violence always shadows ideology. In this case the shadow is the firing squad at dawn.

b) The situation at the site. In a fire or earthquake there is a stampede. It sweeps me along with it although I might wish to return to the fire to rescue someone. This takes the form: My vote is useless, my act is lost in the multitude. I may be powerless at the site even if free in the sense of 12a) above. 12a) concerns Nothingness, 12b) concerns Someness. There is also the real limitation of knowledge. Alexander believed there was ocean where in fact there is India. But knowledge generalises itself. If I have the technology to build a vehicle to take me to the moon I will not take a cheese cutter with me because I believe the moon is made of cheese. But Newton worked out the general consistencies of the universe yet as a creationist spent much of his energy on alchemy – on a game of Nothingness. Theoretical and even practical knowledge does not (*pace vulgar* materialism) lead to the creative logic of humanness. SS scientists used Nazi camps as laboratories. As all this is so, we can say that when on 7 January 1660 Galileo saw through a telescope the moons of Saturn, Auschwitz became inevitable. Intellectual and technological discoveries are made in societies, within the limitations of ideology. Marx describes 'sight' not as biological but as socially encultured. An age of technology thinks of knowledge as hard-edged, as self-validating. It is not. Reason does not – cannot – think except tautologically. Reasoning does not conform to the consistencies of evolution. A mathematical truth is true in all instances. Whether it relates to phenomena in earth, water, air or mind it is categorically true – but not dialectically true. The logic of imagination is evolutionary and dialectical. It is created, not discovered or learnt. Humanness is not linear but profoundly dialectical. A rational truth *creates* nothing, and if society uses it creatively it will involve Nothingness and its dangers. An evolutionary event may occur without human involvement (and involve only Someness). But a creative act or perception must involve imagination and Nothingness. Nietzsche said 'live dangerously'. Do we have a choice?

13 Why must we talk of Nothingness instead of 'ignorance' or 'the unknown'? Nothingness is not negative but positive. It must be so for ideology (and not mere violence) to be possible. Really, Nothingness is 'lies' but in the complex paradoxes of humanness it may also contain truths. We are not simply complex embodiments of Someness, we carry Nothingness with us in our mortality and vulnerability. Nothingness gives us the possibility of creativeness, of choice and freedom. Imagination is logical but not categorical – and so makes Nothingness its site. Without Nothingness we could not be human. Van Gogh said that few painters knew the terror of the white canvas (we may add: no painters except those as creative as Van Gogh, but many painters use art to escape from imagination). That is an image of uninscribed Nothingness. Van Gogh indicates the basic problem. Art is also a skill and we like to think that a skill is humanising, belongs to the art of being human: that Homo Faber is synonymous with Homo Sapiens.

What is sapience? I admire the brick-laying skill used to build a gas chamber. We take this skill for granted but it is of enormous signifiance in the universe because it delays entropy. I admire the technological ingenuity in a complicated torture instrument. A skill may humanise only at a delay, when its use has passed through the sieve of Nothingness, which for a time may make the use of the skill dehumanising. Technological use is not the same as social use. Nothingness is an abstraction and so has no logic. It is the *use* of Nothingness which (in the final analysis) is logical and (in the short term, also) has logical consequences. Brick-laying a gas chamber might in the final analysis lead to humanness. Certainly the Final Solution led to a deeper understanding of Nazism. In the short term it was barbarism. Now we have technological means to destroy the social world, as if we could put the whole human race into one

gas chamber. More probably we would use technology to
dehumanise ourselves, to solve our paradox instrumentally.
We would become the apparatchiki of Nothingness. (This is
the problem of The Faustian Trap, analysed in *The Hidden
Plot*.) Civilisation is not a straight road but an obstacle course.
Many people might not be conceptually aware of these
dangers, but they act them out in the apprehensions of their
daily life.

14   We have to talk of positive Nothingness because of the
nature of the human mind. I will summarise what I have
written elsewhere about the neonate, infant and maturing
child. When does the brain become a mind? This must be the
occasion which initiates self-consciousness. The brain becomes
aware and so becomes a mind. This makes humanness
possible. Only humans have a self. Other animals are sentient
but are not 'sentient they are sentient'. I say 'not sentient' of
this, and not merely unknowing of it, because it has
consequences in imagination. If it were not so then, say, if I
were ill, for me it would be painful – but it would not be
tragic, not concerning for me because of my mortality, my
dependants and so forth. I have not used the word 'emotion'
because creativity is not based on emotion or feeling, or
derived from them (though it may be provoked by or end in
them) but is an idea, derived from an interpretation which
gives meaning. The moment when the brain becomes a mind
is the foundation of humanness. The neonate is *in extremis*, that
is why it struggles and cries. Imagine the shock if you suddenly
found yourself in deep space without knowing how you came
to be there. Or if you died and then found you were still alive
(the shock would be enough to kill you). What bystanders
think of as the neonate's 'arrival', it 'thinks' of, knows as, a
loss. To arrive in the world you lose the ground under your
feet and the sky over your head. Even this is an adult's way of
describing it. To the neonate it is more extreme. The neonate
'knows' it is somewhere – the brain is cognisant of Someness,
but it does not know it has a body *or* that there is a mind –
body problem. That comes with developed consciousness.

   We have to understand the situation of the brain cognising,

and cognising that it is cognising: so that 'consciousness
exists'. Then it must exist before there is a self, that is before
(self-)consciousness. This does not depend on genetic-
biological brain function (except as sea waves depend on the
existence of water) – it is an activity of consciousness, it is
consciousness *itself*, and so it must create a self (which is at the
lowest level, events in consciousness) just as the brain, if it were
a physical object outside the head, would throw a shadow.
The neonate's mind takes the world into itself and so is
conscious that it is in the world. You can tell a child to be
quiet. You cannot tell a neonate not to be conscious that it is
conscious. The act of awareness must create a self, provided
there is a memory to receive the self, and the biological brain
provides this. But at this stage the mind cannot distinguish
between the world and self. The body might be part of the
world or all the world, or the mind might be the world's mind.
All that is sure is that there is a conscious mind – not a
separate world. It is axiomatic to this mind that it has a right
to be. I do not see that this conclusion can be mistaken. The
right is synonymous with the act of consciousness and does not
need a differentiated act. It is axiomatic to consciousness that
it has a right to *be* (in the world, to be itself). All that is
inappropriate here is the word 'right', which is an adult
definition of what the neonate knows. What the neonate
knows is nearer to what is called morality than to law. At the
moment which creates the mind and its relation to the world,
'is' and 'ought' are the same – 'is *is* ought'. This is part of the
mind's coherence and if it were not so the mind would vanish
back into the brain. It is important to note this self-revealing
right because it is the origin of the later need for justice. A
physical object needs no 'right to be'. But consciousness – that
is, the self – *is* the right to be conscious – this is inherent in the
fact that consciousness is *conscious* that it is conscious: the right
exists in the italicised word. An animal is without the italics.
The italics mark the node of our humanness, the origin of our
freedom and repressiveness. History, humanness, tragedy,
Nothingness are all derived from the italics.

How is the adult word 'right' extrapolated from the
neonate's 'is-ought'? If the brain is to contain its own tensions,

and the tensions it gives rise to through consciousness, and the tensions that rise from the double system (the mind may make the brain dysfunction, and vice versa) – then the problem becomes psychological and not ontological. If the mind cannot bear its site it can only vanish into unconsciousness. In effect the mind would erase *its* self. Adults can retreat from the unbearable into madness, and children and adults into delinquency. The unbearable contradictions may be acted out in the world – really, on a deep level of drama, as if the imagination were creating the world differently, and these are the poetics of madness and crime. They are sophisticated mental processes.Ultimately they are ways of searching for sanity and justice. But the neonate mind has nowhere to go, has no character or culture to manipulate and hide in or recreate. It might pass through trauma back into the brain. Instead, if it survives, it *enters* the Nothingness which contradicts its right to be in the world. An adult would flee but this requires an elsewhere. The neonate cannot flee because it *is* the world for it there is no elsewhere, and so it is also its own Nothingness. That is why the neonate needs a 'theory of Tragedy'. This encounter is part of the origin of humanness. When the neonate enters Nothingness its right to be is not erased but strengthened. It has a right to enter Nothingness. It enters it sanely. To most adult understanding – and experience – to enter it is to become mad. Adults may enter it consciously and coherently only in drama. For the neonate Someness is not so abundant that it obscures Nothingness or can be the screen on which ideology is displayed. The neonate faces Nothingness in its pristine state, without its cultural violence or mystification. Nor is the neonate a tap that is turned on and off by the need for food or comfort. Even that sort of deprivation must be generalised in its imagination, even at that level deprivation must become existential Nothingness. The neonate's anxieties are creative, most later anxieties are not – because our culture cannot contain them as expressions of itself, as part of its explanation of itself. The Greeks could. Marx said that Greek art represented the childhood of humankind, that it had an innocence that might not be recaptured. Really, when the Greeks became conscious of humanness they sought to de-ideologise Nothingness. Later, because of their historical limitations, ideology re-blurred the encounter. But we are concerned with what they did, not what they thought they did. Humanness can proceed only through paradox, know truth only in the ghetto of lies. Greek drama was an anti-religious rite staged by priests. It invoked its gods to show that humankind stands alone. Ultimately tragedy is cultural not ontological. The universe – time and space – is indifferent to our understanding of anything at all. For the Greeks the encounter with Nothingness belonged to human freedom and the Promethean joy of radical innocence. That is what Greek art shows. It is why the Greeks created tragedy.

15   The neonate's creation of its self makes it susceptible to the later ideological use of Nothingness. For instance, because a child cannot intellectually understand the natural world, it (with adult encouragement) anthropomorphises it. Animals and trees talk, storm and wind are angry, the chair groans. These 'beings' are arranged into stories which provide meanings. A story is a form of philosophy. It involves imagination and so it involves the self – that which first sought meaning, an existential relation to the world. Usually the story reveals a secret – unveils part of Nothingness. The originating search for meaning – the original encounter with, between, Someness and Nothingness which creates the self – may become lost under complex, baffling layers of experience, exegesis, learning – all distorted by ideology. In the end the self may have the triviality of an anecdote but the import of a tragedy. Ideology makes a sort of social life possible but trivialises it. The self loses itself. Drama is not a form of psychoanalysis, which is concerned with the individual's vicissitudes. If drama were that, each member of the audience would need a different play. Drama is concerned with the need for understanding, which means understanding the present situation. Drama takes place on the contemporary site, but it must relate to the original *need* to be a self, to the 'right to be' and all that followed from this.

16   The radicalness of the neonate
The neonate is radically innocent. It has no concept of right

and wrong, only of Someness and Nothingness. As it grows, its
right to be, which is structural in the mind, encounters
conflicts. It no longer *is* the world, it must share it with others.
The child's behaviour springs from innocence because its right
to be is for it paramount. Later it is tempered by experience.
The self is a relationship to the world – it is not simply that the
child may choose to behave so that it lives harmoniously with
the world: the child and later the adult *is* the relationship. The
child acquires a character: the habitual expectations of its
relationship to the world. And because self *is* this relationship
to the world, the child's self – and later the adult's – is a
habitude. The relationship to the world is reciprocal, because
the world is not passive – that is, is not totally enterable as it
was for the neonate. For the neonate Nothingness is a theatre
of drama – for the adult ideology may make Nothingness a
prison which encloses the whole world: then the self is the cell
and the conduct of others is the institutionalised behaviour of
prisoners going about their affairs in a prison drama. All
drama is on the site of the habitude – in effect, the self, society
and the wider, ontological, world. In drama the self seeks the
meaning of things, but as it is itself part of its habitude it
cannot do this in freedom, intellectually, by pure thought. It
would be like being able to see the back of your neck. The
individual is in the situation, not free to observe it, but part of
it. Only drama is the mirror in which the Medusa-self can see
its face.

17 Freedom
The individual is not part of the situation in the sense that
each tessera is part of a mosaic. Within the situation, binding
it together, there is Nothingness and the self-creating self.
Nothingness is fluid, mutable (because knowledge, technology
and social organisation change) as well as draconian, rigid,
linear, imprisoning (through ideology and the ownership of
society). The origin of the self is in its right to be and that the
world should be its home. All later meanings are
developments, often contortions, of this. The child's
imagination makes a bond with the world, and this is totally
real for the child, real from within. This is the origin of the

need for justice, which supersedes all other incidental needs because it is synonymous with the right to be. If this were not so we would remain egotists, incapable of the altruism which may even prompt us to die for others. The neonate's world is Promethean and tragic. Prometheus knew the fate of Zeus (God), and Zeus (God) did not – so Prometheus and not Nothingness (God – because Zeus is the ideology of Nothingness) is the meaning of the world.

As the child becomes intellectualised, the initial meaning (in which the self is synonymous with justice, and imagination is the means of knowing this) is extended into the complexities of the world and in particular of society. Then social ideology decrees the meaning of the world. The original human meaning – the need for justice which is synonymous with the self-creating self – may always be returned to unless it is reduced to the chaos of clinical madness. The story, or rather *storiness*, may be found under the accumulation of anecdote and violence produced by ideology. The original need is radical innocence, so that the world should be innocent so that it might be a home. The world is made innocent only through the understanding of Tragedy and the child makes the tragic innocent by entering it. But society is not innocent, it is unjust. Ideology justifies its injustice. And so the self's need for justice becomes the need to act injustly, to take revenge on the crime of innocence. That is why dictators, reactionaries, do not say they act injustly but for the common good, to make the world the human home. That is the paradox of humanness. The paradox must not be reduced to determinism (the innate need to aggress, original sin, socio-biology, social-Darwinism) but must be understood because the human future depends on understanding it.

18   Imagination cannot be taught

This is because you cannot talk sanity to a madman or stage a drama that would convert Hitler to socialism. Because unjust society depends on understanding (within the confines of the lie-ghetto) injustice as justice, the paradox is always already there, prepared and waiting: so Hitler would say it was because he was the *real* socialist that he called his politics

National-Socialism. Each day we live with similar contortions of the paradox. That is why theatre does not teach. To change the individual's habitude, to make society more just, it must *create*. This cannot be reduced to reasoning because the habitude is held in the vice of ideology. The encultured participant in injustice *is* his or her ideology.

19   The self's contortions (1)

It is said that evil is banal. It should also be said that if the self is not radically innocent it is an anecdote. Or rather, the common sense self is an accumulation of anecdotes, one triviality confirming another, and italicised by violence when confirmation fails. The self is an anecdote unless it can be returned to the first Nothingness, see common sense vanish, and be confronted with the responsibility of innocence.

Ideology has these two main supports:

a)   The initial human state passed on by the neonate to the adult. This makes the adult mind apprehensive and receptive of anthropomorphism and ideology. The neonate is not apprehensive because it interprets the tragic as being innocent. The neonate dramatises itself, is the author of itself, and creates its (the) world. The author of a suspense novel is not apprehensive because he or she knows the plot. An author's suspense comes not from what is created but from the act of creation itself, it is Van Gogh's terror, the approach to Nothingness which exactly reverses the noumenal routes of birth and death. It is as if, to survive, the neonate made Nothingness and Something part of itself. The self possesses them by situating them in the world.

b) Historically people have been in economic and social need. This negativity reflects Nothingness. Ideology organises society and gives a meaning to the self so that need may be met. That is why except in extreme crisis ideology must contain the human good – truth exists in the lie-ghetto. Ideology is repressive, punitive and revengeful, but it must articulate the need for justice. Justice is not an essence or fixed state of affairs. It is the way in which the need to seek justice may be met in existing conditions. Justice is the world home – and because that must be sought by each individual (no doubt forming approximate bands of generations), the seeking for justice is permanent, innate, in the human condition. As a species we cannot grow old, though we can destroy ourselves. Humanness is as young as Blake's Glad Day. The seeking for justice is ahistorical but can be expressed only in historical forms. The creative evidence of humanness changes historically. The belief in a God is not always evidenced in the same way, as if God were an essence. The Greeks' belief in Zeus and other deities, and their later deanthropomorphisation (but mystification into Platonic Forms) produced in the Greek imagination the Parthenon and tragic drama, and doing this enabled them to create the first democracy and what we understand as politics. But the Greek lie-ghetto also promoted slavery. The medieval Christians' belief in God (and the godlings in the Christian heaven) produced in their imagination Gothic cathedrals, Western art, scholasticism and the rudiments of science. They also burnt heretics and waged crusades. The sites of the two cultures were different but the human imperative was common to both.

20 The self's contortions (2)

Innocence seeks justice, the world home. So the individual must act to create justice. Many of the acts ideology requires make the world dangerous, destructive, antagonistic, more unjust. The ideologised individual is split: the world is not his or her home but the enemy's home. This leads to fear and then the need for justice becomes the desire for revenge, the need to create becomes the necessity to destroy. This is not an innate need for aggression. The meaning ideology gives to the world provokes aggression, the natural capacity for aggression becomes the institutional need – psychological and chronic – for revenge. The greater the aggression, the more it is justified by the conditions it creates. The need for revenge can never be satisfied because however many victims fall to it, it cannot make the world just and innocent. There are social institutions for exploiting this aggression and the existential guilt that goes with it: scapegoats, delinquents, aliens. Revenge could only be satisfied when it had made the world an image of Nothingness.

Ideologically, even death does not satisfy the need for revenge, that is why the returning unquiet dead are called *ghosts*. Ghosts wear the shroud of Nothingness. (Visionaries never say they see the ghosts of dead saints, they see the saints themselves. This is because saints do not seek revenge, and so they return not as Nothingness but as ideologised Embodiments of Justice. This creates a problem for the Holy Ghost, who is obviously a contradiction in terms. Theologians helpfully explain this by reminding us that as the Holy Ghost was never born he did not have a body in the first place.) Justice, like revenge, can never be fully accomplished, but for a different reason: the infinite subtling of human relations. Society's Law and Law Courts do not give justice. It is not even their role to give it, they give only administration (which may be more bearable or less bearable). Justice is far too subtle to be given by the Law. Justice means understanding the reasons for crime, but the Courts cannot even understand the motives for it. Only drama can give justice, by laying bare the need for it. Only a self-understanding society can understand that. Really, Auschwitz is an anecdote, the site of human triviality. And social Law is anecdotal and banal – the threadbare, unhoused tragedy of newspapers.

21   The self's contortions (3)

Historically ideology had to contain the human good. This meant meeting economic and social needs. So, meeting needs was involved in the search for justice and was not always a sign of egotism, selfishness, greed and so forth. It's as if by expressing elements of human goodness, ideology relieved its believers of part of their self-responsibility. Society took responsibility for justice, spoke with God's mandate, fought the sinner and the human animal. This created a host of complexities. We each fit into society in individual ways, our biographies cross-hatch with the general determinations of social being. Each of us is dialectical in relation to the site, the habitude is specific and general: all fish swim but not all fish swim in one direction. Given that, the way needs were met was not simply a way of meeting physical needs but of expressing the human need for justice, so meeting needs was the way we created humanness. That is the logic of imagination, the logic of the relation between individual and society. That structure is now breaking down. Instead of *needs* we have *wants*.

22   For the first time in history ideology seeks to withdraw from Nothingness and instead to insinuate itself into Someness. It is as if the relationship between Nothingness and Someness were being reversed. This happens because *wants* replace *needs*. Fulfilling needs in relation to ideology (both its positive and negative aspects) enabled us to follow the logic of humanness. The necessity to meet needs provided a logical relationship between state and society, and this created a community fulfilling its needs. The fulfillment of a need satisfies the need. A want is not fulfillable because it extends itself into other wants. It is structurally like revenge, it is unfulfillable. Wants are not fulfilled, they are consumed – and the never-ending construction of further wants is an act of revenge on the deepest structures of humanness. That is the malaise of modern society. We take revenge on ourselves for being human. It is as if civilisation were caught up in a film running itself backwards.

The number and variety of rooms I can inhabit, meals I can consume and clothes I can wear is limited. Yet wants lead to other wants. This is psychologically so because they do not meet the original need of the self to be at home in the world by making it more just. So modern consumption is chaotic. At first it seems bizarre that the structural logic which created humanness has now moved elsewhere: it is now the economy that has a *need* – the need to make profit. Really it is not bizarre, it is a consequence of the logic of evolution and a warning that evolution could abandon humanness altogether and both exponentiate and precision itself elswhere: we would be caught in the Faustian Trap. To sustain the economy that creates wants – to meet the *need* for profit – new wants constantly must be manufactured. The logic of meeting human needs is the creation of living humanness, and this is structured in community. The consequence of manufacturing wants is the manufacture of 'life styles', which are not satisfying or humanising. You might as well say that light that came through a Nazi lampshade made of human skin at least helped you see better.

A society which is not a community seeking justice must become vengeful and punitive in order to control the chaos it creates. Modern consumer society is trapped in ancient paradoxes. One of these is that ultimately crimes are the criminal's means of seeking justice, not in the conformist masochist sense (in which, because it is less terrifying, seeking punishment replaces seeking justice) but because in an unjust society a crime is itself an act of justice, an assertion of the criminal's right to be at home in the world. That paradox is far beyond administration's understanding, but it is a commonplace of the dramas which history has made classics. The more we have of what we want, the less we have of what we need. This is not an argument for asceticism, or that hunger and want are good for you. They are not. But it means that we can only socially have the benefits of science and technology when we understand ourselves, and that means understanding the drama of our situation.

23   The consumer is famous

Every consumer shares in the glory of the famous. Fame becomes a possibility which every consumer anticipates. In the past the repressed saw themselves reflected in the repression of those around them. The presence of repression was ubiquitous, even in the ebullience of working-class culture. Now the barrier between classes is reduced to money, any winner might become a millionaire or, perhaps soon, a billionaire. Now on TV people see themselves reflected in famous idols, or as ordinary holiday-makers and shoppers and prize-winners already taking part in the rainbow world of the famous. This (for the sake of completeness and to reflect distant memory of the self's vulnerability) is shadowed by disaster movies and hospital dramas and above all police dramas which instead of struggling like the Greeks to define innocence seek only revenge on scapegoats. Nothingness is no longer inscribed with the old idols – iconoclasm is sudden and ruthless. Now Nothingness itself appears in daily life, infiltrates it like black smuts from the bonfire which burns the past. And so young people live in a paradox: on the one hand there is *joie de vivre* and on the other *joie de mourir*. Between these two extremes there is no conceptual or practical understanding of life. The possibilities open to the young would have fulfilled their ancestors' aspirations – but unlike the aspirations, the possibilities do not have in them the chance of a better society. As more and more consumption less and less meets the self's need for justice, society degenerates. Even despair becomes inarticulate. Soon the ultimate banalities will be reached. A company will provide a take-away suicide service.

24   New faiths posture in Nothingness: genetic determinism, New Ageism, Esoteric rituals and cults. Old faiths become fanatic, chiliastic or apocalyptic. An incipient barbarism is replacing the Enlightenment. Theatre is rational but the young are told to seek its 'spiritual dimension'. Spirituality used to be inscribed on Nothingness – now the global market uses it as a billboard for its garish advertisements. Imagination is plundered to provide ingenious novelties for consumption. And humanness is not created because that only comes from creating something else: community, which is the foundation of the world home. Creativity flourishes only in communities. But 'life styles' cannot create them. In the past society has sometimes excluded its artists, but that was part of the blight of technology. Creativity is in its nature gregarious. I am not saying we should replace modern manufacturing and technology with handicrafts. Modern manufacture and technology would be part of a just society. In themselves they do not require injustice. *That* is required by the economy. The global market does not just require injustice, it *necessitates* it.

25   The future
I describe a possible future in *The Crime of the Twenty-First Century*. In crisis the impossible becomes necessary, the unimaginable becomes inevitable. If we understood why this is so, we could explain most of society's torments. It is easy for the unthinkable to become common sense and even culturally desirable, as it does in Fascist societies, because it is already implicit in the irrationalism and vengefulness of liberal

democracies. The violence of the past astonishes us, so might
the violence of the future and for the same reason: we are not
in its lie-ghetto. There is no human nature to fall back on,
humanness must be constantly recreated. In 1900 mass
gassings were unimaginable. Fifty years later they were not. In
fifty or seventy-five years' time what will be imaginable and
even common sense? Post-modernism works on techno-
reasoning, it thinks that imagination is irrational 'play' and has
no logical relationship to humanness. It is not concerned with
answers because it does not think there are any serious
questions any more. There are only problems and solutions.
In future it might be desirable to gas all criminals, even petty
ones, and all dissidents, even the merely habitually fractious.
Shoplifters might be particularly suitable for gassing because
they are conspicuously disruptive in consumer society. My
incredulity (which experience shows me is unjustified) makes
me think it more likely that (if it were possible) there would be
genetic screening to eliminate thieving and select for
conformism. It would be spurious but it might work for a time.
People told they were genetically incapable of theft might for a
time believe it – in the way that people told there is a God
pray to him and even see him. It wouldn't last. The
imagination is not genetically determined. To achieve
conformity you would have to wound the self in the process by
which it creates itself. That would be a deep genetic wound, a
wound to humanness – and ironically it would itself produce
people who wouldn't object to mass gassings.

26   The need for justice may be turned into the desire for
revenge. Enacting revenge psychologically destabilises the
revenger. This adds to the complex cross-hatching in society,
the meeting and clashing of behaviour and beliefs, the
corruption and idealism that ricochet off Nothingness into
Someness. Originally all significant behaviour is driven by the
self's need for justice. Society can become human only when
this need is radically confronted. That is the origin of drama.
Without this confrontation reason is vulnerable and even
corrupting, because 'reason cannot think'. The self must stand
in the practical site where justice is needed. Unless the Nazi

stands in the gas chamber and looks out through the doorway
over the heads of those entering it and sees himself standing
outside, he cannot when he stands outside see into the gas
chamber over the heads of those entering it. It is the question
of Galileo's telescope. We have to find the way to turn
'linearity' into 'dialecticality'. How? It is useless to argue with
the Nazi (some of those going into the gas chamber tried). He
must stand on the site of the self. Drama must create that site.
This is an abstract formula but I will try to explain it. The site
is not an 'essence' or even an earlier self. It is the site where
the self created the self, where it accepted responsibility for its
(the) world. This creation is constantly recreated in changing
experience, especially of the shifting structure of society as it
institutionalises injustice in the form of law. Ideology may
corrupt imagination but its *need* for justice cannot be
corrupted, it is synonymous with the self. It is that self-
imperative which drama must confront.

27   The self is the extreme site. Not all dramas need be set in
extreme situations. All that is necessary is to enact the
articulation of the paradox, the way the self's need for justice
is misused in society. In the end drama cannot be contained in
words because it is prior to language – but it must seek words.
A reason we learn language is to speak our need for justice.
Many young people have a sense of community and of the
need of mutual support. They have this perhaps because they
are nearer to their self-creation, not yet confused by social
madness. Sometimes they may be raw in intolerance, but this
comes from the urgency of their imperative for justice. It is not
the adult need for revenge. Drama should allow young people
to experience – become – their own dialecticality. They are
especially prepared for this because they are rapidly changing
from infant to child to young adult.

28   Articulating imagination
Imagination has historically been manipulated through
Nothingness. Entities in the real world are imaged in
Nothingness. The transcendental is made of natural elements
in unnatural combinations. The unnatural is given natural
power because the imagination is a reality, having real

potency in the natural world. Entities are mirrored in
Nothingness and then returned back to the world from which
they came but in changed forms, with other meanings, under
different control and cathected with new powers. Nothingness
becomes inhabited by the transcendental, which is an
unreality which through imagination has real power. There is
a dialectic between natural reality, imagination and
Nothingness. Imagination does not achieve a synthesis – that
is an act of reason. Imagination's dialectic may reveal
humanness as a paradox. The Athenians created the real
Parthenon to honour their transcendental goddess. But the
Parthenon's beauty and order is newly created, human-made,
in the real world – it is not a fantasy inscribed on Nothingness.
Nothingness has no beauty or order, it has only what we give
it. But it is like a dark mirror in which we see whatever we put
into it. People cannot be reshaped like the Parthenon's stones.
That is why drama is needed. Antigone and Creon are not
equally right. Sophocles consciously dramatises the human
rightness of Antigone's paradox. The paradox confronts the
audience's self, is involved in the self's dialectics.

Nothingness is not only the site of our freedom, it *forces* us to
create. Otherwise we fall into Nothingness, go mad or are
imprisoned by ideology. We cannot abolish imagination. If we
could we would cease to be self-aware selves. Only
imagination gives us self-awareness. Imagination becomes the
way we are in the world. Historically we empowered
Nothingness to become its victims. But the oracle gave its
pronouncements as riddles, there was always some truth in the
lie-ghetto, the need for justice could not be eliminated. Now
the situation changes. Then we needed Nothingness, *now we
want it*. Its fake spirituality fills the emptiness in consumerdom.
As *need* loses its structural use and gives way to *wants*,
Nothingness is like a broken mirror that reflects us back in
distortions. Imagination's humanising logic is destroyed. We
cease to be creative and become reactive. Imagination
becomes the nihilistic search for nihilism. This is still balanced
between *joie de vivre* and *joie de mourir*. But the consumerism of
the world market extends nihilism. It isn't a matter of attitude,
to be changed by persuasion. It is a matter of structural logic.

Modern culture gives birth to the monster of its own anti-culture.

29   It is not a question of persuading by reason because you cannot talk sanely to the mad. It is as if society could become a prison camp in which robots destroy robots. Our defence against this is imagination, and its only language and activity is drama. We have to remove all transcendentalism from Nothingness. But we cannot put rationalism in its place because this would instrumentalise imagination. Nor can we destroy Nothingness, because we know our finitude, and because the self's creation of the self includes Nothingness – we meet it in our beginning. Instead we have to return imagination utterly to *this* world.

There are three reasons why imagination cannot relate to Nothingness in the way it did in the past.
a)   We are technologically too powerful to share the world with ideology.
b)   A society without *needs* does not need a heaven, which was a truth in the lie-ghetto.
c)   In consumerdom self and society degenerate into revenge and its violence. And when we cannot recreate our humanness we take revenge on ourselves, just as the mad mutilate themselves.

30   Creativity can still confront the self's need for justice. But as reason alone cannot do this, we must trust drama again. If we remove ideology from Nothingness we can site creativity entirely in *this* world, in *joie de vivre* and – in place of nihilism and *joie de mourir* – tragedy. This would not be vulgar materialism (which even consumerism could become if it re-ideologised injustice) but creative-materialism. This can be done only on the site of the self-creating self, which originally accepted responsibility for (being in) a world which was not its home. Only by accepting this responsibility can the self be a force for justice and not revenge. It is also the site of Greek drama. We have to use it for drama based on the praxis of creative materialism.

31   What drama is creative-materialistic? A play showing the

dangers of smoking cigarettes is staged for young people.
Afterwards they smoke. In Nazi Germany a play is staged (if
actually possible) showing that it is wrong to gas ideological
victims. Afterwards the gassing goes on (who could doubt it?).
A play is staged showing the consequences of social madness.
Afterwards more prisons and armaments factories are built.
There are several reasons why these plays cannot achieve their
aim. In effect you cannot preach to the *un*-converted. You
must free the self from its rigid linearity so that it must
experience – enact – its creative dialecticality. That is its self-
imperative, which ideology distorts. Do not try to teach what
is right and what is wrong. These words are distorted by
ideology, and their meanings made even more confused by
social experience. We have to turn street-wiseness (which is a
truth in the lie-getto, a means of survival) into world-wiseness,
which is the means of creating the world home. We can do
this by making fiction a tool of reality, which is what ideology
already does. We can use fiction to show – enact in
imagination, not explain in reason – how reality depends on
its fictions. This is the self-praxis in which the self created the
self. We can call it the 'self module'.

32   The self-module
This could be enacted through everyday simplicities. They
could be extended to show the consequences inherent in the
everyday. A young person outgrows clothes. They must be
changed. This is a natural process. You could say the body
was in dialectical relationship with its clothes. To a being from
Mars it might seem obvious that the clothes were shrinking,
not that the body was growing. How can you be sure of what
is happening in more complex situations?

Drama does not teach right or wrong or create escapist
fiction. It confronts the participants' self-module. Only when
that is done can reason reason. An actor acts the story, the
audience enact it in their self-module. For the actor the story is
fiction, for the audience it is reality – the fiction is real in the
self-module. This uses the structuring of ideology, but in
reverse. Ideology uses reality to create fiction, drama uses
fiction to create reality.

There is no absolute difference between fiction and reality. Each may be causal in the other. Social reality has depended as much on fiction as on tools. Fiction and reality relate in the self-module, which creates the self. The neonate's self-module is created in a site bare to its ontological elements. The neonate becomes a self in a no-self-land. This self is not static but is a praxis. It is not yet enclosed in ideological restraints and defining experiences – when the infant's cradle rocks the world rocks. Later the self-module's primal openness persists even under repression. It may be made the site of drama. Then it may modify the ideology and experience accumulated over time. Because the self must always be recreated in the present, it is vulnerable and open to ideology and drama. This does not conflict with the notion of 'self habitude', because that is structured in the self-module.

An empty stage is a replica of the gap in the self. When it is used it becomes the site of the self-module. People enter and leave the gap. Objects are placed in it. Actions take place in it. This follows the ideological structure in which reality is projected onto and from Nothingness. In drama the process is reversed. Without this structure there can be no fiction or self-awareness and so no humanness. Animals' minds have no fiction.

Fiction may infiltrate reality and create new reality. This is always so in ideology and may be made so in drama. Ideology is reinforced by social and economic reality, fiction in drama may be reinforced by the reality created in the self-module. Imagination is real, people are unexpected. People are epic, reality is dialectical.

33   The Cap

An incident from the Second World War is recorded in *The Cap: the Price of a Life* by Roman Frister (Weidenfeld & Nicholson, 1999). This incident may be dramatised in the following way to show the mutual dependence of fiction and reality:

In the Second World War Nazis imprisoned a boy in a camp. The lowest level of authority in the camps were the Kapos. Kapos were 'trusty' prisoners. They behaved with special brutality in order to retain their power. If they lost it other prisoners took revenge on them. One night a Kapo raped the boy. The boy could report the Kapo to the SS. The Kapo would be shot.

Each prisoner was issued with a cap. Each morning the prisoners were paraded for roll-call on the Appellplatz. Each prisoner must wear his cap. If he does not he is shot. To stop the boy reporting him to the SS the Kapo stole his cap. That morning the boy woke early. In camp it was better to wake early even though lack of sleep meant the work would kill you sooner. The boy reached under his body for his cap. It was gone. The boy carefully got up from his sleeping plank. He crept through the barrack along the ranks. His head was lowered like a dog's sniffing for bones. He gently probed. The sleepers' faces guided him in the darkness. They shone with the pallor of sickness. He saw a cap peeping out from under a sleeping boy's shoulder. The sleeper has a number but no name. He is X. The boy stole X's cap.

Two hours later eight hundred prisoners stood rigidly in ranks on the Appellplatz. The boy stood in a middle rank. All the prisoners in front of him wore caps. He did not look behind him. If you looked behind you were shot. The camp commandant took the parades. He could have ordered his adjutant to take them. The camp commandant enjoyed taking them. Two junior officers accompanied him. The camp commandant inspected the prisoners' turn-out. The two junior officers each counted the prisoners. At the end their totals must tally.

The inspection began at the rear rank. The boy heard the officers' boots grating on the gritty dust. In the distance a lorry engine kick-started. Nearer a door banged. The boy did not know X's face. He had seen it as a blur in the fetid darkness. A dead face under water. The boots stopped. A pair of boots slid in the dust. An officer had bumped into the officer in front of him. This officer must have stopped abruptly. He had seen the capless head further along the rank. Silence. The door banged. The footsteps started. Perhaps the pace was a little slower. The footsteps stopped.

Between the barrack blocks an Alsation barked. Perhaps someone had gone through the door and come out again with a bone and thrown it to the Alsation.

The shot. The Alsation did not bark. A flopping sound as of water thrown on dust. The side of a boot grated briefly in the dust. The death throes. A slight sound. Prisoners' boots were paper-thin. They had no welt. No one moved on the Appellplatz. Silence. The bootsteps started again.

In what way did the boy survive?

34 This is a different version of the story. The commandant marches onto the Appellplatz. He reaches the first prisoner. At that moment a gust of wind blows away all the prisoners' hats. Some hats are swept over the barbed wire fence. They tumble across the open land into the nearby forest. Some are blown against the walls of the barrack huts. They slink along the bottom of the walls. They seem to shudder and cower as if they were trying to hide behind each other. Some hats are caught on the barbed wire. They spin and flap like dead birds. The barbed wire is electrified. The prisoners are weak. Their mouths open but no cheer comes. The officers are tight-lipped. Their hats were not blown away. The wind was a miracle sent by Nothingness.

Does the miracle change the world? Look at the ranks of prisoners before the inspection begins. You can tell which one is X. His jaw is clenched. His face is even paler in daylight than it was in the dark. When the officers had marched along the ranks they had not stopped because they saw X's capless head in the rank ahead of them. They stopped for another reason. Let us say it was to let the commandant blow his nose. The moment the officers had marched onto the Appellplatz they had seen X's bare head. It stood out like a rock floating on water. Even though all the hats were blown away he would be shot. He had come onto parade without his hat.

But there was no wind. No caps were blown away. That is a fiction inserted into reality to show that reality is already fictional. Many real events happen *because* they are fictional. In the First World War soldiers on both sides really died. On both sides they believed they were dying for God. On at least one side that *must* be a fiction. Why not on both sides? How will the soldiers decide which side God was on? – fight another war over it (with God on their side)? Putting fiction into a real situation dialecticises it. It 'agitates' the self-module so that it must respond in some way.

There was already fiction in the real story before the fiction of the wind. The officers were there because of fiction. Orders were orders. The officers obeyed them with rigid linearity. To shoot someone because he is hatless you must be involved in fiction: the fiction of ideology, which is made from Nothingness. Nothingness receives and returns our fears and wishes – but that changes material reality only through imagination. Those who receive back from Nothingness their self-image cathected with God can erect stones into cathedrals and prisons. Those who receive it back cathected with injustice can shoot someone for being hatless – and gas millions. In time they could also gas shoplifters. That is the reality of fiction – of ideology metamorphosed into reality by social violence.

35   Introducing fiction into reality is almost a definition of drama. A better definition would be: introducing reality into fiction. If we do this purposefully we destabilise rigid linearity, which is the law of Nothingness. The self-module must respond to this. *Within* imagination – inside the self-module – this has the consequences of a miracle, consequences as real as those which would have enveloped the camp commandant if a real miracle had blown away the prisoners' caps. The effect in the self-module might be or not be immediate. Effects may take time and be accumulative. And the clinically insane may be beyond reach. But though drama cannot teach, its fictions can change reality.

What would a miracle have accomplished? The officers would not have thought their own hats had stayed on because the wind miraculously left them on. They would have known that their hats stayed on because they were a better make and a better fit. A more effective miracle would have blown away the officers? Even that wouldn't work: there are more officers? It should have blown away the prisoners? There are more

prisoners. And anyway, what would have happened if the
wind had blown away the hats, prisoners' and officers'? The
officers would have shot all the prisoners. This seems *pure*
fiction, but such events took place in reality. Several hundred
children were waiting to be gassed when the camp ran out of
gas. The children were machine-gunned. It was no more
significant than turning a page of Nothingness. A delivery of
prisoners waited at a station and the train did not come. They
were machine-gunned. Another page. Such things happen
because fiction – the text written on Nothingness – infiltrates
reality. In drama, putting fiction into reality can isolate and
dialecticise the fiction already in it. It is a practical way to steal
ideology's clothes.

36   There is another version of the incident. The wind blows
away the prisoners' caps. They run round the Appellplatz
each trying to catch a cap. They fight, kick, bite, tear, gouge
and scream at each other. They curse God for sending his
miracle. How they ask could God know so little of the ways of
men? The officers roll about laughing. Sentries on the watch
towers join in. Some prisoners try to snatch caps from the
wire. They are electrocuted. The officers point at the
cascading sparks and howl with laughter. The Alsation tears at
the prisoners and behaves as badly as men do. The camp
commandant shouts 'Enough!'. Everyone is still. Some
prisoners wear caps. Some wear bits of caps. Scraps of rims.
They stretch them to cover a little more head. The hatless
huddle in groups. The officers punctiliously examine the
scraps of hats. When is a not-a-hat a hat? The officers discuss.
Such is the glory of humankind. Those selected as being
hatless are sent to the hatless groups. They are shot.

37   Once (upon a time) I stopped at a motorway petrol
station. There was a people-carrier packed with schoolboy sea
cadets. They were immaculately uniformed. They wore
sailors' white flat caps with blue bands. A petty officer
standing by the people-carrier was filling its tank with petrol.
A sea cadet came from the toilets. He had taken off his cap.
He walked towards the people-carrier. The petty officer saw
him. He screamed. His face was red. His jowls shook. His eyes

burnt like pistol shots. He screamed and screamed that the hatless cadet was letting him down, himself down, and the cadets in the people-carrier, his officers, the navy, the public . . . Petrol splashed round his boots. Everyday you encounter fictions in reality.

38   We are victims of the Nothingness we turn into reality in accordance with the logic I have described. Because the prisoner X was shot then – for the same sort of reason – within seventy-five years petty shoplifters could be shot. In the past the unthinkable became the inevitable. It did for these officers and prisoners and – for the same sort of reason – it could do so in the future. It is the logic of rigid linearity. It is not possible for drama to say do this but not that. That is more linearity. You can put up a notice saying: Do Not Walk On The Grass. That may work because it is anecdotal and administrative. Imagine a group of prisoners squatting on the grass. Can you put up a notice saying: Do Not Shoot Prisoners Sitting on the Grass? Many teachers of drama in schools – and many political dramatists – try to use drama to do just such things. Often they are told to do no more. Drama must exercise the self in the practice of the self by confronting it beyond anecdote and administration, at the site where the mind creates itself out of its situation. That would be creative-materialism. It is the reality of drama.

(Written in January 2002 for the annual conference of The National Association of Teachers of Drama)

Olly's Prison

Olly's Prison was first broadcast by BBC TV in spring 1993
with the following cast:

Mike	Bernard Hill
Sheila	Charlotte Coleman
Vera	Mary Jo Randle
Frank	George Anton
Barry	Bryan Pringle
Smiler	Jonny Lee Miller
Prisoner 1	Peter Sproule
Prisoner 2	Anthony Trent
Prison Officer 1	Stuart Barren
Prison Officer 2	Michael Irving
Prison Officer 3	Charles Cork
Ellen	Maggie Steed
Oliver	Richard Graham

Also included in the cast were Lucy (a child), Lucy's mother
and other prison visitors.

Directed by Roy Battersby
Produced by Richard Langridge

The first stage production of *Olly's Prison* was on 23 September
1994 in Berlin by the Berliner Ensemble.

Mike	Hans Diehl
Sheila	Anna Thalbach
Vera	Tanja von Oertzen
Frank	Matthias Bundschuh
Barry	Volker Spengler
Smiler	Steffen Schult
Ellen	Traute Hoess
Oliver	Ingo Hülsmann
Prison Officers	Christian Drommer
	Fritz Roth
	Thomas Schumann

Directed by Peter Palitzsch
Designed by Karl Kneidl
Lighting by Johannes Karsch

The play is set in London and the country, in the present and
eleven years earlier.

Part One

Section One – The Flat – Living-Room

A small living-room in a small block of working-class flats. There are three doors: one leads to the kitchen, another to the hallway between the living-room and the front door, and the third is a cupboard door. The cupboard and the door to the hallway are shut. A glass-fronted sideboard with a telephone on it. Fitted patterned carpet. Two armchairs and a bare table which is slightly larger than is usual in such a room. Its surface is slightly polished so that vague reflections appear in it. Four chairs are set at the table and in one of them **Sheila** *sits with her forearms on the table. She is sixteen and is wearing a buttoned-up street coat. She does not move.*

Evening. Electric light.

Off, a sneeze from the kitchen.

Mike *comes in from the kitchen in his stocking feet. He wears a pale shirt and grey trousers. He is in his late thirties.*

Mike (*casually friendly*) Didnt hear you come in.

Mike *goes out to the kitchen.*

Mike (*off*) Good time?

Sheila's *expression doesn't change.* **Mike** *brings in an ornamental wastebin (bought at a stately home) and sets it down by the gas fire. He goes to the sideboard, opens a drawer, takes out a small ornamental place-mat, shuts the drawer and sets the place-mat on the table in front of* **Sheila**.

Mike Goin out again? Not this time a' night.

Off, a kettle starts to whistle. **Mike** *goes out.* **Sheila** *doesn't move.*

Mike (*off*) Do the curtains.

Pause. **Mike** *comes in with a cup of tea with a teabag and a teaspoon in it. He places it on the place-mat. He goes to the window and draws the* *curtains. His jacket is on the back of an armchair. He goes to it, takes a newspaper from a pocket, sits in the armchair and reads the newspaper.*

Mike (*grumbling contentedly*)   Not cold. Bloody ridiculous. (*He looks in the newspaper to see what's on.*) Heatin's not goin on this time a' year. Should eat properly. (*Still studying the newspaper.*) Lad left t'day. No job to go to. Didnt tell his missus. Be ructions round his place. (*Folds newspaper.*) You're no company. Quarrel with the boyfriend? Dont bring your troubles here and take it out on the home. (*He holds the folded newspaper as if he's going to let it fall open, but doesn't. Suddenly.*) Did you want to use the phone? Why didnt you say? I'll wait in the kitchen . . . (*No response.*) You're not talkin to him either. (*Lets the newspaper fall open.*) Not leavin the room so you can sit and sulk. You've got your own room for that. Some people dont even have a roof. (*Shakes the newspaper as he prepares to read it.*) Sorry about the noise. (*Reads.*) Soon complain if I sat there. (*Looks up.*) Did I say somethin? (*No answer.*) I didnt start you off. Just bein awkward. If I'd said somethin the whole world'd know by now. You're not workin me up. Read the paper in peace. Im comfortable. (*Reads.*) That tea'll get cold. Lad just left . . . (*Still reading.*) If you could see yourself. That's a sign of real rotten ignorance. You're in a mood so you're entitled to impose it on everyone else.

Mike *stops reading, lays the newspaper down open on his stomach like a sheet, lies back and shuts his eyes.*

Mike   God I hate this carry-on. Work all day, come home, cook a meal, tidy up – then this. 'S not human. Dont you get enough of it outside? Least we can treat each other like human beings in our own place. Suppose I should've asked if you wanted it: 'Want a cup a' tea?' No one's forcin you to drink it. You heard the kettle. If you didnt want it you should've said. If somethin's botherin you tell me. I'll listen. If you're affected Im affected. Muggins pays in the end. You know what they're like round here. 'Why didnt you find out?' 'She wouldnt say.' 'Fine father! – you're supposed to know not wait to be told.' D'you want a doctor? (*Goes back to reading the newspaper.*) Be in dead trouble then. He'd put you in a loony bin – that's your trouble.

Well this time you've chosen the wrong day. You're not leavin this room till you drunk that tea.

Slight pause. **Mike** *gets up, goes to the kitchen door and closes it.*

Mike   You're not the only one who can play at silly buggers. Come too much of it!

Mike *goes back to the armchair and sits.*

Mike   I've got all night. You drink it before you leave this room. (*Pause.*) I worked for this house. Not goin to sit in it and be treated like dirt. (*Pause.*) If you dont like it move out. No one's stoppin you. Do what you like in your own place. Soon find out when the bills start comin in. Yeh, that's what you'd like! Have a fine old time then! Well you're not goin. You can show a few signs of responsibility before I let you out of my jurisdiction. Not havin people say I let you live on the streets. That's where you'd end up. While you're under my roof you live by the rules. They're not hard. Just a bit of mutual consideration.

Mike *gets up, goes to the table and feels the cup.*

Mike   Be cold. Serve you right. (*Pause.*) You can have some hot in if you like. Im not forcin you to drink cold tea.

Mike *goes to the middle of the room. He hesitates and looks at* **Sheila**.

Mike   Let it stay there. You sit and think it over miss. I'll phone the manageress in the mornin and tell her you're not comin in.

Mike *goes to the armchair and sits.*

Mike   Dont think I wouldnt! (*Pause.*) Talkin t' meself. (*Sudden rage.*) Drink the tea!

Slight pause. Suddenly **Mike** *gets up, takes a chair from the table, goes to the kitchen door and wedges the back of the chair under the door handle. He goes to the armchair and sits.*

Mike   Told you. Im not in the mood. (*Pause.*) And dont dribble it on the table to show us you're clever – dont mean a thing round here. If we cant treat each other with respect at

least we can respect the furniture. That came out of this
pocket. (*Slight pause.*) Not markin that. Turnin the place into a
pigsty. Suppose you want me to force you to drink it? Put me
in the wrong. Slosh it down your coat so you can get a new
one out of me. If I took it in my head I could get you out of
that coat. I know fathers who'd pour it down your collar. Soon
be out of it then! (*Pause.*) What d'you think my life's like? Too
busy thinkin about yourself. As long as I pay the bills, that's all
you worry. I know I should've asked. I put myself in the
wrong. That's no excuse for this carry on. Doesnt matter who
started it. Im head of the household and Im askin you to stop
it. (*Reads newspaper.*) Come in – not a dicky bird – I didnt
bellyache – made a cup a' tea – a father makin a nice friendly
gesture, tryin to behave in a civilised manner – I thought
you'd like a cup a' tea and a chat, tell me what sort of day it
was: you cant even say good evenin! No this is a big joke!
Laugh for your mates. Really chuffed if I chuck it in the sink
and broke the cup. Well you're not gettin me worked up.
Entitled to peace in my own home. (*Pause.*) You're not a child
now. Young lady your age in the house. We've got to adapt.
(*Stops reading.*) How can I get it right if you dont give me a
chance? It's not easy. (*Puts down the newspaper.*) We've got to sort
ourselves out like a family. Well what's your suggestion? (*No
response.*) It's the same with this tea. I let this drop, there'll only
be a repetition t'morrow. It'll be back to square one. Stop it
now before it gets out of hand.

Pause. **Mike** *gets up and pushes the other armchair against the hallway
door.*

Mike I know – bloody stupid: a cup a' tea! But Im goin to
have it drunk. It's only right.

Mike *goes to the armchair and sits.*

Mike You wont go through that door till. (*Pause.*) I'd fall
asleep on me way to bed. What do I get out of sittin here?
Nothin on, missed the forecast. I've got to go in t'morrow even
if it is Saturday. Drink it up like a good girl.

Mike *gets up, goes to the table and sits in a chair facing* **Sheila**.

Mike   You know I worry. If your mother was alive she'd talk
to you. Table too big. Bargain. Couldnt afford to let it go. Sat
here when she was ill. Didnt go in the armchair case I didnt
wake up when she called. What's the use of talkin back? –
'nough trouble now. I talk to make you talk. It just shuts you
up. Wont get a word now I mentioned your mother. That put
the lock on the lid. God you cried when she died. The water
didnt pour out your eyes like a kid. Poured out your whole
face. I thought it was broken – skin ruptured or somethin –
and the water poured out the cracks. When you lose
somethin like that you lose touch with everythin. Think it's all
goin. I wiped the tears off and your face was still there. You
looked different – as if you'd been cryin for all your mates. I
felt ashamed of bringin you into the world. Let me put your
coat on a hanger. Nice on you. Shame to let it crease. Hope
the boyfriend appreciates it. Suppose you dont want me to
touch you.

Mike *goes back to his armchair and sits.*

Mike   Pour it down the sink. Drink it under threat you'll be
ill – end up with tummy ulcers. Pour it down the sink, wash
the cup and hang it on the dresser. That wont make you ill. So
now there's no excuse. It comes down to your attitude.

Mike *goes to the kitchen door and takes the chair away from it. He goes
to his armchair and sits.*

Mike   Now we'll see.

Pause. Suddenly **Mike** *twists so that he's lying on his side facing away
from* **Sheila***, with his legs stretched straight out and the upper part of his
body hunched forward. His eyes are shut.*

Mike   . . . If you were a knife you wouldnt need lessons in
sharpness. Perhaps you should go and live with the boyfriend.
See if he can knock some sense into you. I dont blame *you*.
What can you know at your age? The welfare said have you
adopted. No, you think, love comes first. Times I wished she'd
died before we had you. Least we'd be spared this. You work
hard, try, where does it get you? You dont even know what's
in their heads. I dont even know if you're listenin. Are you

still there? Perhaps you had the sense to walk out? – it's
finished. Im too bloody tired to open my eyes. Day after day
the same. Why did I bring your mother into it? Bloody
whiner.

Mike *opens his eyes and turns to look:* **Sheila** *sits as before.*

Mike   I wish you'd gone Sheila. It's such a pity.

Mike *gets up, pushes the armchair against the hall door so that it's
blocked. Then he wedges the back of the chair under the handle of the
kitchen door and sits in it.*

Mike   Stupid. Stupid. This bloody chair. (*He runs his hands
through his hair.*) You're really goin for it tonight. You're out of
your depth. Im not givin in. Arent you ashamed of doin this to
your father? – look at me. (*Suddenly sardonic.*) Did I serve it in
the wrong cup? I feel sorry for you. Off you go in your new
coat – nose in the air – clippity-clip – not a thought in your
head. If you could see yourself, you're like a dog draggin its
kennel round on a chain. Right: you've got half a minute. (*His
watch.*) Twenty seconds. (*Pause.*) Eleven. Ten. Nine.

*After another twenty seconds he goes to the table. With the teaspoon he
presses the teabag against the side of the cup, lifts it out, carries it across
the room and throws it into the wastebin.*

Mike   In.

Mike *goes back to the table and puts the teaspoon next to the teacup on
the place-mat.*

Mike   You will drink it. There's got to be some order. (*He
leaves the table.*) We're barricaded in.

Pause. **Mike** *goes back to the table and picks up the teacup.*

Mike   God! – there's a ton of it. Heavy! That's what arguin
does. You wouldnt have the strength to lift it! Right: Im holdin
it up for you. (*He puts the teacup to her mouth.*) That's the most I'll
do. It's up to you. You dont have to drink it all. Let me see
you take one sip. Then we'll forget it. One sip. Try. Shall I
take a sip? It's not poisoned. No that's not why you wont. You
could've said at the start 'Dad I dont want a drink' – 'Sure luv

that's okay' – I'd've drunk the lot. Now it's too late. Gone
beyond that. It's not a cup a' tea any more. (*He puts down the
teacup.*) No you wont will you? You have to go on with it.

Mike *goes back to the armchair and sits.*

Mike   My hand didnt shake when I lifted the cup. (*Pause.*)
You think t'morrow there'll be some smart alec way out.
You'll want a sub so you'll *have* to talk. 'Scared me with the
chairs dad. Upset me over mum.' That worked in the past
Sheila, it won't work t'morrow. Be careful. You could be sittin
in a room with a lunatic. It's all got on top of me. Run up
debts. Got the sack. Off me head. You dont know. All sorts of
things happen these days. (*Pause.*) Must be some sort of
satisfaction bein as ignorant as you. If you were a pig you
wouldnt know the smell of muck. You think it's big to say no.
Anyone can do that. I pity your kids. What sort of future
d'you think you're makin for them? Perhaps people cant learn
any more – put on the headphones and shut it out. People
dyin – bein robbed – goin crazy – and you sit. The world's
bein handed over to people like you – and you dont even
know your own street. You're nothin really, because you dont
want to understand. If you did you'd be on your knees beggin
me to help you – talk to you. You changed our whole lives this
evenin Sheila. You'll drink the tea but it wont repair the
damage. If you only knew, you're runnin round this room
puttin a wall across it – you cant chuck the bricks up fast
enough. I can see you from the cradle to the grave. When you
marry – have kids – get old – you'll still be in that chair. You'll
end up like the little old woman down the road. She lives in a
corner of her room behind a wall of bags. When they want her
they call her out as if she's an animal in a hole. Why why why
did I mention your mother? That's the one thing I blame
myself for . . . You're more dead than she is. Your sort of
stubbornness is worse than bein dead. You want to run the
world? – one cup of tea – under your nose – and you cant put
out your hand. You're trapped. Well well well.

Mike *twists to one side, as before, and shuts his eyes but his shoulders
do not hunch.*

Mike   I've seen real pain. Grown-up people cryin. You cant help, cant do anythin. An old man in the papers. They found him sittin straight up on a box. The skin crumblin off like paint – fallin off like feathers on a bird flat in the road. His tongue was hangin out like a toilet roll. He'd forgotten his own language . . . Why'm I tellin you this? Take your arms off the table. This wont blow over t'morrow. It'll take more than that. All this for one cup of tea. It's terrible.

Mike *jumps up and goes to the table.*

Mike   Arms off! You want me to knock them off! – fight! Then you've got bruises to show. Go round in short sleeves – put powder on 'em to pretend you dont want 'em to show and make sure the whole street stinks of powder for weeks!

Mike *pulls the table away from* **Sheila**. *Her hands fall into her lap.*

Ha! Ha! Gotcher! Didnt think of that! The table moved! The world doesnt always do what you want it to! Bang! Now she knows what the mouse feels when it goes for the cheese! I'd've liked the privilege of bein inside her head when the table moved! And I didnt spill a drop! (*He sits in the armchair blocking the hallway door.*) Have to be childish when you're dealin with a child. Bang! (*He calms down.*) . . . The lad just left. The shift didnt make a collection. Not even voluntary redundancy – self-inflicted. Why should they put their hands in their pockets? Could go off an' do the same the next place. Make a regular racket . . . I nearly went to Australia. Then I met your mother. Everythin changed. Work offered me trainin plus a rise at the end. Then it's all over. I never hit you. I pinched the top of your arm when I was puttin you in your school coat and you dawdled. I darent be late. You could've drunk the tea. It wasnt much to ask. No you wont. Too easy. Got to be the hard way. A tragedy. One cup of tea and the world's got to end.

Mike *goes to* **Sheila** *and stands behind her chair. He picks it up with her in it and places it at the table where it was before. Her hands are in her lap. The tea is in front of her.*

Mike   Where there's a will. Pushed your pram for hours.

Row of little dollies on the hood. Made out of wool on a
string. Had the hood up even when it was sunny. Washed you.
Ugly little toes. Put you to bed. Dished your food up on the
plate – I made the tea out of habit. Said 'eat it up, it's good'
and you believed it. Had more sense then. Now I say be a
good girl – drink it up – it's good because it'll get us out of the
mess – you wont. It's all got to go in the bin. If you drink it *I'd*
taste it. You watch a mother feed a kid. She scoops the grub
up on the spoon – shoves it in its little gob – and goes gobble-
gobble as if *she's* enjoyin it. Even has to wipe her chin. Daft. If
she didnt do it we'd still be in caves . . . 'Drink your tea or it'll
swallow you up!'. Once you said 'If I eat it will mummy come
back?' If it was that simple . . . I didnt mean it about a wall.
People hurt each other all the time – you'd think that's what
we're here for – but you live through it. We dont have to
punish each other for survivin.

Mike *pulls the chair and armchair from the doors and leaves them
haphazardly in the centre of the room. He picks up the teacup and goes out
to the kitchen.* **Sheila** *doesn't move. After a moment* **Mike** *comes back
with the teacup. He puts it where it was on the table.*

Mike   Made some tea. Nice evenin?

Mike *sits in his armchair.*

Mike   No it's not that easy. Only the other way now. With
pain. You're right: I put you on the spot, I've got to stick with
it. It's worse than that. All this damage. . . when you drink it
you'll make it worse. You'll drink it like an insult. Like spittin
it in my face. A cup of tea. That decides now. Have you heard
a word I said? Dont even know if you saw the table move. I
wish it wasnt late. Before you get into this you need time to
finish. No use after midnight. Talk. Nothin's done. Threats.
Crawlin for sympathy. If I hadnt – !: why why why did I bring
your mother into it? That's the last tea I make you. The lad
just left.

Help me Sheila. You dont know what's happenin. People are
cruel. I dont know why. They make you suffer. What we're in
now – this teacup – that'll happen all your life. One way or

another. That's all there is. Learn to handle it. You've got a chance. In a few years it's over. I try to help you – talk and talk – we're the only people in the room – and I cant tell you – because you wont have it! Somethin's got to be done. (*He goes to the table.*) Sheila I made the tea and put it on the table. That's an order. (*Wanders off.*) No she wont. I said one sip. I held the cup. She wont, she wont.

Mike *goes to the table and sits.*

Mike   Drink it. Please. *Please.* Will that do? (*Sprawls with his head on the table, bangs the table with his fists.*) Help me. A daughter should. We lived here sixteen years – we wont fight over a cup! For nothin! Give me your hand. *Dont* understand! If it's hard! No need for a reason! Give me your hand. (*Pushes her hand towards the cup. She doesn't respond.*) Touch it. Touch it. Somethin must belong in this world. Somethin must have its place! (*He stares at the cup, holds one hand round it as if he's protecting a candle-flame and hammers his other fist next to it on the table.*) Take it! Take it! Somethin take it! Smash it! Smash it! No no there's nothin! No help! (*The side of his head is on the table. He draws his neck into his shoulders.*) The wood on my face. I cant see. I wont look. Cant. You wont lose. Drink it. *Dont* drink it! Say! Just say! Lie! Lie! Lie! Say you drank it! (*He gets up and leaves the table. Turns to face her.*) Tell me you drank it! (*No response. Violently.*) Drink! Drink! Drink! Help me! Help me! No no . . . (*Rapid mutter.*) No she wont the hard-faced little bitch – grinnin inside her head – she'd let it stand there on her mother's grave till it's colder than the corpse. A laugh. The bitch. The dirty little bitch. (*Looks at* **Sheila***. Pleads.*) Sheila . . . is it too much to ask? Then what! Pick up a spoon? Shut the door? Too much! (*Mutter.*) You brought her in the world. What'll you do about it? I'll do what I must do! You cant! I will! (*Pleads.*) Sheila! . . . My god one day *you'll* ask and no one'll listen! You're my child – you hard-faced little slut. . . You bitch! I will! I will! They kick you out of doors and make you shut it! (*He goes behind the chair.*) My child, my child!

Mike *slams his hands round* **Sheila***'s neck, lifts her straight up out of the chair and strangles her. For a moment she is too shocked to react. Then* *her hands go up and claw at his hands. Her body wrenches round once so that it is sideways to the table – the chair comes round with her. The shape of her body is contained in his body as if they were one piece of sculpture. The struggle is concentrated and intense – their bodies shake, vibrate, violently judder – like a magnified drop of water on the end of an icicle before it falls. Her hands claw more weakly, they seem to be patting his hands. No sound except breathing.*

When **Sheila** *is dead* **Mike** *lowers her into the chair. She sits bolt upright, sideways to the table. He moves away. After a moment he looks at the table. He goes towards it. Stops. Turns to the kitchen. Stops. Goes to* **Sheila**. *He picks up the chair – with her in it – and turns it to face the table. The tea is in front of her as before. He goes to the armchair and sits on the arm.*

Mike   Drink your tea. (*He glances vaguely at his arms as if they hurt.*) Phew! . . . That chair's . . . well . . . I told you what would – . Work in the mornin. The lad just left. Come on Sheila. (*He gets up and goes to the table.*) Sugar. Diet. Boyfriend. It's in now, drink up. You might as well.

Mike *sits at the table and puts his hands in his lap.*

Mike (*Gently*)   I dont want us to come to any – Im sorry if I – . I'll put the kettle on and – . Dont punish me. You were so quiet. Perhaps you're still . . . ? I cant put out my hand to see. Afraid, in case – .

Mike *stands, picks up the cup and goes towards the kitchen. Stops.*

Mike   She doesnt have to be – . No need. That can be said when it's time. (*Cradles the cup.*) You can pretend it hasnt happened. (*Calm amazement. Flat.*) How wonderful. The room – the night – all this – it's free. How wonderful to live here. (*Tears.*) So lucky . . . (*Hurries to the table.*) There was – there – was – . (*He finds the teaspoon, fills it with tea and holds it to* **Sheila**'*s mouth.*) If you could drink. To help . . . No she wont. Stubborn. (*Tea dribbles.*) O Sheila your new coat. The money. Ruined. What will she be buried in! Bills. Bills.

Mike *goes to the sideboard, opens a drawer, takes out envelopes, stamps, a chequebook, a biro and a few bills. He goes to the table and sits.*

Mike   Sort all this. Bills. Bills. Electricity. Estimate again. (*Writes cheque.*) I should complain. Call when we're in. Bills. What's this. Your credit card. More shoes. (*He is going to write another cheque. Stops.*) She's dead. You must let it happen. Her right. Be fair. It's all she's got. (*To* **Sheila**.) I took the rest. All that – so easy. (*Touches her arm.*) Can you feel my – ? Perhaps it takes a little time to go. They'll punish me. Is that what you want to hear? The last words. They're true. I wouldnt lie to you now. Our life isnt that bad. The last words must be true. Perhaps you're screamin at me: 'Bastard! Bastard! Killer!' Dont! I called you slut. I thought I had more time to – . Bills. Bills. These are facts. Milk? (*He tries to read a bill but puts it down.*) It doesnt matter.

He puts the cheque in an envelope and seals it. He gets up and goes to the window, lifts the curtain and peers out.

Mike   Empty. All asleep. Wake up in the mornin. Then the fuss. Your coat's caught on the chair. You used to watch here for me when I came home.

Mike *switches off the light. Street lighting comes through the curtains. He sits in the armchair and immediately goes to sleep.* **Sheila** *sits bolt upright in front of the tea.*

Section Two – Living-Room and Hallway

Morning. Daylight comes through the drawn curtains. **Sheila** *lies face down on the table with the cup beside her.* **Mike** *sleeps slumped in the armchair. A doorbell. He does not react. A few moments pass and he opens his eyes and concentrates, trying to recall if he has heard a sound. The doorbell again. He gets up, notices the curtains are drawn and opens them. He goes out into the hallway.*

Mike *walking to the front door. He opens it. Beyond him* **Vera**, *a neighbour. She is about thirty and is in indoor clothes.*

Vera   Rang four times. Standin there. Your curtains are drawn.

Mike   What time is it?

Vera (*coming along the corridor*)   You'll be askin me what day it is next. Thought you were workin this weekend. I cant stop. Came to see Sheila. She up?

Mike's *face: he remembers. He starts after* **Vera**.

Mike   No no she's not – you cant –

Vera *is entering the living-room followed by* **Mike**. **Sheila** *is slumped as before.*

Vera   She drunk? She's not startin all that? Sheila . . . !

Mike   Leave her.

Vera (*picks up the teacup*)   Eugh! She come home in that state? No wonder you didnt want to let me in.

Vera *speaks in a low voice.* **Mike** *copies her.*

Mike   Im goin out.

Vera   And you – all crumpled! Suppose you slept like that. Fine pair!

Mike   Got to go out.

Vera   I was on my balcony and saw your curtains. The frowse in this room! (*She goes to the window.*)

Mike   Dont.

Vera (*opens the window*)   Let some honest-to-goodness pollution in.

Mike   I've got to go to work –

Vera   Im glad I caught her like that. (*She glances at the bills.*) Poor kid. She needs another woman – with a bit of experience. Talk about make-up – clothes – have a good row. A man's no use. Dont worry, she cant hear. If they dont have someone they turn in on themselves. Dont say you havent been warned.

Mike   What did you want? Is there anythin – ?

Vera   You're half her trouble. More than half. (*Shrug.*) It's

none of my business. You let me know where the line is. That
was made very clear from the start. Im useful for the washing
an' tidying – an' your visit once a week – an' even then you
dont always stay after. You wouldnt find many women so
understandin. (*Shrug.*) I accepted it. Im not being used. It's
more than that.

Mike   I cant listen. Im late.

Vera   She hasnt got a mother – and she's only got half a
father. You're all over the place – so what's she got to cling to?

Mike (*trying to explain*)   Vera somethin I – I want –

Vera   I should be here full time. That's what both of you
need. You wouldnt have to cope with it all on your own. We
ought to get married. Why *dont* we?

Mike   I cant talk about that – I've got to –

Vera   This isnt a good life. Tell me what rights we've got?
We cant make demands on each other. Im allowed to worry
and fret and that's all. Im not even entitled to that. Half the
time Im afraid to open my mouth. If I cried I'd be told to
mind my own business. It's no different for you. We let
everythin go to waste. Well you're certainly in no hurry to
answer.

Mike   I cant think now.

Vera   Dont give me that. (*Sour.*) This has gone through your
head more than once. You've got your answer ready! (*Tries to
reconcile.*) There isnt anyone else. And Im not tryin to replace
your wife – that only happens once. But she's dead. We're not
teenagers, we dont expect the earth. There'd be two salaries
comin in. Why dont I shut up? Her lyin there seemed the
golden opportunity. She makes my point for me. I should
keep it to myself! We'll go on as before. I think you deserve
better.

Mike   Keep it to yourself? You're always sayin it!

Vera (*idea*)   Unless you're plannin to ask her permission?
Even you wouldnt be so daft! Girls that age are little madams

when it comes to bein jealous. An older woman in the house –
she wouldnt get her own way all the time. O I wont shut her
out – I know my responsibilities. But I wouldnt encourage *this*
for a – (*Stops suddenly.*) When did I say it before?

Mike What?

Vera You said Im always sayin –

Mike Last week – a few weeks back – ! You're always hintin
– goin on –

Vera No Im not! It's been on my mind – I dont deny it –
but that's why I know what I said. I went out of my way not to
say! – so I couldn't be accused. Now this! You're twistin my
words. I said she'd move out when –

Mike It doesnt matter!

Vera It matters to me! A lot! Always sayin? Hintin? You
make me sound like a – . I dont have to go beggin for it!

Mike It's always somethin! Who opened the window?
That wasnt you? O god I'll go mad. Leave me alone. I've got
to go.

Vera The woman on my landin's sellin her carpets. (*She gives
the teacup to* **Mike**.) Sheila was thinkin of one to go by the bed.
(*She picks up the sealed envelope.*) D'you want anythin if I pass by
the shops?

Mike No no.

Vera (*takes the teacup from him*)   And Im right. You'll see.
When she's ready she'll be off.

Vera *goes into the kitchen.* **Mike** *puts the envelopes, stamps,
chequebook, biro and bills into the drawer. He closes it.* **Vera** *comes
back without the teacup.*

Vera I've come up here cleanin six years. I know your dust
better than I know my own. You've never given me a key. All
that time. (*Envelope.*) I'll post this. Im only thinkin of your
convenience. One of you wouldnt always have to be in for me.
Shall I have a key cut?

Mike *shuts the window.*

Vera   Dont know how you can live in it. An' dont shout at me again! 'S not human after I've shown my feelins! Will you come down in the week?

Mike   I've got to go.

Vera   Well it's not my place. I've no rights here.

Mike   Thanks about the carpets.

Vera   I might not be in.

Vera *goes out into the hallway. The front door is heard closing.* **Mike** *hesitates a moment. He goes behind* **Sheila** *to the cupboard. He opens the cupboard door.*

It is full of neatly stacked domestic appliances and stores – a radio, vacuum cleaner, hair dryer, portable electric fire, a box of Christmas decorations, bottles of cleaners, dusters, etc. Clothes on hangers on the walls. In a corner at the back a set of mail-order luggage. **Mike** *pulls out the biggest case.*

Mike *leaves the cupboard door open. He puts the suitcase down by* **Sheila**. *He opens it but immediately turns away and goes to the phone. He dials. Waits.*

Mike   Frank please. (*Pause.*) Did you row? Mike. When Sheila came in, she –. Come here. You must! Now! (*Pause.*) All right, Im sorry. It's not important. Yes yes. This evenin. Thank you. Yes.

Section Three – Living-Room
'The Hand on the Telephone'

That evening. Darkish. **Mike** *is getting up from the armchair. He goes out to the hallway. Off, the sound of the front door.*

Frank (*off*)   Well what was so urgent?

Mike *follows* **Frank** *into the room.* **Frank** *is in his early twenties. He wears dark trousers, a green shirt and a maroon blouson.*

Frank   Sheila? (*To* **Mike**.) Is she all right?

Frank *puts on the electric light.*

Mike   She's dead.

Frank (*trying to understand*)   Ill is – ? The doctor? Mike? (*He goes towards* **Sheila**.)

Mike (*stopping him with his voice*)   I killed her.

Frank   O yeh you and Jack the Ripper? You're payin me back. Both of you. (*He tiptoes towards* **Sheila**, *miming holding a dagger.*) I've got a nasty big knife to –

Mike   Aah!

Frank (*realises*)   O no. (*Goes to phone.*)

Mike   Dont! An arrangement's got to be made.

Frank   You said you'd –

Mike   A cup of tea.

Frank (*goes towards* **Mike**)   You – have you sat there all day with – ? (*Squeezes* **Mike**'s *arm.*) You didnt kill her. O you poor – . You disturbed someone and – the shock. (*Sees the suitcase.*) Look they were – . A cup of tea?

Mike   I forgot.

Frank (*realises*)   No you wouldnt sit there all day if you'd disturbed a . . . (*Goes to phone.*) Tell me. It's quiet. When I phone they'll all come. What did you put in her tea?

Mike   Terrible things have happened here. Terrible. I didnt know they – you could be pushed so far.

Frank   The tea!

Mike   Last night. Was it? We rowed. I slept. The door. An' I forgot!

Frank (*watch*)   You've got half a minute.

Mike   I killed her an' forgot! Forgot! Forgot!

Frank   It was someone else. (*Dialling.*) The police'll know
what to –

Mike   The arrangement! Take the flat. (**Frank** *stops dialling.*)
I sat here all day. I worked it out. You can afford the gas and
electricity and upkeep and the tax. There's no mortgage. It
was a struggle. The interest was higher than they said. I dont
know what happens to your stuff when you've done this. Get a
lawyer. Make it legal. It's worth the cost. Say we arranged it
weeks ago in case it makes a difference. Im sorry I shouted. I
was afraid you might not want it because she died here. You
cant afford to think like that. I've lost everythin. (God Im an
evil bastard!) Take the flat. Then somethin's saved. Yes you
will – I can see from your hand on the phone.

Frank   You mean the freehold? Not a lease?

Mike   Yes.

Frank   I always liked this flat. (*Doubt.*) Wait. What if people
say Im mixed up in the . . . ? It's your idea. You said to help
you.

Mike   It would've been hers one day. So when you
married . . .

Frank   She'd've wanted me to have it. I cant believe she's
dead . . . People my age dont often get a chance to own their
place. I need some cover. If you change your mind – I warn
you –

Mike   I forgot.

Frank   Scribble somethin down for the lawyer.

Mike   I'll do it.

Frank   It's furnished too.

Mike (*dismisses him*)   . . . Now call the police . . .

Part Two

Section One – Visiting Room in a Closed Prison

Day. The room is partitioned with a barrier across which visitors and prisoners talk. Two wardens – one on a high stool – watch by the door.

Vera and **Mike** *face each other.*

Vera I didnt bring anythin. Didnt know you could. Should've come before. Dont know where all the time went. I had to sort it out in my head. Decide what to do with my own life. I'll stand by you. The man said I could've brought magazines in.

Mike Long journey.

Vera Nothin's changed. The flats are still there. You know Frank's got a new girl?

Mike He didnt keep in touch.

Vera I'll never know how you . . . You're not a violent person. We all lose our temper. How could you kill your daughter? . . . It was the stairs. Me downstairs, you up. You had a row. If I'd been there to say wait a minute . . . she'd be alive. If I'd just come up to borrow somethin!

Mike Frank's got a new girl?

Vera I want us to get married.

Mike Vera Im here for life.

Vera That's only their way of puttin it.

Mike It's nine or ten years minimum. Or twice as long. They can change the rules when they like.

Vera You're not puttin me off this time.

Mike No no. This is my life. No past, nothin in front of yer, just day t' day. It's the only way t' survive. If I've got another life out there I could still be livin *if* I 'adnt . . . The world ends at that door.

Vera   The time'll go –

Mike   Stop it!

Vera   – then what? You'll be a lost kid – come out and grab the first hand you see. God knows what sort of woman'll get her claws into you. You cant look after yourself – it was all pretence. That's why you're here.

Mike   That's 'outsider' talk! If I thought like that I'd go round the bend.

Vera   I'll be waitin with a home. You wont have to worry your secret'll be found out. Im doin it for me as well as you. Im not an angel.

Mike   Why did you 'ave t' come 'ere? I stopped meself thinkin. Chriss woman cant yer see what yer've done? I could be in that room with 'er body now! Why did yer come?

Vera   More self pity. You'd feel sorry for yourself if you won the lottery. Im glad I never met your wife.

Mike   Dont talk about her!

Vera   You put her on a pedestal. If you worship someone dead the rest of us are bound to seem shop-soiled: we've got to cope with life. Your wife put you here.

Mike   O go away.

Vera   She's in the cemetery and you're in prison – isnt that far enough apart? I've learnt a lot these last few months. If you cant be free in here you never will be. (*Gently.*) You're a good man. None of this should've happened. You do what you say: go on day t' day and forget everythin. It'll be like fallin asleep for a long rest. It's a fairy story. You'll be away so long all the nasty things'll vanish. The past never happened. When you wake up you'll be cured. Forget *me*. I'll be so busy it'll be enough for both of us. I'll live your life for you. Im glad you're in prison. I can see the way clear now. I blame her for Sheila's death – but I thank her for bringin us together. When I saw the warders in their uniform at the gate I wanted to rush up and kiss them. I felt so safe.

Mike   I forgot.

Vera   What did you forget luvvy?

Mike   I was with her body all night. Then you rang and I opened the door. I forgot she was there. I didnt know I was a murderer.

Vera   Of course not. If you were wicked you'd've known. That sort of person has their wits about them. Last thing they do is let anyone in.

Mike   I forgot.

Vera   Shock.

Mike   I could've gone out to work – or Timbuctoo. I wouldnt 'a known till someone told me. If I'd killed a stranger – there'd be no one t' tell me.

Vera   What magazines d'you want?

Mike   If you can forget for one night – with the body under your feet – you can forget for the rest of your life. It's terrible. It just drops out of your mind –

Vera   Dont talk daft.

Mike   – an' yer think you're innocent! There's people walkin round who've done terrible things an' dont –

Vera   Stop it.

Mike   *You* might think you're innocent only because yer dont know what you've done!

Vera   I beg your pardon? I didnt come here for all this tommy rot! You murdered your daughter! She's in her grave. You had a proper trial. You're in prison. I dont want to hear another word.

Mike   How could I forget?

Vera   I told you: shock. You frighten me when you're like this. It's not right. Havent we suffered enough to satisfy you? I've got to go back on the train with all this whizzin round in my head. You sit here ten years thinkin up any more of this and they'll never let you out! You murdered your daughter.

Mike   I know.

Vera   Then dont accuse me. Tellin me I dont know what I've done! There's nothin to be ashamed of in my life – unless it's slavin for you! Im not sittin here being accused. When I rang your bell I didnt know you had a body inside. You could've let me in and strangled *me*! Then I suppose you'd've forgot! I never blamed you. Came here and offered to devote myself – like a bloody fool! *You murdered your daughter.* Say it to yourself every day. It's your only chance. If we cant face what we've done we'll all end up murderers! You always make me sound so harsh. It's a real gift. You dont know the hurt you cause.

Mike (*flatly*)   I didnt say I didnt do it. I did. Then I forgot. That's worse.

Vera   If you'd been murdered you wouldnt need the police to tell you. I suppose this is why you gave Frank the flat. Yes, let's have it all out! You gave Frank the flat because you forgot me? That it? How could you give it to him?

Mike   Didnt think I –

Vera   I dont want to know! It'll only be more rubbish. Not that Im entitled to ask. Blast, blast! I promised myself I wouldnt mention it. Gettin involved in all this worry for nothin! – Why did you give Frank the flat?

Mike   To get shot of it.

Vera   The other flats said you did it to stop him killin you when he found Sheila's body. Anyway his new girl's moved in. You've got a stranger there now.

Mike (*shrug*)   It's his place.

Vera   I *know*. (*Slight pause.*) Some of them said it's not right him havin another woman there. I hope it's not haunted. (*Half-shrug.*) Well you cant live on spilt milk. The first visit was bound to be difficult. You're like a minefield. If someone looks at you you blow up in their face.

Mike   . . . I could've walked out in the street – got lost in all that out there – gone to bed. It was easy. Why? Why? (*Cries.*)

Vera (*silently watches him cry. Pause*)   I've nothin against Frank or his girl. I told her to change the wallpaper. She always let me in when I knocked, till Frank stopped it. I remind him of Sheila. You men only know how to love ladies when we're dead, dont you. Then you soon know how to cry for yourself. They wont stay in the flat. Some stains you cant wash out. We'll wait till it gets to him.

Mike   Sorry. I'll be all right next time. You will come Vera? Please. And write. (*Tearfully puts his hand on hers.*) You've been a saint to me. I dont deserve it.

Vera   As long as you behave. No more pretendin. I cant go on like that. Cry. You have to cry to get used to these places. I can manage the fare once a month. I worked it out. There are other things to save for.

Section Two – Association Area

Day. A bleak space with doors and a cupboard. Tables, chairs and a few games.

It is empty except for **Mike** *and* **Barry** *sitting at adjoining tables.* **Mike** *is turned away with a vacant expression.* **Smiler** *comes in. He seems under twenty and is blond, good-looking and at home in the world. He crosses the Association Area with a mug of tea.*

Smiler   Late for din-dins. (*Warning.*) Closin the 'atch.

Barry   Smiler?

Smiler   Drop dead.

Barry   *One.* Go on!

Smiler *goes out through the far door.*

Barry (*mutter*)   Little runt. (*Looks at* **Mike**.) You're bloody depressin. That cow stopped visitin yer? Yer give 'er the push. Should'a let 'er come. Somethin t' look at, bit a' sniff. Dont 'ave t' listen. (*No answer.*) Your fourth year. Always the worst. Cant 'elp, cant say nothin. Used t' think the clock 'ad died.

Smiler *comes back without the mug and crosses the Association Area towards the other door.*

Barry (*offers*)   Give yer three? Cant offer fairer. Be a sport.

Smiler (*crossing*)   You owe me two weeks.

Barry   I'll settle up.

Smiler *stops and leans on the back of a chair at another table: arms straight, left knee bent, left toe behind right heel.*

Smiler   Dont try your duff tricks on me grandad. Fly little bleeder. Im the lad 'oo sells the worms t' the early dickybirds. Out next week, so yer reckon yer wont 'ave t' pay me. News for you. Wait till yer see 'oo's runnin the bag when Im gone.

Barry   'Oo?

Smiler   Ain nice natured like me when it comes t' owin – or anythin else.

Barry   Give us a ciggie Smiler. Im bloody dyin.

Smiler   Congratulations – only go an do it outside in the dustbin. When yer goin t' settle?

Barry   It's all arranged.

Smiler   You couldnt arrange a knife an fork if the plate gave yer lessons.

Barry   Givvus.

Smiler   Scroungin git. You wouldnt show your arse to a blindman if it'd restore 'is sight – which ain likely.

Barry   Farewell pressie?

Smiler   Pressie? If I was Santa Claus an you was the last Christmas tree on earth I wouldnt give yer a shovel a' reindeer manooer. You owe me fifty-five.

Barry   So what difference's one more?

Smiler   Geriatric old scrounger.

Barry   Givvus a ciggie. (*Points to* **Smiler***'s shirt pocket.*) 'Ole bloody packet there! Look at it! Could put out me 'and an' touch it. (*Dry tears.*) I'll pay. I promise.

Smiler   Look at 'im pretendin t' cry. Got runny eyes lookin through key'oles.

Barry (*rage*)   'F I wanna be a fool, thass *my* right! I take what's comin when I cant pay. Never 'ear me whine! (*Softening. Wheedles.*) You're a vicious little turd Smiler. I bet all the best sewers put in bids for you. Be a pal, givvus. I settled it with Clarkie. 'E pays what 'e owes on the trannie an I pay you. 'E give 'is word.

Smiler   Never 'eard you whine? You sound like a fart that cant afford music lessons. Shouldnt put young blokes with you geriatric trash. Corruptin the nation's future.

Mike *gets up and slowly walks out.*

Barry   Just one. Keep me goin. Avent 'ad a ciggie since slop out.

Smiler *takes the cigarette packet from his shirt pocket.*

Barry   Good lad! Knew yer wouldnt let a mate go without.

Smiler *takes a cigarette from the packet. Then he fishes down behind the cigarettes and takes out a thin blade.*

Barry   You sod! Yer dirty little toe-rag! Yer'd steal the maggots off a corpse.

Smiler *lays the cigarette packet, the cigarette and the blade in a neat row on the edge of the table. Surveys them.*

Smiler (*offer*)   Yes or no?

Barry   Yeh yeh. Givvus. You'll want one day. I wouldnt lend you a straight corkscrew.

Smiler   If it was straight yer wouldnt know what it was. You're so bent yer bump in t' yerself comin back.

Smiler *cuts the cigarette in two with the blade.*

Smiler   Like a tit in a baby's gob.

Barry (*walking up and down in agitation*)   When you was born yer mother only let yer live cause she'd run out a' toilet roll.

Smiler *holds up the two halves to measure them against each other. With quiet satisfaction he finds they are exactly the same length.*

Smiler   Jesus couldnt tell the difference if they was two nails. I was lookin forward t' givin you the little one.

Smiler *tosses half the cigarette onto the table. It rolls onto the floor.*

Barry   Dont spoil my fag yer runt!

Barry *kneels and gropes for the half cigarette under the table. He knocks over a chair. He gets it. Still kneeling, he lights it and inhales.*

Barry   God I needed that.

Barry *goes to the middle of the room to smoke in peace – as he inhales he bows his head to concentrate.* **Smiler** *puts the other half cigarette back in the packet. He meticulously cleans the blade and slips it in the packet behind the cigarettes. He puts the packet in his shirt pocket. He takes a notebook from his hip pocket and a pencil stub from behind his ear. He writes in the notebook.*

Smiler   Put a sign on me nose when you're around: trespassers will be prosecuted. Yer get right up it. Thass fifty six an a 'arf.

Section Three – Mike's Cell

Day. **Mike** *lies on one of the two beds. Through the open door a prison officer is seen passing along the corridor outside. He is followed by a prisoner pulling a trolley loaded with bundles of dirty washing. Pause.*

Smiler *passes by. A few seconds later he comes back and leans on the wall opposite the open door. He looks at* **Mike**.

Smiler   They keep that face in a bin an 'and it round. Year four. Yer look like snow thass bin pissed in just after they made the thaw illegal.

A **Prisoner** *passes between* **Smiler** *and the door.* **Smiler** *collars him.*

Smiler   Three days! Out! Will yer miss me?

Prisoner (*friendly aggression*)   Yer'll spend three bloody years in 'ospital!

The **Prisoner** *goes.*

Smiler (*to* **Mike**)   Come t' say cheerio.

Mike   Monday . . . ?

Smiler *levers himself off the wall and comes into the cell. He half closes the door behind him.*

Smiler   Three days. If I last. Wont be time for cheerios then. (*He sits on the other bed.*) 'Ave t' console the mob. What yer in for: frightenin ol' ladies with that mug? If you laughed yer'd go to the medic with a dangerous symptom.

Mike *makes a friendly, tired gesture with his hand.*

Smiler   Ain so bad: four years then it's downhill all the way. (*Hand gesture.*) The sunny side. I'll keep yer company for a bit. That all right? (*No answer.*) Dump eh? Architect put the rat 'oles in when they built it. That ol' crap-'eap get on yer nerves? If I let 'im 'e'd smoke the 'ole camel. Way beyond 'is means. I mix it with 'im so 'e keeps out a' real bother. Even a wimp like 'im can go the distance with the champ when it's shadow boxin. Puts a bit a' shape in 'is life. 'E ain grateful. (*Slight pause.*) Thass it then. (*Suddenly stands and puts a finger to his lips.*) On Monday Im goin t' chuck all me ciggies in the air an let the lads scramble. Freebies!

Smiler *tiptoes to the door and suddenly opens it:* **Barry** *comes in as if he's just arrived.*

Smiler   You're so bent your arse knows more words than your mouth.

Smiler *goes.*

Barry   Watch it.

Smiler *goes away down the corridor.* **Barry** *sits on the edge of his bed with the cigarette butt in his hand. He opens his locker and takes a pin from the shelf.*

Barry   The little sod'll be back. Read 'is palm even if 'e was born with no arms. Give 'im a week. Six months at the most. (*He sticks the pin into the end of the butt.*) You're dead? – make the most of it. The chaplain says it doesnt last. They come round and wake yer up. Dont suppose Smiler drop yer any ciggies? Might'a lashed out cause a' Monday. If 'e slashed an Jesus walked on the puddle 'e'd charge 'im for a ticket. Know where . . . (*He lights the stub and inhales.*) . . . 'is stash is. Dont finger it. Do it all verbal. Not mixin it with 'im an 'is mates – even if 'is ciggies was a mile long. Know what 'e's in for? 'E dont mind 'oo knows. Tell anyone for a packet a' twenty. No, tell *that* for nothin – only thing 'e dont charge for. (*He removes a shred of tobacco from his lip and examines it on the end of his finger.*) Carved 'is mate in a bar. Mate, mind – not an outsider. Cut 'is eye out. Not normal, like slashin a cheek. Made a proper job they say. Methodical. Talent for it. Would'a bin a surgeon if 'e'd come from a proper family. Poor ol' National 'ealth. (*He slides the shred of tobacco onto the smouldering butt. Inhales.*) Went for the other eye. Ambitious. Mates pulled 'im off. Bloke saw 'is own eye in the broken glass. 'Ad t' go somewhere. New meanin t' gazin in t' the crystal ball: Smiler's little joke when 'e tells it. Comes up every time. Know 'im from the cradle t' the gallows, as they used t' say. (*Small wince as he burns his lip.*) Wass 'e put in 'is fags? Fluff off a gorilla's groin. Think they're number one. The ocean couldnt dilute the piss they talk. (*Calls.*) Smiler! – See 'em in the visitors room. Their mothers an tarts. White faces. Starin great eyes. Like the eyes on those tree rats – or monkeys is it? – yer see on telly. (*Calls.*) Smiler! (– Watch me put 'im through 'is paces). In the visitors room. Then they give birth t' their kids. An yer see it in the kids.

Even the little toddlers. Same little murderers' faces.
Animals're descended from 'uman beings. (*Calls.*) Oi! – You
watch. Looks down on me cause a' me 'abit. That ash's got
more life in it than their kids.

Barry *cleans the pin.* **Smiler** *comes in.*

Smiler   Three days! Three! Three! Three! (*He picks up a
pillow and beats* **Barry** *with it.*) Dont oi me yer git! Oi! Oi!Oi!

Barry   Lay off yer bleedin nutter! Yer lost me pin!

Smiler   'Oo you oi-in? (*Chucks the pillow down.*) Im 'ere!

Barry   Tell us what yer'll do on Monday Smiler.

Smiler   When they say on the news there's bin an earth
tremor thass me on the job. (**Barry** *finds his pin.*) One day yer'll
bend that pin an 'ave a twin.

Barry *puts the pin on the shelf of his locker and shuts the door.*

Barry   Yer'll be down the boozer too pissed t' get the
wrinkles out.

Smiler   Mine dont 'ave wrinkles grandad. Thass where I
notch up the virgins. Wass it worth? All the details before I sell
it t' the press?

Barry   Tell us Smiler. You're a lad. Slip it in eh?

Smiler   Yer lecherous ol' lag! (*Yells.*) Three days! (*To*
Barry.) Forty ciggies on account?

Prisoner 1 (*off*)   Put a sock in it Smiler!

Prisoner 2 (*off*)   Yer sayin yer prayers?

Prisoner 1 (*off*)   Pullin me plonker! Show some respect for
the workin man!

Smiler (*to* **Barry**). Get 'ard on it t'night? Yer couldnt get 'ard
if they give yer an iron spike an cement injections. No Im not
tellin you. Ain wasted time in 'ere – I learnt. Not the garbage
they feed yer. I watched the lot that put us 'ere – thass where I
learnt. They're the crooks – an they get away with it. They

can't fail. It's their set-up – all that out there: the rich man's racket. From now on it's number one. I give that poxy shower enough a' my life. Ain comin back next time. (*Yells.*) Three days! (*Off, groans. He yells.*) Out! Screwin boozin cars Costa Brava lolly!

Prisoner 2 (*off*)   Thank chriss! Then we'll get a bit a' shut-eye!

Barry   You're a lad Smiler. Slip it in eh? Tell us.

Smiler (*suddenly still*)   I cant. I told yer. Screwin boozin cars trip-t'-the-sea lolly: 's foreign language in 'ere. Yer cant understand nothin in 'ere. I only know what it means cause the door's openin for out. If I tried t' tell yer it's like writin on a sheet a' paper an' the words come out on the other side: all you see's blank, 's out there where it means.

Barry   Six months. You'll be back.

Smiler (*very still*)   Yer see? Yer cant understand. Givvus givvus givvus: it's freedom innit? (*Jumps up and yells.*) What sod said put a sock in it?

Smiler *runs out. Off, prisoners' yells and shouts of 'Shuttit nutter!'*

Section Four – Association Area – Cupboard – Washroom, Prison Yard – Mike's Cell

Mike *holding a rope. It has been made by tying two ropes together. Low electric light.* **Mike** *is standing in a cupboard. The cupboard is the blocked-off part of a corridor. Longish and darkish. Near the top along one side there is a shelf backed by a wooden plank. Pipes on the walls and ceilings. Mops, squeegees, floor-cloths, blocks of industrial soap and buckets with mop-grills in the top – one bucket stands under a tap in a corner. Two domestic chairs, one inverted with its seat on the seat of the other.*

Mike *takes down the top chair and wedges its back under the door handle. He stands the other chair under a pipe that crosses the ceiling. He begins to tie the end of the rope into a noose. He is weak and sits on the chair to finish it. He climbs onto the chair. From a trouser side-pocket he* *takes a small envelope – blue, crinkled, with worn edges. He props it against the plank behind the shelf.*

He passes the end of the rope over the pipe on the ceiling and knots it. For a moment he stands in silence. His hand strays to his side in the gesture of a child that wants to wee. He steps down from the chair – and doing this moves it so that it is no longer directly under the noose. He takes away the chair wedging the door and opens it.

Mike *closes the cupboard door behind him. No one else is about. He crosses the Association Area and goes down the corridor till he comes to the washroom.*

He crosses the washroom, passes the urinals and goes out of sight into a cubicle. He doesn't close the door. Pause. The toilet is flushed. **Mike** *comes out of the cubicle, crosses the washroom, goes into the corridor and along it till he reaches a window.*

Mike *looks down into the yard from the second storey. Dusk. The yard is surrounded by security fencing and lit by security lights. On the far side of the yard there is a long one-storey utility hut with a row of brightly lit windows in the wall facing the yard.*

It is after office hours but in one window a **Prison Officer** *crosses with some files. He wears a shirt with rolled-up sleeves and a tie. He crouches, opens the bottom drawer in a desk, puts the files into it and closes it. He goes away.*

Mike*'s hand gently brushes the pane – a gesture like a segment of a handwave.*

In one movement he turns and continues calmly along the corridor. He reaches the Association Area. He crosses it and goes to the cupboard.

Still calm he puts his hand on the door handle and opens the door. **Smiler** *is hanging in the noose.*

A chair lies on its side under the body. The other chair is where **Mike** *had left it.* **Mike** *runs into the cupboard. He tries to support the body and loosen the noose. He can't. The body swings round, twisting away from him as if it's fighting him.* **Mike** *whimpers and tries to support it and hook the chair towards him with his foot but his foot pushes it further away. He lets the body swing, picks up the chair, stands it by the body*

*and climbs onto it. He tugs the body towards him. The legs flop against
the chair – it almost topples. He hitches the weight of the body off the rope
and loosens it. He drags it over the face, squashing and grazing the nose
and cheeks and yanking open the mouth. He stands on the chair holding
the body and breathes into its mouth. He climbs down. The chair lurches
from under him, crashes into the wall and bounces away. He stumbles to
the ground with the body and falls on top of it. He shakes it.*

Mike Smiler. Smiler. No. No. (*Stands, lost, blank.*) I – where
is the – ? What 'ave – ? (*Looks down at the body. Slowly he kneels by
the body, hits the chest, breathes into the mouth.*) Please.

Mike *stands. Looks round, sees the chair, picks it up, puts it under the
noose and starts to climb onto it: one chair leg tangles with the body, the
end of the chair leg pressed into its hand.*

Mike No! No! Let go! Give me the chair! I will! I will!

Mike *savagely kicks the body away – the chair is free. He climbs onto it
and reaches for the noose. It is much larger than it was – stretched when it
was pulled from the head.* **Mike** *holds the bottom of the noose with both
hands and pulls it open so that it forms a perfect equilateral triangle. He
holds the bottom straight and pulls down to keep the triangle rigid. He
puts his head into it. He feels with his foot to kick the chair away.*

Mike*'s head, hands and the rope triangle. His hands grip the bottom of
the triangle as if it were a rail. Pause. Suddenly his face cracks – it seems
to burst into pieces – and water pours from his eyes and the cracks as if
his face were breaking up and washing away in a flood. Dribble spills
from his mouth. He makes a sound. Slowly he lets go of the rope, creeps
down from the chair, huddles against a wall and cries. He runs out of the
cupboard.*

Mike *runs.*

Mike 'Elp! 'Elp! 'Elp! You bastards! 'E's dyin!

There is a moment before two **Prisoners** *come into the corridor.*
Mike *turns to run back.*

Mike *is kneeling by the body breathing into its mouth. Two* **Prison
Officers** *come into the cupboard.*

Mike 'E pulled the chair when I stood on the –

Prison Officer 1   Out!

Mike   'E's alive!

Prison Officer 2   Out! Out! Out!

Prison Officer 2 *pulls* **Mike** *from the body and throws him from the cupboard.* **Prison Officer 1** *bends over the body and gives expert resuscitation treatment. Through the open door* **Mike** *is partly seen getting to his feet in the Association Area.* **Prison Officer 3** *appears behind him, jumps round him, comes to the cupboard door and looks in. He says nothing. Other* **Prisoners** *come into the Association Area and come towards the cupboard.* **Mike** *stands with his head bowed.*

Prison Officer 2 (*low*)   Get that shower out.

Prison Officer 3 (*turning*)   Cells! Cells! Cells!

Prison Officer 2 *slams the door in the* **Prisoners**' *faces. They try to open it.*

Prison Officer 3, **Mike**, **Prisoners**.

Prison Officer 3   Move!

Prisoner 1   Whass up?

Prisoner 2   'Oo they got?

Prisoner 3   'Oo's on the floor?

Prison Officer 4 *comes into the Association Area. He bangs on the cupboard door.*

Prison Officer 4 (*calls*)   'S Jenks! (*The door is opened slightly. He looks in.*) Chriss.

Prison Officer 4 *helps* **Prison Officer 3** *to clear the Association Area.*

Prison Officer 4   Move! Let's 'ave yer!

Prisoner 3   Dont bloody push! 'Oo they got?

Prison Officer 3   Move! Nothin t' see!

Corridor.

Mike, *other* **Prisoners, Prison Officer 3** and **Prison Officer 4**. *Hassle. An alarm starts.* **Mike** *stalks through the others like a zombie.*

Prisoners   Bastards! Bastards! 'Oo they got? What they up to? Dont want no witnesses!

Prison Officer 3   Move or there'll be trouble!

Prisoner 2 (*to* **Mike**)   Yer said dyin!

Mike *doesn't respond.*

Prisoner 3   'S a rope!

Prisoner 4 (*calls*)   Rope!

Prisoners   It's rope! Rope! Rope! Another one!

Prison Officer 4   Not a rope!

Prisoners   Rope!

Prisoner 4   A massacre!

Prison Officer 3   Accident!

Prison Officer 4   Yer'd queue t' see an empty piss pot!

The **Prisoners** *shout as the* **Prison Officers** *hustle them to the cells.*

Mike's Cell.

Electric light. Door shut. Off, the alarm, doors banging, feet and shouts: 'Rope! Another one! Bastards! Move!'

Mike *half-sits, half-crouches on his bed with his face to the wall and gasps as if he's run round the world. His hand slides along the wall, and then he levers himself off it and slowly, still crying – without fuss, like a mechanical toy – crawls off the bunk, creeps under it and goes out of sight.*

Inside the cupboard.

Prison Officer 1 *and* **Prison Officer 2** *with the body.*
Prison Officer 3 *and* **Prison Officer 5** *in the open doorway.*

Prison Officer 1 (*interrupts his resuscitation for a moment*)   Kill that bloody racket. It's not wakin 'im up an it's givin me an earache.

Prison Officer 2   Would choose the end a' shift!

Prison Officer 1 *looks up – his expression changes. He sees* **Barry**'s *head peering over the backs of* **Prison Officer 3** *and* **Prison Officer 5**.

Prison Officer 1   'Op it scrag!

Prison Officer 3 *spins round and frog-marches* **Barry** *away.*

Mike's Cell.

As before but seemingly empty. Off, the alarm – it stops abruptly and **Mike**'s *sobbing is heard: a brief downward scale.*

Mike (*unseen*)   Uh-uh-uh-uh-uh.

Inside the cupboard.

Prison Officer 1, **Prison Officer 2** *and* **Prison Officer 5** *and the body.* **Prison Officer 1** *stops resuscitation.*

Prison Officer 1   'E's gone to the great prison in the sky.

Prison Officer 2 *sees the envelope on the shelf. He takes it down.*

Prison Officer 2   Remembered t' post early for Chriss-mass. Shall I . . . ?

Prison Officer 5   It's 'is thank you letter.

Prison Officer 1 *takes the envelope and opens it.*

Prison Officer 1   Might've left a forwardin address . . . (*Takes out a note and sees the signature.*) No 'e aint.

Section Five – Mike's Cell

Day. **Barry** *and* **Mike** *alone.* **Barry** *sits on the bed with an open cardboard suitcase on it in front of him. In the suitcase, assorted packets of about eight hundred cigarettes. A few more packets on the bed beside the case.*

Barry (*looking at the packets*)   Could'a left 'im me pin in me will. (*Looks up at* **Mike**.) Know where 'e 'ad it 'id? That cupboard. Be'ind the board on the shelf. Not some little bog 'ole. Move arf the wall t' get at it. Smart.

Mike *takes no notice of* **Barry**. *He stands close to the window looking at it. A noise at the door.* **Barry** *quickly and neatly drops a blanket over the case and the loose packets. The door opens slightly and a uniformed arm comes through and beckons.*

Prison Officer 2 (*off*)   Visitor.

Section Six – Probation Office
'Four Lumps of Sugar'

Day. A small room with a desk. Behind the desk an office chair and in front of it a visitor's chair with padded back and pads on bent wood arms. On the desk a lamp, a computer, empty office trays and two cups of coffee. Four sugar lumps on the desk beside the cups. A wastepaper basket. Wall charts, lists, rosters, holiday postcards, etc.

Ellen, **Smiler**'s *mother, stands at the desk. She is in her forties and has longish hair. She wears a street coat. She is making an effort to control her grief.* **Mike** *sits in the visitor's chair.*

Ellen   I said I didnt want to go in the visitors room. The Probation Officer said we could use his office for half an hour. He was nice about it. I cant understand what happened.

Mike   There'll be an inquest.

Ellen   The Probation Officer said you were the last one to speak to him.

Mike   No 'e was dead when I got there.

Ellen   Two days. He'd've been out. His room was ready. We were going to celebrate. I know what he'd done was bad. It would've been different – he'd grown out of it. But they put them in these places. Like living on the edge of the cliff. They make them worse.

Mike   Everyone liked 'im.

Ellen (*she sits*)   Why did he do it?

Mike   Im sorry.

Ellen   You gave him the rope. The Probation Officer –

Mike   I cant 'elp yer missus.

Ellen   If you hadnt given him the rope he couldnt have done it.

Mike *stands to go.*

Ellen   You must've passed him in the corridor? I dont care what it is. Tell me. They smile or they're busy and shout at you. Now you! I thought if I spoke to someone inside . . . Didnt you see he was in trouble? Everyone liked him? They didnt like him very much if they let this happen. And who are you to like my son? You're criminals – half animals – not boys like him. If you could like anyone you wouldnt be in these places! . . . If he'd come out for a few days – then been run over! – he'd've had something. You had years before you came here. He had nothing. I want to know what happened!

Mike   I tied the rope. It's quiet in the evenin. 'Our before they lock us up. I wouldnt be found too soon. They just 'ad t' get rid of what's left. These places can handle that. Part a' the routine. Few extra forms.

Ellen   You left the rope there?

Mike   When I'd worked out what t' do I shut off. Kept my mind blank. Went round like a zombie. Didnt think – in case I lost me nerve. Then when it was all ready – I realised I wanted t' pee. I'd even shut that out. All day. They say when yer 'ang yer lose control. I didnt want t' be found like a baby wettin itself. At least I'd learnt somethin while I was alive.

Ellen   You wanted to pee so he . . . ?

Mike   . . . Screws laughin . . . detail a lad t' mop up . . . didnt want that. I was away three minutes. The shock of findin the rope. . . must've bin the last straw . . . ?

Ellen   It was a joke. He found the rope – knew it was you because he saw you leave – and you said you were fond of him

– so he wanted to joke you out of it. Everything was a joke to him! He stood on the chair – when the door opened – he was excited – so he slipped . . .

Mike. 'E was dead when I got back.

Ellen   In three minutes? He found the rope and did it in three minutes!

Mike   It could 'a bin four or five. I didnt look at the watch. There'll be an inquest.

Ellen   What good's that to me? They didnt find out why he was alive at his trial, why should they bother to find out why he's dead at an inquest? Im the only one who wants to know the truth. He wasnt anybody. They'll blame him because it's easiest. They'd've lent him a rope! I want to know why! . . . I wont let you down. I wouldnt tell them if they *were* interested. They're nothing. I cant live through the rest of my life with it preying on my mind. If I'd nursed him. I didnt even say good-bye. See you on Monday it's a date.

Mike   'E was scared.

Ellen   You mean the other lad? No no even he said it could've been the other way round – he could've hurt my son. He didnt hold a grudge. Sit down. Your coffee's getting cold. Perhaps you'll think of something you forgot in all the upset. Or someone's said something since?

Mike *looks at his watch and sits.*

Ellen   I used to pass the empty prams by the wall. Visitin 'im. Smelt of milk and washing. Empty baby straps. Nappies squashed up in plastic bags. Even the devil'd cry here. He died here. Like climbing down into a grave to hang yourself. (*Pause.*) Well I certainly came on a fool's errand. I suppose they dont let you out of their sight.

Mike   I shant try it again.

Ellen   No. You wouldnt. Had a chance to see. Put on a show. What did he look like on the end of a rope? Tell me. Then the journey's not wasted. Did he have time to pee?

(*Silence.*) You look the sort that makes other people do your suffering for you. Your face is like a mincer with sympathy coming through. Yes you keep quiet. I'll find out. You'll pay. I wont bother with their trials and tribunals. There must be somewhere to turn for – I'll make my own justice! God this is a rotten world. I hope you hang. Open a cupboard and there's the rope! You should be dead. He's here but you're stood in front of him. You cant change everything: I'd've smiled at him – I hate you! Get out of his chair!

Mike *stands abruptly: the empty chair.*

O he's dead. Sit. Sit. Sit in his chair. (**Mike** *sits.*) Rather my enemy than that emptiness. I know what he did, but he was good. I want him back.

Mike   I cant 'elp.

Ellen (*order*)   Sit there. It helps. (*Pause. Slow with hatred.*) You look at your watch? I'll tell you when it's time. You took his life, you can give me half an hour. You're breathing his air – everything you do now's a swindle. I'll hate you when Im dying. Look forward to it. No distractions then, shopping, catching the bus, all the little things you have to do to stay alive . . . just you, to hate. Lie in my bed and hate. Im glad I came. My pulse is hammering away. D'you take sugar? (*Puts the four sugar lumps one by one in her coffee.*) I dont take it. But you're not having it. (*Stirs coffee.*) A little practice in hate. (*Sips.*) Muck. (*Puts the cup down.*) I forgot you're fed on swill. Can I ask you a question? (*No answer.*) How long you in for?

Mike   Life.

Silence. She gives a short sharp giggle.

(*Quietly.*) Im sorry your son died. This is the pits, really. The morgue where they put the living. Me – 'im – some other number – 'oo's it matter 'oo used the rope? I could be dead. Out a' this. I should a' done it when I found 'im. 'E wouldnt a' minded about the piss. Let the screws laugh. Now I cant. Cant get the courage up twice. 'E stole my rope. If 'e was a cannibal 'e'd steal off 'is neighbour's plate. I dont know what was wrong between yer. Dont take it out on me. Dont cry – I seen through that. See through too much in 'ere. When they lower me in my grave I'll be starin in t' my tears on the bottom.

Ellen (*absently*)   He changed in here. He wouldnt tell me. After a while I dont think 'e knew me unless I told him my name.

Mike (*fumbles with a piece of paper*)   My suicide note. (*Holds it out to her.*) Might be some use. (*She doesn't take it.*) It'll be read at the inquest.

Ellen *reads the note as he holds it in his hand.*

Mike   A copy. Wouldnt give me the original. Thass the property a' the court.

Section Seven – Mike's Cell

Day. **Mike** *lies on the only bed. On a shelf beside it there is a mug of tea with a spoon in it. Without looking at what he does he takes the mug from the shelf. He holds the spoon for a moment. He begins to stir the tea.*

Section Eight – Visiting Room in an Open Prison

Day. Prisoners and visitors sit at separate tables and drink coffee, tea and fruit juice. Some of the adults nurse infants and older children on their knees. Other children stand and stare or wander or play with prison toys. A Prison Officer.

Mike *stands at his table and looks towards the door.* **Vera** *has just sat. She wears a brown coat and a baggy beret of loosely knitted pale string.*

Vera   Arent you excited?

Mike   Yer said Frank was comin.

Vera   Outside, bein tactful. Sit down.

Mike Whass 'e want?

Vera Didnt bring anythin. Only extra to carry out. You dont want to leave anythin behind. He hasnt said.

Mike *sits.*

Vera Hardly seen him since he sold me your flat. Found him on the front door in his uniform. I knew he joined the police when he moved. I thought: panic – he wants the flat back! The thoughts go through your head. The flat's mine. He cant touch it. Payments up to date. He wanted me to ask you to send him a visitin order. Suppose he wouldnt write to you in case you said no. They train the police in social work now. He'll offer to stand by you, say he doesnt hold a grudge. Ask me, he owes *you*: you *gave* him the flat. He certainly didnt think of that when he sold it to me!

A **Child** *wandering with a glass of orange juice leans on her knee and offers her the glass. Without looking at it she steers it away.*

Vera There's a luvvy go to mummy. – Cant wait to see your face when you see the flat. All new – even the – ! No you'll see it for yourself! I had to struggle. You're worth it. (*She is going to pat his hand but doesn't.*) This isnt the place for emotions. Frank'll know what to do if you get into trouble.

Mike I wont get into trouble.

Vera We wont let you. As long as you dont get upset and dont try to do everythin yourself. It's all changed. Ten years is what ten lifetimes used to be. A day or two's rest, then we'll look for a job. Wont rush it. Two to keep, an' the mortgage. You wont believe the prices. Frank brought me in the car. I'd love to know what he's after. I'll pop out and send him in. Make a note of everythin he says. He might drop little hints you dont understand. All right?

Vera *stands and goes towards the door.* **Mike** *watches her. At the door she turns to mouth, emphasising the words with stabs of her index finger:* '*Don't worry – it'll be all right – I'll be back soon.*'

Mike *stares at the door when she has gone. The wandering* **Child**

comes to his table and plays sliding its glass of orange juice on the table top. **Mike** *doesn't notice.*

Child   Brr. Brr.

Frank *enters. He is in civvies: a white woollen polo-neck sweater, dark trousers and shoes and a light brown hound's-tooth tweed jacket with a folded newspaper in a pocket.* **Mike** *stands as* **Frank** *comes towards him and holds out his hand.* **Frank** *stops before he reaches* **Mike**'s *table.*

Mike   Frank. Thanks for giving Vera a lift. (**Frank** *hasn't taken his hand.* **Mike** *hesitates.*) The flat seems to have kept her busy. (*No answer.*) Policeman must feel funny visitin 'is pal in prison.

Frank *speaks in a low voice, but naturally so that it doesn't attract attention.*

Frank   You bastard. That's all.

Child (*sliding the glass on the table*)   Brr. Brr.

Frank *turns and walks away.* **Mike** *stares after him. The child spills orange on the table top and writes in it with a finger. Three-quarters of the way across the room* **Frank** *turns and comes back.* **Mike** *realises now that he is white with anger.*

Child   Slop. Slop.

Frank (*as before, but now as if his mouth is almost paralysed with anger*)   You shouldnt be – all you should be hanged – pollute the streets. You see me – first word: flat. You didnt buy me. Duty.

The **Child** *turns to* **Frank** *and with one hand pulls at his trousers and with the other offers him the glass of orange juice.* **Frank** *doesn't notice it.*

Frank   Im glad I saw you – your box.

Child's Mother (*off*)   Dont wet the gentleman's trousers Lucy.

Frank   You're not out – your time starts. You're tied to my eyeballs.

The **Child's Mother** *comes and gathers it away without noticing* **Frank**'s *anger.*

Frank   You look forward – hands on innocent people. Your first move it's your last.

Frank *goes.* **Mike** *stares after him with a blank face. The spilt orange juice glistens on the table.*

Part Three

Section One – The Flat – Living-Room

Vera *has 'modernised'* **Mike**'s *old flat with new furniture, carpets, covers, wallpapers, lights, ornaments and objets de kitsch. The flat is small and over-crowded but the triviality of the things over-crowding it makes it seem empty.*

Mike *is in a chair at the table.* **Vera** *is at the sideboard. She picks up a tray on which are a sherry decanter, two glasses and a glass bowl of nuts and raisins.*

Vera   The look on your face! You didn't expect all this! All the changes are mine. Frank only tinkered when he had it. Sit in an armchair.

Mike   Im all right.

Vera (*points*)   You had your table there. I put mine so you can see the street. (*Remembers.*) O! (*She goes to the stereo and plays a James Last CD.*) Too late to play it loud. You can hear the volume t'morrow. (*Sherry toast.*) To us.

Mike   Us.

Vera   Want a bite to eat?

Mike   No.

Vera   You're tired.

Mike   No.

Vera   The long journey. We should go to bed when you're ready.

Vera *goes out through the hall door. From time to time* **Mike**'s *eyes flicker round the room.*

Vera (*off*)   Im nervous.

Mike   Why did you want t' live 'ere. Yer could 'a moved out.

Vera (*off*)   You've got a perfect right to be in that room. Anyway – a single woman – it was all I could afford. No removal van. Two lads downstairs carried it all up. I only set out to change the furniture but you could see the marks in the pile where yours had stood. So I got a new carpet. It's all paid for – except the mortgage. The bank statement tells me where I am every month. (*Slight pause.*) *You murdered your daughter and spent ten years in prison.* That doesnt make you worse in my eyes. You suffered so you're bound to feel nibbled round the edges. Makes you appreciate what we've got! No use blamin the past if we do wrong now. You've got to have good thoughts – learn to accept responsibilities again.

Vera *comes in wearing a nightgown, a quilted dressing-gown and mandarin slippers.*

Vera   That's the first time you've been in this room since it happened. Left you alone on purpose. You feel better now you've faced it.

Mike *goes to an armchair and sits.*

Vera   You do like it?

Mike *raises his eyebrows, compresses his lips and shakes his head to show his admiration.*

Vera   There's lots more sherry. You're not worried about livin in sin? Be modern for a bit! You're here that's the main thing. You'll soon be proposin. (*Gesture.*) All this – the extra stability – your probation officer'd be pleased. If you go wrong this time you'll be in for good – it wont be a long weekend.

Mike   I might sit 'ere t'night.

Vera   I understand. Let me fetch you a blanket.

Mike   There was a lad inside. Only young. 'E was due out in two days: 'e 'anged 'isself. I thought about it all those years. I was goin t' serve my time quietly – then two days before the end do a runner: escape. I even 'oped – cause I'd taken the risk – I'd find out why 'e'd done it. Why all the other things. It'd come t' me while I was runnin. Then Frank came – an

put the fear a' god in me. Dont suppose I'd'a done it anyway.
No guts. I cant now: ten years down the drain. I dont know
'ow t' live. I don't know what t' do.

Vera   Thank god for Frank! If you'd done that they'd've put
you in Broadmoor for life.

Mike   I didnt murder Sheila.

Vera   You're not goin to start all that Mike? I thought we'd
got over it. You know it frightens me. O! – dont let me forget:
your key.

Mike   I didnt murder her.

Vera   You told the judge you did! Everythin's been so nice.
Dont spoil our first night. (*Gestures round.*) Im sorry it's nothin
better. If you hadnt gone to prison you'd have somewhere
much nicer by now. You're a hard worker. You'd've taken
advantage of all the new opportunities. Or found yourself a
good-looker with money. You missed out once, dont miss out
again. We deserve our bit of happiness.

Vera goes out and comes back with a blanket. She covers **Mike** *and
kneels beside him.*

Vera   Warm? I dont expect I make the most of myself. (*Rests
her head on his lap.*) T' tell the truth I let myself go. Didnt have
the time. Now you're here I'll get rid of the strain. (*Laugh.*)
T'morrow I'll be ten years younger. Or you'll be runnin after
some fancy pair of legs. No more silly talk. We havent got the
time.

Mike   Did yer choose it all yerself? – all the colours.

Vera   There you are! See how nice you can be! I knew you'd
have a little crisis. Now it's over. (*Strokes the back of his hand.*)
You try to understand too much, instead of lookin for the way
out – like the rest of us. It was bound to go wrong. You don't
want this silly old blanket?

No response. **Vera** *goes out and comes back with another blanket.*

Vera   Not leavin you alone t'night. I know the signs. (*She sits*

in the other armchair and covers herself with the blanket.) Frank'll be
your guardian angel.

Mike   I didnt do it.

Vera   That's enough Mike.

Mike   I cant 'elp it. Thass got t' be the basis from now on.

Vera (*sudden anger*)   It's not right to play me up! Are you goin
to appeal? Whose money? You're not throwin my savings
down the drain. Get up a petition for the flats? They wanted
you to hang. You'll be the laughin stock. Turn into some old
crank goin round in slippers with a billboard on his back 'I
never did it!' Never heard such rot! Look at this carpet. In that
cupboard there's a set of these glasses for when we have
people in. You're not to sit there and smash the home for me!
It's always number one! (*Calmer.*) Sorry Im on edge. Im the
one entitled to be overwrought. You havent said one nice
thing about all my work. I ask you if you like it and you pull a
funny face. Now your blanket! Worse than a child! Cant even
keep a blanket on! (*She wraps his blanket closer around him.*)
Someone did it. You'd still've lost a daughter. Everythin
would've changed. Let's stop it Mike. (*She folds up her blanket.*)
Come to bed. We'll just go to sleep. Or lie there. At least we'll
be each other's company. It's not easy to get back into life.
They gave you a booklet. The longer you put it off the harder
it is. Do it for the –

Mike   Stop it! Stop it! . . . I dont care about the flats! It's not
even the prison! And god knows I cant bring Sheila back! I
want t' tell the truth in my own 'ouse. You sit there an tell me
Im a monster an then say get back t' normal! Whass normal?
– murder? I didnt do it.

Vera   You did.

Mike   Im sorry. This isnt what you planned.

Vera   O I knew you'd have this row. Been lookin forward to
it! I didnt call you monster. I dont know why you cant *say* it.
You did it – is sayin it worse? You killed her.

Mike   I didnt! Men dont do that!

Vera   They do!

Mike   Where's my jacket?

Mike *goes into the kitchen.* **Vera** *stands.*

Vera   You're goin out. You cant. You havent got a key. I'll ring the probation. They left an emergency number.

Mike *comes back.*

Mike. I cant live 'ere. Yer put me jacket somewhere.

Mike *goes towards the hall.*

Mike's *small suitcase stands flat against a wall.*

Vera *overtakes* **Mike** *in the hall and blocks the front door.*

Vera   Please. Please. Nothin's the matter. You dont like the furniture. We'll change it. You can do that nowadays. Let me get you a warmer blanket. Tell me what you want. I've got money if you need it. Is it your own room? Sleep alone. You be in charge. That's what I want. I *want*! Im tired of doin all the thinkin. You decide. Please Mike. Dont leave me.

Mike *turns and goes back towards the living-room.* **Vera** *follows* **Mike** *in.*

Vera   They catch you in the streets at night without a jacket they'll put you away. You made your point Mike. You win. I wont say another word. I wont even tell them if you hit me. (*She takes his jacket from the seat of a chair and gives it to him.*) There's your jacket. I'll have to sew that tear before it gets any bigger. I wanted it to go so well. My fault. Im such a silly cow. I go on an' all you need is rest. We're both tired. What d'you want me to think? Im the sort of woman a man runs away from the first night after ten years? I know it's true but dont do it to me. You cant ask me to live with that. I waited so long. It doesn't matter if it hurts you. Stay. Think of me for once.

Mike   Yer knew I wouldnt stay. It's obvious – yer can think out 'ere. Inside yer kid yerself about everythin.

Vera *sits sideways in the armchair, drawing up her legs so that she seems to crouch, facing away from him.*

Vera   Dont go. Dont go.

Mike   It's a shock because it's finished so soon. Yer thought yer could draw it out for weeks – months – go through all the details. Yer need that. I cant. Sheila could've bin in that chair all these years. Waitin t' be told I didnt do it. She wants a good man for 'er father. I didnt kill 'er.

Vera *(crouches as before)*   I dont understand when you talk like that. You need your ideas. That's why I love you. But you have to live in our world. Someone must wash and cook for you. They did it for you in prison. I could do it for you. My hands feel grubby when I touch you. Show me the other things. I want to know. But dont go. Please. Please.

Mike   It's best. Im a fool, I –

Vera *(curls tighter still facing away from him)*   Other people are happy. Why cant I be? O please. *(Cries.)*

Mike *(putting on his jacket)*. I'll take my things. You neednt see me again. I'll always say I didnt do it. That's no use t'you. You wish I did.

Vera *falls out of the chair to his feet. She grabs the ends of his trousers and squeezes them into two fistfuls.*

Vera   Dont leave me. Dont leave me. Please. I dont understand. I'll go out of my mind. I hate this place! Hate it! *(She bites a fistful of trouser.)* Hu – hu – hu – hu. Hate it. Hate it. Hate it. Or kill me – and let me get out that way.

Mike *helps her to her feet.*

Vera   Yes. Yes. That's better. So kind. *(Wipes her face with her hand.)* So kind. Scarin me. There's no one like you in the world. Give me your case. Wait till mornin. Then you can –. O god you make me sound like your gaoler. You'll wait till I sleep and then escape. I've got to sleep – cant stay awake all my life. *(Dabs her eyes with her hands.)* You could walk out next week. Anytime. Doors are everywhere. I'll never trust you now. Doors, doors. There's nothin I can do. (*She sits on the edge of the armchair seat, facing away from him. Talks almost automatically.*) Someone – I heard them on the stair – you said – the police confuse you – strangers come in as they like – because the area – the flats are poor – no they'd've stopped her in the entrance – unless they wanted money – and came up with her to the . . . someone . . .

Mike *sits on an arm of* **Vera***'s chair. He faces away from her, leaning his elbows on his knees so that his hands hang in space.*

Mike   I've bin angry for ten years. Five prisons. Cant think inside. *She's* not sittin there. They ground 'er up long ago. Im not angry. It's the sky. Not used t' it. I killed 'er: but I didnt. 'Ow can I answer that?

Vera   I wish I'd killed her. Another woman's jealousy. I could tell you you didnt do it. I'd be so happy. I hope she's in hell. The little bitch. She made me suffer.

Mike   I'd better go.

Vera (*whispering to herself*)   Ten years . . . in prison every day. Get up. Work. Save every penny. I couldnt afford to look at other people's faces. They were happy. The faces would've been a knife in me. (*She clenches her fist and presses the side of her index finger against her teeth.*) I've given my life up for today. That's what it cost me: you standin there. It's not murder. When you murdered her you paid. You murder me and I pay. She sent you – all those years ago – you've only just found what she wanted. You murdered the wrong one. It should've been me. You're evil – that's why you're always askin for the truth. (*She puts her hand in the pocket of her dressing-gown. She takes out a little ring of keys and throws it on the floor.*) I locked the front door when I got ready for the night. Anyone who lies down next to you's already in their grave. You used to be a weak little man. I shouldnt be surprised if you had periods. You're changed. I dont want you here.

Mike   Per'aps later – if I –

Vera   No. Take your filth away. (*With her foot she straightens a* *ruck she made in the carpet when she was on the floor.*) Dont want your dust and dirt and smut. This place is sacred. All of you stay out. (*She straightens the carpet with her hand.*) You're all murderers makin excuses. I'll keep this place holy. Talk to myself. My mother used to sing to me. Play my CDs. It's in my name.

There is water in her eyes but she doesn't cry. Mike picks up the keys. He goes out with his case.

Section Two – Ellen's House – Front Doorstep – Hall – Living-Room
'Two Shoes'

Night. The front door opens. **Ellen** *stands there. She raises her eyes to* **Mike**'s *face.*

Mike   You dont remember me.

Ellen *closes the door a fraction.*

In prison.

Ellen   What d'you want?

Mike   I come out t'day.

Ellen   It's late.

Mike   About your son.

Ellen (*hesitates*)   Come back t'morrow.

Mike   I 'ave t' go away.

Ellen *thinks for a moment.*

Ellen's Living-room.

The room is about the size of Vera's but is comfortable, with simple furniture and decoration.

Mike *and* **Ellen** *stand looking at each other. He holds his case.*

Mike   I couldn't stay at home.

Ellen   You want to tell me somethin about my son?

Mike   Can I sit? (*He remains standing.*)

Ellen   You haven't got anything to tell me. Go. I cant talk about him. He's been dead six years. (*She moves towards the hall door.*)

Mike   I tied the rope to 'ang meself. 'E found it an 'anged 'isself. (*Confused.*) I should be dead. Your son give me my life – or 'is – or I took it –

Ellen. You didn't kill him?

Mike   No.

Ellen   Please go. I shouldnt've let you in. I cant help you. He mixed me up in trials and inquests and wounds – I dont understand those things. I go to work, do the shopping, get on with life. I've forgotten him.

Mike   I murdered my daughter. We rowed about a teacup. You dont murder over that. I loved 'er. I thought about it for ten years. I wanted it t' go slower so I could think. There was just three words: Im innocent. They joke when they're comin out: swillin, screwin. They dont believe it. They kill – or break somethin – t' go back in. If they dont it's no different: there isnt any 'out'. Your son knew, 'e mastered that. 'E killed 'isself when 'e was comin out. If I knew why, I'd know all the rest. I'd'a put a piece a' chalk in 'is 'and so 'e could scrawl it on the prison wall while 'e was swingin. Inside they're cruel an' stupid: but I can respect them. They are what they are. Out 'ere people are like beetles under stones: only they live under other people. 'Ow can I live out 'ere? I dont know what t' do.

Ellen   You must go.

Mike (*he sits on his case*)   I spent me money on a taxi. Didnt want t' be too late. If Im found wanderin . . . conditional release. Used t' little rooms. The streets scare me. (*Glances round.*) There's no photo of 'im.

Ellen   Sleep in the chair. You'll have to leave when I do – I go to work in the morning.

Mike (*sits in the armchair*) Per'aps between us we could think . . . ?

Ellen I lay awake for years. There's nothing. I wish you hadnt come. It's not fair.

A doorbell: three short rings – **Ellen** *looks up in surprise. The front door is heard opening and slamming.* **Oliver** *comes in. He has been drinking but is not drunk. He is twenty-six, stocky, with greasy dark hair and is dressed in a dark suit, a white shirt unbuttoned at the collar and no tie. He has one eye.*

Oliver Company! (*Pecks* **Ellen**.) 'Ad a party?

Oliver *flops into an armchair and leans back with his legs spread. He raises his hand in Indian Chief greeting to* **Mike**.

Oliver Hi. Olly.

Mike Mike.

Oliver (*mimes shaking hands across the distance*) Please t' meet yer.

Oliver *eases off his shoes with his feet.*

Ellen (*to* **Oliver**) We used to know each other.

Oliver 'Ad a take-away in the street. (**Mike**'s *case.*) Goin far?

Mike I was lookin for a place. Somewhere cheap local.

Oliver Let 'er put yer up. Got plenty a' room.

Ellen Nowhere's made up.

Oliver That chair!

Mike (*stands*) Dont want t' be a –

Oliver Suit yerself. (*Bends forwards, picks up his shoes and tosses them behind his armchair.*) Wont get nowhere local this time a' night. (*No answer.*) If no one else is puttin the kettle on . . .

Oliver *goes into the kitchen. Sounds of kettle, water, etc.*

Ellen He'll stay for a week or so. Turns up when his

drinking's got him in a state. Then he's off for months. He's the one my son – destroyed his eye. (*Shrug.*) I let him use his old room.

Section Three – The Same
'The Empty Vase'

The next afternoon. **Mike** *sits at the table. His jacket is on the back of his chair. He wears a sleeveless pullover.* **Oliver** *comes through the kitchen door. He wears slacks, sweatshirt and a crumpled baseball cap.*

Oliver   Stoppin?

Mike   She said a few days was all right.

Oliver   Where yer from?

Mike   Prison.

Oliver   Knew it. What for?

Mike   Murder.

Oliver   'Ave t' lock our doors at night. So what's the business?

Mike   I was in nick with 'er son.

Oliver   Ah. Well. Serves yer right for doin murder. Yer ain stoppin. I got the spare room.

Mike   Why d'yer come 'ere?

Oliver   I drop in. (*Shrug.*) Me lady 'eaves me out when Im obnoxious.

Mike   Why d'e 'ang 'isself?

Oliver   Little prick got it right for once. (*Shrug.*) All the rackets inside. Mixed up in somethin.

Mike   Why'd'e knife yer eye?

Oliver   Bloody 'ell! Leave it eh? (*An angry gesture – he controls it immediately.*) Party got out a' 'and. Under all the Mr Fix-it stuff 'e was crude. Couldnt 'andle knives.

Mike   Why did 'e—

Oliver   Forget it. 'E's out a' it – I live with it. One eye, two a' the rest? Always gets a pint. The big joker! I carry 'im round with me. One eye, yer twist yer neck t' see all the time – gives yer a slight deformity. Pretty Polly! I got a dead man's 'and on me shoulder. The longer 'e's dead, the more 'e's there. Lets 'ope 'e dont go for the neck. They'll bury me with the bastard.

Mike   Why go an' sleep in 'is room?

Oliver   Same difference. If they take yer leg yer spend the rest a' yer life 'oppin after it. When they take yer eye they get right inside. Talk t' 'im when Im drunk. Give us the price of a pint an I'll ask 'im why 'e done it. Not every ventriloquist 'as a dead dummy.

The front door is heard opening and closing.

Oliver   Dont let on what we said.

Ellen *comes in with a parcel. She wears a street coat.*

Ellen   'Lo. You two all right?

Mike   Listenin t' 'is patter. 'E should do the clubs.

Ellen *goes into the kitchen.*

Oliver   I told yer not t' upset 'er. Bin through enough with that bastard for a son. I dont blame 'er for this. I knew 'e was crude. There was a moment in the fight when 'e went out 'a control – an I missed it.

Front doorbell. **Ellen** *comes from the kitchen wearing a pinafore.*

Ellen   You expectin?

Oliver   Yer bin followed. (*Wolf whistle.*)

Ellen *goes through the hall door. Off, the sound of the front door and voices.*

Oliver (*calls*)   Tell 'em we ain buyin.

Ellen *comes in and shuts the door behind her.*

Ellen   The police. Shall I say you're here? Perhaps the probation –

The door opens behind her and **Frank** *comes in in uniform.*

Frank (*to* **Ellen**)   He lodging here?

Mike   What is it Frank?

Frank (*suddenly finds it difficult to speak. Hides it*)   Change of abode sir – should be notified.

Mike   I was goin round. Who told you I was 'ere?

Frank (*looks at* **Oliver**. *Turns back to* **Ellen**. *Hides under formality his difficulty in speaking*)   I'd advise you not to shelter him madam. He assaulted a woman last night.

Mike   Ha! Is that what she said?

Frank   Soon as I saw the state she was in it all fell into place. I knew where he'd be next. Some of them carry bits of their victim round in their pocket. Relics. You're the nearest he can get to reliving what he did without paying for it. There must be a forensic name for your role madam. He gets your sympathy and wallows in being cunning. (*Glances round. He has found his own voice.*) He sees your son swinging in every shadow in this room. That's what he's here for. He hanged him.

Ellen   Is that true?. . . You've found something out?

Frank   He put the rope up. So he's holding the smoking gun and the dead man pulled the trigger?

Ellen   Is that all you know? Nothing new? (*No answer.*) No! What d'you want? I won't listen!

Ellen *goes into the kitchen.*

Frank (*calls after her*)   Your son couldnt've killed himself – he was going out! (*Turns to* **Mike**.) It clicked when I saw that woman. Your first day. You cant keep your hands off.

Oliver   Hoo hoo hoo now it's interestin.

Frank *goes into the kitchen. His and* **Ellen**'s *voices are heard.*

Ellen (*off*)   Go away! I wont go through all this again! You know nothing!

Frank (*off*)   You should be grateful madam. I've told you the truth about your son!

Mike   'E's mad.

Ellen (*off*)   Leave me alone! Leave me!

Frank (*off*)   Im not leaving you with him! A public danger! (*A door slams.*) I saw that woman! I know when someone's been terrorised. Too scared to come to the door. I had to climb to a window. *She* welcomed him with open arms: he *crept* in here! – god knows what he'll do!

Oliver   Naughty naughty.

Ellen (*off*)   Get out of my way!

Frank (*off*)   He's got nothing to lose! They'll stick him away for life because of that woman! Rape! Assault! Think what goes on in the head of a man like that!

Ellen *comes through without her pinafore and putting on her street coat.* **Frank** *follows her.*

Ellen   Leave me alone!

Frank   But madam –

Oliver   Love it. Love it.

Ellen   I'll go to your superiors!

Oliver   Better than the boozer!

Frank   What sort of mother are you? Would your son invite his killer in his house? You're in more danger than he was! Why should he kill himself when –

Ellen   Because he was afraid! He was a boy (*Sweeping glance to* **Oliver**.) – someone threatened. (*Turns away buttoning up her coat.*) Find out who threatened him! Then come here! (*Silence as she finishes fastening the last buttons.* **Oliver** *and* **Frank** *stare at her.*) Who sent him the letter? After that they all joined in. You know what prisons are! They terrorised him. Played with him till he – . (*To* **Mike**.) You didn't kill him? Tell me!

Oliver   'Old on, 'old on! *I* wrote a letter – thass what you mean! I didn't write a letter! 'E topped 'isself because 'e knew what 'e'd do next time 'e 'ad a blade in 'is 'and! Why should I touch 'im? 'E'd come to a rotten end without *me* for a pen pal!

Mike   I couldnt kill 'im! 'E could kick me t' matchwood!

Frank   Murderers have the strength of a mob. Everyone knows that.

Oliver   Not 'avin that pinned on me. Suffered enough for that bastard.

Ellen   You couldnt kill him! – then come and let me take you in – treat you like my – ! *But you gave him the rope!* You never explain it! Did you kill him?

Mike   No.

Frank   How d'you know?

Mike   For chrissake! I told the inquest what –

Frank   How d'you know?

Mike   I didnt do it!

Frank   Perhaps you forgot.

Mike   Forgot? 'E's mad! 'Ow could yer do that an' forget! Forget yer'd – . (*He stops. Realises. He gets up and walks away.*) No . . . it's not like that . . . I didnt 'urt 'im . . . I wouldnt 'arm a . . . Dont let them say I did it. Please give me some 'elp. A little 'elp. Accusing, accusing. On an on, always accusin . . . Someone speak for me. I didnt kill 'im or my daughter. We learn when we get older – we know what we've done. Dont we? Surely? Isnt there something we can know?

Frank (*reassurance*)   I've got his number.

Mike   I cant go through it again. Im not strong now. This 'appened when they died. I was in this place. *It's 'ere.*

Ellen What is it? Tell me!

Mike Go away! You've no right 'ere! All of you! Leave me with them! They know what I am! Sheila! The boy! . . . (*He stretches his hands as if he touched them.*)

Oliver Bloody 'ell! The bloody limit! 'E wants us out! 'E wants this place!

Ellen *goes out through the hall. The front door is heard.*

Frank I'll tell you the truth. That woman: I saw the state she's in. She's covering up. She'll come round. There'll be charges. Now this! I started it – but it was waiting to be started. I know how it would've ended if I hadnt been here. Look at her running away! When you're around they're running from the morgue! Why did you come here? With you it's always that first morning – when you killed – and phoned me. The body was under your feet. You forgot. You dont know what you do. I know. I know what it's like to be *killed* by you: when you gave me your flat you were chucking flowers on my hearse. Why do I talk to you? I'll put you inside for ever.

Frank *goes out through the hall. Door heard.* **Oliver** *goes to the sideboard and looks in a vase.*

Oliver (*turns the vase upside down. It's empty*) Keeps 'er change there. You 'ad it? No you'd 'a took the vase. If yer lent us a tenner I could leave yer in peace? You're not strapped for readies. Your sort stash it away for when they come out. Robbed the taxi driver last night. (*No answer.*) That copper's mad. They dont notice cause a' the uniform. I could blackmail you. Tell 'im what 'e wants t' 'ear. Me eye's goin t' throb. Does that when Im upset. All that shoutin. I'd swap a pint a' blood for a pint a' piss flavoured with stout. Givvus, givvus. (*Sits in the armchair facing* **Mike**.) God rot this place. If I go out I come back. Stuck with 'er – another nutter. No wonder people top theirselves. It wouldnt take much, it wouldnt take much. Cant even cry – one eye cant cope with all I feel. If I did a muggin I'd be Jack the Ripper. After the torments I suffer Im supposed t' 'ave sympathy for others.

They take yer eye an yer 'ave t' be a saint.

Section Four – Stairway of Ellen's Flat

A little later. A flight of stairs and a landing where a corridor joins.

A door slams in an upper storey. Clattering feet. **Oliver** *comes downstairs singing short phrases to calm his anger. He comes into view getting into his jacket.* **Frank** *steps out of the passageway.*

Oliver   O yeh? Waitin for 'er? (*Going on.*) Dont talk t' nutters.

Frank (*following him for a few paces. Functionally*)   Want to earn?

Oliver (*stops*)   Shop 'im? 'Ow much?

Frank   I cant prove he strung up the lad. I'll get him but it'll be late. If he gave you a hammering I'd get him –

Oliver   Give us a tenner. We'll 'ave a natter sometime. Do business. In a 'urry now.

Frank   – and you apply to the criminal injuries board. Second time victim. You'd clean them out.

Oliver   No one give me for the eye.

Frank   No board then.

Oliver   You rough me up – I point the finger at 'im – an I get paid?

Frank   We use her flat. Call me when they're out – I'll give you a number. Bit of damage. Few bruises. Your word against his. His record? Open and shut.

Oliver   'Ow much?

Frank   Thousands.

Oliver   Sound nice people. What do I lose? It's on. Lend us a tenner an I'll pay yer back when I get me money.

Frank   D'you want the number or not? Memorise it. Nothing written down.

**Section Five – Ellen's Living-Room/The Grey Room
'Training'**

A few days later. Evening. Electric light. **Oliver** *in sweat shirt, slacks
and trainers. He picks up the phone and his face concentrates as he recalls
the number and dials.*

Half an hour later. **Oliver** *leads* **Frank** *into the room.* **Frank** *is in
police uniform.*

Frank   How long?

Oliver   'Bout an 'our. Probation's give 'im a late
appointment.

Frank *takes off his jacket.*

Frank   Uniform. Mustn't mark. (*He takes off his shirt and
trousers.*)

Oliver   . . . Dont wan' it too rough.

Frank   Got to be genuine. No pay otherwise. More you take
the more you get.

Oliver   I know, I know. I know all that. They always pay?
Government dont run out a' money? Dont trust that lot.

Frank *picks up the TV set and gives it to* **Oliver**.

Frank   Break it. (**Oliver** *looks at him.*) Go on. Get the
adrenalin pumpin. Charges the atmosphere. Dont feel it then.
Like takin the medicine before you're hurt. Fact. I could cut
off your dick and you wouldnt know till you kissed the
girlfriend goodnight. (**Oliver** *hesitates.*) Break a few things.

Oliver *breaks the TV. He giggles.* **Frank** *hands him some glasses
from the sideboard.*

Frank. Break them.

Oliver *breaks the glasses.*

Frank   You've got it. Bright lad!

Frank *gives* **Oliver** *a chair.*

Oliver   An that?

Frank   Smash it. They'll pay. It's your money. Smash it. Smash it. Smash it.

Frank *hits* **Oliver** *in the face.*

Oliver   O yer bastard!

Oliver *smashes the chair.* **Frank** *takes a looking glass from the sideboard and gives it to* **Oliver**.

Frank   Smash it.

Oliver   Yeh. But not so rough. That 'urt.

Frank   You're a time waster – plonker! (*Hits* **Oliver** *in the face.*) Smash it. You're not smashing enough. That's why it hurt. Your fault!

Oliver *smashes the looking glass.* **Frank** *kicks him.*

Frank   That 'urt?

Oliver   Ow bastard! (**Oliver** *kicks* **Frank**.) That 'urt – like *that*!

Frank   . . . We're getting nasty. Down to the little worm.

Frank *punches* **Oliver**.

Oliver   Bastard.

Frank *gives* **Oliver** *china ornaments.*

Frank   Smash it! Smash it! Smash it! Or I'll break your bloody neck!

Oliver (*Shying china at the walls*)   Bastards! Bastards! Why did I get in t' this? Bastards! Smash it!

Frank *attacks* **Oliver** *viciously.* **Oliver** *retaliates on the furniture.*

Oliver (*smashing*)   Bastard! Bastard! Bastard! The bastard's 'ittin me! The bastards! I'll kill the bloody lot! O 'er poor stuff – she paid for that – that was a bit a' – 'ad it for years – . (*Stops. Cries.*) Enough. 'S enough.

Frank   This? It's junk! Junk! It should be smashed!

Oliver   We done enough.

Frank   You wimp! Your money! They owe you for the eye!

The Grey Room.

The action is continuous. **Frank** *and* **Oliver** *are in a large grey space with plain walls and a ceiling. The doors are dark blanks. The debris and furniture are the same as in the first room, and the same pictures hang on the walls but everything is grey.*

Oliver   The bastards! The bloody bastards took my eye! Where are they? Pay what yer owe me! Smash it! Smash it! Smash it!

Frank *grabs* **Oliver**'*s collar and shakes and mauls him.*

Frank   Come 'ere yer little bastard! Yer couldnt shake 'ands with a fractured wrist! (*Hits* **Oliver** *in the back of the neck.*)

Oliver (*screams with shock*)   You bastard! (*He hits* **Frank**.)

Frank   You little dog. You dangerous little tyke. That'll cost. You'll pay for that. Hit me you bastard? Im the law! (*He uses his fist as a hammer to beat* **Oliver** *down.*) Came here. On a public service. (*Hammering.*) Line your pockets. Put that bastard away. (*Kicks* **Oliver**.) And you hit me! (*Walks away from* **Oliver**, *turns and faces him.*) Gratitude? (*He takes a running kick at* **Oliver**.) Say sorry sir you nasty bit of snot!

Oliver (*dodging*)   I'll murder yer! I'll bloody kill yer! When I get me money! I'll bloody run yer down! I'll run yer under the bloody road!

Frank   Run me down? Yer couldnt run yer finger up yer nose t' pick it! (*Gestures round.*) Bomb it!

Oliver *goes wild and smashes up the place.* **Frank** *follows him round urging him on with hits and kicks.*

Oliver   Bomb it! Bomb it! Bomb it!

Frank   Bomb it! Bomb it! All this! All yours! Your kingdom! Bomb it! You little shit! King shit – are we? Come 'ere!

Frank *puts both hands on top of* **Oliver**'s *head and forces him down to a standing crouch.* **Oliver** *protects his head, sides and crutch with his hands and arms.* **Frank** *moves round him kicking and punching him.*

Frank   You bastard! Threaten me! The best pal you got! I give you money money money money money money!

Oliver *(through clenched teeth, as if repeating his prayers weakly)* Money . . . money . . . money.

Frank   The face! The face! The face! Give me the face! I want the face!

Oliver *stands in the same crouch. Slowly he raises his face – eyes and mouth screwed tight.* **Frank** *takes a breath and hits his face. Repeatedly.*

Oliver   O dear. O please. O god no please. Dont. Sir. Dont.

Frank   Love it! Love it! Scum! It's good for you you snot! It's money!

Oliver *(crying)*   No more . . . I'll make the bastards pay . . .

Oliver *turns to hobble away.* **Frank** *trips him.* **Oliver** *falls.*

Frank   Get up! Get up!

Oliver *stands and heaves over a table.*

Oliver   Pay! Pay! Pay! Pay!

Oliver *picks up an empty broken frame and clutches it to himself for comfort.* **Frank** *hits him with a chair.* **Oliver** *sprawls into the debris and lies still.*

Frank   Get up. *(Kicks* **Oliver**.*)* The man's berserk. Killer. Attacks women. What sort of man's that? *(Walks round surveying the mess.)* Yes . . . Yes . . . Not bad . . . Looks good . . . A mess . . . His footprints everywhere. *(He chucks a broken cup at* **Oliver**.*)* Look! My god – no wonder we need prisons: thugs like you . . . *(Smashes a glass.)* Bit of law and order. That'll do. Phew. You lucky man. They'll ram it down your throat. Piss the milk of human kindness.

Oliver *(flat)*   I cant see.

Frank   Soon's he's in the door. Dial the law. Not before.

Oliver *is still sprawled in the debris.*

Oliver (*flat*)   I cant see.

Frank   Tell them what I said. Dont embellish. The woman'll back you up. Goes berserk, out of the blue. Lost my cap. (*Searches.*) In this junk. If that's marked I'll thump you for real! . . . I could do with some water.

Oliver (*flat*)   I cant see.

Frank (*looks at him*)   Get the blood off your – . (*He goes to* **Oliver** *and gets down beside him.*) Ugh. Wipe your mug. (*Searches for a rag. Finds his cap. Brushes it.*) Dirt. (*Puts it on.*) Wipe your – . (*Finds a rag.*) God's sake yer look like a dead rat in a drain.

Oliver (*flat*)   I cant see.

Frank (*giving* **Oliver** *the rag*)   Get a grip of yourself! Mind my jacket you oaf! (*Pushing the rag into* **Oliver**'s *hand.*) For chrissake! – catch hold of this. What're you going to tell them? Everything depends on that!

The rag falls from **Oliver**'s *hand. His hand feels round to find where he is. He doesnt hear* **Frank**. *His voice does not change – flat, rather like a child's.*

Oliver (*flat*)   I cant see.

Frank   No – cause you're running in muck! (*He tries to force the rag into* **Oliver**'s *hand.*) Wipe yourself. Im not paddling in your gore. Blood's too dodgy these days.

Oliver (*flat*)   I cant see.

Frank   There must be some concussion. (*He kneels by* **Oliver**.) You knocked your head and – . Shake your head – clear it. (*He grabs* **Oliver**'s *head and shakes it. Then he cuffs it.*) Look. (*He waves his finger in front of* **Oliver**'s *face.*) My finger. (*To himself.*) O god he's . . . (*Clenches his fists and bangs the heels of his palms together. Triumph.*) He's lost an eye . . . The other eye! I've got him! Fixed him! He'll go down for – yipppeeee! (*Pity for* **Oliver**.) And. Wipe it. Wipe it. It may not be. Wipe. You'll see. I promise – your pal – you'll – and spend the money.

Oliver (*flat not hearing* **Frank**)   I cant see.

Frank (*low, gleeful*)   He cant see! He cant see! He – . Tell me it's true!' (*Stands. Dances a few steps.*) He cant see! (*Goal-scorer's triumph: bends back his head, bends his knees and elbows and shakes his clenched fists.*) I did it! I scored! (*Pity. Goes to* **Oliver**.) O no no no no it's nothin – only a little – you poor – poor – it'll pass – they'll make it go.

Oliver (*flat*)   I cant see.

Frank   I didnt want this. I only needed a little – . Not necessary for my – . You know I didnt want it. (*Tries to control himself.*) The time. Late. (*To* **Oliver**.) I didnt do it. You threw yourself about and – . Did it to yourself. We nailed him the main thing is we . . . (*Still trying to be calm.*) So you suffer. He's mad. They all suffer if he's not put away. What is the story? Tell me.

Oliver (*flat*)   I cant see.

Oliver *crawls round the floor in a circle trying to reach the door.* **Frank** *walks round in the opposite direction.*

Frank   Shut in. Shut in. This prison. With that. O god what shall I do? Could I – ? He broke the telly and got into a – no control. Useless. Useless. I work with trash. The job's impossible.

Oliver *reaches the wall and tries to climb it.*

Frank   O god he's going for a doctor! Now I've got to be his nurse! (*He goes to* **Oliver**.) All right. All right. Im here. (*He examines* **Oliver**'*s face.*) Im trained. Medical work. Keep still. (*Dabs* **Oliver**'s *eye with the rag.*) How can I help you if – ? Waste time getting to a doctor. Attention now. (*Stares at the wounded eye.*) O god it's beautiful . . . (*Gently touches the wound.*) How kind. My life. It's beautiful . . . (*He hangs his head in awe.*) They'll take twenty year from him for this . . .

Ellen's Living-room.

The action is continuous. **Oliver** *crawls away along the bottom of the wall. From time to time he tries to climb it and edge along – he falls.* **Frank** *watches him crawl – then follows him, squatting and moving forward on his haunches, leaning over him, sometimes rising when he rises, sometimes looking up at him.*

Frank   You must hear this. Your eye's bad. I think. I know. You're blind. Perhaps. *You're blind. Face it* – get it over. Stick to the story. Your only chance. You need money now – you know that more than I do. You're lucky. The story's gone up in price. It's worth hundreds of thousands now. Im sorry – people like him – there's no defence against the – that's the world. (*He stands and combs his hair.*) Now listen. (Am I talking to myself?) My superiors'll never own up to this. The force'll stick behind me. They'll hound you till you wish you had another eye to give them. You tell the truth an' you get nothin. Even if they believe you. You entered a criminal conspiracy with me: nothin! Tell the story. It's your big chance. You're rich.

Oliver (*flat*)   I cant see.

Frank (*grips* **Oliver**)   What is the story? (*He lets* **Oliver** *go. Tired.*) You're on your own. I've got to go. Do what you like: you attacked me – I hit you in self-defence.

Frank *picks up his jacket, goes to the middle of the room and crouches on his haunches to think.*

Frank   So still. I havent got the strength to walk downstairs: and I've got to put up all the bluff. Some good'll come of it. (*Suddenly becomes very weary.*) Some day people'll be good – no violence then. I try. I take the risk. It always ends in mess. One house I kicked a door down, when we brought the villain out the rats were feeding on the splinters. It's him. He killed her. It comes from him. Sometimes Im frightened of myself. I dont know where it's going. (*Fingers the dust.*) Dee-dum. Dee-dum. (*He looks calmly at* **Oliver**.) Can I trust him? That's why you chose him. Little crooks take the money.

The sound of the front door.

Frank   O god.

Frank *gets up and goes into the kitchen.*

Mike *comes in holding his jacket in his hand. He stops.*

Oliver *sits on the ground like a doll with his back to the wall and his legs stretched out before him. The bloody rag is on his knee. His hands stray feebly over the floor and walls. He has not heard* **Mike**.

Oliver (*flat*)   I cant see.

Mike *takes a few steps towards him, half crouches and holds out a hand. A sound behind him: steps on broken glass. He turns.*

Frank *is coming out of the kitchen towards* **Mike**. *He wears his cap and uniform and has tied Ellen's pinafore over it.* **Mike** *stands as he reaches him. He viciously punches* **Mike** *twice in the face, takes the jacket from his hand, rips open a pocket, tears a lapel and throws the jacket onto* **Oliver**. *He stares at* **Mike** *a moment and then speaks – at the normal speed, but he is so exhausted that no sound comes out of his mouth.*

Frank (*silent*)   Im tired.

He backs, takes off the pinafore, drops it and – still calm – goes out to the hall. The sound of the front door.

Section Six – Hospital Ward

Day, natural light. A small single-bed room in an NHS hospital. A locker and a visitor's chair beside the bed. The bed is made up. **Oliver** *sits next to it in an adult version of a child's high chair; it has a table top that swings across as a gate to hold the sitter. On it, an invalid's plastic mug with a spout.* **Oliver** *wears yellow pyjama trousers and a printed sweat shirt. His head is gauzed unevenly so that parts of it show through.*

Mike *sits on the visitor's chair.* **Ellen** *sits on the edge of the bed. They wear street clothes.*

Mike (*to* **Oliver** *trying to see if he remembers*)   Frank? (*No answer.*) Was it? (*No answer.*) Criminal injuries pay-out? They might not. I'll tell the truth. What use is money now yer cant see? Let Elly look after yer. Yer need 'er.

No answer.

Ellen   Olly.

No answer: **Oliver** *doesn't listen to them.* **Ellen** *leans forward in despair.* **Mike** *puts his hand on her to comfort her.*

Oliver (*runs his finger round the edge of the table top*)   Thass the map a' my world from now on.

Section Seven – Ellen's Bedroom

Night. **Ellen** *and* **Mike** *in the large single bed. Naked, still.*

Mike   The law'll speak t' 'im t'morra. 'E'll take the money. Piss it down the drain. In that state yer cant see anyway. When it's gone he'll fall down on your doorstep – you send 'im away?

Ellen   'E cant sit in the dark year after year knowing 'e put you back inside . . . The blind cant lie . . .

Mike   Frank murdered my daughter an' your son. 'E wasnt there when it 'appened – didnt 'ave t' be. 'E did it – just as 'e blinded Olly. For the same reason. 'Ow can I make anyone understand that? See the connections. They cant. That's why we go on sufferin. Olly's prison. 'E'll never get out. We're all in it now.

Olly's Prison – Stage Version

Author's Note

The play was written for TV. A few changes are necessary for the stage. Most of these are in Part Two. The Association Area takes up most of the stage. The visiting rooms are to one side, Mike's cell to the other. The cupboard is upstage. It has two doors, one to the front and one to the rear.

The hallways and stairs in Parts One and Three should be cut. In Part One it is possible (but not necessary) to cut the day that passes between Sections Two and Three. Section Three could begin with Mike at the door opening it to Frank. Later in the section 'day' would have to be changed to 'night' in Frank's lines 'Have you sat there all day – ' and 'No you wouldnt sit there all day if you'd disturbed a . . .' At the end of Section Two Mike's line 'This evening' would have to be changed to 'Soon as you can'.

It might seem that difficulties are created for the stage by the destruction in Part Three, Section Five, and the shortness of the following two sections. The difficulties may be turned to advantage. The destruction is not an indulgence in chaotic violence. It is a lesson in destructiveness, taught by Authority. Authority carefully chooses the objects to be broken. Its actions have precise aims. It trains its victim efficiently. It is not till the end that it becomes its own victim. I saw a rehearsal in which the fight was staged as a 'TV punch up'. It was disastrous. It showed that Authority owned even the violence on TV and made it a commercial product. It did not show the social cause and psychological cost of violence. There was no 'Theatre Event' (TE) of the sort I have described in the Commentary to my *War Plays*.

Sections Six and Seven should be staged 'ruthlessly' in the chaos of the living-room. Anything needed to create the different venues should be done and shown openly. There should be no attempt to create an illusion of naturalism. Naturalism is created from fictions, from the illusion of reality. Theatre must show the reality of this illusion. When it does this it changes reality – the fictions by which we live. Fiction, illusion, false pretences – these are the enemies of art.

Part One

Section Two – Living-Room

Morning. Daylight comes through the drawn curtains. **Sheila** *lies face down on the table with the cup beside her.* **Mike** *sleeps slumped in the armchair. A doorbell. He does not react. A few moments pass and he opens his eyes and concentrates, trying to recall if he has heard a sound. The doorbell again. He gets up, notices the curtains are drawn and opens them. He goes downstage right to the door that leads onto the outside stairs. He opens it.* **Vera** *stands there. She is about thirty and wears slippers and indoor clothes.*

Vera Rang four times. Standin there. Your curtains are drawn.

Mike What time is it?

Vera You'll be askin me what day it is next. Thought you were workin this weekend. I cant stop. Came to see Sheila. (*Passes by him into the room.*) She up?

Mike (*remembers. He spins round on the spot to stare after* **Vera**) No no she's not – you cant –

As **Vera** *walks into the room she sees* **Sheila** *slumped as before on the table.*

Vera She drunk? She's not starting all that? Sheila . . . !

(*No other changes in the section.*)

Section Three – Living-Room
'The Hand on the Telephone'

That evening. Darkish. Doorbell. Immediately **Mike** *stands, goes downstage right to the door and opens it.* **Frank** *is there.*

Frank Well – what was so urgent?

(*No other changes in the section.*)

Part Two

Section One – Visiting Room in a Closed Prison

A table with two chairs. **Vera** *and* **Mike** *sit facing each other. There is a barrier between them across the table. Two Prison Officers – one on a high stool – watch upstage.*

(No other changes in the section.)

Section Two – Association Area

Day. A bleak space. Tables, chairs, a few games. The Association Area is empty except for **Mike** *and* **Barry** *sitting at adjoining tables.* **Mike** *is turned away with a vacant expression.* **Smiler** *comes in. He seems under twenty and is blond, good-looking and at home in the world. He crosses the Association Area with a mug of tea.*

Later, when **Mike** *gets up and slowly walks away, he goes to his cell and lies on his bed.*

(No other changes in the section.)

Section Three – Mike's Cell

Mike *is lying on one of the two beds.* **Smiler** *passes, glances in at* **Mike** *and goes on. After a few seconds he comes back. He leans on the end of* **Barry**'s *bed and watches* **Mike**. **Barry** *is still bowed over his cigarette in the Association Area.*

Smiler   They keep that face in a bin an 'and it round. Year four. Yer look like snow thass bin pissed on just after they made the thaw illegal. (*Yells.*) Three days! Out! Yer're goin t' miss me!

Prisoner 3 (*off. Friendly aggression*)   Yer'll git three bloody years in 'ospital!

Smiler (*to* **Mike**)   Come t' say cheerio.

Mike   Monday . . .

Smiler   Three days. If I last. Wont be time for cheerios
then. (*He sits on* **Barry**'s *bed*.) 'Ave t' console the mob. What
yer in for: frighten ol' ladies with that mug? If yer laughed
yer'd go t' the medic with a dangerous symptom.

Mike *makes a friendly, tired gesture with his hand.*

Smiler   Ain so bad: four years then it's downhill all the way.
(*Hand gesture*.) The sunny side. I'll keep yer company for a bit.
That all right? (*No answer*.) Dump eh? Architect put the rat
'oles in when they built it. That ol' crap 'eap get on yer
nerves? If I let 'im 'e'd smoke the 'ole camel. Way beyond 'is
means. I mix it with 'im so 'e keeps out a' real bother. Even a
wimp like 'im can go the distance with the champ if it's
shadow boxin. Puts a bit a' shape in 'is life. 'E ain grateful.
(*Slight pause*.) Thass it then. (*Gestures to* **Mike** *to be silent. Raises
his voice slightly*.) Im goin t' chuck all me ciggies in the air and
let the lads scramble – freebies!

Barry *patters into the cell.*

Smiler   Ain it marvellous! 'E'd 'ear a fart if a brass band was
playin in a thunderstorm. (*To* **Barry**.) You're so bent yer arse
knows more words than yer gob.

Smiler *goes.* **Barry** *mutters after him.*

Barry   Know a few words for you.

Barry *sits on the edge of his bed with the cigarette butt in his hand. He
opens his locker and takes a pin from the shelf. He sticks the pin into the
end of the butt.*

The little sod'll be back. Read 'is palm even if 'e was born with
no arms. Give 'im a week. Six months at the most. You dead?
Make the most of it. The chaplain says they come round an
wake yer up. Dont suppose Smiler drop yer any ciggies?
Might'a lashed out cause a' Monday. If 'e slashed an Jesus
walked on the puddle 'e'd charge 'im for a ticket. Know where
. . . (*He lights the stub and inhales*.) . . . 'is stash is. Dont finger it.

Do it all verbal. Not mixin it with 'im an 'is mates – even if 'is ciggies was a mile long. Know what 'e's in for? 'E don't mind 'oo knows. Tell anyone for a packet a' twenty. No, tell *that* for nothin – only thing 'e dont charge for. (*He removes a shred of tobacco from his lip and examines it on the end of his finger.*) Carved 'is mate in a bar. Mate, mind – not an outsider. Cut 'is eye out. Not normal, like slashin a cheek. Made a proper job, they say. Methodical. Talent for it. Would'a bin a surgeon if 'e'd come from a proper family. Poor ol' National 'ealth. (*He slides the shred of tobacco onto the smouldering butt. Inhales.*) Went for the other eye. Ambitious. Mates pulled 'im off. Bloke saw 'is own eye in the broken glass. 'Ad t' go somewhere. New meanin t' gazin in t' the crystal ball: Smiler's little joke when 'e tells it. Comes up every time. Know 'im from the cradle t' the gallows, as they used t' say. (*Small wince as he burns his lip.*) Wass 'e put in 'is fags? Fluff off a gorilla's groin. Think they're number one. The ocean couldnt dilute the piss they talk. (*Calls.*) Smiler! – See 'em in the visitors room. Their mothers and tarts. White faces. Starin great eyes. Like the eyes on those tree rats – or monkeys is it? – yer see on telly. (*Calls.*) Smiler! (– Watch me put 'im through 'is paces.) In the visitors room. Then they give birth t' their kids. An yer see it in the kids. Even the little toddlers. Same little murderers' faces. Animals're descended from 'uman beins. (*Calls.*) Oi! – You watch. Looks down on me cause a' me 'abit. That ash's got more life in it than their kids.

Barry *cleans the pin.* **Smiler** *comes in.*

Smiler   Three days! Three! Three! Three! (*He picks up a pillow and beats* **Barry** *with it.*) Dont oi me yer git! Oi! Oi! Oi!

Barry   Lay off yer bleedin nutter! Yer lost me pin!

Smiler   'Oo you oi-in? (*Chucks the pillow down.*) Im 'ere!

Barry   Tell us what yer'll do on Monday Smiler.

Smiler   When they say on the news there's bin an earth tremor thass me on the job. (**Barry** *finds his pin.*) One day yer'll bend that pin an 'ave a twin.

Barry *puts the pin on the shelf of his locker and shuts the door.*

Barry   Yer'll be down the boozer too pissed t' get the wrinkles out.

Smiler   Mine dont 'ave wrinkles grandad. Thass where I notch up the virgins. Wass it worth? All the details before I sell it t' the press?

Barry   Tell us Smiler. You're a lad. Slip it in eh?

Smiler   Yer lecherous ol' lag! (*Yells.*) Three days! (*To* **Barry**.) Forty ciggies on account?

Prisoner 1 (*off*)   Put a sock in it Smiler!

Prisoner 2 (*off*)   Yer sayin yer prayers?

Prisoner 1 (*off*)   Pullin me plonker! Show some respect for the workin man!

Smiler (*to* **Barry**)   Get 'ard on it t'night? Yer couldnt get 'ard if they give yer an iron spike an cement injections. No Im not tellin you. Ain wasted time in 'ere – I learnt. Not the garbage they feed yer. I watched the lot that put us 'ere – thass where I learnt. They're the crooks – an they get away with it. They cant fail. It's their set-up – all that out there: the rich man's racket. From now on it's number one. I give that poxy shower enough a' my life. Ain comin back next time. (*Yells.*) Three days! (*Off, groans. He yells.*) Out! Screwin boozin cars Costa Brava lolly!

Prisoner 2 (*off. Friendly aggression*)   Thank chriss! Then we'll get a bit a' shut-eye!

Barry   You're a lad Smiler. Slip it in eh? Tell us.

Smiler (*suddenly still*)   I cant. I told yer. Screwin boozin cars trip-t'-the-sea lolly: 's foreign language in 'ere. Yer cant understand nothin in 'ere. I only know what it means cause the door's openin for out. If I tried t' tell yer it's like writin on a sheet a' paper an' the words come out on the other side: all you see's blank, 's out there where it means.

Barry   Six months. You'll be back.

Smiler (*very still*)   Yer see? Yer cant understand. Givvus givvus givvus: it's freedom innit? (*Jumps up and yells.*) What sod said put a sock in it?

Smiler *runs out. Off,* **Prisoners**' *yells and shouts.* 'Shuttit nutter!'

Section Four – Association Area – Cupboard – Mike's Cell

Night. **Barry** *sleeps in his bed.* **Mike** *goes to the cupboard in the Association Area. He opens the door and goes in. The second door at the back of the cupboard is open. He shuts it. Inside the cupboard along one side near the top there is a shelf backed by a wooden plank. Pipes on the walls and ceiling. A few mops, squeegees and buckets with mop-grills in the top. Two domestic chairs, one reversed with its seat on the seat of the other.*

Mike *takes a rope hidden in the corner. He lifts down the top chair and stands it under a pipe that crosses the ceiling. He starts to tie the rope-end into a noose. He is weak and sits on the chair to finish it. He climbs onto the chair. From a trouser side-pocket he takes a small envelope – blue, crinkled, with worn edges. He props it against the plank behind the shelf.*

He passes the end of the rope over the pipe on the ceiling and knots it. For a moment he stands in silence. His hand strays to his side in the gesture of a child that wants to pee. He steps down from the chair – and doing this moves it so that it is no longer directly under the noose.

Mike *leaves the cupboard. He closes the door behind him. He crosses the Association Area and goes to his cell. He picks up the night bucket. He carefully urinates against the side, making no sound.*

Prison Officer 1 *comes into the Association Area. He is bent and grey. He carries a large stack of files before him in both hands. He drops a sheet from one of the files but does not notice. He goes out.*

Mike *goes back to the Association Area. He sees the sheet of paper on the ground. He stops. He stares at it dully. He steps over it. He goes to the cupboard. Calmly he opens the door.*

Smiler *is hanging in the noose. The door on the far side of the* *cupboard is wide open. A chair lies on its side under the body. The other chair is where* **Mike** *had left it.* **Mike** *runs into the cupboard. He tries to support the body and loosen the noose. He can't. The body swings round, twisting away from him as if it's fighting him.* **Mike** *whimpers and tries to support it and hook the chair towards him with his foot but his foot pushes it further away. He lets the body swing, picks up the chair, stands it by the body and climbs onto it. He tugs the body towards him. The legs flop against the chair – it almost topples. He hitches the weight of the body off the rope and loosens it. He drags it over the face, squashing and grazing the nose and cheeks and yanking open the mouth. He stands on the chair holding the body and breathes into its mouth. He climbs down. The chair lurches from under him, crashes into the wall and bounces away. He stumbles to the ground with the body and falls on top of it. He shakes it.*

Mike   Smiler. Smiler. No. No. (*Stands, lost, blank.*) I – where is the – ? What 'ave – ? (*Looks down at the body. Slowly he kneels by the body, hits the chest, breathes into the mouth.*) Please.

Mike *stands. Looks round, sees the chair, picks it up, puts it under the noose and starts to climb onto it: one chair leg tangles with the body, the end of the chair leg pressed into its hand.*

Mike   No! No! Let go! Give me the chair! I will! I will!

Mike *savagely kicks the body away – the chair is free. He climbs onto it and reaches for the noose. It is much larger than it was – stretched when it was pulled from the head.* **Mike** *holds the bottom of the noose with both hands and pulls it open so that it forms a perfect equilateral triangle. He holds the bottom straight and pulls down to keep the triangle rigid. He puts his head into it. He feels with his foot to kick the chair away.*

Mike's *hands grip the bottom of the triangle as if it were a rail. Pause. Suddenly his face cracks – it seems to burst into pieces – and water pours from his eyes and the cracks as if his face were breaking up and washing away in a flood. Dribble spills from his mouth. He makes a sound. Slowly he lets go of the rope, creeps down from the chair, huddles against a wall and cries.*

Mike *runs out of the cupboard into the Association Area.*

Mike.   'Elp! 'Elp! 'Elp! You bastards! 'E's dyin!

Mike *runs back into the cupboard, kneels by the body and breathes into its mouth.*

Prison Officer 1 *and* **Prison Officer 2** *run into the Association Area.*

Mike   'E pulled the chair when I stood on the –

Prison Officer 1   Out!

Mike   'E's alive!

Prison Officer 2   Out! Out! Out!

Prison Officer 2 *pulls* **Mike** *from the body and throws him from the cupboard. An alarm siren starts.* **Prison Officer 1** *kneels by the body and gives expert resuscitation treatment.* **Mike** *gets to his feet.* **Prison Officer 3** *comes in, goes to the cupboard and looks in. He says nothing.* **Prisoners** *are heard shouting.*

Prisoner 2 (*off*)   Whass up?

Prisoner 3 (*off*)   'Oo they got?

Prisoners (*off*)   Bastards! Bastards! 'Oo is it? What they up to? Dont want witnesses!

The **Prisoners** *kick and hammer the cell doors. Shouts.* **Prison Officer 1** *interrupts his resuscitation drill for a moment.*

Prison Officer 1 (*to* **Prison Officer 3**, *calmly*)   Kill that bloody racket. Ain wakin 'im up an it's givin me an earache.

Mike *goes to his cell. He half-sits, half-crouches on his bed with his face to the wall and gasps as if he had just run round the world.* **Barry** *sits upright and motionless on his bed watching him.* **Mike***'s hand slides along the bed, he levers himself up and to the side and slowly, still crying – without fuss, like a mechanical toy – crawls off the bed, creeps under it and goes out of sight.*

Barry *does not move, he stares at the bed – then he stands and creeps on tiptoe to the Association Area.*

Prison Officer 3 (*yells*)   Shurrup! 'Eads down! Bloody shut-eye!

Prisoner 3 (*off*)   Dont bloody shush me!

Prisoner 2 (*off*)   'Oo they got?

Prison Officer 3 (*yells*)   Shut it or there'll be trouble!

Prisoner 2 (*off*)   'E said dyin!

Prisoner 1 (*off*)   'S a rope!

Prisoner 3 (*off*)   Rope!

Prisoner 2   Another one!

The **Prisoners** *shout and bang in unison.*

Prisoners (*off*)   Rope! Rope! Rope! Rope! Rope!

Prison Officer 3 (*yells*)   No rope!

Prisoner 2 (*off*)   Massacre!

Prison Officer 2 (*yells*). 'S'n'accident!

Prisoner 1 (*off*)   Listen! Listen! Shurrup!

Prisoners (*off*)   Shurrup! Listen! Rope! Murder! Bastards!

Prisoner 1 (*off*)   Shut it! Listen what's goin on! That's what they dont want! Listen!

Prisoners (*off*)   Rope! Listen! Listen!

The **Prisoners** *are silent. The alarm siren stops.* **Prison Officer 1** *works at resuscitation.* **Prison Officer 2** *and* **Prison Officer 3** *stoop over the body. In the silence* **Mike** *is heard under the bed. He sobs in a brief downward scale.*

Mike (*unseen*)   Uh-uh-uh-uh-uh.

Prisoner 3 (*off*)   Rope!

Prisoner 2 (*off*)   Shut it! Listen! I'll bloody rope *you*!

A few **Prisoners** *shout 'Rope' and others shout 'Shut it!'. A communal hiss as the* **Prisoners** *call for silence. Silence.* **Barry** *is peering into the cupboard.* **Prison Officer 1** *looks up and sees him.*

Prison Officer 1 (*half-weary*)   'Op it scrag!

Prison Officer 3 *frog-marches* **Barry** *to his cell.* **Prison Officer 1** *stops the resuscitation drill.*

Prison Officer 2   'Ad t' choose the end a' shift!

Prison Officer 1   'E's gone t' the great prison in the sky.

Prison Officer 2 *sees the envelope on the shelf. He takes it down.*

Prison Officer 2   Remembered t' post early for Chrissmass. Shall I . . . ?

Prison Officer 1   'Is thank you letter. (*He takes the letter and opens it.*)

Prisoner 4 (*off*)   Whass 'appening?

Prisoner 3 (*off*)   Rope!

Prison Officer 1   Might've left a forwardin address . . . (*He takes a note from the envelope and sees the signature.*)

No 'e aint.

Section Five – Mike's Cell

The next day. **Barry** *and* **Mike** *alone.* **Barry** *sits on his bed. On it in front of him he has an open suitcase. In the suitcase, assorted packets of about eight hundred cigarettes. A few more packets on the bed by the case.*

Barry (*gazing at the packets*). Could' a left 'im me pin in me will. (*Looks up at* **Mike**.) Know where 'e kep 'em 'id? That cupboard. Be'ind the board on the shelf. Not some little bog 'ole. Move arf the wall t' get at 'em. Smart.

Mike *takes no notice of* **Barry**. *He stands head bowed in thought. Suddenly* **Barry** *jerks a blanket over the case and the loose packets. A few seconds later* **Prison Officer 2** *comes in.*

Prison Officer 2 (*to* **Mike**)   Visitor.

Section Six – Probation Office – Association Area – Mike's Cell
'Four Lumps of Sugar'

A table and two chairs. **Ellen** *enters with two mugs of coffee and four lumps of sugar. She puts the mugs on the table and the four lumps of sugar by the cups. She stands and waits.* **Prison Officer 2** *brings* **Mike** *in.* **Mike** *sits at the table.* **Prison Officer** *waits outside.*

(No other changes till the end.)

Ellen *reads the note as he holds it in his hand.*

Mike   A copy. Wouldn't give me the original. Thass the property a' the court.

Ellen *goes without looking at* **Mike** *or speaking to him.*

Prison Officer 3 *comes in.*

Prison Officer 3   Take that with yer.

Mike *stands. He picks up the two coffee mugs. He goes towards his cell.* **Prison Officer** *follows him.* **Mike** *stops. He stares dully at the two coffee mugs.*

Prison Officer 3   Move. Paralytic twat. *(No response.)* Move!

Mike *goes into his cell. He puts the two coffee cups on top of the locker. He lies on his bed facing away from them.* **Barry** *is not there.* **Prison Officer 3** *goes out.*

Section Seven

Delete.

Section Eight – Visiting Room in an Open Prison

Day. A table with two chairs. **Prison Officer 5** *sits upstage and reads a newspaper. From time to time, the sounds of visiting children and their mothers.*

Vera *sits at the table. She wears a brown coat and a baggy beret of loosely knitted pale string.* **Mike** *stands at the table and looks towards the door.*

Vera Arent you excited?

Mike Yer said Frank was comin.

Vera Outside, bein tactful. Sit down.

Mike Whass 'e want?

Vera Didnt bring anythin. Only extra t' carry out. Yer dont want to leave anythin behind. He hasnt said.

Mike *sits.*

Vera Hardly seen him since he sold me your flat. Found him on the front door in his uniform. I knew he joined the police when he moved. I thought: panic – he wants the flat back! The thoughts go through your head! The flat's mine. He cant touch it. Payments up to date. He wanted me to ask you to send him a visitin order. Suppose he wouldnt write to you direct in case you said no. They train the police in social work now. He'll offer to stand by you, say he doesnt hold a grudge. Ask me, he owes *you:* you *gave* him the flat. He certainly didnt think of that when he sold it to me!

Mother (*off*) Lucy come an kiss da-da bub-bye. Got to catch our train.

Vera Cant wait to see your face when you see the flat. All new – even the –! No you'll see it for yourself! I had to struggle. You're worth it. (*She is going to pat his hand but doesn't.*) This isnt the place for emotions. Frank'll know what to do if you get into trouble.

Mike I wont get into trouble.

Vera We wont let you. As long as you dont get upset – an dont try to do everything yourself. It's all changed. Ten years is what ten lifetimes used to be. A day or two's rest, then we'll look for a job. Wont rush it. Two to keep, an the mortgage. We wont have a kid, you dont want to be bothered with that again. You wont believe the prices. Frank brought me in the car. I'd love to know what he's after. Wouldnt let me help toward the petrol. I'll pop out and send him in. Make a note of everythin he says. He might drop little hints you dont understand. All right?

Vera *stands and goes towards the door.* **Mike** *watches her. At the door she turns to mouth, emphasising the words with stabs of her index finger: 'Don't worry – it'll be all right – I'll be back soon'.* **Mike** *stares at the door after she has gone.*

Mother (*off*)   Lucy! Da-da's going! Mind that orange juice!

Frank *comes in. He is in civvies: a white woollen polo-neck sweater, dark trousers and shoes and a light brown hound's-tooth tweed jacket with a folded newspaper in a pocket.* **Mike** *stands as* **Frank** *comes towards him and holds out his hand.* **Frank** *stops before he reaches* **Mike***'s table.*

Mike   Frank. Thanks for giving Vera a lift. (**Frank** *hasn't taken his hand.* **Mike** *hesitates.*) The flat seems t' keep her busy. (*No response.*) Policeman must feel funny visitin 'is pal in prison.

Frank *speaks in a low voice, but naturally so that he doesn't attract attention.*

Frank   You bastard. That's all.

Frank *turns and walks away.* **Mike** *stares after him. Three-quarters of the way across the room* **Frank** *turns and comes back.* **Mike** *realises now that* **Frank** *is white with anger.*

Mother (*off*)   Lucile!

Frank *tries to speak. His anger almost paralyses his mouth. Forces words through his teeth.*

Frank   You shouldnt be – all you should be – hanged – pollute the streets. You see me – first word: flat. You didnt – buy me – duty. Im glad I saw you – your box.

Mother (*off*)   Look at the state you're in! Your dress!

Frank   You're not out – your time starts – you're tied to my

eyeballs – you look forward – hands on innocent people –
your first move – 's your last.

Frank *goes.* **Mike** *stares after him with a blank face.*

Part Three

Section One – The Flat – Living-Room

There is no hallway. The front door is downstage right. When **Mike** *leaves at the end of the section he unlocks the door from the inside, goes out and shuts the door, leaving the keys inside in the lock.*

Section Two – Ellen's House 'Two Shoes'

There is no hallway. The front door is downstage right.

Oliver's *arrival*:

Oliver *gives his three code rings.* **Mike** *and* **Ellen** *turn to stare at the door.* **Oliver** *opens it and comes in. He sees* **Mike** *and pauses.*

Section Three – the same 'The Empty Vase'

Frank's *arrival*:

Frank *gives one long ring.* **Ellen** *comes from the kitchen wearing her pinafore.*

Ellen   You expectin?

Oliver   Yer bin followed. (*Wolf whistle.*)

Ellen *goes to the front door.*

Oliver   Tell 'em we ain buyin.

Ellen *opens the door.* **Frank** *stands there. She tries to shut the door as she turns to* **Mike**.

Ellen   The police –

Frank *comes in behind her. He wears uniform.*

Frank (*to* **Ellen**)   He lodgin here?

(*No other changes in the section.*)

Section Four – Stairway of Ellen's Flats

No stairway. **Frank** *loiters downstage. His posture shows he is outside.*
Oliver *has just left* **Ellen**'s *flat and is still pulling on his jacket.*
Frank *stops him.*

(*No other changes in the section.*)

Section Five – Ellen's Living-Room 'Training'

The Grey Room. This is not staged. The whole fight takes place in
Ellen's *living-room.*

Section Six – NHS Hospital Ward

Oliver *sits in an adult version of a child's high chair. It has a table top
that swings across to hold in the sitter. On it, an invalid's plastic mug
with a spout. A drip-feed apparatus is attached to the back of the chair.*
Oliver *wears yellow pyjama trousers and a printed sweat shirt. His
head is gauzed unevenly so that parts of it show through.*

Ellen *sits in the visitor's chair.* **Mike** *stands at her side.* (*No other
changes in this section.*)

Section Seven – Ellen's Bedroom

Ellen *and* **Mike** *could undress on stage and lie on a blanket or
mattress on the floor.*

Notes on Imagination was written for the International
Quarter Studio's Group, in conjunction at the invite of
Education of the University of until England Ph. and
Head is Patron of the Centre.

Notes on Imagination

An introduction to **Coffee**

Notes on Imagination was written for the International Centre for Studies in Drama in Education at the Faculty of Education of the University of Central England. Edward Bond is Patron of the Centre.

Notes on Imagination

1 A child's mind should not be described as a circle of light that increases as the child learns. Its mind is a totality and it brings the world into it bit by bit as if increasing the brightness. Before, it knows the totality ignorantly, with knowledge it knows it knowledgeably. From the beginning the child needs a total explanation of the world. For it, all the problems of ontology and value are presented by its rooms and their objects; and the child must give meaning and value to them from its limited learning.

2 A child's world is meaningless, is presented to it without meaning. The child asks of its world all the basic questions of classical and modern philosophy; questions such as why there is anything rather than nothing; how it is that we can act; why there are good and bad. Questions to which there are no answers, only the ramblings of sages.

3 A child's world is a mosaic. Every object and event is a tessera; each must form part of the picture, which is the meaning of the whole. Tesserae have the meaning they have in the picture and of the whole picture and of being in it.

4 A child's world is a map. It learns to live in the world by mapping it. Its map of the world is its means of being. A child could not think or move without its map of the world. The map must contain and describe both the known and the unknown places. Nothing may be unmapped. Anything unmapped would be like a hole in nothingness. A child's mind resembles a ruler, if part of the ruler moves the whole moves.

5 For the child the unknown is a place to describe, a place of values. There nothing is something, emptiness moves and nowhere is somewhere. When the child goes there it finds nothingness cannot be known. It is everywhere.

6   The child's map may be compared to an early mariners' map of the world. It shows that the world's unknown regions contain the fabulous – Eldorado, Atlantis, anthropophagi, dragons, the world's edge. If such things were not mapped, mariners could not sail between trading ports. The human mind must know the unknown as the context of the known. It makes a topography of nothingness, it is a condition of its sanity.

7   To know the objective meanings of things requires concepts beyond a child's understanding. But its map must make it possible for the child to be in the world; its map must be rational, practical, utilitarian. It can be this only by being imaginary. The fabulous inhabits the mundane. Later, ideology reverses this; that is psychological terrorism but it passes unnoticed as the stuff of our daily life.

8   Science is value-free. It studies the world in itself, not as a source of value. Science usefully mines diamonds in order to study rocks. But everything in the imagination has value, nothing is imaginable without value. To imagination, value is what resistance is to touch.

9   Value cannot be dissociated from the valuer. This is so in the way a thing must be seen to have three dimensions; even seemingly flat objects have the third dimension of distance from the viewer. Value is what the valuer knows; it is presence and being. The valuer may equivocate, be cynical, be unsure, but cannot abscond from value; reverence and cynicism are equally values. For this reason the child is part of its map of the world. The child is inscribed in the map and the map in it. It cannot think or move without being part of the map. It thinks and moves on it. Value makes the map co-extensive with all that is. The map states the child's right to live: that is, its authority as the map and the map maker. The world and the child are a monad. The child creates the world, its world. The world is the place of the child's radical innocence.

10   A child is produced by its map of the world in the same process in which it maps the world; the process continues through life. If the map is torn, the map maker is torn.

11   Imagination creates a self which is both protean and stable. It encompasses change but the story-teller does not change. The self is the story that imagines itself. The self pays attention to the story because the self is also the valuer.

12   There is no homunculus in the brain, no 'ghost in the machine', no soul in the imagination, no centre in the psyche. The brain is a complex nexus of relations to the world and itself. The brain structures a map not a person. There is no unified ego, instead there is a 'chorus' which is collectively the self. Imagination is an aspect of the brain's ability to function consciously, at first at the need of the child's body and later also of its mind. The brain's interrelations perform the imagination's story. Imagination, in the world, is theatre and its story is drama.

13   All value must originally have been referenced from the body as feeling. This changed when the brain had activity of its own apart from caring for the body. Thinking is embodied and cerebral; that is why imagination combines reason and value.

14   One of the difficulties of change arises because the self is part of its map of the world. This is more fundamental than material ownership in the world, because as the world is inscribed in the imagination it is to that extent created by the imagination. We imagine the real. But we do not describe and evaluate the world once and for all; the imagination is protean and constantly responds to material and social change; but it is protean only by remaining the same. The mental and objectively material interrelate and so value, in the imagination, alters not merely the story but may even alter the appearance of things.

15   As the brain is a physical organ it may malfunction. It may then be mad and not maintain the map created by imagination. But this is not a failure of imagination; when the imagination goes mad it is not controlling or obliterating reality but playing serious games with it. The first madness is an organic or chemical malfunctioning; the second is true madness. It may be creative and useful and is a province of drama. If it is still functional, then in a mad environment or a mad society it passes as sanity.

16   Madness is an excess of rationality. The mad are reduced to relying entirely on their reason; in madness, value and reason are dissociated and autonomy given to reason. This happens when the imagination (which must ordinarily combine reason and value) cannot create a story to explain whatever it is that is the cause of the incipient madness; it is therefore prudent for it to rely on reason and sustain itself by going mad. We may become mad only because imagination must give priority to reason. In crises this either debases action or leads to re-evaluations in the imagination – which depends on the extent to which the existing map becomes too impractical, too lacking in utility in the objective world, or too lacking in vision.

17   'Nothingness' is a threat of great seriousness and urgency to a child. Children map and create their world of events and things in the presence of nothingness. Nothingness may be endangering or engendering; but only after imagination has apprehended nothingness can it use the real to present nothingness.

18   The child's map of the world is a lie and so the child is a lie. Its descriptions of the world and itself are lies. Yet rationality is the product – is confirmed by – its lies. Its elders teach it to anthropomorphise the world. They tell it lying tales; and indeed, to love a child in this world is to lie to it. But if a child is not lied to, and if it does not lie to itself, its mind is incoherent and cannot bear reality. Perhaps the child's only ontological truth is nothingness and the consequent need to describe and value. The map is a lie but the mapless mind is autistic. We humanise children by lying to them. And the wolf-child maps the wolves' world.

19   The self's description of itself and the world is not merely false but a lie because its elders connive with the falsehood. Later, many factual lies are discarded. But evaluation, which is also made mendacious, endures. In the beginning was the lie and it is the source of all value. Outside the imagination the world is mere ordered chaos, a watch made by a maniac and

read by a clown. The mind is incoherent without a story; the
story contains meaning and makes the map traversable. Later,
when ideology reifies imagination as objective reality, it makes
the mind a disciplined chaos.

20   A child understands the world in terms of itself. 'Trees
speak.' Later the child learns that trees do not speak; but once
a tree or any other such object or such animal has spoken, a
mark is made on the map which remains a site on which
something else must be marked. Because once trees spoke,
people may grow to be speaking trees and utter strange things.
Theologians call speaking trees God's brain. Politicians call
them the voice of the people.

21   We have values because once we were children. Our
ability to evaluate comes from our childhood. A thing,
attitude, event, has value when it is creatively part of the story;
'creatively' means that it mutually articulates with all other
parts of the story. A child gives value to everything. For
example, it will use a piece of wood to be something else in a
story; the piece of wood is then cathexed with its part in the
story and with storiness; it has the aura Walter Benjamin
found in art, not because it is a special piece of wood but
because it is any piece of wood. Later the child is told to give
the piece of wood a price instead of a value; the piece of wood
then becomes property, part of a house, say; and then
ideology finds ways to stabilise property by appropriating the
original, unpriced value; so, for example, a piece of wood may
be turned into an image of crucifixion and bear the myriad
values of a culture; and then a wooden maquette of the cross
can hang on the wall of the house to give a special value to the
money that buys houses and other property. Ideology retards
the adult's mind to a child's mind in order to control the adult.

22   The growing child learns the objective falsity of its map
of the world. Imagination's need for truth is prudential; but it
also desires it, because it must dramatise nothingness which is
the opposite of itself.

23   The child is the origin of value yet the self is a lie. If the
self were not a lie we could not respect the truth – I do not

mean not respect it as an alternative to lies, but because it would not have the existential value with which lies justified themselves to the child. Truth must have the value of lies. It's because imagination needs the truth, the factual, that its respect for truth is nurtured in lies: at first only lies can give meaning to facts by placing them in the story. Lies are our first humanity and it cannot be discarded when we have greater rational understanding: it is our means of gaining greater rational understanding. The lies of childhood persist in the way grammar persists in language – though the child's lies are utterance. It is not that imagination is a 'grammar of perception', but that it is its own oracle. Adults do not speak as children; every day they forget their childhood language, but it is always spoken by the imagination; it is a firework illuminating mundane things.

24   Childhood is more ancient than adulthood; to the child the adult comes later and is the child; the adult forgets but the child remembers; it is as if the child lives on in the adult and gives life to the adult by remembering it – because the child has known nothingness and it cannot be forgotten, but the adult has bartered nothingness for the day's bread.

25   Imagination takes nothingness into its story, into the site of events and things. Our early recognition of nothingness makes us human. Not only is the map drawn on nothingness, but because we take nothingness into ourselves it is as if we drew the map on the far side of the 'paper'. Imagination constantly retraces the map or nothingness will erase it. Nothing is forgotten, and new knowledge is written on the map's palimpsests and so on nothingness. Nothingness is always new and always old; it gives us possibility by demanding our attention and care.

26   Imagination's story is false yet without it reality would not be real or truth significant. Arithmetical facts must be imagined before their proofs have meaning (not merely use). Imagination needs logic but logic cannot eclipse imagination or nothingness; logic is the masquerade of nothingness. An arithmetical sum of things is a fact, but a thing is held in the imagination, and in this sense 'sum' is also a thing. But if imagination is so all pervasive, it seems to disappear – isn't it as if its functions are undertaken by other, mostly mental, means? An imaginary monster may be imagined to do arithmetic but this makes the monster part of its world as well as ours. Nothingness has no corners behind which things may vanish. Facts are in the world and imagination is the map of the world; one is not the place of the other. The gap between cause and effect is not filled by Humean habit and a game of billiards or by Kantian categories, but each instance is sustained by the imagination. All facts enter imagination through one gate: the meaning of the story. Only the people in hell are spectators.

27   The child grows and its map describes the world more objectively. The world functions objectively and its utility has practical value; but objective utility does not replace imagination's valuing; the imagination *en*-valuates facts.

28   The body's sensory experience is not utility. Appetite does not desire nutrition. Utility is first inscribed in the map and our sensory experience is the performance of this inscription. This makes us individuals and explains the great variety of human desire and behaviour. Otherwise we would have souls and each soul would be a clone; each of us would be the others' homunculus.

29   The imagination is primary in its own mind, the body secondary in the imagination, and everything else tertiary in the imagination. Everything is plotted in the imagined story. Yet we are human only when we recognise the imagination in others.

30   *The Tales of the Thousand and One Nights* are an image of the working of the imagination. They show the relationship between the story and death. The imagination's story exponentiates itself so that the teller may live. But the listener is not one caliph; for each story there is a new caliph because the caliph is the teller in the story. The listener tells the story and the story listens.

31   A child's imagination inscribes its early learning onto a

map which is also the self and so the acquirer of new facts.
The growing child inscribes more of the factual onto the map.
Facts are acquired by being placed in the story. Imagination is
where all things are.

32   The child believes it is God. God is the only sort of being
the child knows. The child believes that it creates the world. If
children did not believe they were God we could not be
human. Because the child believes it is God it also behaves like
the devil. If it did not behave in this way we could not be
human. When anyone loses their Godlikeness they lose their
humanity, their responsibility for the world, and then they
behave like the devil behaving like God. All children have the
innocence of God and the innocence of the devil. Authority
made the Son of Light the Prince of Darkness by giving him
an official title and the work to go with it.

33   A child's story interprets authority and the factual. Its
imagination cannot ordain that its elders will always acquiesce
or that fire does not painfully burn. But the child makes its
submission its own and not authority's, and its submission
becomes part of itself. Really, it submits not to authority but to
the world and the world's guardian – nothingness. The tree
spoke the child's language, and thereafter facts must speak the
imagination's language. The sane imagination abhors no fact,
it desires the other. It learns to anticipate the factual and may
be shocked but not surprised.

34   The material is the imagination's profoundest resource,
its profoundest knowledge and experience. Materialism
achieves its forming power through the imagination. Direct
and mutual response between the material and imagination
would be perfect knowledge, uncontaminated by mysticism.
Ideology misled the German Mystics into describing
nothingness as God and finding God in all things; but clearly,
only a world could create a God. In ideology, truth is never
more than a variation of a lie.

35   When persuasion that is not empowered by imagination
remaps the imagination it does so in violence and is a source
of violence.

36 A child maps the world anthropomorphically. All terrors in the unknown are *its* enemies – the terrors know the child. The child is at home in the imagination and places all objects in it just as it places objects on a table and sits down to it to eat. The child imagines the world so as to be in it. It needs and has the right to evaluate itself as the source of value and not only of satisfaction.

37 The child owns the world it creates but everything in the world is owned by others.

38 Because the child's imagination creates and owns the world, the child creates and owns itself. Social ownership is legally maintained by forces outside the child. Ownership of property not only entails ownership of others, it is founded on it.

39 A child's ownership of the world is not a fiction but a necessary corollary of its being and owning itself. And so each of us creates the world and forfeits it to others. Our world becomes their property. How is the child induced to accept this? It learns to obey authority and live for rewards and punishments. Because this happens over time in its daily life it may not notice it, but the imagination notices everything. Each line on the map is congruent with all other lines and depends on them.

40 There must be an event or events, a rite or rites of passage, a shock, in which imagination abdicates responsibility for the world and loses its first proximity to itself. Social organisation is the means by which we live together and maintain social relations with one another, metabolic relations with the natural world, and technological relations with knowledge. Yet society is not a collective but a utilitarian structure.

41 Authority owns society as the child owns itself. How does authority establish its ownership? Submission is achieved by force, as in slavery; but co-operation is achieved only by ideology. Authoritarian ownership uses ideology to relate technology and self to each other and to itself. Ideology turns

upside down the lies of childhood and projects them into the
adult world: infantilism, not maturity. Ideology's one truth is
its technological utility, but even in this it is inefficient.

42   Authority inscribes the adult world onto the child's map,
and the newly injected facts extrude from the map the old
existing values; it is not as if putting on new clothes but as if
flesh ingested new bones. Because valuing is the way the self
owns itself, ownership of society necessarily entails ownership
of others.

43   Authority obtains acquiescence in many ways: need,
reward, ambition, fear, the granting of limited authority and
limited ownership: all these are bound together by ideology.
Ideology turns desire into mere attitude.

44   Ideology is the child's map of the world transposed to the
world of ownership and authority. The child's map was a
truthful lie, ideology reverses this to a lying truth. The child
imagined and so was made human. Existentially, ideology
dehumanises; but utilitarianly it may in part humanise,
because organisational authority can temporarily incorporate
technology into existing forms of ownership. But technology
develops and initiates, and this increasingly disturbs the
existing forms of ownership. It is as if new machines always
demanded new stories; all new things – machines and children
– require the telling of new stories. Those required by children
and machines humanise; those authority requires to maintain
existing forms of ownership corrupt. Children live in a world
of speaking machines; but in owning societies, machines give
adults orders, and only in a truly just society could it be
otherwise. Machines are on the side of children and
imagination, but technology owned by authority is
infanticidal.

45   Ideology institutes the growing child into the owned
world. It projects the child's map into social reality and
reverses its meanings. Now the nation is the motherland or
fatherland, we become our nationality or race, tsars and other
leaders are fathers, the armed services are sister arms. The
relationship between real things is made fabulous; history is

made mythic. Often much of this is expressed as religion.
Christianity projects the child's family and its tensions onto
the universe as the holy family; the Oedipus and Antigone
stories are stultified as doctrines – God the Father kills God
the Son out of love and the mother standing between them is
a virgin. The church institutionalises imagination and helps to
submit it to social ownership. Other religions use nothingness
or childhood fables. Ideology is idolatry. It was to preserve
ownership that heretics were burnt, and that modern states
imprison and sometimes kill.

46   When the child filled the unknown regions of its map
with monsters it unwittingly prepared itself to receive ideology.
Ideology enters the unknown regions and colonises the
monsters it finds there. So adults live and die for childhood
phantoms and pass their lives in no-man's-land.

47   Hitherto politics have been the childhood of the adult
world; the adults' toys are machines and weapons; military
uniforms, insignia and regalia are toddlers' clothes worn by
adults; the battlefield is their nursery floor; prisons, barracks,
death camps and execution sheds are their dolls' houses.

48   Weapons and owned machines are more autonomous
than toys, more able to elude imagination and submit to
ideology; imagination possesses them less creatively and can
do so only when it has submitted to ownership; and perhaps at
first the submission was a clumsy defence against nothingness.
When imagination is autonomous the relationship to
machines, to all things, humanises, and the self becomes itself
and not the site of nothingness. But as machines are less
passive and benign than toys they disturb ownership and its
hold on imagination. Then it is as if ownership used all
machines as weapons to repress imagination and – if it is
necessary to the preserving of ownership – to kill.

49   Authority corrupts imagination by making it fearful. It
makes nothingness the site of its enemies – not, as does the
child, of tragedy and creation. Corruption is a desire to escape
from the self and abandon autonomy to authority. The
obedient are responsible not for acting but for obeying: it is

their duty to obey. Obedience is adult autism. The obedient
have no unmediated access to imagination because authority
occupies it. Often those living in this way think they are being
their most real, authentic self, when really they are least
themself. They die for king, country, leaders, race, God,
civilisation: that is, for ownership, for toys and fairy tales.
They are slaves who die for their chains, their chains are their
rosary. With unconscious accuracy authority demands from
them their *selfless* obedience.

50   We are human because we were once children and our
imagination was ours. The desire for truth is prior to its utility,
play is prior to work and teaches us seriousness, the need for
art is prior to the wish to own, the story is prior to the facts.

51   Genetically we are human but we behave inhumanly.
This is not because we are half-feral animals. We have
capabilities and what is made of them depends on imagination
and story. We have the capability of language – organs of
speech and language modules in the brain – but which
language we speak depends on which language we are taught.
It is the same with our other capabilities. Ownership teaches
us badly, it teaches the worst of lessons.

52   Instinct is not creative. Instincts are set, circumscribed
responses to stimuli; at their most complex instincts are no
more than adaptive and contriving. We are able to live in
diverse ways in diverse habitats because our behaviour is not
instinctive.

53   It is as if imagination is evolved from instinct, as if the
brain's instinctive structures have come to interrelate with its
prefrontal lobes of consciousness; as if imagination were free,
undesignated instinctual ability. What in us concerns
imagination, in other animals is regulated by instinct. But if
imagination is instinctual freedom, it must be free to be either
creative or destructive, but not necessarily either one or the
other as instincts necessarily are. Imagination is unstructured
capacity, instinct without instinct's structures of prudence and
security. And so human freedom is possible only at the risk of
inhumanness. If our creative ability were not necessarily at the

risk of being destructive, it could not rise above instinct to be creative. But we are not destructive for socio-biological reasons; precisely the area socio-biology describes as being instinctually determined, is the area in which we are instinctually undetermined and *necessarily* free.

54   Imagination and reason are closely symbiotic. The story which is imagination's structure is acquired through reason, through description, explanation and evaluation. When imagination is destructive it uses the morphology that before was at the service of instinct. If we had a viper's fangs, when we are angry we would spit. Instead we use our fists. It is an article of faith to ideology that we are creatures of instinct. But really when we behave like animals we do so specifically because we are not animals. We drop bombs on people not because we have animal-like instincts but because we can reason; and so there is a reason why we drop bombs on people. Animals cannot change their instincts, but we can change our reasoning and reason differently. The problem is that reason is guided by ideology and is the product of ownership. We bomb each other because we are free not to do so – blatantly that is entailed by our ability to make anything as complicated as a bomb – but are taught we must. To behave humanly we do not have to curb our instincts but to change our society.

55   Imagination gives us the possibility of being peaceable, ownership makes imagination destructive and changes it into the simulacrum of instinct. When imagination is made destructive it may seem to be anti-life. This is the half-truth behind Freud's theory of Thanatos, and its derelict, political version in fascism. All owning societies must produce Cultures of Death; both slave-owning societies and modern consumer democracy are Death Cultures.

56   A child's imagination relates directly to the material and so is creative. No person or authority intervenes between its imagination and the world. Children are helped, encouraged, taught, coerced, loved, whipped – but they cannot retreat from self to obedience. This is seen most clearly in the learning of language: a child learns its teacher's language so it can 'speak for itself'. Nowhere on the child's map may be consigned to another's authority. With adults and their map it is otherwise, because of their more urgent need to compromise with utility. Compromise may usurp creativity. On the adult's map there is a no-man's-land which is a place of cemeteries.

57   Acts are produced by the interrelation of objective and subjective. But this does not mean that when X is ordered to do Y, X does it because X's imagination is stimulated by the order to do Y. X acts from fear of punishment for disobeying or hope of reward for obeying; or perhaps just because the act passes unheeded in the great host of unheeded, prudential acts that make up the habit of living. Y is not mapped on the imagination – at most what is mapped is a general submission to authority, though this may allow authority to order acts which are against the imagination's will. In the end all acts committed without imagination are destructive.

58   'When I was a child I spake as a child, I understood as a child, I thought as a child: but when I became a man, I put away childish things. For now we see through a glass darkly; but then face to face: now I know in part: but then shall I know even as also I am known.' This is an ideological statement; it reverses truth and contains it in a distorted and finally impractical form. Most ideologies that tell you how to live expect you to die for them. How else could they prove they work? Ideology is a dark glass.

59   What is the creativity of a child's imagination? A child learns to move, speak, understand, act – to live; its power, its autonomy, comes partly from others' co-operation but also from constantly learning the ways in which imagination is utilitarian, so that the story facilitates the objective, the material, the real, as well as having its own meaning. Day by day the map extends in scope and proliferates in detail. Children's understanding of the world is more profound than that of most adults. Adults are entangled in the chaos of ideology, lost in the dark mirror, and struggle for understanding. The child's world has a more profound meaning for it because its questions are its own and not authority's. Most adults think their understanding is more profound than the child's because they are more practical, they know how to use the tool. The child knows it is the tool.

60   Children trust their parents and rely on their parents' knowledge but they still live with their imagination. They grow and pass from truthfulness to facts; and ownership turns facts into lies, as before the child turned lies into truth – the wheel spins for the farm-cart and the machine-gun. Because authority cleans the streets it establishes its right to build H-bombs and gas chambers. Adults and children have a human need for the unreal reality of fables, but adults do not need lies. Lies enter the adult world through the gate of ownership because only ownership needs them. Adults have no need to lie amongst themselves. Adult lies, like crime and social violence, are only conventions of ownership.

61   Imagination makes self-autonomy necessary. Without it there is no coherence. But society owns the self, and imagination creates submission in the guise of freedom. This leads to the negative freedoms of crime and vandalism. These are not caused by psychological faults, with biological, instinctual components, but are assertions of the imagination in a society corrupted by ownership. Such societies confuse justice with law-and-order and co-operation with discipline; and the more right-wing a society the more violent it must be. Right-wing ideology is produced by authoritarian ownership and it either stimulates rational opposition (prompted by imagination) or enforces a submissive disjunction between reason and imagination, story and fact – and this is disciplined chaos. In the end ideology disrupts, and discipline is the etiquette of thugs.

62   Only societies commit crimes, individuals cannot. Someone who commits a 'crime' transgresses against the self, but when society is criminal it transgresses against others. Society holds us responsible for our acts not our imaginations. This is because authority owns people and must be criminal, must create gods and must wage wars.

63   Punishment is the generalised cause of crime. In owned society the imagination may conform to ideology, lose its autonomy and take part in society's crimes; or it may seek autonomy in the only way ideology and social thinking leave open to it – that is, commit crime. Punishment corrupts criminals. They are corrupted when fear or need forces them to believe that their crime should be punished: then they have accepted authority's false story – the ideology which justifies society's injustice and which was the cause of their crime. No wonder many criminals are right-wing reactionaries who support imprisonment, flogging and capital punishment. All crimes are attacks on injustice and are gestures of support for the victims. Of course such statements sound meaningless and absurd. That is the tragedy of our situation. It is as if we lived in two parallel sets of actions. In the first, criminals cause their victims grievous suffering and authority punishes them. All well and good! In the second, the same acts are part of a total social structure in which ideology reverses meanings for the sake of ownership. This second interpretation is not an abstraction. Ideology is embodied in bricks and mortar, in customs and attitudes and psychology; it becomes a motive for action. Ownership uses the first, practical explanation to justify its authority: and so ownership depends on theft for its existence.

64   We should ask not for mercy but sanity. It is a serious undertaking to disentangle our tragic chaos, but it becomes more urgent: if we do not, there will be starvation and war. It is no longer a matter of sparing ourselves present suffering. Technology is now too powerful to let us take refuge in the irrational, as we have always done in the past. We are moving towards disaster. Society can afford its criminals but it can no longer afford its laws or the people who obey them.

65   Action and ownership, crime and law, folly and justice are intermeshed in chaos. And yet, behind these two parallel worlds, there is a strange simplicity in our lives: meaning is reversed because the map is turned upside down.

66   Criminals, vandals, racists act and speak on authority's

behalf. Authority's corruption of imagination is an act of
violence against itself, against the owners of authority; and this
self-violence is projected into others who become violent in
turn; money, rewards, honours and so on, are other forms of
violence. Corruption proceeds in two directions, against the
self and – through the philosophies and institutions of
ownership – against others. And so crime is the representative
of law, violence the representative of order and discipline the
representative of chaos. It is not simply the platitude that law
often incites crime, provokes it by reaction – it is more: crime
speaks for and on behalf of law, is the spirit of law; and violence
is the spirit of law-and-order; war of peace; repression of
democracy. Owning societies have only the simulacra of law,
justice, peace and democracy. Even Utopia may establish
laws, but they will not corrupt truth as our laws do; in our
society crime is the necessary guardian of property and
violence of public order, because our laws serve the servitude
of imagination to ownership; for us, crime and violence are
reason trying, under the existential necessity of imagination, to
protect itself against irrationalism.

67   The mad go mad to protect their understanding, and
criminals commit crimes out of respect for justice; on their
map it is written that crime is an attack on the injustice of a
whole society – even when the imagination is repressed, the
accuracy of its understanding is uncanny. But in such a society
many lives are mere proxies for death.

68   All criminals are innocent; and all punishers are corrupt
because they misdescribe reality. This offends the last
innocence left in their imagination, and so they offend against
themselves. That is why so many of them are fanatical and
belligerent. In punishing, punishers deny their own innocence
– otherwise it would reveal to them their guilt. Self-
righteousness is self-hatred.

69   While a person can still act utilitarianly, there may be a
functioning – even a propitious – relation between reason and
imagination, even while the relationship is declining. A
bureaucratic psychopath (such as a Nazi functionary) need not

be a psychopath in private. Psychopathic functionaries must still be able to co-operate with the inertia of the real; it is, for example, more complicated and demanding to organise train timetables than to gas the passengers when they reach their destination. But a 'private psychopath' does not try to adapt facts to the story, he disputes facts. He acts as if he owned the world, not as if he created it. He has no responsibility, only culpability.

70   To be creative, imagination must constantly inscribe new facts and utilities into the map. For this it must be autonomous. If it were to lose autonomy but still be sane, there would have to be no new facts or utilities – the world would have to stand still. But daily life and technology require imagination to change, even if only to retain some coherence in the chaos of ideology. The map is always under a stress which ownership denies. And so conservatism must be reactionary and in times of great change fascistic. Creative imagination must inscribe the new into the existing map so that it becomes more utilitarian and rational and a source of greater satisfaction of desire.

71   The difference between reaction and progressivism lies in the way imagination functions; either it denies change or it recreates itself in change.

72   Reaction and progressivism do not always coincide with the ostensible political right and left. Conservatism cannot be progressive because it is literally *unimaginable*. It holds that a technological tractor is a social horse, a rational scientist an irrational druid, an H-bomb a chivalric bow-and-arrow. To sustain ownership and its legal and cultural supports, ideology must repress the present and its utility. Over time the pressure of resisting change becomes so great, that these supports – institutions and doctrines – become independent and take on their own fetishistic violence. The fanatic of law-and-order is like an oarsman without a boat who plies his oars in the open sea.

73   There is a profound and irresolvable conflict between capitalism and conservatism. They do not belong together.

Capitalism welcomes technology, conservatism abhors and indeed fears it. It can accept technology only by becoming fascistic. Hitler combined technology and teutonic myth in a truly farcical way. This split between capitalism and conservatism is very dangerous: our consumer democracy is built on a fault-line, and the heap of consumer products cannot hide it. Capitalism must degrade democracy – it is why our world becomes more barbarous.

74   Conservatism cannot preserve the past and its attempts to do so destroy the present. But progressive politics has its own difficulties. It has to deal with an existing social situation that is opposed to it. It cannot do this by inscribing a new society onto each individual imagination. That was the error of Stalinism. The imagination must autonomously inscribe each new reality into itself. Stalinist social-realism was as reactionary as socio-biology in denying autonomy to the imagination. When it is attempted to impose freedom, then even an objectively freer, better society rapidly deteriorates into a less free, worse one. We cannot be forced to be free, freedom is learnt.

75   Politicians think they can impose a changed reality on others and in this way reorganise society. But if reality is to be in the present, it must be imagined. There is no silver bullet to kill the past. Only a free society could freely recreate itself. Till then, progressive politics must find ways to disentangle the present from the past.

76   For humans to act humanly the material must be the source of imagination. The child relates to the material creatively: it sees the union between the superficial and the profound. It directly stories the material into the imagination's map. In our societies ownership intervenes between self and reality; ideology describes reality in ways which support the ownership of reality, of things and their relationships and meaning. Unlike violent tyranny, democracy succeeds in transmuting opposition into affirmation and its weaknesses into strengths. It does this through ownership of the imagination. But the cost is appalling.

77   War and crime are taught.

78   War memorials are the trademarks of ownership.

79   The Russian Revolution turned revolutionary strengths into weaknesses; fascism turns its own weaknesses into strengths. Both must fail but it is a dangerous error to describe them as being the 'same'.

80   Some illnesses have direct physical causes; others (mental and physical) are or are caused by disorders of the repressed imagination. Society treats both sorts of illness in the same way, and so its cure for the illnesses of repressed imagination is another disease. Curing the disorders of repressed imagination obstructs the possibilities the imagination's vicissitudes give us of acting humanly. These vicissitudes need not be reduced to medical symptoms; that happens when the sickness or the cure deprives the sufferers of responsibility for their actions. Society owns its sicknesses and propagandises them in its ideology; then its social practice promotes sickness and suffering. There are no cures for the problems of being human, there are only stories.

81   One social disease is the traumatisation of children. Sometimes this has a natural cause, but usually the cause lies in the way ideology teaches us to treat children. A child is traumatised when it must face a situation too brutal or confounding to be used creatively in its story. Punishing a traumatised child complicates and deepens the trauma; and medical 'cures' and attempts to change the child's 'nature' are only well-meant punishments. The child must be helped to redramatise its mind and change its story.

82   New housing estates reproduce the social malaise of old tower blocks because only the design is changed – not social ownership. In a property-owning democracy you may legally own a house but ideologically, culturally you are no freer in it than a prisoner in a cell; you and the house are still owned by society. Really, the Englishman's home is his dungeon.

83   Deconstruction shows that there is no 'closure' in thought, nowhere meaning may be secured or value confirmed. But value comes from the imagination *because* it cannot be stabilised by closure. Authority corrupts it when it tries to impose closure and calls it the soul or atavistic instinct. Theoretical thought is a singularity which cannot reflect itself and thus create closure. Imagination is a duality of itself and reason, itself and the material, of the story-teller and the story. Its dualism requires it to describe and evaluate so as to know that one side of the duality 'is' and the other side 'is-not', and vice versa; and the reality of the distinction is assured by nothingness. Imagination functions through the mental and the material and objective; it is the matrix of relationship between things, utility, necessity and freedom. Evaluation is implicit in imagination's responses.

84   When our imagination is not autonomous we behave irrationally. Imagination does not 'recognise' rationality but 'authors' it for its own ends of existing in reality. When rationality and social judgement are imposed they are repressive. It is not that imagination innately rejects the imposition of reason, but that the imposition deprives imagination of the vulnerability and vitality it must have to recognise itself in others. Imagination is rational and human when it recognises imagination in others and in society.

85   Authority strives to make imagination static; by ideologising imagination, it objectifies all the psyche's movement into industry, invention, money, weapons, war and so on. The forms of ownership change but its control of imagination remains.

86   Our society changes dynamically. The economy depends on the constant innovations of commercialism. It is not that we are subjected to every changing fashion, but that imagination's resistance to repression is recouped by fashion as greed, envy, sentimentality, cruelty, fear. This gives the system a gravitational cohesion so strong in its denial of imagination's truths that it finally collapses in on itself.

87   Technology and commercialism now provoke change too rapidly for society to be able to stabilise imagination and make it static in, say, religion; instead the whole former

process is reversed, and now imagination is forced to
constantly change. This apparent freedom is repressive. It
serves the same purpose as violence in feudalism and tyranny.
It subordinates imagination to the biological and to
consumption, to satisfaction within the story instead of in
changing the story. The story becomes its own, hermetic
subject instead of the subject being reality. The map is
redrawn as a grid. The apparent dizzying changes are no
more than the repetitions of a mantra, the anecdote repeated
by an obsessive. Each morning we dig up the same corpse,
and at nightfall we bury it. And as imagination cannot be
static it regresses to sectarianism, nationalism, racism,
religiosity, new ageism, social division – the things inseparable
from capitalist democracy. Imagination is made the site of
violence.

88   Capitalism controls people by owning their imaginations.
In the past imagination was strictly systematised and ordered,
now it is agitated. It is diverted into consumption, and then
consumption is projected into conduct. The greater the
consumption, the more it produces of conduct that authority
may approve. As the poor and feckless consume less, naturally
their production of approvable conduct is less – it is as if the
poor consumed poverty. Consumption penetrates the whole
society. It becomes a structural (not necessarily always
psychological) fiction which ramifies like a disease. Consumer
capitalism fictionalises the material.

89   Ownership is now as regressive as religion was in the
witch-burning crazes of the sixteenth and seventeenth
centuries. They occurred when changes in the technological
foundations of ownership and authority led to a crisis; as
change accelerated religion became maniacal. Capitalist
democracy replaced the old order, and now *it* is entering its
crisis.

90   Owning societies can afford their criminals but not their
wars. Technology, logistic complexity, the military juggernaut
– such things overtask ideology's ability to control reality.
Giving bombs to politicians and soldiers is like giving matches

to children playing in an oil refinery. For a while victory postpones problems, but the problems of peace are the problems of war.

91   Children interpret the cosmos domestically and the domestic cosmically; for children they are the same. And so each of their acts relates to the whole world: therefore it is natural for them to take responsibility for the world. And for them that responsibility is not something less serious than it is for adults: a child finds in its toys all that Blake found in a grain of sand. The smallness of the child's world does not decrease its responsibility for the world, it enlarges it – because, like God, it sees everything in it, the fall of the sparrow, the chipped arms of the doll. When authority deprives its imagination of autonomy, the child loses responsibility for the world and so for itself. We act responsibly, in a way which those affected by our acts will recognise as responsible, when we are responsible for the world. Our democracy deprives us of both responsibilities. Formally, we own ourselves, but existentially authority owns us. Slaves and animals cannot be corrupted because they are not required to act responsibly; but democratic citizens are corrupt because they act 'responsibly' but have no self with which to act. When they feed and clothe themselves it is as if they did it to an alien figure that stood outside them – such people live their lives as if they were diseased statues.

92   Can corruption be so radical that it cannot be reversed? Authority supports corruption with militarism, patriotism, nationalism – with all the ideological manias and their psychological consequences. But authority is insecure. When reality can no longer support the fantasies of ideology, the mind may be driven mad by what living asks of it. If the mad possess political power, it will protect their madness so long as it also enables them to manipulate reality. But people go mad, the world does not. When reality in the imagination is at breaking point, facts speak for themselves. In the end reality imposes its materialism on imagination. The world is not a secure asylum for the mad.

93   The child's map is of itself and the world, of itself in the world. Authority's map is never as complete. It cannot totally describe nothingness because that is already inscribed in the child's first map, in the self. Nothingness is the only thing that can never change. It endures in the mind as a questioning and apprehension that authority cannot silence with answers or force. The self has the power of nothingness. Authority has the weakness of nihilism.

94   Authority refracts imagination in an amalgam of the occult and the rational and this creates a vicious ideology. Creativity is left to be fostered by unacknowledged educators: anarchists, artists and – negatively – criminals and the unpolitical mad. They do not have ingress to imagination free of ideology, but they do not confuse the ruins of ideology with the ideal city.

95   Reality imposes crises, dramas, on us. We can anticipate them in drama and other arts. Madness cannot be abreacted into sanity. It is a form of corruption or shock and cannot be cured by punishment, drugs, prisons and executions. The mad may be made sane only by a story.

96   We would be human – all our acts would be human – if the childhood autonomy of imagination extended into adulthood. This seems the antithesis of adulthood, which depends not on imagination and responsibility but on organisation, discipline and duty. Children create the world in their own image but take the image from the world. When society appropriates the image it imposes on it the image of ownership: it covers our life mask with its death mask. Its chief justification is practicality. Ideology creates problems such as violence and crime which take on their own dynamic and become practical problems. In this way the huge fantasies of ideology are propped up by practical common sense; we do not die for our country every day, but every day we shop and do not want to be robbed on the way to the shops. But common sense cannot explain the paradoxes of our life, and human behaviour bewilders it. Practical, commonsense people are unprepared when things go wrong, they do not understand; and so in any crisis they fall immediately into the most dangerous pits of ideology. Commonsense people are at heart fanatics.

97   No society has enabled autonomy of imagination to survive from childhood to adulthood, except in admonitory and compensatory forms such as sport, religious fantasy, war. Now capitalism commercialises these things. It prizes sport over art because of the two sport is closer to war.

98   Whatever its transitory historical characteristics, the source of humanness is imagination. Authority replaces humane responsibility and initiative with conformity. This limits creativity to the administration of existing utility. Education could create an understanding in which authority could not disguise itself as the self. To do this it must dramatise imagination. If it does not, then there is instruction but not education. Instruction is destructive if imagination is not autonomous. You can be instructed in bricklaying. Who will teach you whether to build a hospital or a gas chamber? – the imagination. We act humanly when our imagination recognises the imagination in others, but only an autonomous imagination can do this because only it can recognise the human in itself. In a just society we would map our imaginations onto the real world, and then our actions and even our economy and institutions would replicate our humanness.

99   Education should not dramatise the imagination constantly and obsessively. It should do it as often as is needed to free the mind to creatively receive all the other knowledge it needs. In everyone's life there are occasions which change the meaning of their life. It is the same with education. Dramatisation should show the imagination in society, and present it not with the needs of authority, discipline, organisation, compulsion – but with the imagination in others. No other lesson is as serious. Tragic necessity far exceeds the compulsions of any prison, school, house of correction or barracks. Dramatising the imagination is not a 'soft option'; what is the frivolousness of a short-sharp-shock compared to the grave learning of tragedy? The first merely discomforts the body, the second demands knowledge of the mind. What is to be gained by a short-sharp-shock when so many lives are a long, dull, aching one? It is tragic understanding that teaches us the strength of comedy, which otherwise is trivial and cruel. If older people find this too serious, it is because they are too afraid, too cowed, to be as serious as their children at play.

100   Tragic heroes and heroines are alone in feeling no guilt at their acts or recrimination at their fate. They turn the child's creation of value into responsibility for justice. The sublime is made practical.

101   Nothingness draws our attention to tragedy. Avoiding it leads to triviality or fanaticism, and triviality turns to fanaticism when common sense despairs. Fanaticism, whether of the crowd or the solitary, is joy at surrendering responsibility to nothingness: nihilism. Belief is always belief in 'nothing'; this gives it a conviction as strong as the grip of the dead.

102   In drama the imagination directly confronts itself, and when it does this it is always drawn to an extreme because it remembers nothingness: the space which the self wishes to enter with its humanity. Our strength needs to do this, our weakness needs to hide in authority.

103   Tyranny and Western democracy are both unstable because they are based on our weaknesses. Weakness is open to penetration but produces little in response. The weak lack vulnerability because they protect themselves in cruelty, conformity, fanaticism. Vulnerability makes change and creativity necessary, and only strength is vulnerable.

104   The problem of our society is that the teachers do not know.

105   Imagination may not be examined; it is recognised.

106   To prehominids the language of the first humans would appear as magic.

107   A child's imagination may be exuberant, perplexed, traumatised. It reads and is not read because it confronts nothingness which cannot read. Even more than events and things, the border with nothingness gives imagination its concern for the world. Imagination has the exuberance to endure and know tragedy.

108   It is as if children pass freely in and out of death – the border is not barred to them – till the body claims the mind for life. As we grow older we must remember.

109   The child's radical innocence accepts responsibility for the world. If our mind could be unconscious, automatic, till puberty and then become conscious, aware of itself – we would have no problems; we would be as pure as machines but we would not be human. If a child's imagination survives as it grows, its radical innocence is secured from corruption. We cannot entirely lose our innocence, but education ought not to teach us to try. Formal instruction and formal socialisation create a non-person – a statue fidgeting with its bandages.

110   Nothing else has the dignity of a crying child.

111   Theatre dramatises imagination in small, seemingly insignificant incidents, and in incidents of obvious significance. Drama cannot instruct, it confronts, perplexes and intrigues imagination into recreating reality. This cannot be systematised and generalised; if it could, authority would use it to stabilise ownership. Art brings nothing of its own, but it defines everything else. Its confrontations force some people deeper into reaction, but then they must take responsibility for it and cannot leave it to authority.

112   Theatre dramatises society's critical structures. There are no right answers to its questions though there are many wrong ones. It puts each of us into the situation of Lear, Hamlet, Macbeth, Oedipus, Antigone, Hecuba, Cassandra, Medea. These are situations in which imagination seeks its innocence and to take responsibility for the world; they are not situations in which it is easy to act humanly, and our imagination does it only at a cost to ourself – really, at the cost of being ourself. Authority handles these situations by giving orders or by talk of transcendental authorities. Both are ways of avoiding the situations, but we must confront them to be human. When we come to die we can have no proxy for ourself, nor can we when we live.

113 At present human beings stand between instinct and freedom. Imagination frees us from instinct; but when authority takes away responsibility from our imagination, it reduces us to a state which is more animal-like than the animals', to instinct which has no instinctual restraint. When one thing is owned everything is owned. We cannot be free and human till imagination is autonomous throughout our life. The world I have described is often bleak and tragic, full of needless suffering, a desert of ash and grey winds. We live in a Death Culture and arm death with terrible weapons; and the most terrible of these is ignorance.

(1994)

Coffee

A Tragedy

Coffee was first staged on 12 May 2000 at Le Théâtre National de la Colline (Paris). The cast was as follows:

Girl	Stéphanie Béghain
Gregory	Carlo Brandt
Jelly	Rodolphe Congé
Nold	Clovis Cornillac
Zemlinsky	Gilles David
Simon	Vincent Garanger
West	Guillaume Lévéque
Young Woman	Lisa Pajon
Jolly	Lionel Tua
Woman	Dominique Valadié

Directed by Alain Françon
Designed by Jacques Gabel
Costumes by Patrice Cauchetier
Lighting by Jöel Hourbeigt
Sound by Luc Charles
Artistic Adviser Myriam Desrumeaux
Movement Adviser Caroline Marcadé
Assistant Director Barbara Nicolier
Assistant Costume Designer Isabelle Flossi

The First House

An upstairs room in a block of flats. Upstage a table and chair. Behind them to the right a door. Some early morning light.

Nold *comes on stage right. He is an engineer and part-time student. A little over average size. He wears shirt and trousers. He carries a knife, fork and place cloth. He lays them on the table and goes out right.*

Silence. **Gregory** *comes in through the door. He looks older than he is — grey, gaunt with wiry muscles. His face is lined as from grimacing in the open air and the rims of his eyes are a little reddened. A strip-bandage is wound round his head, blood-stained to the left. He wears an old crumpled suit and shirt, no tie, and carries another jacket. He and his clothes and the bandage seem to be lightly sprinkled with quarry dust.*

He walks slowly to the middle of the room. He stops and stares in the direction taken by **Nold**. *His face is dully expressionless. He turns, goes to the door, hangs the jacket on the inside knob and goes out.*

Nold *comes in from the right. He carries a plate of food and a mug of tea. He stops and stares dumbly at the jacket. He puts the plate and mug on the table and throws the jacket into a corner. His face is concentrated but almost as expressionless as* **Gregory**'s. *He goes to the table. He is about to sit but stops himself with a short sound of annoyance. He goes out right.*

Silence. **Gregory** *comes in. He walks slowly to the middle of the room, stops and looks after* **Nold**. *He picks up the jacket. With one hand he makes a half-hearted gesture of dusting it but the hand does not touch it. He goes to the table and drapes the jacket on the back of the chair. He turns to go — but turns back to look at the food, puts some of it into his mouth with his fingers and chews, staring off in* **Nold**'s *direction. He licks his finger and goes out through the door.*

Nold *comes back with a textbook. The bright orange cover is stained with oily fingerprints. He reaches the table and stops when he sees the jacket. He goes to it and hesitates, unsure what to do. He sits down brusquely and jerks the chair in under him. He props the open book against the mug, forks food into his mouth and eats and reads. Suddenly he stops and noisily pushes back the chair. He stands and goes out right.*

Short silence. **Nold** *bursts into the room and stops as if expecting to see someone. Pause. He goes to the table, sits and quietly pulls in the chair under him. He eats as if forcing himself to concentrate on reading.*

Still chewing he stands and picks up the book. He holds the top edge with his two fists and the book rests on his wrists as though they were the top of a lectern. He takes a hand from the book and puts a forkful of food in his mouth. He puts down the fork and holding the book as before he walks to the middle of the room. He stops, still reading and chewing. After a few moments he takes a hand from the book, a pencil from his pocket and underlines a sentence in the book, chewing all the time.

Woman's Voice (*off*)   Give them the list.

Nold *shows no sign of hearing the voice. For a moment he chews and reads. Then he goes back to the table and sits. He presses his left hand on the top edge of the book to hold it upright on the table. He eats with the fork in his right hand and reads.*

Gregory *comes on. He stands in the open doorway and stares at* **Nold***'s back.* **Nold** *stays in the same position but his gaze falls from the book to the table.*

Nold   What yer want? D'yer live in the flats? Yer see different people comin 'n goin. Ain see you.

Woman's Voice (*off*)   They do the rest.

Gregory *glances expressionlessly in the voice's direction and then looks back at* **Nold***.* **Nold** *shows no sign of hearing the voice.*

Nold (*touches the table top*)   I got a good job. Tech one day a week. Savin up. Get married. People get on with me, I get on with them. Why should I . . . ? I should'a sent yer packin first time yer come. What d'yer want?

Gregory *goes.*

Nold   Yer'll 'ave t' tell me in the end. I ain goin nowhere. Where to? – Tell us what yer want.

Nold *lifts a forkful of food towards his mouth – abruptly he puts it down, stands, turns and picks up the coat to thrust it at* **Gregory***. He sees the empty doorway.*

Nold (*shouts*)   Take it! Don't drop yer trash in my . . . ! I ain
goin nowhere!

Nold *looks down at the jacket. He puts his hand in a side pocket.
Empty. He puts on the jacket. It is a little too small for him. He pats the
outside of the side pockets with his flat palms. He goes to the door and
turns back to look – he sees he has knocked over the chair. He takes a few
steps towards it but turns and goes out. He shuts the door behind him.*

The Second House

A dark opening in a forest. At the back a hole leading to an underground hovel.

Gregory *comes in followed by* **Nold**. **Gregory** *stops*. **Nold** *stops*.

Nold   Why yer stopped? It's late.

Gregory *wearily looks round for a place and then sits.*

Nold   Where are we? We wan' t' get on. (*Looks round.*) This ain where yer were takin me?

Gregory *bows forwards over his knees.*

Nold   'Ow long yer goin t' sit there?

No answer. **Nold** *finds the entrance to the hovel.*

Nold   D'yer know whass down there? It's a 'ole. (*He looks in the direction they were going. Decides.*) I'm goin back. 'Nough a' this caper. (*He starts to go, stops, turns to* **Gregory**.) Can't yer talk? . . . Too dark t' find the path. (*Loiters.*) If yer wan' t' rest . . . ? Bin walkin all day. (*No response.*) Where yer takin me? Tell me. If I go back now I'll spend the rest a' me life wonderin where I'd'a got to if we'd gone on . . . Why did I follow yer? Least tell me *that*!

Gregory *stands and starts to walk.* **Nold** *follows him, stops and watches.*

Nold   What is it? Make a sign if yer can't talk! (*Realises.*) Yer don't know where we are. . . Yer lost. O god. I'm off. You wander round till yer find some other idiot daft enough t' – . (*Stares at* **Gregory**.) 'E's kippin. O god. 'E could a' bin akip the 'ole time I followed 'im!

Gregory   They're draggin the river through the bridge . . . under the arch . . . red bricks drippin . . . Take the pain away . . .

Nold   Is it yer 'ead?

Gregory   She took the bones out a' 'er body 'n thrashed me
with 'em . . . it made little 'oles in 'er bones, she blows on the
'oles . . . thass where I feel my pain . . . I'll wait a 'undred
years 'n see if she dies. (*Slight pause.*) She didn't – she's cuttin
the bread – the sides a' the 'ouses fall . . . I'll 'ang 'er on every
tree in this forest – on every branch . . . the rope 'anged little
children – all the innocence a' the world – 'n never made a
murmur. . . when it 'angs 'er it'll cry at its own pain . . . Take
this pain away from me, I can't live with this pain . . .

Nold (*gently*)   Sit down. (*Leads him.*) – 'Ere – yer sat 'ere
before.

Nold *sits* **Gregory** *down. He takes off the jacket and drapes it round*
Gregory. **Gregory** *whimpers in vague protest.*

Nold (*insisting*)   It'll keep yer warm . . . Least yer can talk!
Less see what yer done t' yer –

Nold *starts to unwind* **Gregory**'s *bandage.* **Gregory** *wakes.*

Gregory   What yer on at?

Nold   Yer was talkin in yer sleep.

Gregory   Where am I? (*Rewinds the bandage.*) 'Oo said yer
could look at my – ? 'Ow did I get 'ere?

Nold   Yer brought us 'ere –

Gregory. Me? Us? I never seen yer in me life!

Nold   Never seen – ? Yer come t' my 'ouse – kep comin – 'n
I –

Gregory *puts his hand in the jacket pocket – realises he has on two*
jackets. He snatches out his hand.

Gregory   What the – ! Why I got two jackets? (*He throws the*
jacket on the floor.)

Nold   It's your jacket!

Gregory   Mine? I never set eyes on it!

Nold   Yer was talkin in yer sleep – a woman –

Gregory   Yer was goin through me pockets!

Nold   Yer must remember me! I followed yer!

Gregory   Wass goin on? Yer playin tricks? (*Looks round. Bewildered.*) It's all trees! We're in a swamp. The trees're fallin down. Yer can't tell which way they're supposed t' stand up!

Nold   Yer wanted t' 'ang 'er –

Gregory   I *what*! (*Stares at* **Nold**.) . . . Did I? I ain bin well. Couldn't look after meself. (*Touches his bandage.*) They must 'a 'ad me in casualty. Rows a' people on seats. I walked out. Wouldn't expect yer t' understand, yer young . . . Things go wrong. Yer wander round the bricks. Kids everywhere. When yer die they come 'n stare at yer open mouth. Old man's gob, no teeth. They think it's yer throat bin cut. Next they put yer in the ground. Slip a bit a' wood between you 'n the earth. That soon rots 'n lets the earth through. I 'ate the earth. Soil. (*Pauses.*) That it? . . . When I walks out a' casualty yer must 'a saw me in the street – likely through a window – 'n come up with some cock 'n bull story 'n followed me. I kep goin cause I was bein followed. Yer drove me 'ere. This could 'a bin the world's rubbish tip one time, now it's empty . . . What d'we do?

Nold   When it's light we'll find the path. Must be night. The trees make it dark. People come 'ere. There's a 'ole – yer can see where they go in 'n out. Someone'll 'elp us.

A **Woman** *rushes in. She is short and fat. Her long hair, white face, red hands and clothes are smudged with dirt. Her clothes seem wrapped on her, her dress and coat flap loose. Her cracked shoes are bound with string.*

Woman   Get away! Get away from my – ! (*She stops, holds out her hand to beg.*) Food! Food! Food! Pity 'n ol' woman! (*She brings out a knife.*) Yer bin down! Both a' yer! I'll kill yer!

The **Woman** *flashes the knife at* **Gregory**. *He runs out and she follows him.*

Woman   I'll kill yer! (*Stops, turns back to* **Nold**.) I'll gut yer like a fish!

Nold   No! We're lost!

Woman   Lost? 'Spect me t' believe that? (*Jabs the air with her knife.*) 'Oo are yer? This is mine! I live 'ere!

Nold   We're lost!

Woman   If yer bin down I'll gut yer like a fish. (*Guts the air.*) From crutch t' gob! (*Wipes dribble from her mouth.*) The flies'll scour yer out! They swarm like wire wool for anythin like that 'ere! (*Suddenly exhausted.*) Yer got all the rest – leave this place t' me. Nothin 'ere for yer. I walked all day. No one gives. Don't even look now – the streets too full a' ghosts 'n follies. If yer bin down –

Nold   No – we're lost in the wood 'n –

Woman   Why? Why were yer lost in the wood? (*No response.*) If yer bin down I'll smell yer stench – it'll still be there. I'll gut yer like a fish. The flies'll scour yer.

The **Woman** *goes into the hole.* **Gregory** *comes back – beckons* **Nold** *to the side.*

Gregory   Get rid a' 'er!

Nold   'Oo is she? Yer know 'er?

Gregory   This is your place. She took it.

Nold   This? – This dump? Is this where you were leadin me? (*Stops in despair.*) She's a poor ol' woman livin in animals' filth. I'll take 'er t' the city – she needs proper –

Gregory   The city! They'd burn 'er alive! They drove 'er out! She's the plague! If I 'ad a rope –

Nold   Yer know 'er?

Gregory   No – worse! I never 'eard 'er – never saw 'er – but she got inside me when I slept! Thass 'er I said I'd – . We could fill in the 'ole – bury 'er alive – but rats 'a got more than one way in 'n out! Get rid a' 'er! When I dreamt – I 'anged 'er with this bandage!

Nold   I'm not 'urtin some poor ol' woman t' satisfy –

Gregory. 'E don't see! 'E don't see! Once when I was in the bricks – I spend the days countin the doors 'n windows – I saw a broken bottle in the street. The bottom 'arf was gone – there was a jagged edge – 'n just the top – the neck 'n shoulder – left. The cap was still in the neck. Never opened, never touched. Thass when I saw what my life was – 'n the kids 'oo'd come t' stare at me when I'm dead. (*Pause.*) Even if this weren't yer place when yer set out, it is now. Yer 'ere, yer seen 'er. When yer kill 'er she won't leave yer alone. She'd follow yer round the world. When yer think yer rid of 'er she's waitin round the next door. When the goin's good, thass when she's preparin the worst. This is the one place she wants: it's yer grave. No one can't live without a grave. Yer spend yer life tryin t' keep it. Yer must've brought me 'ere t' tell yer that.

The **Woman** *comes from the hole.* **Gregory** *runs away.*

Woman (*shouts after* **Gregory**)   Run! The end a' yer shadow's tied t' me 'ands. Stretch it! Stretch it! – It don't break! Yer won't get far! (*Turns to* **Nold**.) Yer ain bin down. I thought two men'ld treat themselves t' my lamb. (*Stares at* **Nold**.) Didn't yer 'ave time? Are yer still a child?

Nold   We wouldn't 'urt yer. 'E's just a poor ol' – like you – 'e's –

Woman. 'E's wicked!

Nold   No!

Woman   I know 'is face. I seen it in the streets. All the time. Pavements're cracked because 'is like walk on 'em.

Nold   'Ow long yer bin 'ere?

Woman   Long enough. A long time. Out a' the way, no one else's come. (*Listens.*) 'E's still there. 'E's scared a' yer – don't trust 'im. Listen, get 'im back – talk t' 'im – make 'im sit. I'll come be'ind 'im. The knife don't take long. When 'e's dead look at 'im closely. Brush the flies off 'n look at 'is eyes.

Nold   'E said yer were wicked.

Woman   No – I'd kill for my daughter. I stay alive for 'er. Otherwise I wouldn't put up with it for five minutes. I could be in the ground under yer feet. I wouldn't feel yer stand on me. Thass my peace. In the city my daughter played with the kids. It frightened them because she's big. They threw stones. So we left. Every day I scavenge. She cries when I come back empty-'anded. She thinks I'm punishin 'er – but she ain done nothin. She says if I loved 'er I'd make the world good. She 'asn't eaten for three days. I rock 'er 'n try t' tell 'er things pass if yer wait. She can't learn. She thinks any little pain'll last for ever. If she cuts 'er finger it 'urts 'er more than all the pain we'd feel if we were in 'ell 'n the devil 'ated us more 'n all the rest. She can't see things as they are. She thinks the sun's a fire with 'n empty stake in it. I'm 'er mother but she's never seen my face – it could be the back a' anybody's 'ead. In the city yer pay the kids t' bury yer. When I die she won't know – yer can't tell from the back a' the 'ead. She'd sit in the grass beside me 'n pull me 'air till she starved. I'd 'ave a livin gravestone till it toppled over on me.

Nold   Where's 'er father?

Woman   Look in yer pockets. Yer might find somethin there.

Nold (*shakes his head*)   No.

Woman   If yer'd made 'im sit down like I said – I'd'a killed yer first – 'n when 'e looked up in surprise killed 'im. I don't trust yer – yer got a kind face but it ain bin scratched.

The **Girl** *comes from the hole. She is in her late twenties. She is thin and taller than the* **Woman**. *She wears a white skirt, black jacket and plimsolls – all are dirtied with mud.*

Girl (*coming up*)   I'm 'ungry. (*Sees* **Nold**.) Mum-ma?

Woman   The man won't 'urt yer. 'E's 'armless as a babe.

Girl   Is there any –

Woman   Yer should be asleep.

Girl   – dinner?

Woman   'Ave t' cook it first.

Girl   Let me see it.

Woman   I'll call yer when it's ready.

Girl   Show me.

Woman   If yer get under me feet I can't cook yer –

Girl (*takes out a rag doll*)   The doll 'asn't eaten for three weeks.

Woman   Go back t' sleep. Take dolly with yer. When yer wake up the food'll be cooked . . . Somethin must 'appen, somethin must be given to us . . . 'Old me my precious, I walked so far for yer t'day. I earned a 'ug.

Girl (*to* **Nold**)   Did yer bring me some food?

Nold   No –

Girl   When did yer eat?

Nold   This mornin I –

Girl   Did yer eat it all?

Nold   I –

Girl   Yer didn't save me any?

Nold   I didn't know I'd –

Girl   Yer could'a met anyone. A crowd! Yer didn't save anythin for them? Look in yer pockets.

Nold   'S nothin –

Girl   Look!

Nold (*perfunctory search*)   Nothin.

Girl   The doll'll die.

Woman   She won't . . . (*To* **Nold**.) The starvin don't arst for food, they never do. I pass 'em when I'm beggin in the streets, they just follow yer with their eyes.

Girl (*scraping the ground with the side of her plimsoll*)   Look I'm scrapin out a place for 'er t' die. (*To* **Nold**.) It won't 'urt. When yer dead yer don't worry or feel cold or see the sky. (*She drops the doll on the ground.*) *You* 'ave t' see the sky every day. Thass yer punishment for eatin the food. Look – thass 'er last breath. (*She points her finger to the side and with it follows the breath to the doll's mouth.*) There – 's goin down like a mouse bustlin in t' its 'ole. Now the sawdust's stiflin it. Don't take long t' die. Just a big hiccup.

The **Woman** *picks up the doll and turns to peer into the forest.*

Girl   It only seems like us. All the dolls died long ago. We're sillier than them: we play with little dead things 'n pretend they're alive. Did yer eat yesterday too?

Nold   Yeh.

Girl   'N the day before? 'E eats nearly every day. Mum-ma didn't get any food t' cook. She lies. She thinks when she gets t' the end of what she's sayin I won't remember the beginnin so I won't know she's told a lie. I know when she starts so I don't listen.

Nold   If I fed yer doll she'd come t' life.

Girl   Then she'd die again. Anyway yer ain got any food.

Nold   At 'ome. I left some on me plate!

Girl   Food? – On yer plate? Yer left it on yer – ? No no stop them they're eatin it!

Nold   There's more – plenty more –

Girl   More? More food? On yer plate?

Nold   Yeh yeh – in the 'ouse – cupboards full –

Girl   Fetch it! Fetch it! Quick! Mum-ma 'e's got food!

Woman (*turns to look at them*)   Food? Why should 'e share it with us?

Girl   'E's got lots 'n lots!

Nold (*to* **Woman**)   I'll fetch it from my –

Woman   No no! (*To* **Girl**.) Yer mustn't arst! (*To* **Nold**.) I
left our food – it's on the path! It was too 'eavy t'– – (*To* **Girl**.)
I'll fetch it when I'm rested! Go down 'n let me be!

Girl   What food? 'Ow much? Where? Liar!

Woman (*holds the doll against the side of her mouth. Whispers*)
'E knows this place now! 'E'll come back with other men –
'n – ! I'll kill 'im! We'll go through 'is pockets! (*Aloud.*)
There's a man out there – 'e won't let 'im feed us! (*To*
Nold.) 'E'd kill yer first! – (*To* **Girl**.) I can't! I can't! I can't
do any more! Go down! I'll lock yer in down there for ever!
Go down when I tell yer!

Girl   The doll 'asn't eaten – yer don't –

Woman   She's dead!

Girl   – care! Don't care!

Woman   Dead! (*Suddenly tearful.*) Come 'ere! Come t' me
precious! Let me 'old yer! I'll rub yer tummy 'n make the pain
go!

Girl   I'll scratch! I'm 'ungry! 'Ungry! The pain's worse!
When I scraped the ground my foot wept! The people're
breakin in 'is 'ouse 'n stealin my food from 'is plate! (*To* **Nold**.)
Don't listen t' 'er! Fetch it! Fetch it! Food!

Woman (*to* **Nold**)   Wait till mornin – then yer'll 'ave a
chance! If yer've come t' feed us, if yer our luck at last – 'n we
lost yer now! – Stay t'night! (*To* **Girl**.) I've got t' 'old on t' 'im
as if 'e's my son!

Girl   'Er son! Don't be a child of 'ers! She starves 'er
children! Thass 'ow she keeps 'er 'old! I'm silly cause she won't
let me eat! She's frightened I'll get well 'n leave 'er t' rot in this
'ole!

Nold (*to* **Woman**)   I'll take 'er with me!

Woman   No no thass worst of all! Yer see 'er now she's
be'aved – but when she's mad –

Girl   I'm not mad! Not mad!

Woman   She can't stand the light! She'll run – get lost – (*To* **Girl**.) Then the man in the trees'll kill yer!

Girl   I'll be good! I'll be good!

Woman   Yer don't know 'ow! (*Suddenly changes.*) Go with 'im! Go! – 'n let me get some peace. A little rest! If yer wasn't mad would I live in this 'ole? I 'ide yer so they won't lock yer away! We live like animals because yer be'ave like one! Eat like 'n animal! Eat the dirt! They do!

Girl (*panic whisper*)   Mum-ma Mum-ma please not not not Mum-ma –

Woman   When I'm gone yer'll know it! Feed *me*! Yer young 'n strong! Look at my poor body! Yer couldn't make a cobweb out a' it! D'yer know what bein weary is? She sharpens 'er claws in 'er *sleep*! When she was a baby she never chewed 'er nails she sharpened 'em! (*Claws out.*) I'll claw back! I'll open yer skin as easy as turnin pages in a book!

Girl (*submissive whimper*)   No no Mum-ma not – please – no –

Woman. Then she whines! I said she was an animal! Let 'im go! Let the man kill 'im! Then the animals'll eat 'im! 'E's the food!

Girl (*whispering to* **Nold**)   Fetch it. Fetch it. Food. I'll talk t' 'er. – No Mum-ma Mum-ma let 'im fetch the food! I'll give yer mine. I won't touch a crumb till yer can't eat any more! (*To* **Nold**.) She works 'n works for me 'n takes such care – good Mum-ma – I'm ungrateful – I wish I was as good as 'er. Bring 'er lots a' food!

Nold   I can be back in a few 'ours. I'll see the lights a' the town. Wait for me. Don't quarrel. Yer 'urt each other.

Girl   What'll yer bring?

Nold   All sorts a' –

Girl   Yer'll need a big bag. A big box. Yer'll bring lots – yer might as well if yer goin all that way. – Yer mustn't think we always quarrel. We only shouted cause we're 'ungry.

Nold   I'll bring a 'aversack! Keep me 'ands free t' fight off wild animals!

Girl   O clever!

Nold *starts to go.*

Woman   Wait!

Nold *goes out. The* **Girl** *runs to the side to watch him.*

Girl   Quick! Quick! Quicker than that! No quickly! They're breakin in 'n eatin my food! – 'E's gone. I can't see 'im in the dark. (*She turns to the* **Woman**.) Give it t' me. Yer 'id some bread in case it was the last. Yer must 'ave or we'd'a starved. Yer needn't 'ide it now – 'e'll feed us every day! (*Turns back to shout.*) Whass yer name? (*No answer.*)

Woman   Come down 'n sleep.

Girl   Give it t' me!

Woman   Let me rest. There was no food t'day.

Girl (*realises*)   . . . Then if 'e 'adn't come we'd'a starved. (*She turns, looks for* **Nold** *in the trees.*) 'E will come back. 'E ran so fast – it shows 'e wants t' 'elp us . . . (*She follows the* **Woman** *to the hole.*) P'raps 'e was runnin away?. . 'E'll come when we're asleep 'n think we've gone! 'E knows people're ungrateful. 'E'll eat my food!

Woman   We'll be awake long before.

Girl   But –

Woman   If we're not 'e'll call us.

Girl   I'll leave the doll out. 'E knows I couldn't go without it. (*Drops the doll by the hole.*) It's dead, it can be left on its own.

The women go into the hole. **Gregory** *comes in and goes to it. He stares down it. He picks up the doll and puts it in his jacket. He goes to the side, sits and watches.*

Nold *comes in exhausted. He sits.*

Gregory   There'll be a war.

Nold   Couldn't find the town. Searched – 'unted – two days. We crep' 'ere in a few 'ours! Saw lights flashin through the trees. Lorries 'n voices. There was a light in the sky. When I got there 's not the town – 's shacks or factories burnin. I couldn't find me 'ouse. I started in the wrong direction, I couldn't get back t' the – . Why couldn't I find it?

Gregory   Nothin matters in a war. (*Looks round.*) These trees – 'ere's like a burnt 'ouse – rafters on the ground. They came up 'n called yer several times.

Nold   Why can't I get back?

Gregory   I tell yer everythin. Yer can't listen. I tol' yer t' get rid of 'er. Now there'll be a war.

The **Girl** *comes from the hole.*

Girl   She's gone. I tol' 'er t' play by the 'ouse. (*Wrings her hands and searches.*) Why d' children play? They still die. Men take them from the doorsteps 'n corners. (*Calls.*) Come in! (*Cries gently.*) She's in the river – the 'and's comin through the pebbles on the bottom – the pebbles are eyes – I can see 'er drown.

Nold   Stop 'er – she mustn't cry like that –

Girl   'Er little body's stitched a' canvas.

Nold (*to the* **Girl**)   Stop it! Stop it! Yer mustn't do it!

Girl   The runnin water presses 'er down in t' the 'and –

Nold (*to* **Gregory**). 'Elp 'er! (*He calls down the hole.*) The girl's cryin! She's 'urtin 'erself! (*To* **Girl**.) Yer mustn't cry like that!

Girl (*crying gently*)   Under the pebbles there's another world – the 'and's tuggin 'er down – 'er little dress is wavin at me –

The **Woman** *comes from the hole.*

Woman   The food!

Nold   She mustn't cry like that!

Woman   The food!

Nold   There ain no food! Somethin's breakin inside 'er! – can't yer 'ear it?

Woman   Go! – I'll tell 'er yer dead – got killed in the –

Nold   That ain 'er cryin! – she's tearin inside –

Woman   She's asleep. 'Er sleep takes care of 'er. – Cry my precious, yer sleep won't let yer come t' arm.

Girl (*lifts her face and stares sightlessly at the* **Woman**)   It's not 'er dress wavin – it's little tongues – the mice are drownin – if I could lift them out – the water's cruel, it shows me everythin – the doll gave birth t' little mice when it drowned – their little tongues are lickin at the sky –

The **Woman** *sees* **Gregory**.

Woman   O god – 'e's seen 'er! What can I do?

The **Girl** *wakes and sees* **Nold**.

Girl   Where's my food? (*Sees the* **Woman**.) Mum-ma! – 'Ow long 'as 'e bin 'ere? (*Laughs.*) Yer've eaten some already! While I was asleep!

Nold   There's no food. None.

Girl   'E's 'idden it!

Nold   I couldn't find me 'ouse!

Girl   The plate was empty? They licked it clean? Yer 'ad more! – Yer said!

Nold   I couldn't find the –

Girl   Scraps! Scraps! Give me yer scraps! The 'aversack, the cupboards full a' – I didn't believe all that! But scraps yer can carry in yer 'ands – ?

Nold   I couldn't find my way back t' the –

Girl   'E don't know what 'unger is! 'E can't! 'E still remembers what 'e ate! Even the dead 'ave food stuck in their teeth! – That reminds them! Surely the scraps? The bits yer carry in yer fists! Look – 'is fists! Open 'em! Open 'em!

Nold (*shakes his fists to the sides*)   Nothin . . . !

Girl   Open 'em!

Nold (*opens his fists*)   Nothin! I couldn't find me –

Girl   Yer must've found it! Yer went wrong – yer found yer way back 'ere! Yer must've found yer way t' – . Don't tease. It's wrong. I left the doll so yer'd – (*She sees the doll has gone.*) Please – if yer ever felt pity for – if yer ever pitied – give me food . . . 'E lied, 'e lied. 'Oo took the doll?

Woman   I think if we don't eat now it'll be too late. We reached the point where food don't 'elp. Yer die with it in yer mouth. (*Half grins.*) It's 'ard. There's food somewhere if we could find it. (*Looks at* **Gregory**.) 'E'd run in front of us 'n eat it first.

Nold   Why couldn't I find me 'ouse?

Woman (*takes bread from her skirt*)   Bread. The last bit. Take it.

Girl (*stares at the bread*)   I should keep the doll in me pocket when it's dead.

Woman (*holding the bread*)   I found it in the road. A bird dropped it 'n was too frightened t' come back – or it fell off a lorry.

Girl   In yer skirt all that time. Yer must be 'ard-'earted t' take such care a' me. Yer could'a said 'e's gettin food, I'll eat it. I was asleep. I wouldn't know. (*Looks at* **Gregory**.) Why does 'e stare at us?

Woman   'E's come t' watch us starve. I thought this was just a 'ole in the trees. This *earth's* 'is buried treasure: it's where we'll die – p'raps where yer scuffed yer foot. 'E'll live 'ere when we're dead. Get up in the mornin 'n stare at the spot. 'E'll spend all day like that.

Girl (*to* **Gregory**)   Did yer bring me food? Look in yer pockets – that one. (*To the* **Woman**.) I'll look after yer now. I'll be good. I'll go out beggin. (*She goes to* **Gregory** *and holds out* *the bread to him.*) Take it 'n go away. Mum-ma doesn't want yer 'ere.

Woman   No stop 'er! No! – Thass the last I can give! It's 'er life!

Gregory *takes the bread.*

Woman   Yes – 'e gets everythin. 'E'd take the bread out'a the mouth a' the child in my womb. Eat it! – I'll poison it when it's in yer guts. The worms'll crawl through yer as if yer was the earth.

Gregory *puts the bread in his mouth and chews.*

Gregory (*grimace*)   She feeds yer muck.

Girl   Now go.

Gregory *chews and then calmly spits out the bread.*

Gregory   Didn't eat.

Girl   . . . Mum-ma?

Woman   Nothin I can do.

Gregory (*laughs*)   Don't let 'er teach yer nasty thoughts about me. I brought yer a present.

Woman   Don't listen! 'E'll 'umiliate yer.

*The **Girl** turns her back on **Gregory**. He takes out the doll and holds it out to her.*

Girl   Go away.

Nold *takes the doll from **Gregory** and gives it to the **Girl**.*

Nold   Take it.

Girl   A dead doll? – Is that all? (*She holds the doll upside down by a leg.*) I'll eat that.

Woman   No my precious, no more . . .

Girl   I'm 'ungry.

*The **Girl** throws the doll in the air – a string is fastened to it. She jerks it back by the string.*

Girl/Doll   Eeek no Mummy!

Girl (*tearing the doll with her teeth*)   Mum-ma must eat! Mum-ma must eat! Mum-ma 'ungry!

The doll hops away across the ground. The **Girl** *jerks it back on the string.*

Girl/Doll   Eeek Mummy no – please Mummy –

Girl (*tears the doll with her teeth*)   Mum-ma eats! Mum-ma eats! Thass what Mum-ma's precious is for!

The doll flies in the air.

Girl   Look at the little darlin – bless it – 'arf a body flyin off! Cavortin in the air! Come back yer little bugger! Fowl for dinner! Fowl's on t'day!

The **Girl** *jerks the doll down and tears it with her teeth.*

Girl/Doll   Mummy! Mummy! Mummy! Don't 'urt precious! Don't bite so deep! It was lovely t' fly in the air! Away!

The **Girl** *stares at the doll for a moment then tosses it in the air and jerks it back.*

Girl   On the plate! On the plate! Thass the place for you till yer go in Mum-ma's tum-tum! (*She tears the doll with her teeth.*)

Girl/Doll   Ah!

Girl   Rags 'n bones – rags 'n bones!

Woman (to **Nold**)   Why yer starin? Yer searched for two days? I search every day! Why did yer come 'ere – yer can't 'elp! A man, a man! 'E ain ashamed, 'e don't blush! Still starin? Go away! I seen kids so starved the dogs sit in front of 'em 'n stare at their bones.

The **Girl** *holds the bits of doll in her hands.*

Girl (*covers her ears with her hands*)   She's in me shoutin 'unger 'unger! I've eaten my own 'unger! (*She puts a shred of the doll in her mouth.*) My tears tasted a' salt, they fell on 'er while I ate . . .

(*She lies on her side.*) Yer'll see me changed now. (*Feels the ground.*) The earth's 'ungry. I can feel it in my 'ands. It 'as so many dead t' feed.

Nold   Why did yer tell me not t' look? One day I'll crawl on the ground. Yer thinks yer in pain? – Thass just the dirt grinnin on yer. I'll feed 'er. I won't get lost again. I'll look at the dark – thass all the map I need. I'll find my 'ouse if I 'ave t' cut the forest down t' find it! (*He goes to the* **Girl**.) Don't eat any more a' this. (*He takes a shred from her mouth.*) I'll bring yer proper food. Two days ago I was sittin at my table by the window – everythin in its place. I'll find it, it's still there.

Girl   . . . Will yer feed me.

Nold   Yeh.

The **Woman** *goes into the hole.*

Girl   She's gone t' fetch 'er needle 'n thread. When I eat the doll she sews it up. Threads 'er needle 'n sews 'n sews. 'Er knuckles go up 'n down like teeth eatin 'er inside.

Nold   When yer cried it was like stitches breakin inside yer.

Girl   'Ave yer got mittens in yer 'ouse? If she wore mittens I'd only 'ave t' see 'er fingertips. When she sleeps 'er 'ands look like animals waitin by the cookin pot. Go! – Yer'll stand there till I starve.

Nold *goes out. For a moment the* **Girl** *watches him going then she jumps up and runs to the side.*

Girl (*calls*)   What'll yer bring me? Bring me lots 'n lots this time! All sorts! A sackful on yer back! 'Ow much can yer carry? (*No answer.*)

Gregory   What'll yer do when she dies? Yer can't carry 'er round in yer pocket.

Girl (*singsong*)
Somebody spat the bread out.
Somebody spat the bread out.

Gregory   Yer said yer'd start bein sensible like the rest a' us.

Girl She won't die. 'E'll look after 'er. The way 'e ran! – 'e'll be good at lookin after!

Gregory 'E'll get lost – run round like a flea on a dog's arse'ole – come back 'n expect you t' feed '*im*!

Girl When Mum-ma 'as t' die I'll nurse 'er so well she'll know I can look after meself when she's dead. Then she'll be 'appy. Dogs die on their side in the gutter. Their lips pull back. Their gums 'n teeth grin – like yer grinnin now. 'Somebody spat the bread out'! Yer'll grin in the gutter. The ants'll sit on yer teeth like tiny Buddhas 'n meditate for ages . . . 'n then walk down yer throat.

Gregory Yer bitch. I started that sentence long ago. Now it's finished.

Girl (*picking up shreds of doll*)   There's one. There's one.

The **Woman** *comes from the hole with needle and thread.*

Woman Collect all the bits. It won't go if any's missin.

Girl What'll 'e bring me?

Woman We'll see.

Girl Yer don't think 'e'll come.

Woman I'll feed us. I did before.

The **Girl** *goes into the hole.*

Woman (*sewing*)   There was a man fishin in a ditch. 'E didn't see there wasn't any water in it. 'E was so pleased with the little fish on 'is line. 'E didn't know the 'ook was in 'is mouth. 'E tugged 'n tugged all day. 'Is eyes screwed up. 'N every time 'e cursed the 'ook went deeper down 'is throat.

Gregory Yer was lyin in the ditch with 'im.

Woman I'm not afraid a' yer now I seen 'im. If she goes mad I'll take 'er round on a lead. 'Er 'owlin won't put me off. Yer'll never get 'er. (*Stops sewing.*) Besides, what could yer do? 'Er 'ead's so empty there's nothin in it for yer t' twist. She knows more than yer'll ever know. It don't make 'er 'appy.

She doesn't know nothin lasts, gets broken, worn out like 'n old coat 'n dies. She thinks it lasts for ever. Yer can't add t' 'er sufferin. Ain that enough?

*The **Girl** comes from the hole with a lighted candle.*

Girl   Look! – it's better than a doll. (*She sets the candle by the hole.*)

Woman   'E won't see it that far.

Girl   Silly! – it's for when 'e's near. Thass when 'e'll be tired 'n make mistakes. 'E'd pass by 'n wander for years 'n go mad 'n eat the food. That'd be a tragedy. Don't use the red thread. Yer fingers look as if they're bleedin.

Woman (*sewing*)   It shows up when I stitch.

Girl   Yer see the red spots when it's finished.

Woman   I do what I can.

Girl   Stitch – stitch – stitch. – Less use the good things!

Woman   What good – ? No!

Girl (*tugs the **Woman**'s arm*)   Yer don't think 'e'll come!

Woman   I can't stitch if yer –

Girl   Use the good things! Please!

Woman (*sewing*)   If there's food we'll eat – there's no need t' –

Girl   There is, there is! If it's all laid out 'e'll 'ave t' come!

Woman   The mud'll spoil my –

Girl (*snatching the doll from the **Woman***)   Please! Please! 'E was so angry – 'e'll bring lots 'n lots t' spite yer! We 'ave t' use the good things!

Woman   Stop it! If yer spoil it I won't do it again! My eyes won't let me –

Girl   I wan' it t' be nice for *you!*

*The **Girl** goes in the hole.*

Woman (*sewing*)   Some boys were throwin stones at the sea. The sea took its revenge. It made one of the stones float. The boys threw stones at it – it didn't sink even when they 'it it. 'N when they were so angry they went in after it, it floated out t' sea. They followed it – throwin their stones. When the stones were gone they still followed it – tryin t' beat it with their fists. They drowned. – 'E found 'is 'ouse. Yer'd set it on fire. 'E stood 'n watched it – 'e didn't know.

*The **Girl** comes from the hole with an old wicker picnic basket.*

Girl (*laughing*)   It's our 'appy day!

Woman   I said no! The mud'll –

Girl. It's mildewin in the damp! I'll clean it if it gets dirty!

*The **Girl** spreads a white picnic cloth and lays plates, dishes, glasses and cutlery.*

Girl   My picture book showed all the things t' eat 'n all the things t' eat 'em with! They ate the fields – the trees – they drank the sea – they didn't mind the bleatin of the little lamb when they cut its throat – its little feet shivered as if they were standin on red 'ot coals – it 'ad t' go in the pot! O all these things! What are the glasses for? Mum-ma don't sulk!

Woman   The glasses were . . . I can't tell now, it's in the past.

Girl   Don't lick yer plate. Don't eat off yer knife. All dos 'n don'ts! An yer 'ad t' talk t' yer guests while they ate yer food! We'll invite lots a' pretend-guests so they can't eat ours! Yer exchange the news 'n gossip! (*She looks at the picnic.*) O Mum-ma . . . It's beautiful. What are all the things for?

Woman   It was the lady's I worked for – she –

Girl   Such beautiful things! It's a spell! 'E must come! When 'e sees it 'e'll know we're grateful cause 'e went so far for our food.

*The **Girl** runs down the hole. The **Woman** picks up a glass and stares at it. The **Girl** comes from the hole with a filthy bundled-up grey greatcoat.*

Girl   What yer doin . . . ?

Woman   Lookin at the glass . . .

Girl   Why?

Woman   I –

Girl   T' see the light! – yer see it on the rim! – even in the dark. (*She holds a glass and tries to imitate the* **Woman** *– but it is upside down. She puts it back on the cloth.*) It frightens me. I'll put it away.

Woman   It's there now, let it be.

Girl   I don't know 'ow t' use the things! No one taught me! 'E'll laugh at me 'n go away! We'll starve with all the empty plates around us! Let me eat in a corner – where I belong – with me back t' 'im. Don't offend 'im with the sight a' me! 'E's our prince!

Woman   We'll eat t'gether.

Girl   We 'aven't got a butler!

Woman   Good 'eavens it's a picnic – yer don't need no –

Girl.   The book said! If there's no butler 'e'll take 'is food away! (*To* **Gregory**.) Be our butler! Be! Be! Be! It's easy! I'll teach yer it!

Woman   No!

Girl   'E must! 'Oo else? 'E can't poison our guests, they're too grand! 'E wouldn't *dare* when the man's 'ere! (*Walks round in agitation.*) Yer won't 'ave a butler! Yer won't let me eat in the corner! Yer spoilin the feast! (*Looks at the* **Woman**. *Stops.*) Yer face – look – whass 'appened? – it's white. (*She goes to the* **Woman**.) The white cloth's shinin on yer face. Yer beautiful. Sit. (*She puts down the coat.*) Sit on the cushion I brought for yer. (*The* **Woman** *sits.*) Yer face is even whiter. For the solemn feast. (*Gently.*) I can see where the lies live in it. (*Checking.*) Knife 'n fork, knife 'n fork. (*She raps her plate with a spoon.*) The butler must practise!

Gregory *hands the* **Girl** *a plate.*

Girl (*cross whisper*)   The lady a' the 'ouse. (**Gregory** *offers the plate to the* **Woman**.) Don't keep the servants waitin. The book says it teaches them idleness.

The **Woman** *takes the plate.*

Girl   'Er glass. Pour somethin.

Gregory *pretends to fill the* **Woman**'s *glass. She takes it.*

Girl (*points to the glass*)   Do what yer did before.

The **Woman** *half raises her glass. The* **Girl** *imitates her.*

Girl (*mystified*)   What does it mean? (*She touches her glass.*) Can I guess? . . . (*Decides.*) It means drink mine! (*She touches her glass to the* **Woman**'s *lips.*) Drink mine! Drink! (*She puts down her glass, takes her fork and pretends to offer the* **Woman** *food from her plate.*) Would the lady care t' toy with this morsel? Don't stint yerself there's plenty more where that come from! What fun! A family outin! Dad's not 'ere 'e's off 'untin for the pot! Our life'll change! More picnics! 'E'll bring real food! If 'e ran too fast it'd spill. (*Pretends to eat.*) Yummm! Why do the dead sweat when they're still? Our chef cooks foreign dishes for our guests from round the world. My mother's knuckles on the glass – dead sheep grazin the pasture. Why don't the glass break? The sheet's turned 'er tears white . . . she's cryin milk. The little pearls a' ignorance. When 'e comes I'll cover 'er 'ands 'n 'e won't 'ave t' run away. It'd be better for children if they never saw their parents' 'ands. The lady's glass is empty.

Woman   Fetch me a bowl a' water.

Girl   Why?

Woman   T' wash yer 'ands before the meal.

Girl   Me 'ands! I put dirt on the glass! – the plates! O look! – dirt on the cloth!

Woman   It doesn't matter, it's a picnic. Fetch the water.

Girl (*running to the hole*)   Yes yes. (*Stops.*) 'E'll be back before I

washed my – ! 'E wouldn't be so cruel! If 'e comes tell 'im
I'm –

Woman   'Urry!

Girl   Yes! (*She goes into the hole but comes back almost immediately.*)
The butler must be the footman! Take 'is coat 'n arst if the
journey was – I forget! I forget! It's in the book! I 'ad it once!
Everythin's lost 'ere!

Woman   Quickly!

Girl   I 'aven't got a picnic 'at with ribbons! They give me
nothin!

The **Girl** *goes into the hole.*

Woman (*calling*)   Be careful with the stoup! Pour gently –
gently! – Yer splash!

Girl (*off*)   Yes yes gently not splash!

Woman (*listening*)   'Er feet are 'oppin from side t' side . . .
(*Calls.*) Bring a cloth.

Slight pause. The **Girl**'s *head comes from the hole.*

Girl   Why?

Woman   T' dry yer 'ands.

Girl   Yes yes wash me 'ands 'n dry 'em!

The **Girl** *goes out of sight into the hole.*

Woman (*listening*)   . . . 'Er feet . . . from side t' side . . . I can
feel the ground tremble under 'er feet . . . a little pulse . . .

The **Girl** *comes from the hole carrying a towel and a bowl of water.*

Girl   Is 'e back? Thank god! All the food slows 'im down!

Woman   Give me the bowl. (*The* **Girl** *puts down the bowl beside
the* **Woman**.) Give me the towel. (*The* **Girl** *hands her the towel.*)
Give me yer 'ands.

Girl (*hands behind her back*)   Can't.

Woman   I must wash them.

Girl   Shut yer eyes.

Woman (*shuts her eyes*)   If yer wish.

Girl (*brings her hands from behind her back and looks at them*)   The dog with broken legs. It grinned 'n tried t' dance. Its 'ead sank on the stones – 'n it didn't try again. Why did it break its legs?

Woman   Let me wash yer 'ands.

Girl   If I was good they'd be soft like a daughter's ought t' be.

Woman (*holding the* **Girl**'*s hands*)   They're soft – feel inside the fingers.

Girl   The mud flakes off where yer 'old them. I can't show 'im me 'ands! They're ugly.

Woman   When I wash them . . . It's what I'm for. (*She puts the* **Girl**'*s hands in the water.*) There.

Girl   The water's gone dark.

Woman (*opens her eyes*)   Then I can look. Yes see the skin – it's clean – warm – they're like a child's 'ands in an old woman's gloves.

Girl   They're ugly.

Woman   No they never struck a blow in anger.

Girl   The doll.

Woman   They tore some rags. Yer silly rages, there's no anger in them. These 'ands always did good.

Girl   I scratch.

Woman   I'd rather be scratched by these 'ands than see these fingers covered in rings.

Girl   They scar.

Woman   Look at my face. Is there any sadness there? No only peace – even 'ere. Why did I walk the forest – till I'm tired 'n old 'n ill? – because yer 'ere – I can come t' yer – see yer – touch yer 'ands –

The **Woman** *dries the* **Girl**'s *hands.*

Girl   Yer 'ands 'it people. I can see the scars. All the faces yer struck – the things yer stole – the gates yer entered – the little animals yer killed – they left their marks. (*The* **Woman** *cries.*) There – they're not your tears – the animals – the people – they've got no eyes t' cry in now – they're cryin in your eyes – (*Touches the* **Woman**'s *face: holds up her finger.*) – look, their tears shinin on my finger – it's the kindness in yer that lets them use yer eyes t' cry in – yer 'ave t' let them cause yer made them suffer once. Yer 'ands aren't ugly now.

Woman   When I washed yer 'ands the water ran over mine.

The **Woman** *and the* **Girl** *hold each other's hands.* **Gregory** *puts out the candle with his foot.*

Woman   If I do anythin t' 'urt yer –

Girl   I forgive yer –

Woman (*trying to pull away her hands*)   No – yer mustn't touch my 'ands – let go –

Girl   Let me wash them. (*She puts the* **Woman**'s *hands into the water.*) The water's clear. There was so much dirt it sank so quickly. Yer 'ands are clean. They were already washed in the tears. Be still, 'n let me dry them.

Woman   Now I 'ave t' wash yer face.

Girl   For a picnic? – do people 'ave –

Woman   I washed it all yer life. Even *your* face changed – dirt, little tempers, 'unger – leave their marks. The water's washed them nearly all away. It's left only a tired child.

Girl   Trickles – my neck.

Woman (*drying with the cloth*)   There – caught it on the cloth. Close yer eyes. Your breath's on me 'ands. Me skin's tremblin like the lamb that licked me knife when it thought I'd come t' nuzzle it. I've finished.

Girl   Yer face.

Woman   No. Finished. Done. (*She empties the basin.*) My face is an ol' pit for rubbish t' be left in.

Girl   Why d'we wait?

Woman   A little longer.

Girl   What'll 'e bring? 'E came before – that proves 'e'll come! I never seen yer eat real food. I should'a arst 'im t' bring what yer like – but I don't know what it is –

Woman   The light's gone out.

Girl   What? (*She goes to the candle.*) When? We were washin! 'E came 'n went!

Woman   No –

Girl   We'll never see 'im again! 'E went by! 'E's lost! Why did we wash?

Woman   I –

Girl   Why? Why? Why? She won't tell me!

Woman   Don't – don't today –

Girl (*throws away the empty basin*)   Cruel! Cruel! Cruel! Look at our rags! Look! What could it matter if our 'ands are filthy? I 'ate yer!

Woman   No no – yer don't –

Girl   My claws're out! They want t' claw yer! Claw! Claw! Claw!

Woman   Yes claw my precious. . . it doesn't matter . . .

Girl   I'm clawin the air! It's bleedin!

Woman   Pick up the bowl. We must be tidy for –

Girl   Claw! Claw! I'll peel yer skin off yer bitch! My claws 'd peel a stone apple! Yer did it on purpose! I must find 'im! Stop 'im before 'e gets away! (*She goes to the side and calls.*) Come back! Give me my food! I won't waste it on that 'ag! She can starve 'n watch us eat! (*Turns to the* **Woman**.) Mum-ma make 'im come! (*Turns back to the forest.*) Please come!

Woman   'E'll come.

Girl   Look! – 'e's there – it's 'im – it's 'im! No no the trees! Mum-ma where is 'e?

The **Woman** *gathers up the picnic sheet – the picnic things crash.*

Girl   Ah! A shot – ! No – music! Is 'e dead? A bird? They wouldn't let 'im run – now 'e's a bird! – the angel from the mud! – 'e flies! – with my food in its beak! I 'eard 'is music! – or the branches – they're chasin 'im – branches breakin!

The **Woman** *throws the sheet over the* **Girl**.

Girl   Ah! (*Turns.*) You! – it's you! Mum-ma 'e's 'ere! 'E's playin tricks! 'E blew the candle out – 'n crep up with my food! O lovely tricks tricks tricks! Is 'e changed? Tell me 'ow 'e looks! Mum-ma are yer playin too? I won't peep! I'll play! My 'ands in prison at my sides! 'E's layin out the meal – Mum-ma whass 'e layin out for me t' eat?

The **Woman** *walks away from the* **Girl**.

Woman (*muttering*)   'Elp me – 'elp me – 'elp me –

The **Woman** *tries to go back to the* **Girl** *– turns away and stops – turns back and tries again – walks up and down muttering to herself.*

Girl   Shall I come t' table now? (*She moves forwards, sweeping the ground with her feet.*) If I sit down – open my eyes – there – see it all at once! I'll die with joy at – ! (*She feels the sheet with her hands.*) This sheet is – is it the sheet we – ? (*Searches with her feet.*) I can't find the – . 'E brought *'is* sheet because – ! O god – 'e brought a *table*! It's a *feast*! Mum-ma I said! – yer wouldn't 'ave it! What can I feel under my feet? Mum-ma can we finish now? Let me 'ear 'is voice? I'm goin t' be afraid.

Woman (*walking and hugging herself and muttering*)   – 'Elp me – 'elp me – 'elp me –

Girl   O Mum-ma what shall I see when they take the sheet away?

The **Woman** *puts her hands on the sheet over the* **Girl**'s *head. The* **Girl** *steps back sharply.*

Girl   'Eek! It's 'im! Make the butler lay the table – it's quicker – quicker – ! (*Feels the* **Woman**'s *hands.*) Damp. Still wet. 'N old man's 'ands. Knuckles.

Silence.

Girl   Put some food under the sheet. A bit. Then I'll play. (*She waits a moment.*) I'm the doll. Stitch stitch. A straitjacket full a' sawdust.

The **Woman** *tightens the sheet round the* **Girl**'s *neck.*

Woman   If – I – all my strength – !

Girl   'Eek no! No – no –

Woman   – take it, don't waste it – I –

Girl   Mum-ma 'elp me! Come back!

Woman   When I bore yer I wrenched – yer came in the world! 'Elp me – *wrench* – 'n break yer neck in my 'ands! . . . Please. I can't. I can't. I can't. Too weak.

The **Woman** *turns away. The* **Girl** *sits on the ground under the sheet – one hand feebly tries to raise it.*

Girl   Mum-ma somethin's 'urtin. Did we eat the meal? The pain in my neck . . . is that good food? (*The* **Woman** *starts to retch.*) You're sick. The good things we ate (*Half giggle.*) . . . 'urt us now . . .

The **Woman** *goes to* **Gregory**.

Woman   Give me one 'and – (*She lifts* **Gregory**'s *hand and fondles it.*) – this 'and – I'm beggin – lend me this 'and – t' put on one side 'er neck – my 'and on the other – between two 'ands – t' strangle 'er.

The **Woman** *lets go of* **Gregory**'s *hand – he raises it to feel his smile.*

Woman   'E won't.

The **Girl** *falls over.*

Woman   I'll never 'ear 'er voice again. Silence now. She owes me that.

Girl Sew sew –

Woman No more, no more – . (*She kneels beside the* **Girl**.)
Don't arst me again – I can't put up me 'ands again t' – I
can't! If yer was dead I'd do it – t' make sure for yer sake. Give
me a sign yer dead. Some blood on the sheet. A little sign.

Gregory (*singsong*)
Somebody don't want t' be dead.
Somebody don't want t' be dead.

Woman She's dead. She did it out a' kindness.

Girl Mum-ma.

Woman Ah she's mockin me. Do the dead want revenge so
soon? 'Er voice is worse than claws.

The **Girl** *stands under the sheet.*

Woman No no! Yer must die for my sake – I can't 'elp yer
any more –

Girl Mum-ma was it you?

Woman (*walking away*) Tell 'er – tell 'er – I'm not 'ere, not
'ere. My poor baby – she still smells a' me when I wash 'er –
The **Girl** *begins to walk slowly.*

Girl Don't do it again – not not – I won't be a nuisance –
won't arst for things – let me live with yer –

Woman (*goes to* **Gregory**) She's still – she's sick 'n starvin
but she's still alive! Kill 'er for me! She 'as no right t' live after
she made these 'ands take – . (*Stands behind* **Gregory** *and rails
at the* **Girl**.) 'Elp me! 'Elp me! (*Takes a few steps towards the* **Girl**
and screams.) 'Elp yer mother! Die! (To **Gregory**.) Kill 'er – the
little madam! – One bit a' 'uman kindness. Yer always 'ated
us! Was it a lie? Do it t' 'elp me 'n enjoy yer 'ate! I'll bless yer
or 'ate yer if yer want. 'E won't! 'E won't! (*She walks away.*)

Girl Mum-ma take the sheet away.

The **Girl** *tries to take off the sheet. She can't.*

Woman No one'll kill yer for me! – there's no pity! – or make the sky come down 'n be a 'ammer on us!

Girl   I want t' see the trees – I want t' see the broken picnic –

Woman   I'm old, old – if I was in a wooden box – the wood's more comfortable 'n soft than these clothes I 'ave t' live in – so soft they turn t' rags –

Girl   Let me see yer –

The sheet comes off. The women stare at each other.

Woman   Yer mustn't want t' live . . . it's over now . . . (*Turns to* **Gregory**.) Kill us both! I'll sing t' yer in the grave!

The **Girl** *falls over. The* **Woman** *goes to her.*

Woman   Ah – that was why – she walked t' get rid of 'er last breath – drive it away . . . Cover 'er. (*She nurses the* **Girl** *on her knees and covers her in the sheet.*) It's easy now. (*She presses one hand on the sheet over the* **Girl**'s *face.*) There. (*She takes away the hand and kisses the sheet over the face.*) Thank yer. My good daughter. Yer 'elped me. (*She stands. Calm.*) Now I regret it. Regret. That 'as t' start. (*She walks away.*) No right t' be near 'er now. (*To* **Gregory**.) If yer'd put one 'and on 'er neck – I arst – I could pretend I'd never strangled 'er – my 'and was strugglin with yer 'and t' pull it away. She'd still be my daughter. If yer knew what that word says. . . It's spoken by the dumb, men never 'ear it.

Girl   Mum-ma.

The **Woman** *half-hears the* **Girl**, *turns.*

Woman   Was it the wind . . . ?

The sheet ripples.

Woman   Look – life – a little life still under the sheet – or did I spill the water 'n it's runnin under it – or a little mouse – she fell on the poor little creature 'n it struggles t' get free – 'n find its 'ole.

The sheet is still.

Woman It's dead too . . . Glass. Can't cut me wrists. Can't
pick it up. I couldn't scratch on water. (*She straightens the sheet.*) I
can't love yer now. It'd 'urt. Cover yer t' show respect. Yer a
corpse. I see 'em on the street. They stitch their eyes so they
can't see. Stitch their mouth so they can't use our names. I'll
love yer t'morra. There's no more food. The mouse was
lookin for it when it died. It ate the last crumb in the world.
Thass why yer died. The man won't come.

Nold *comes on. He wears a soldier's battledress without equipment.*

Nold I'm 'ere. There's soldiers everywhere. I 'ad t' steal a
uniform . . . Call 'er. We must go.

Gregory She's dead.

Nold Dead? (*He sees the sheet and goes towards it.*)

Woman No – !

Nold (*stops*) I come t' take 'er t' the – (*He goes to the sheet and
lifts it.*)

Woman Nothin I ask for'll be done now. I told 'im not t' lift
it. If I said close the door they'd leave it open. They'd open
every door in the street.

Gregory *begins to collect the picnic things in the sheet.*

Nold We can't do anythin 'ere – we'll understand this
t'morra. The soldiers are –

Gregory (*clearing up*) If they find this they'll look for us.

Woman I laid 'er out while she was alive. I couldn't touch
'er when she was dead. I'd sooner break 'er neck while 'er legs
were in my womb. I washed 'er face 'n 'ands. She washed my
'ands – the kindness of a dead woman.

Gregory She killed 'er.

Nold (*stares at the* **Woman**) No – the soldiers were 'ere –
they –

Woman I forced 'unger down 'er for years. Yer came 'n
said yer'd feed 'er. Yer was famine itself. Put 'er through that

again – dirty bits a' bread like footprints t' 'er grave? She's better off like this. She deserves it.

Nold (*to* **Gregory**)   You killed 'er. (*To the* **Woman**.) Tell me. Don't lie for 'im! 'E killed 'er. (*To* **Gregory**.) Yer came 'n dragged me 'ere – 'n killed 'er! (*Takes the* **Woman**'s *knife. Turns to* **Gregory**.) I'll kill yer!

Gregory *stands by the hole. The picnic things are bundled in the sheet – it hangs like a long sack on his back. He points at* **Nold** *– his arm and finger straight.*

Gregory   Pity me! Pity me!

Nold   'Oo are you!

Gregory   An old man! I live on the streets! I own a tin! Yer put pennies in it at my feet! 'E blames me for 'is 'orrors! I'm old! – the soldiers torment the old! Pity me 'n let me go!

Gregory *goes into the hole.* **Nold** *turns to the* **Woman**.

Nold   Tell me what – ? (*The* **Woman** *has gone. He shouts after her.*) 'Oo is 'e? Tell me why I'm 'ere! Tell me 'oo I am!

He jumps into the hole.

Nold (*off*)   Yer won't hide in the dark! I'll kill yer! They won't need t' bury yer! I'll kill yer in the ground!

Silence. **Nold** *comes out of the hole.*

Nold   There'll be a war. That was right. 'Ow many will the soldiers kill? I'll kill 'im – just one – but it's more than all they'll kill. There ain the wood in this forest t' make the coffins 'e'll need. I could kill 'im now with the knife I was eatin with and I wouldn't wipe the blood off before I went on with the meal. It makes me tired even before I done it. I'm carryin 'is coffins on me back. (*Lurches – one leg slips down the hole. He walks away from it.*) Fool. I let 'im go. 'E told me there was other ways out.

Simon *comes on. He is a little thinner and darker than* **Nold** *and wears the same uniform. He carries two mess tins of food and has a vodka bottle sticking from his pocket.*

Simon (*gives one of the mess tins to* **Nold**)   Cop 'old.

Nold (*takes the tin*)   Back yet?

Simon (*nods*)   Sarge made 'em walk. Well chuffed. 'E kep the truck.

The two soldiers eat.

Simon (*points to the body*)   Raped?

Nold (*touches the body with his boot*)   Wouldn't fancy.

The soldiers walk a little aside, sit and eat.

Simon (*vodka*)   Gravy?

Nold (*takes the bottle*)   Where yer nick it?

Simon   Don't arst: CO's pad. 'Ad a good ferret.

Nold (*swigs. Approvingly*)   Officers' issue.

Jelly *comes on. He is thin-faced, a little under average height and slightly built. He wears the same soldier's uniform but has a rifle and webbing.*

Jelly (*calls over his shoulder*)   Them! (*To* **Simon**.) Smelt grub. Done ourn?

Simon   Weren't expected.

West, **Zemlinsky** *and* **Jolly** *come on.* **West** *is thickset and average height.* **Zemlinsky** *is thin and tall.* **Jolly** *is fair-haired and well built. They wear the soldier's uniform and carry the same equipment as* **Jelly**.

West   Knackered ain in it.

Zemlinsky *and* **Jolly** *sit and loosen their gear.* **Simon** *and* **Nold** *eat.* **West** *lies down.*

West   Goin t' kip. Give us a shout if the war ends.

Jelly   Yer sleep long enough we might win.

West *promptly falls asleep.*

Zemlinsky   Done ourn?

Simon   Weren't expected.

Jelly (*starts to go*)   Dosh our own.

Jolly (*stopping him*)   Ain stood down yet.

Simon   Sarge kep the truck?

Jolly   'E's got 'em fillin in the 'ole. Least 'e don't put us on the shovel.

Zemlinsky   They never stand on the edge. (*The other soldiers groan quietly.*) I watch it every time.

Jelly   Give it a rest.

Nold (*to* **Jelly**)   'Ow many yer do?

Jolly   'E couldn't count t' eight if 'e lost a finger off both 'ands.

Jelly   Yeh well get rid a' that.

Jelly and **Zemlinsky** *start to drag the body away.*

Jelly (*stops and looks questioningly at* **Zemlinsky**) . . . Yeh we should.

Jolly   Leave the poor cow in peace.

Jelly and **Zemlinsky** *drag the body to* **West**'s *side.*

Jelly   Nice surprise when 'e comes round.

Nold   Put 'is 'and up her crutch.

Jelly *puts* **West**'s *hand on the* **Girl**'s *crutch.*

Zemlinsky (*to* **Jelly**)   Steady.

Jelly   'E could kip on a paper boat in a storm.

Nold   Bet 'is watch is tickin faster.

Jolly   Give me packet for a real tremble.

Jelly   Only 'ole yer'll get 's off stiffs like 'er.

Simon   Least she can't cut yer goolies off.

Jelly   They booby-trap the dead ones. She's got a razor up 'er fanny.

Jolly   That'd give yer a close shave.

The vodka bottle is on the ground beside **Nold**.

Jelly   Give us a wet.

Simon (*to* **Nold**)   Give 'im.

Nold (*refusing*)   '*E* 'as one, they're all entitled.

Jelly   Sits there swillin.

Nold   Choked if yer knew 'ow it tasted. Officers' issue.

Pause.

Zemlinsky   One did t'day though. Stood right on it. I checked.

Pause. The other soldiers are silent. **Simon** *and* **Nold** *eat.*

Zemlinsky   Could a' bin stood on the edge of a sheet a' paper.

Jolly   On 'n on.

Zemlinsky   'E knew where 'e was. Look straight down the 'ole. Some of 'em moving. Still got the death fidgets.

Jolly   'E's lookin for 'is relative or some tart.

Zemlinsky   O yeh. Never thought a' that. Thought it was 'is bit a' defiance: 'e knew 'oo we was 'n what we's up to.

Jolly   Long as they don't put me on the shovel.

Jelly   Give us a wet.

Nold   Whass that supposed t' mean – 'what we was up to'? They bump in t' yer in the dark with a knife yer'll know what *they're* up to. 'S what a fish feels when yer bone it. They ain got faces. Two backs like the targets in the butts. The one-arm man with the scythe mowin down the world, thass war. They won't be no trouble dead. Just stack 'em up. It's their land, let 'em be buried in it. Then we can go 'ome in peace, where the

sun shines 'n the shit smells as if it's come out a' civilisation.
More poor sods're drowned in the milk a' 'uman kindness 'n
all the blood baths since some shise-'ouse invented carnage.
It's orders, thass all. (*Swigs vodka. Gestures with bottle.*) Thank god
someone's got some initiative. . . 'Stood on the edge', what
was yer in civvie street, shoe-salesman?

Zemlinsky   Never said don't – said get it organised.

West (*asleep*)   'Orses comin up the 'ill – bringin the ropes –
evenin – sweat in the sky after rain –

Jolly   They couldn't organise piss out a leaky fanny.

Jelly (*nods at* **West**)   'E bettin on the gee-gees?

No response.

Simon   Yer'll be organised t'morra. They're truckin us out.

Silence. The others wait for **Simon** *to go on.*

Jolly   Well? Where to?

Nold   'E 'ad a ferret in the COs.

Jolly   Up the front?

Simon   T' the rear my son. Two 'undred kilometres.

Jelly (*nods*)   Same job then.

Nold (*explaining*)   'S where 'e nick the bottle.

Nold *passes the bottle to* **Simon**. **Simon** *drinks.*

Simon   They found a ravine – a ditch – a cliff on both sides.
We set our guns up on one cliff – the other cliffs four 'undred
metres away on the far side a' the ditch. Thass the point a' it:
'arf way up that cliff there's a ledge – runs right along it. Wide
enough for one t' walk on. There it was, ready waitin – a
natural piece a' architecture. They push 'em out on the ledge
in groups. Thirty – forty – at a time.

Jolly   No diggin? They drop straight in the ditch?

Simon (*offering the bottle to* **Jelly**).   One.

Nold *gets the bottle before* **Jelly** *can.*

Nold   Wastin officer issue on 'im . . . !

Jelly   I 'ope the CO counted 'em.

Zemlinsky   They'd never walk.

Simon   I told yer: it's organised. They truck 'em in – unload 'em down the back out a' sight a' any nasties – strip 'em off – chase 'em up the top between two lines a' squaddies – kapos – local gendarmes – lay in t' 'em with truncheons – lumps a' metal – chains – anythin t' 'and – the dogs join in – when they get t' the top they don't know their tit from their arse'ole – scientific fact. They walk out on that ledge like kiddies on the way t' school. They'd 'old 'ands if there was room.

Jolly   They got a town? – A proper civvie one?

Jelly *(ironic)*   O yeh! – a 'ome postin.

Zemlinsky   They won't walk. They'd see the bodies in the ditch.

Simon   Never look. They got their own blood on 'em by then remember. They look down? – just dead stiffs sunbathin in the snow. Last thing each day the squad goes down 'n bumps off any still breathin.

Jolly   Thass t'morra then.

Nold *(to* **Simon***)*   Chuck us the top. (**Nold** *catches the bottle top and picks up the two mess tins.*) I'll rinse. My turn I think.

Zemlinsky *tries to grab the bottle from* **Nold***. They grapple mechanically round and round in silence. The others watch without interest.*

Zemlinsky   I'll break the bottle 'n –

Nold   Shite!

Zemlinsky   I'll break the bottle 'n –

Nold   Kill yer yer shite-'ouse puke!

They grapple. The vodka splashes.

Jelly   Waste! Waste! Waste! Waste!

Nold *gets the bottle. He fights off* **Zemlinsky** *with one hand and with the other puts the cap on the bottle.*

Zemlinsky   I'll smash it in 'is face –

Nold   Shite-'ouse puke. (*He holds the bottle upside down and swings it tauntingly.*) Take a shufties at what's mine 'n me mate's – yer pissy shit-'ouse door.

Zemlinsky   I'll break it 'n twist the jagged bits in yer guts – (*Breathes slowly, straightens his clothes.*) – like spaghetti on the forks they use in graveyards.

Jolly   Right! (*To* **Zemlinsky**.) If 'e wants t' be a slimy git, let 'im. (*To* **Nold**.) It wouldn't take *you* much ambition. (*To* **Zemlinsky**.) Yer started it – all that 'on the edge' crap. I'll squash the pair a' yer so small yer'll fit in that bottle 'n still leave room t' drown. We got our enemy already – in the trees – (*Kicks the ground.*) down there. (*Nods at* **Jelly**.) Get rid a' that.

Jelly   Where's yer stripe?

Jolly   Get it got rid of! (*To the others.*) 'S kids say yer do this 'n I'll do that! . . . We put up with each other. Yer wan t' kill yerself for a 'arf-empty bottle – wait for peace-time. One's threatened, we're all threatened. I got a 'ome too – where the sun shines 'n shit don't just stink it knows its limitations. I'm goin there in one bit if I 'ave t' murder me father in me mother's bed t' do it.

Jelly *drags the body out.*

Nold (*takes the cap from the bottle and swigs*)   Officer issue.

Simon *watches him with a faint grin.* **Jolly** *watches him blankly.* **Zemlinsky** *goes out.* **Nold** *puts the cap back on the bottle.*

Jolly (*to* **Nold**)   Yer the sort a' 'eap that gives excrement a bad name.

Nold (*picks up the mess tins*)   My turn t' 'old these under the tap.

Simon and **Nold** go out. **Jolly** kicks **West**. **West** staggers awake without making a sound.

Jolly　You people appal me.

Jolly goes. **West** looks round.

West　Wha'?

West sees he is alone and goes out.

The Big Ditch

A cliff top. One edge of the cliff is downstage. There is a vertical path on this which is not seen. The cliff's other edge is upstage facing the ravine and the opposite cliff. This cliff and the ravine are not seen, only the sky above them. When soldiers look towards the ravine only their backs are seen.

Upstage, two MGs (machine-guns) are trained on the opposite cliff. Centre stage, a portable field canteen, Primus, coffee-pot and billy-can. Scattered over the cliff top ammo boxes, food scraps, cigarette packs, three empty schnapps bottles and other litter.

Full afternoon sunlight.

Simon *and* **Jolly** *begin to dismantle and clean one MG,* **West** *and* **Zemlinsky** *do the same to the other. The barrels are hot.* **Jelly** *makes coffee – lights the Primus, puts coffee in the filter and pours water from the billy-can into the pot.*

Silence except for shuffling feet and a few clinks of metal. The soldiers are quietly tired, collars and buttons undone. **Jelly** *puts a schnapps bottle to his lips – empty. He puts it down.*

Gregory *comes on downstage left. He is younger than before, mid-forties. He is a sergeant and wears the same uniform as the other soldiers. He walks along the bottom edge of the cliff looking over it.*

Gregory *(aloud to himself)*   Where's the little sod got to? Skivin 'ound.

Silence.

Simon *(to* **West***)*   Loan us a bit a' pull-through.

West *throws the roll to* **Simon***. He catches it, tears off a strip and throws the roll back to* **West***.*

Simon   Pay yer back.

Simon *oils the pull-through, loops it in the landyard and pulls it through the gun barrel.*

Gregory *(as before)*   Takes the lazy little tyke three 'ours t' deliver one little packet. Soon sort 'im out when 'e turns up. (*To* **Jelly**.) Ain that coffee ready yet?

Jelly (*working*)   Give us a . . . (*His voice trails off.*)

Gregory (*claps his hands*)   Less 'ave yer! Bloody morgue attendant'd die a' boredom if 'e 'ad t' deal with you lot.

The soldiers work at the same pace as before. **Gregory** *inspects* **Simon**'s *barrel against the sky.*

Gregory   Got enough gunge down that t' grow potatoes for a famine. Pull it through.

Simon   Just 'ave.

Gregory   Yer couldn't pull a fanny if it 'ad welcome tattooed round it. Do it proper this time. (*He wanders to the coffee and adjusts the Primus flame.*) 'Ow much yer put in? Coffee's all right, 's the way yer make it.

Off, a voice calls indistinctly from the other cliff.

Jolly   Oi sarge they're callin yer.

Gregory (*peering across the ravine*)   Wass 'e on about?

West   Bound t' be somethin wrong if 'e's in the –

Gregory   Shut up! Yer all mouth! (*Shouts across the ravine.*) We'll be down in 'arf 'n 'our. (*To* **Jelly**.) Get them boxes sorted out. Bloody rubbish tip.

Jelly *ignores him and collects the mugs from the soldiers.*

Off, the indistinct voice.

Jelly   Bloody determined 'bout somethin –

Gregory   Will yer shut up 'n let me listen! You rabbitin, 'ow'm I supposed t' 'ear? (*Shouts.*) Say again!

Off, the indistinct voice.

Jolly   They got more.

Gregory   They said we finished. (*Points across the ravine.*) Got the gas cape on the rock t' say finish for the day. Blind git. (*Shouts.*) Whass goin on?

Off, the indistinct voice.

West   Pretend we never 'eard 'em –

Gregory   Will yer wrap up! I'm tryin t' 'old 'n intelligent conversation! (*Shouts.*) We stood down!

Off, the indistinct voice.

Simon   Less scarper sarge.

Jolly   Tell 'im we never savvied.

Gregory   Belt up! – They're like a pack a' bleedin monkeys. (*Shouts.*) 'Ow many?

Jolly   Use yer fingers.

Gregory (*wags his fingers in the air*)   'Ow many? (*To himself and the soldiers.*) Wass that supposed t' mean?

Jolly   'S few.

Gregory (*shouts*)   Can't they wait till mornin?

Jelly (*speculating*)   Found 'em in the back a' the trucks. Why can't they look before?

Gregory (*to* **Jelly**)   Will yer belt up!

Zemlinsky   Done enough for t'day. Me mind's off it now.

Gregory (*peering across the ravine*)   Now where's 'e off to . . . ? (*Turns and goes back to the coffee. To* **Zemlinsky**.) Pity about that. – Get them guns up.

Simon   Less wait. See if they finish 'em off.

Gregory (*sudden temper*)   Ain arguin with me superiors for the sake a' you lazy snots! Nough brass over there t' open 'n ironmongers. (*Calmer.*) 'S one a' them things. Don' wan' no incident: them out on the ledge 'n we ain ready. (*Fiddles with the Primus.*) Bloody gas runnin out now . . . – Get set up.

Jolly   Can't do it.

Gregory   O? Why?

Jolly   No ammo.

For a moment **Gregory** *glares at* **Jolly**. *He goes to the ammo boxes, kicks one aside and then examines all of them carefully. The soldiers watch in silent derision.*

Gregory   I always tell yer keep a reserve! Every bloody time the same! Yer do it so yer don't 'ave t' donkey none down! This time they caught yer out!

Simon *starts to dismantle his MG.*

Gregory   Leave that! – get it set up.

Simon (*quiet satisfaction*)   No ammo.

The coffee begins to filter. **Gregory** *looks at the soldiers.*

Gregory   The skiver'll bring a box up with 'im.

Silence. For a moment the soldiers are at a loss. **Jelly** *walks across to the coffee-pot, picks it up and empties it with a whoosh across the stage. No one reacts. Silence.*

West   Yer sit in one place all day till yer spine's comin out yer back . . .

Gregory   Whass the point a' that? Whass 'e do that for?

Jelly   They don't want sweat they want our blood.

Gregory (*sudden anger*)   Get them guns up 'n get be'ind 'em! (**Simon** *bangs his MG as he reassembles it.*) 'Ack that again 'n I'll 'ack you! – yer life may depend on it one day! (*Shouts across the ravine.*) Oi! (*To the soldiers.*) All this shise-fuss for a few they – can't be many, they'd a' find 'em before. (*Shouts.*) Oi!

Jolly   That fetched him.

Gregory, Simon, West, Jolly (*a ragged call*)   'Ow many?

Jolly (*counting the signals*)   Ten – twenty – whass that?

West   Thirty.

Jolly   Twenty-five.

Simon (*shouts*)   Keep 'em for t'morra.

Gregory (*to* **Simon**)   One more word out a' you – ! (*Shouts.*)

'Ang on till I give the OK. (*To* **West**.) See what that jerk's skivin at.

West *goes downstage and looks over the cliff.*

Simon   Don't need two sarge. Do that with one.

Gregory (*to* **Jelly**)   Could've 'ad coffee while we wait.

West (*nearly at the cliff edge*)   Reckon 'e ain comin.

Gregory   'E is. Seen 'is nut. Weren't no mountain goat – yer ate all them. (*To* **Simon**.) Two. One of 'em's bound t' jam t'day. (*To* **Jelly**.) Yer chuck that coffee again I'll 'ave yer on orders for wastin army property.

Simon   We could do twenty-five on one.

West (*calling down the cliff*)   Oi! – Move it!

Gregory   I fiddle 'em good coffee – not that turnip muck – 'n 'e chucks it! (*To* **Simon**.) The trouble with your conversation 's yer learnt t' talk.

Simon   Two . . . !

Jelly *packs away the coffee things. The soldiers set up the MGs and wait.* **Gregory** *gazes across the ravine.*

Gregory   . . . That line a' red where the bullets splash 'em – when it rains the cliff looks like it's bleedin . . . Dump. (*Pause.*) Yer never know where yer goin till yer get there. The map's stuck on the soles a' yer feet. One night the looey's in a good mood – which is a bloody miracle 'n a 'arf in itself – gets piss in the sergeants' mess – drops 'is ciggie case – afternoon a' the day followin, we runs out a' ammo – they find a last lot playin 'ide 'n seek in the back a' the trucks: trouble! As it 'appens I sent my laddie down t' return the ciggie case to its owner – 'e comes back with a box a' reserve: the 'and a' fate don't always thump yer, sometimes it gives yer a wank.

Simon   Still don't make two right.

Gregory   That ciggie case is a work a' art. 'N 'eirloom. 'E's only a looey but 'is family go back. They 'ad that ciggie case

before ciggies was invented. Looks too piss-elegant thin t' get
the ciggies in. Real gold – not this gypsy muck yer get.
Chamfered edges, chased corners, engraved escutcheon on the
lid. The ciggies ain 'eld in by a common strip a' elastic as per
normal: 's got a gold bar – see yer fingers through it but it
don't bend. When I pick that case off the floor some dick'ead
'ad stood 'is 'obnails on it: smooth as silk 'n not a scratch. A
way a' life in that. Fits yer 'and like a well-formed tit.

West   'E's always flashin it.

Jolly   Never offers me.

Gregory   Officer 'as t' keep 'is distance from scum like us.
Give one t' a stretcher case – 'n a light. Some wouldn't.

Zemlinsky (*to* **West**)   Give 'im a yell.

West *does not respond.*

Gregory   The precision on that 'inge: yer press the button
'n the lid flies up like a sparrer landin on a puff a' smoke. If yer
was 'n ant kippin on it yer wouldn't lift 'n eyelid.

Simon   Can't be content with one like anybody normal.

Pause.

Gregory   Bet 'e was cross when 'e woke up. 'Ead like a lead-
rock – 'and out for 'is fags – no case – mater'll give 'im a right
bollockin if it's lost. State 'e was in, 'e could a' drop it anywhere
– some squaddie pick it up 'n flog it. Big Brass visitin t'day. 'E
likes t' flash it round for the nobs. Press the button: Turkish on
the left, straight on the right. Nobs choose – the echelons a'
wealth. If I was a man 'oo could be tempted I could 'a 'id it
where Jesus couldn't find it on judgement day – 'n I don't
mean up 'is arse. (*Half shrug.*) Let 'im flash it round. I'll be well-
in with 'im when 'e gets it back. (*Gives a little private snigger.*)

Nold *comes on from below. He is in uniform with webbing and rifle.*

Gregory   Well? – Give it 'im?

Nold   Sarge.

Gregory   Whass 'e say?

Nold Narked.

Gregory Never said 'e was chuffed?

Nold Arst why yer brought it up 'ere in the first place.

Gregory What you say?

Nold *shrugs.*

Gregory Whass that supposed t' mean? (*No response.*) All kitted up for 'is conference was 'e?

Nold Sarge.

Gregory Bet 'e was chuffed when yer give it to 'im before 'e set out?

Nold 'E 'ad 'is driver lookin for it in the road.

Gregory O?

Nold Mud on 'is trews. Bloody ugly mood. Face like Siamese pigs.

Gregory Did 'e count the ciggies?

Jolly Can 'e count?

Nold (*answering* **Gregory**) Not t' my knowledge.

Gregory I know 'ow many's in it.

Nold That coffee?

Nold *goes towards the coffee.* **Gregory** *takes a few steps towards the bottom cliff edge.*

Gregory Where's my ammo?

Nold What ammo? Yer finished – I 'eard yer 'arf 'n 'our back. (*He starts to untie his mug from his pack. To* **Jelly**.) Yer better 'ave 'ad saved us some!

Nold *has untied his mug. He looks round and sees the other soldiers watching him.* **Gregory** *goes down to the edge and looks over it. There is no ammo box. He comes back, picks up an empty schnapps bottle and reads part of the label.*

Gregory (*to the soldiers*)   'E *is* 'avin me on?

Gregory *stands the bottle upright on the ground, goes to* **Nold** *and puts out his arm to grasp his shoulder and turn him to face the other cliff – but stops and walks away.*

Gregory   I never put a finger on 'im. – See that ledge son? In a minute I'll 'ave people stood out there expectin t' be shot.

Jolly   Less pack it in sarge. They made the mess, they can sort it out.

Gregory (*to* **Nold**)   I can't shoot 'em with no ammo. I shouldn't think they brought their own. (**Nold** *shrugs.*) See that? – 'E shrugs at the looey, 'e shrugs at me!

Nold   It was late so I –

Gregory   I never arst yer for the time!

Gregory *picks up the schnapps bottle and reads the label. He goes upstage and matter-of-factly throws the bottle over the cliff into the ravine.*

Gregory   Yer disarmed this unit on active service. Rendered it incapable a' carryin out a military order. 'S court-martial for that. Yer'll regret this for the rest a' yer short life!

Jolly   Less go sarge. We done our job.

Gregory   We ain done our job! We disobliged our officers! That offends every fibre of my bein. We let our comrades down!

Jelly   Coffee on sarge?

Gregory *takes a few steps towards the Primus and looks at it dully. He turns to* **Nold**.

Gregory   Yer *did* bring it?

Nold   I thought I'd meet yer comin down!

Gregory   I give a standin order. No one climbs up that face without a gun or box. Everythin 'as t' be donkeyed up. Beasts can't pick a way – they'd 'ave t' be donkeys with wings. (*Fuming.*) Sometimes I despair. Any minute I'll 'ave bodies waitin t' be dealt with – is that a kindness t' them, let 'em stand? Ain yer got nothin 'uman left in yer?

Jelly   Coffee sarge?

Simon (*looking across the ravine*)   Reckon they lost 'em again.

Gregory   The looey knows yer come up. Can't say we run out 'n never 'ad chance t' resupply. I only sent yer down – the ciggie case was extra – t' bring the ammo up. I knew we was low so I acted.

Nold   Yer sent me with the case.

Gregory   Ah 'e wants t' argue!

Jelly (*to* **Gregory**)   Yes or no? – Chrissake . . .

Gregory   I didn't 'ave t' send yer with the case. I could 'a give it t' me officer meself t'night –

Nold   Yer said 'e 'ad t' 'ave it for 'is –

Gregory   'E'd 'a bin just as grateful if I pick it up be'ind the bogs t'morra mornin 'n I was still wipin the shit 'n vomit off as I *give* it to 'im!

Nold   Didn't think.

Gregory   Yer come up enough times t' think! These lads *dream* a' it! Yer tellin me yer stood there – look up at that face – 'n didn't notice there was nothin in yer 'ands?

Nold   I thought we'd 'ave t' 'od it down again.

Gregory   So? War ain just a slaughter'ouse yer know: carryin comes in t' it. If it was too 'eavy yer could 'a 'ung a couple a' bandoliers round yer neck! (*Walks away.*) What more can I do? Yer won't get away with this. A standin order – that applies t' all that part a' the world thass in my uniform. If this unit was ambushed –

Jolly   By sparrers.

Silence.

Gregory   'Oo says we'd 'ave t' 'od it down? I could'a kep yer up 'ere sat on it all night.

Simon (*looking across the ravine*)   Shit-'ouse! – they're comin out.

Gregory   Well. You're in trouble lad – deep 'n dark. The looey got ratty just cause 'e lost 'is case for one day. If it's left t' that lot over there they'll make a right ruddy blood-bath. They ain got our discipline. They'll use their dinner knives. My advice is trot. Say yer 'ad a nervous breakdown. They only shoot yer for that. Yer under arrest. (*He takes* **Nold***'s rifle. To* **West***.*) Private I'm makin yer responsible for my prisoner. (*To* **Jelly***.*) Get on 'is gun.

West *picks up his rifle and stands escort by* **Nold**. **Jelly** *takes* **West***'s place on the MG.*

Gregory   Well the next ten minutes should make the 'istory books. 'E give yer a ringside seat.

Jolly   We ought 'a stop 'em –

Gregory   A simple order: yer come up – yer carry up. Jesuschriss yer'd think yer 'ad enough savvy t' realise yer in somethin serious.

Jolly   Sarge –

Gregory   That ciggie case is a work a' art. Thass supposed t' teach yer respect 'n responsibility – the value a' things. It offends me t' think I put 'n object a' beauty like that in 'is grubby 'ands. Where was yer – in limbo? (*Anger.*) Stan' straight when I talk t' yer! (**Nold** *stiffens.*) If yer nicked 'is fags – if yer put yer nasty fingers on one t' sniff it! – it'll get back t' me. Yer'll wish yer was on that ledge.

Zemlinsky   Sarge –

Jolly *waves his arms to signal no.*

Gregory (*to* **Nold**)   Yer always was a contrary little sod. (*Sees* **Jolly** *waving.*) Leave that!

Jolly } Sarge we –

Simon } Sarge they're on the –

Gregory. Leave it! (*To* **West**.) Get back over there with yer mates. (*Bangs his hands together and rubs them in satisfaction. To* **Jelly**.) You: get that coffee on – 'n don't ruin it. I fiddle 'em the best coffee 'n 'e makes it taste like 'edge'og shit.

Simon   Sarge they're on the –

Gregory   Rifles!

Jolly   What?

Gregory   Use yer rifles! (*To* **West**.) I tol' yer – over there!

Zemlinsky   We can't!

West *joins the other soldiers at the MGs. They hesitate and look at each other uncertainly.*

West (*to the soldiers*)   Rifles?

Jolly (*to the soldiers*)   For them – at this distance – ?

Gregory (*looks at the soldiers*)   Yeh . . . yer think yer lords a' creation sat with 'n MG between yer legs. I seen yer smug faces. Kids sprayin piss up the playground wall. Now we'll find out 'oo can shoot. Yer'd better make each round score. Yer run out, yer mate'll be in dead trouble. Save 'im one. 'E can put 'n 'ole in 'is 'ead 'n we'll watch the piss run out.

Jolly, **Simon** and **Zemlinsky** *pick up their rifles.*

Gregory   Fire in yer own time. No 'urry. They're still comin out. I'll tell the CO it was my idea for some real target practice.

Simon (*counting*)   Thirteen – fourteen – fifteen . . . twenty-one – twenty-two – the lot?

Jolly   Wait – don't panic 'em –

Gregory   Twenty-eight. 'E said twenty-five.

West (*peering across the ravine*)   They don't know where they are.

Gregory   Down down in case they twig.

Zemlinsky   Won't they see the MGs?

Jolly, **Simon**, **West** and **Zemlinsky** *crouch with their rifles.*
Jelly *makes coffee.* **Nold** *stands at the Primus, his mug held out in his hand, his head bowed in angry thought.*

Simon   They're stood there . . . 'S like doin it in slow motion.

West (*mystified*)   Why's it so . . . ? (*Realises.*) They ain naked! – they ain bin strip off.

Jolly   Weren't worth the bother – last lot.

Zemlinsky (*targetting*)   The ol' sod in the greatcoat.

West   No always start with the nippers. Kid on the left.

West *fires a shot. Pause.*

Simon   'E miss?

West   No!

Simon   'E ain fell.

Jolly   Totterin on the edge.

Silence. The soldiers stare.

Zemlinsky   O no.

Simon   I don't believe it – I'm not seein this . . .

Silence.

West   The silly cow! – look at the silly cow! –

Zemlinsky. She's –

Silence.

Zemlinsky (*shouts*)   Let 'im go yer stupid – let go a' 'im yer stupid cow – !

Silence.

Simon   It ain 'appenin . . .

Nold (*to* **Jelly**)   Any water left t' rinse me mug? The shit 'n dust on that climb.

Jelly (*hands the billy-can to* **Nold**)   Don't waste it. That 'as t' be donkeyed 'n all.

Gregory (*looking at the soldiers*)   Kids gawpin at a circus! Shoot the silly bitch! Get it started!

Jolly   Shoot 'er! Shoot 'er!

The four soldiers fire ragged shots.

West   She's gone.

Simon   They still don't know . . .

West   They see the kid fall in the pit with 'er –

Jolly   They're lookin along the line t' see . . .

Simon   They must know . . . they must know . . .

Gregory (*looks over his shoulder at* **Nold**)   Look at 'im stood there with 'is mug at the ready! 'E's good at that! Get them boxes stack!

Gregory *turns back to watch the firing.*

Nold (*not moving. Mutters to* **Jelly**)   Drink me coffee first. Prisoners're entitled.

Simon   Why don't they see – why don't they – ?

Nold (*to* **Jelly**)   Fall for 'is caper? 'E'd 'ave yer up 'n down 'oddin 'is bloody boxes all day. Ain a bleedin pack-animal.

Simon   They don't even look down t' see where the kid went.

Jelly (*to* **Nold**)   'E 'ad t' get the ciggie case back sharpish. 'E nick it then got scared. If the officers told 'im t' eat shit 'e'd arst for seconds.

Simon   Why don't they see? . . . The ol' dad with the greatcoat – 'is fists're still stuck in 'is pockets –

West   Wha'?

Simon   In the greatcoat tied up with rope! (*Sticks out his hand.*) Glasses – glasses! Give us the glasses!

Zemlinsky *gives* **Simon** *the FGs* (*field glasses*).

Simon (*focusing the FGs on the ledge*)   'E's clutchin somethin in 'is pocket –

West   Wha'?

Zemlinsky   'S where 'is money is!

Jolly   O Jesus Jesus don't let me go like that! Let me know. (*Suddenly yells.*) Yer dead yer shits! Yer the dead! (*Waves his rifle over his head.*) With this! (*Fires a shot into the air.*) I got this!

West (*hand out for the FGs*)   Less 'ave a butchers! Less 'ave a butchers!

Simon (*hands the FGs to* **Jolly**)   The ol' sod in the black coat tied with rope! – The tears're pourin down! – They're runnin in the light!

Jolly (*focusing the FGs*)   Like little maggots rollin on 'is face.

West   Give us a see!

Nold (*showing* **Jelly** *a dark blue paper bag*)   This all the sugar? – empty bag?

Jelly   They pour it in.

Jolly (*looking through the FGs*)   They know where they are now – they know what they're 'ere for . . .

West (*puzzled*)   . . . Then why they just stood . . . ?

Simon   Make the last minute longer innit. They run they know we open up.

Zemlinsky   They reckon if they can stand it 'arf a minute longer the war'll end or we'll be converted –

Gregory   Jesus wouldn't 'ave yer – ain that desperate. Give 'em 'ere. (*He takes the FGs from* **Jolly** *and focuses on the ledge.*)

Nold (*to* **Jelly**)   Give it t' me wrap up. I couldn't check. Any gone – it's 'im.

Simon (*to* **Gregory**)   The ol' grandad in the coat – 'e's got 'is 'ands –

Gregory. Cut the gob: let me see yer do it.

The four soldiers fire a fusillade. **Gregory** *watches through the FGs.*

Jolly   That moved 'em!

West   They ain so bloody clever!

Zemlinsky   O look at 'em 'op! (*Yells.*) Yer bastard scum yer know now! (*Shooting.*) An you! An you! Show us yer death roll off the top ol' son! I'll wipe yer off that cliff like shite off a big stone bum! O don't they run!

The soldiers pick off people at random.

West   Got one!

Simon   Got one!

West (*his magazine is empty*)   'Old it! I'm out! Mag gone! Wait for me!

The other soldiers stop shooting. **West** *struggles frantically to change his mag.*

Jolly   Be sharp or yer'll miss the final action – (*He fires one shot.*)

West   No wait yer greedy bastard! Wait for me! (*He drops the replacement mag.*) Sod it! Sod it! (*Clips on the replacement mag.*) Got it! Got it! I'm in!

West *fires a shot and* **Jolly**, **Simon** *and* **Zemlinsky** *cheer. They all fire at random.* **Gregory** *looks over his shoulder and sees* **Nold** *still standing by the coffee with his mug.*

Gregory (*to* **Nold**)   Oi told yer t' stack me empties!

Zemlinsky   Got 'im!

Nold   Bin up 'n down twice t'day sarge. I'm entitled t' –

Gregory   Yer entitled t' my toe up yer arse! Yer got a bloody nerve! I'll 'ave yer 'umpin crates up there all day

t'morra – yer'll think yer dead 'n come back as the 'uman yo-
yo.

Jelly   Coffee's done.

Nold *begins to stack the ammo boxes noisily.* **Gregory** *puts down the
FGs and goes to the coffee. He fills his mug. It is hot. He sips as he
watches the shooting.*

Zemlinsky   Got one!

Gregory (*to* **Nold**)   My officer 'ates litter. Could come 'n
inspect any time. Don't rely on that climb keepin 'im down.

Jolly   Get them poor wretches 'uddled on the end. They get
on me wick.

The four soldiers fire a barrage. Suddenly they stop and stare at the ledge.

Simon   . . . Whass 'e doin . . . ?

Gregory (*calls to the soldiers*)   Oi get on with it. That don't
take all day!

Simon   No sarge – the ol' sod – the ol' grandad in the coat –
'e's kneelin on the ledge – stretchin out 'is arms t' the gap
where they come on.

Jolly   'S 'e prayin?

West (*shouts*)   The gap's empty!

Zemlinsky (*shouts*)   There's no one there!

Simon   Kneelin 'n 'oldin out 'is arms – O god 'e's 'oldin out
'is money – must be money! – tellin 'em 'is pocket's full.

Jolly   Ain money – the gap wouldn't be empty – the
sergeant'd be out there –

Simon   The one with the squint's got three 'ands – !

Jolly   On each arm!

Simon   Ain money – the ol' sod's strugglin with 'is rope –
it's off! –

West   Wha' the – ?

Simon 'E's kneelin on the end – why's 'e – ? . . . The ol' sod's only tryin t' 'ang 'isself – 'e's only tryin t' –

Jolly . . . The ol' . . .

Simon (*suddenly*) 'Er ! – 'er! – 'er! – 'er! O look at 'er! . . . Thass brilliant . . . (*Puts out his hand.*) Glasses! Glasses! Give us! Glasses!

Zemlinsky *passes the FGs to* **Simon**. **Simon** *focuses on the ledge* – **Jolly**, **West** *and* **Zemlinsky** *stare at it.*

West . . . Yeh . . .

Zemlinsky . . . Yeh . . . that is somethin . . . even I never expected t' see somethin a' that class . . .

Nold *finishes stacking the ammo boxes. He goes to the coffee –* **Gregory** *stops him.*

Gregory (*to* **Nold**) Get yerself 'n yer rifle over there.

Nold Can't. Under arrest.

Gregory I let yer off. Next time yer won't be so lucky! Move!

Nold (*obstinately*) Take me coffee with me.

Gregory Get!

Nold *picks up his rifle and joins the other soldiers at the edge.*

Simon . . . the girl . . . look she's climbin up the cliff be'ind 'er . . .

West . . . tryin t' get out . . .

Jolly . . . she's seen the bodies below . . .

Simon . . . she's tryin t' reach the top – clawin the rock – she can't – 'er claws – 'er claws're slippin where the cliff's bin soak with blood – 'er slippers're twistin off 'er feet – in the wet – 'er little toes – if she could reach up out the blood t' get a 'igher grip – grip 'igh enough – god she'd go up there like a fly with wings on fire – !

Jelly (*calls*) Coffee.

Gregory (*going up to the soldiers*)   Whass going on? (*Peers across the ravine.*) I'm not 'avin that! Bring 'er down!

Simon   No sarge watch.

West   'S only 'er 'n the woman –

Jolly   'N the ol' sod on the end – soon 'ose 'em down, no bother.

Simon   Yer don't see this every day.

Jolly (*shouts*)   Go it darlin!

Simon (*looking through the FGs*)   'Er nails diggin in the rock –

West (*hand out for the FGs*)   Less look! If she was only naked! The bloody fools ain strip 'er off! A naked tart spread out on the rock! Me barrel up 'er arse!

Jelly (*bored*)   D'yer want this coffee or what?

A barrage of feet: **Nold**, **Jolly**, **Simon**, **West** *and* **Zemlinsky** *drum the ground like sports spectators.*

Simon   O chriss 'er claws'd drill the 'oles for dynamite.

Gregory (*hand out*)   Give us a go.

Simon *gives* **Gregory** *the FGs. He focuses on the ledge.*

Gregory (*slow*)   . . . That is a picture . . . One end the ol' man 'angin 'isself – coat flaps goin – got 'is beard caught up in the rope – the other end the girl – stuck up on the rock – arms 'n legs spread out – 'n stretch between the two a' 'em a long red line a' blood.

Simon   Normal yer never see it . . .

Jelly   I'll pour.

Simon   . . . there's never time . . .

Slight pause. **Jelly** *begins to pour the coffee in the mugs.*

Zemlinsky (*suddenly*)   O look at that!

West   The silly mare! – she's draggin the girl down – !

Simon No tryin t' climb up on 'er –

Jolly 'Angin on 'er skirts!

West (*rhythmic clap*)   Drag-'er-down! Drag-'er-down!

Gregory (*to* **Simon**. *Sudden, sober shock*)   What? – yer'd let 'er get away?

The soldiers drum their feet – **West**'s *clapping is drowned out.*

Simon Can't get no higher grip.

Nold Go it! Go it! Go it! Go it!

Jolly Stuck!

Gregory 'Ose 'em off!

Simon No sarge less watch – it ain –

Gregory 'Ose it!

The soldiers fire. Silence.

Nold She's still there.

Zemlinsky On 'er own.

Jolly Stuck.

Nold 'Less she's a floatin ghost.

Simon She'd stay up there all night.

Jolly Still there when yer come in the mornin . . . floatin in the air . . .

Jelly *stands behind the other soldiers with five mugs of coffee. He sips from them.*

Zemlinsky (*warning*)   Agh! – she's –

Nold, **Simon**, **Jolly**, **West** *and* **Zemlinsky** *each fire a shot.*

Gregory She fell before yer –

Jolly 'S all right.

Simon 'S all right – I got 'er on the fall – I got 'er –

Gregory *goes to the cliff edge and peers down into the ravine. He takes out his pistol.*

Gregory (*peering*)   Yer'd think clothes'd stand out in that mess.

Jelly (*low*)   Every time 'e looks at the dead 'e 'as a gun in 'is 'and.

Jolly, **Nold**, **Simon** *and* **West** *stroll to the edge.*

West (*points*)   That 'er?

Gregory   Nah. (*Fires a shot.*)

Jolly (*reassuringly*)   'S all right sarge –

West   The fall 'd've kill 'er anyway – the extra 'eight.

Gregory *stands at the edge with his pistol in one hand and his coffee in the other. The other soldiers take their coffee from* **Jelly**.

Jolly   Ta.

West   Yer bin drinkin out a' this?

Jelly   No.

Jolly (*throws the sugar bag to* **Simon**)   Catch.

Simon *catches it.*

West   Call this a full cup?

Jolly *throws the spoon to* **Simon**. *He catches it, puts sugar in his coffee and hangs the spoon in his lapel buttonhole.*

Gregory   Get that down yer smart. Still the moppin up. (*He leaves the edge, muttering reassurances to himself.*) Yeh yeh got 'er on the fall.

Jolly   'S all right sarge – we 'it 'er.

Silence. The soldiers drink and prepare to go down – tidy up and move the equipment and litter to the top of the path. **Jelly** *dismantles and packs the portable canteen. He puts it in its carrying harness.*

West   The nipper I shot first off. (*No response.*) Tottered t' the edge – goes t' fall – 'is mum grabs 'is 'and – 'e's swingin over the side like a pendulum.

Gregory   Yer wanna keep the 'ole thing quiet. CO'd go spare. They'll put in a complaint as it is – we kep 'em waitin.

Simon   Didn't 'ave t' double clean the MGs.

Jolly *goes round with the coffee-pot and pours the last coffee into* **Simon***'s and* **Nold***'s mugs.*

Simon (*focusing the FGs on the ledge*)   The marks of 'er nails.

West   She weren't naked. Yer never get all the details serve up right.

Jolly   Mankind's story.

Gregory   Give them mugs a good swill. Gingivitis.

Jolly *helps* **West** *and* **Simon** *to strap ammo boxes in the carrying harnesses on their backs.*

Gregory   See they're tight. Don't want that landin on me nut. (*Gestures at* **Nold**.) Give 'im 'n MG. (*To* **Nold**) Yer a donkey all next week.

Jelly *straps the portable canteen on his back.*

West   That climb takes it out a' yer boots. We ought 'a be reissued.

Jolly *picks up an MG.* **Jelly** *goes down first.* **Nold**, **Jolly**, **Simon**, **West** *and* **Zemlinsky** *follow.* **Gregory** *is alone. He looks over the edge.*

Gregory (*calls to soldiers*)   Get them gaps closed!

Gregory *makes a last check. He goes to the top edge, takes out his pistol and stares into the ravine. Nothing. He turns back, picks up an empty cigarette packet and goes down the cliff path.*

The Third House

The floor of the big ditch. It is covered with the dead and dying. (These need not be shown.) The rock wall is some way off the back. High up on it a few bushes hang like little green clouds. No sky.

In the distance from time to time shots and the sounds of the dying.

The **Girl** *pulls on the* **Woman**. *They wear the same clothes as before but they are dirtier and more ragged. Their faces are whiter and their hair more matted.*

Girl   Mum-ma. (*Stops.*) My turn for carry. (*She drags the* **Woman** *a little further. She looks down at her face and stops.*) Face moved – not the bump-a-dee-bump – not dead. (*She tries to nurse the* **Woman**.) Dee-dee . . . (*Looks at the sky.*) The sky's a big empty 'at.

Woman (*unconscious*)   Wha' . . . ?

Girl   O Mum-ma wakes up! (*She stands and tries to get the* **Woman** *to her feet.*) Up! Up!

Woman   Let me be . . .

The **Woman** *falls at the* **Girl**'s *feet. The* **Girl** *wanders away.*

Girl   Where are we? (*Half-calling.*) If someone could 'elp us . . . (*Changes direction aimlessly.*) No cart t' push 'er in . . . (*Stands still and cries. Points to the cliff.*) The row a' houses with no doors 'n windows.

Woman (*hearing the crying*)   Who . . . ?

Girl (*goes to the* **Woman**)   I'm frightened! (*Tries to make the* **Woman** *stand.*) Up! Get up!

Woman (*in pain*)   Ah . . .

The **Girl** *walks away angrily.*

Girl   I'm 'ungry. (*She holds out her hand to beg.*) Once if yer 'eld yer 'and out the passers-by'd stop. In the old days – long before – food fell out a' the sky. If a bird 'opped on my 'and it'd 'op away. I looked in yer pockets when yer was dead. Why didn't yer 'ide some bread? Good mothers do 'n when they die their children find it.

The **Girl** *shuts her eyes and holds out both arms stiffly, a little to the sides with the palms open.* **Nold** *comes on. He holds his rifle horizontally in his hand, the strap hanging loose. He stops and watches the women. They do not see him.*

Girl (*standing as before*)   Feed me. (*Waits.*) If we could eat the air we'd live. No, it smells of people . . . the wet earth smells of people. (*Opens her eyes and examines her dress.*) My hem's wet.

Woman   . . . There were steps . . .

Girl (*half-answering the* **Woman**)   No food there. The rocks looked like bread but they were chalk. (*Gestures round.*) These people sold their clothes for food. Now they're dead. They've still got their 'ands out t' beg. Too many t' feed.

Woman   . . . Steps . . .

The **Woman** *tries to stand.* **Nold** *takes his rifle in two hands.*

Girl   Clever Mum-ma stands!

Woman (*to the* **Girl**)   'Oo are yer?

Girl (*tries to dance with the* **Woman**)   Dance! Dance! I danced when I fell through the air! No stones t' dash me feet on! It's lovely t' dance in the air!

Woman (*fighting off the* **Girl**)   No – !

Girl (*pulling away*)   She tore my dress! Why did she tear my dress?

Woman (*half-remembering*)   Yer my daughter – 'n yer 'ead is . . . Come t' the side – in the open it's –

The **Woman** *tries to keep her balance. The* **Girl** *walks away from her.*

Girl (*pointing to the dead*)   There's one. There's one. All dead.

Nold *aims his rifle at the* **Girl**.

Woman   Come t' the side.

The **Woman** *falls.*

Girl   All the dead look the same. They're wearin my
mother's death mask. (*Looks at the* **Woman**.) Cover it! Cover it!
Are all these dead people yer dolls? (*Stares round angrily.*) Why
are they starin at me! They should 'ide under their sheets!
That one bit 'er lips when she died – 'er teeth're comin
through 'er chin!

The **Girl** *sees* **Nold**. *His rifle is aimed at her.*

Girl   Are you dead? You're standin up. Did they 'ang yer?
Will yer stand like that for ever? Did yer bring food with yer
when yer died?

The **Woman** *has half-risen – she sees* **Nold**.

Woman   'E was with them.

The **Woman** *falls back.*

Girl   She 'urt 'er leg. If she eats it'll get better.

Nold (*to the* **Woman**)   Can yer 'ear my voice?

Girl (*nods briskly*)   She 'ears – I know, I know.

Nold (*to the* **Woman**)   Yer don't ever 'ave t' eat again.
(*Gestures with rifle.*) This is best 'ere. Ask me. It's me job. – She
don't 'ear.

Girl (*nods*)   She won't answer when she's in a mood.

Nold (*to the* **Woman**)   'Er first – that it?

The **Woman** *raises her hand and makes a low sound, almost a growl.*

Nold   Why? Why? 'S no sense 'ere. (*Pause.*) Ask me or I'll
walk away.

Girl   No no don't leave me with 'er. 'Er leg frightens me!
She can't feed me now!

The **Woman** *stops the* **Girl** *with the same low sound.*

Nold   Both t'gether. So quick yer won't know which was
first? Just ask. (*Pause.*) . . . Else yer could lie 'ere all night.

They'll 'ear yer. When the trucks stop yer 'ear everythin. Yer 'ear the dead sneeze sometimes. T'morra when they're shootin she'll run round 'ere singin. If they're busy they leave 'em to it all day. Don't have no time t' notice . . . even god almighty don't want t' watch us play like that. (*Pause.*) I wish I could see over the rocks, whass 'appenin in the town. – Ask. I ain got all day. When yer on the ledge yer give the orders. Ain the officers. Yer say do it, it's got t' be done. Yer ain on the ledge now. I ain yer servant. Yer can ask. Yer can beg. (*Pause.*) I ain got long. (*Takes a small piece of bread from his pack. Eats.*) The army gives me bread. I eat it. Yer 'ave to sometimes. (*Uncorks his water bottle. Drinks.*) I drink – the bottle 'as t' be empty from time t' time.

The **Girl** *stares at him. He soaks a piece of bread in water and gives it to her.*

Nold I soaked it t' make it easier. (*The* **Girl** *stares at the bread.*) Take it. It's surplus. Over.

Gregory *and* **Simon** *come on stage.* **Simon**'*s rifle is slung on his back.* **Gregory** *holds his horizontally in his hand, the strap loose. He gestures to* **Simon** *to keep quiet. The others do not see them.*

The **Girl** *snatches* **Nold**'*s pack and turns out the food on the floor. She rummages and eats like an animal.* **Nold** *steps back in dismay.*

Nold Give 'er!

Girl (*eating*) She don't eat! She's dead! 'Er mouth's always empty! Empty! Don't waste my food pokin it down 'er! (*Eating and crying.*) She wants my food! My food! (*Throws food at the* **Woman**.) Take it! My food! I'm 'ungry! Steal it! (*She goes to the* **Woman**, *eats, nurses the* **Woman** *and puts food in her mouth, cries.*) Yer see! The waste! The waste! My food! (*The* **Woman** *spits out the food.*) Eat it! Eat it now yer stole it!

The **Woman** *chokes, slightly but persistently like a baby. The* **Girl** *stares at her.*

Girl Is she coughin up a baby in 'er mouth? Is that how the dead 'ave their kids?

Nold (*holds out his water bottle*)   Give 'er this.

The **Girl** *holds the water bottle to the* **Woman***'s lips. The* **Woman**
*convulses, shudders, spits – suddenly the water dashes from her mouth as
if she is vomiting afterbirth.*

Woman (*shakes her bowed head*)   No water. Take us t' the
bushes . . .

Girl   I'm wet! She tore me dress now she's made it wet!
(*Apologetically.*) It's painful for 'er t' live like we do. It's bin too
long. She's wasted away. (*She wipes the* **Woman***'s face with the
wet corner of her dress.*) Let me clean yer up. Don't retch – there's
nothin t' bring up, yer dried up inside.

Woman (*gasping. To* **Nold**)   The bushes . . .

Nold (*fastening his pack*)   The night's yer safest bet. Lie 'ere till
mornin. It freezes nights. Lie t'gether. Thass 'ow yer'll die. If
she wakes up when yer dead – she'll 'ave t' play 'er games 'n
god'll 'ave t' look away. (*Finishes packing. Answers her question.*) I
can't.

Nold *turns to go – he sees* **Gregory** *and* **Simon**.

Gregory   Why don't yer shoot 'em?

Simon   I'll do the –

Gregory *stops* **Simon** *with a gesture of his raised hand.*

Gregory   Yer give 'em. (*Lowers his hand.*) Army grub t'
civvies.

Nold   They picked the leftovers.

Gregory   Looters shot.

Girl (*feeding the* **Woman**)   'Is friends'll carry yer t' the
bushes.

Gregory   Water too. (*No response.*) Ah well shoot 'em.

Nold   Let 'em eat.

Gregory   Why?

Nold Yer can't shoot people while they're eatin.

Simon (*coming down, unshouldering his rifle*)   Less put a stop t' –

Gregory *stops* **Simon** *with the same gesture as before.*

Simon They're waiting for us at . . .

Gregory *goes to the women and peers at them.*

Girl (*explaining to* **Gregory**)   'Er legs 're floppy. Yer'll 'ave t' give 'er a piggyback over the bodies.

Gregory (*shrugs and turns to* **Nold**)   D'yer know 'em?

Nold No.

Gregory 'S the clothes. They didn't strip 'em. 'Ad the time but never bothered. Ignored a regulation – then this. My wife keeps a garden. In the winter the leaves come off. Yer never notice. Then a bird 'ops on 'n off a twig – the twig bounces – 'n suddenly yer got a garden a' dead sticks. Same 'ere. 'Is sister or 'is woman's got a coat similar t' this. Clothes remind yer of 'uman bein's. So yer start t' fraternise with bread 'n water. Yer *were* goin t' kill 'em?

Nold Sarge.

Gregory Thass right. Orders is the breath a' life. Break 'em 'n yer in no-man's-land.

Girl (*feeding the* **Woman**)   Save some for the bushes.

Gregory They don't 'ave t' 'ave a last meal. Only 'umans need ceremonies. Would yer give a fistful a' grass to a heifer tied up outside a butcher's? (*Pause. He looks round.*) We might as well all eat while we're waitin.

Gregory *sits and takes food from his pack.*

Simon Sarge I –

Gregory Eat. 'E'll shoot 'em after. (*Looks at* **Simon**.) 'Ave a bit a' common understandin. (*To* **Nold**.) Yer got left? (*He gives* **Nold** *some of his food.*) Get it down yer. (**Nold** *shakes his head.*) I got more.

Nold *takes the food.*

Simon   Ain 'ungry.

Gregory   Eat. Yer will be by the time we get back. One thing, they give us top grub. (*Gestures to the women.*) They ain eat so good in years. (*He takes out his schnapps flask and loosens the top. He stands the flask on the ground beside him.*) Army kills on its stomach as we know.

Nold *crouches, puts his pack on the ground before him and the food on top of it. He eats mechanically with a bowed head.*

Gregory (*repeating his order*)   I tol' yer.

Simon   No thanks sarge I'm all right honest. (*Starts to walk away.*) If yer need –

Gregory (*to* **Simon**)   Eat. (*Eating.*) 'Nough one playin up, 'out you makin it two.

Simon   No! I ain eatin 'ere – with this shit lyin in its – I'd rather eat shit!

Gregory   It may come t' that if they change the caterin corps. Eat. '*E's* got a problem – which I'm sortin out – *yer've* got no excuse. Don't try my patience.

Simon *takes food from his pack.* **Gregory** *eats staring in front of him.* **Nold** *eats mechanically with his head bowed. Behind him the* **Girl** *eats and feeds scraps to the* **Woman**. **Simon** *takes one mouthful and retches.*

Gregory   Sit.

Simon (*coughing*)   Sarge I'm all right 'onest – stood 'ere with –

Gregory   Save yer energy it belongs t' the army. Only animals with four legs eat on their feet.

Simon (*suddenly, stunned, suppressed shock*)   I don't wan' t' sit 'ere! I don't wan' it!

Gregory (*eating. To* **Nold**)   See what yer done t' yer mate?

Simon   'E's a bloody shit-'ouse mate – no mate a' mine after this –

Gregory   *Will yer sit!*

Simon *squats. He tries to turn his back on the others but is facing bodies. He groans and turns back.*

Simon   I can't, I can't. (*He puts down his food but remains squatting.*) It ain 'uman.

Gregory   Yer led a pampered life lad. (*He reaches across, turns over* **Simon**'s *food with his fingers, picks what he wants and puts it with his own food. He does not stop eating. Sighs.*) Long days. The gardens a' war.

The **Woman** *chokes.* **Gregory** *hands his water to* **Simon**.

Gregory   Tip that down 'er.

Simon *stiffens, stands, takes the water bottle and gives it to the* **Girl**.

Gregory (*without looking round*)   Unscrew it.

Simon *unscrews the top and gives it to the* **Girl**.

Girl   Water! The men've brought us more water! (*To* **Simon**.) She's got a floppy leg. (*She puts the water bottle to the* **Woman**'s *lips. The* **Woman** *twists away.*) Water! It's good! (*She dabs water behind her ears coquettishly.*) Good water! Look at me Mum-ma! (*She puts the water bottle to the* **Woman**'s *lips again. The* **Woman** *splutters.*) Don't waste!

Gregory (*without looking round*)   'Elp 'er.

Simon *straightens and steps back.*

Girl   Quiet! If yer cough in the bushes yer'll wake the birds.

The **Woman** *splutters. Still eating* **Gregory** *stands, goes to her and takes her head in his hands. Immediately she is still. She drinks calmly.*

Girl   O 'e put 'n invisible crown on 'er 'ead!

Gregory (*to the* **Girl**)   Enough. Too much'll 'urt 'er. 'Ave some.

The **Girl** *drinks.* **Gregory** *goes back to his place, still eating. As he passes* **Simon** *he takes the food from his hands and throws it over his shoulder to the* **Girl**.

Girl   Food! (*She runs round collecting the food.*) More! More!
They're throwin it from the top! (*Looks up.*) Mum-ma when yer
better we'll walk up there. (*Points.*) Along the red line!

Gregory *sits. He throws his crusts over his shoulder. The* **Girl** *runs
round frantically.*

Girl   No more! No more! The dead'll get it! (*Shouts at the sky.*)
No more! (*Picking up the food.*) Mine! Mine! It came from the sky
for me! (*Kisses the food.*) I kiss it – where 'is 'and touched! (*Stops
and stares at a body.*) Look at 'er tearin 'er 'air! She's vexed! 'Er
mouth's open t' catch it! It's mine! Mine! (*She stamps on the dead
woman's face.*) Shut it! Shut it! (*To the* **Woman**.) Mum-ma the
lady wants my food!

While the **Girl** *runs and gathers food* **Gregory** *leans back, pushes his
hand along the ground and picks up the water bottle. He empties it on the
ground, puts back the stopper and puts it in his pack. The* **Girl** *tries to
hide food in the* **Woman**'s *coat.*

Girl   'Ide it! 'Ide it! Won't go! I tore yer pockets when yer
was dead! Yer didn't need 'em! 'Ave t' 'ide it! 'Ave t' 'ide it!

Gregory (*salts his food and holds up a little paper pack*)   These
little paper screws a' salt 're normally reserved for officers.

Girl   'Ide it! 'Ide it!

The **Girl** *runs out with the food.*

Simon (*unshouldering his rifle*)   Stop 'er! Let me – yer must –
now she's –

Gregory   No! (**Simon** *stops.*) Use yer sense a' proportion.
'Ow far can she get? Just round 'n round. Let 'er play 'er little
games. (*Hands* **Simon** *the schnapps flask.*) Get some a' that down
yer.

Simon *takes the flask and gulps two swallows.*

Gregory   Don't stint yerself. My treat.

Simon *takes two more swallows and chokes slightly.*

Gregory   When this war's over you lads'll look me up. Both a' yer. We're not grand but it's comfortable. I'm suited. The wife cooks. She's got mirrors in every room. Yer'll get a surprise when yer see our town. There's a park. 'Eated swimmin pool. Some a' the streets've got trees in 'em. I'll take yer round the waterin 'oles. Introduce yer t' the local worthies. Show yer off. The lads I served with. Proud a' yer. Yer'll see another side a' me. I'd like that. Yer can't show it 'ere. (*Glances at the* **Woman**.) She's dead. (*To* **Nold**.) One t' go. – The youngsters want lights. It suits me. Thass an invite then?

Simon   Yeh.

Gregory (*to* **Nold**)   'N you.

Nold (*stops eating for a moment*)   Yeh. (*Eats*.)

Simon   If we live long enough.

Gregory   We will. (*He takes a photo from his wallet. Hands it to* **Simon**.) The wife in front of our 'edge. I'm in civvies 'olding the shears. Give yerself time t' think. Shuffle the ideas in yer nut, shake out the dust. Thass what we all need. (*To* **Simon**.) Show 'im.

Simon *hands the photo to* **Nold**.

Nold (*eating*)   Nice.

Simon   We seen it before.

Simon *swigs from the schnapps flask.* **Gregory** *takes the photo from* **Nold**.

Gregory   I show it sometimes. Forget 'oo. (*Slight silence. Calls*.) Girlie don't play too far. Stay where I can keep 'n eye on yer.

Girl (*off*)   I'm playin with the children.

Gregory (*calls*)   Don't play too rough. (*Looks at the ground. Silence*.) I don't understand fear. It comes 'n goes. Where does it go to? Takes a wise man t' answer life's riddles. (*He takes the schnapps flask from* **Simon**. *He does not drink. He tightens the cap and puts the flask in his pocket*.) Blind man with 'is 'and on the globe. Thinks 'e knows. Shall I tell 'im it's square? I know it is cause I live in it every day. Let 'im enjoy 'is ignorance. We're 'uman shit, thass what we come down to in the end: democracy's livin in the sewer a' yer choice. If there was a god would 'e put up with our pranks? 'E'd wipe us off the crack a' 'is arse. (*Chucks a crust at the* **Woman**. *She doesn't move.*) Dead. – There ain no god. Least ways no more. We're just the little piles a' shit 'e left be'ind when 'e skived off t' torment some other soddin place. 'E thinks 'e's got 'is 'and on the globe. Well I could tell 'im somethin: wherever 'e's swanned off to it'll be worse – the shit there won't speak t' 'im. Only 'e never arst me. 'E's officer class, they don't arst shit do they. (*Wipes his mouth with the back of his hand.*) Moved over the face a' the waters . . . ? I 'ope the bugger drowned. (*Suppresses a slight burp with his hand.*) Saw one dirty little tyke pick 'is nose then 'andle my guns. – Right – pack up shall we?

The **Girl** *comes on wearing an old black coat and carrying a rope unravelling at the ends.*

Girl   I found a skippin rope round 'n old man's neck. I tugged 'n tugged. 'E slid along the ground. All the dead people bobbed up t' see. (*She holds the rope as if she's going to skip but the bottom of the loop lies on the ground before her and she only counts the steps.*) One. Two. Three.

Gregory *stands, brushing his trousers with his hands.* **Simon** *and* **Nold** *stand and fasten their packs – they seem to be rising from sleep.*

Gregory   'Er then. (*Nods at the* **Woman**.) She's dead but put one in in case. (*Looks round.*) 'N thass the lot done – we walked over all the rest.

Nold *picks up his rifle and holds it half-aimed.*

Simon (*quietly*)   Sarge if it's –

Gregory   No.

Simon   Permission t' – requestin permission t' –

Gregory   No.

Simon   What yer said before – visitin when it's – yeh – looks good – get our 'eads sorted – . Take 'im away 'n thump some sense in t' 'im. Won't take me a jiff t' –

Gregory   No.

Simon   Please sarge take 'im away. I don't want 'im standin
there like – . 'E's evil! (*To* **Nold**.) Yer bloody fool! Yer bloody
fool! Let the man 'elp yer! 'E's bendin over backwards!
They're shit shit shit! Why can't yer give 'im somethin? Two
dead! Two dead in this morgue! The 'ole place is a morgue
crammed between two gravestones! They'll be dead t'morra
anyway! . . . I should rape 'er. It's expected. I can't. Let the
locals do it, they'll rape 'er t' death. Why're we 'ere? I come t'
kill – not eat 'n talk! My god if I could pull the cliffs down 'n
rub this shit out under the – under the stone paper – 'n sit in a
'eap a' rubble . . . give me some peace. Every day shoot shit,
shoot shit! What do I do t'morra? – say I sat 'n ate with it?

Gregory   No permission.

Girl   There's one. There's one.

Silence.

Simon (*flat, intense. Gestures to the women*)   They done somethin
t' 'im. Them two – they can't *all* be in it? Less go sarge. If we
get out a' the ditch – get t' the other side – it's different there.
We shouldn't a' come down t'day. It's the glasses – we looked.
'S not enough t' kill any more – got t' do more now! (*Goes to the*
Girl.) Give me that rope!

Girl   No no it's mine! The ol' man told me t' play with it
forever or the world'll come undone! – It's a parcel.

Simon   Give it t' me!

Simon *tries to drag the rope from the* **Girl** *– he gives up.*

Girl (*looks at* **Nold**)   'Is face is white . . . ! I thought it was a
light. I can see where the flies'll walk on it. Only birds can be
as white as that. (*To* **Simon**.) O yer poor man why're yer
dressed in them silly clothes? – can't yer afford real ones? (*To*
Nold.) I'll lend yer the rope. The ol' man won't know.

Simon (*jerks the rope from the* **Girl**)   Give it t' me!

Girl No no! It's mine! Mine! (*She runs to the* **Woman**.) Mum-ma wake up 'n punish 'im! 'E stole my rope!

Simon I'll 'ang 'er with it! I'll 'ang that dead 'ag first 'n show 'er 'ow t' dangle when 'er turn's next! . . . They scare me – 'e scares me more.

Simon *stands with the rope hanging in his hands.* **Nold** *stands with his rifle.*

Gregory Shoot 'em.

Nold 'E shouldn't a' took the rope. Why did 'e? She was playin.

Gregory No 'e shouldn't. Yer right. 'S all out a' order now. Yer forgot the ammo box – now this. We ain ready. We go round nice 'n easy rockin on the balls a' our feet – we're asleep. Then two dwarfs – little zombies – come 'n wake us up. They can't 'urt yer. They're dead. Only 'umans 'ave ghosts. 'Elp us – shoot 'em 'n put it right.

No response.

Gregory Yer made a stand. Now yer scared a' losin face. I understand. I'll 'elp yer – I'll turn me back. Just curl yer trigger finger till the spring snaps. Yer done enough of it before. (*To* **Simon**.) Turn yer back.

Gregory *watches* **Simon** *turn his back and then turns his own.* **Nold** *raises the rifle. Suddenly* **Simon** *spins round to face* **Nold**, *aiming his rifle at him from the hip.*

Gregory I tol' yer –

Simon Not that shit! Not that shit! 'E'd shoot me in the back! My god 'e would! 'E's gone mad!

Gregory (*stamps*) Ruined! Ruined! I 'ad 'im – talked 'im round! I stand 'ere stampin on dead corpses cause yer lost 'im for me!

Simon Let me go. Please. Thass all I want now. O god sergeant 'e was goin t' shoot us!

Gregory   None a' this! I won't 'ave it! – Yer wouldn't shoot 'im?

Nold (*half audible*)   No.

Gregory   Would 'e shoot me? – 'E's confused with *them* – 'e knows 'is comrades.

Simon (*to* **Nold**)   Then what is it? Tell *me*. – Let me talk t' 'im quiet sarge –

Gregory   Stay out a' this – I'll –

Simon (*to* **Nold**)   You 'n me . . . ? No it wouldn't work. 'S not enough t' kill now. 'E wants more. I feel so sad. (*Sighs.*) Me 'and aches: I bin squeezin a trigger so 'ard I'd crush the rocks – it ain there . . . (*Bewildered.*) Not my place 'ere now. Let me go – both a' yer. Yer thought this up between yer but I'll pay.

Girl   I 'id my bread in the ol' man's mouth. I put a stone on it. 'E can't eat now – 'is throat's puffed up 'n sore. The dribble on 'is beard's turned 'ard. (*Looks at the coat.*) I think 'e was a labourer. 'Is coat's wore round the waist like animals' skin. 'E pulled a cart. Mum-ma 'is coat's 'eavy. I want t' sleep.

The **Girl** *crouches beside the* **Woman**.

Simon (*trying to go*)   I'll do anythin the army wants – this ain army. Let me go t' the cliffs 'n watch the –

Gregory   Shun! *Shun!*

Simon *shuffles to attention – he groans.*

Gregory   Shun till I say! Stand there stiff – then yer'll be safe. Show 'em what rigor mortis is. They're just dead stiffs – show 'em what a livin man can do!

Simon *at attention groans.*

Gregory (*to* **Nold**)   Soldier port yer weapon – move!

Nold *ports his rifle for inspection.*

Gregory   Bolt! (**Nold** *opens the bolt.*) Rounds – SC off – good.

Gregory *takes the rifle from* **Nold**, *closes the bolt and hands it back to him.*

Gregory   Do it by numbers. Then it's me – yer just part a' the gun. (*Military but low.*) On the command word 'aim' – aim at the girl. Soldier – 'aim'.

Nold *does not move. Silence.*

Gregory   It's the ciggie case. Thass what it is! What else? 'E's still got it. 'E's stood there with it on 'im.

Gregory *goes towards* **Nold**. **Nold** *moves back.* **Gregory** *stops – wavers for a second.*

Gregory (*to* **Simon**)   Frisk 'im. (**Simon** *hesitates.*) Frisk 'im.

Simon *goes to* **Nold** – *runs his hands over his pockets and down his legs.* **Nold** *does not move.*

Gregory   Thought 'e'd say 'e lost it then make a ruck 'n it'd be forgot. Thass why 'e forgot the ammo – 'is brain was set on thievin.

Simon *leaves* **Nold**.

Gregory   'E's 'id it under corpses. Come back in the dark. 'E's diabolical.

Woman   . . . I 'ave a daughter . . .

Simon *snatches up his rifle.*

Gregory   No!

Simon *aims at the* **Woman**. **Gregory** *moves to stand between her and* **Simon**.

Gregory   No no!

Simon *changes his aim to the* **Girl**.

Simon   Let me – let me – I wan' it –

Gregory   No – !

Gregory *goes to* **Simon** – *reaches him.* **Simon** *fires* – **Gregory** *jumps away.*

Gregory   The bloody stupid –

Gregory *yanks* **Simon***'s rifle from him and skews it away across the floor as far as it will go.*

Gregory (*through his teeth*)   O I was ready for yer! I'll crucify yer! I'll put a nail in every bone yer got! The wood'll yell! '*E's* got a reason, not *you*! I said stay shun – so yer were safe – yer couldn't move 'n come t' 'arm – I took care. But no . . . Yer stupid little . . . '*E* does it: not you.

Simon   'Ad to – 'ad to – 'ad to –

Simon *sits on the ground, his head bowed on his raised knees.*

Gregory   Yeh sit – sit there. Out a' 'arm's way. (*Looks down at his hands.*) I don't know. Some nights I talk t' that photo. Only intelligent conversation round 'ere. When I trimmed that 'edge I was ignorant. I thought I knew it all. I'll 'ave somethin t' tell it t'night. This is new. (*To* **Nold**.) Is it just for t'day – or is it for t'morra?

Girl (*wandering aimlessly*)   There's one. There's one.

Nold   Less leave it sarge. Pretend it never 'appened.

Gregory   It did.

Nold   Pretend. That'll get us through. We can walk back t' barracks in 'arf 'n 'our . . . 'n be free.

Gregory   I must 'ave order. I must 'ave order.

Nold   I can't do what yer want. I don't know why. Sometimes yer get that way. When I started I thought I'd leave 'em for someone else. 'E offered – yer should'a let 'im. I'm askin for them now. Now yer got it all. (*He looks round.*) All these dead – they can stand in for 'em. Let 'em walk or crawl away – or do what they got left in 'em. They won't leave no footprints on the bodies – 'oo'd come lookin anyway? It'll be our mystery. (*Looks round.*) The bushes are like big wreaths at some funeral. (*To* **Gregory**.) Let 'em go – yer can do it 'ere – . The three of us 'd 'ave t' stick t'gether. (*To* **Simon**.) Tell 'im.

Gregory   'E ain listened. Don' wan' t' know when 'e's called as witness.

Nold (*to* **Simon**)   Tell 'im.

Simon (*lifts his head*)   . . . I dozed off . . .

Silence. The **Woman** *tries to stand.*

Woman   . . . the soldiers took us in lorries . . .

Gregory (*angry sigh*)   Damn!

Woman   . . . then they . . .

Girl   Let me sleep.

Woman (*calmly. Looks up*)   . . . we stood up there . . . (*Turns to the soldiers.*) . . . and soldiers – . (*Realises. Cold shock.*) Men shot us on the ledge. Old people, women, children on a ledge. Those things can't 'appen in this – (*Looks at the soldiers. Despairs.*) Ah yes . . . *you* shot them. (*Explaining.*) It was difficult to die, they thought they were safe in the lorries. – The girl's a child. Children can't 'urt yer.

Gregory (*shakes his head*)   Useless, useless.

Woman   Yes – soldiers must kill the people they don't like – 'ow else could the world go on? But not 'er. What satisfaction would yer get from killin 'er? She wouldn't know she's dyin. She'd laugh.

Girl (*laughs*)   Mum-ma do the sails! Mum-ma 'old yer coat out! On my birthdays I climb on 'er back 'n float 'n float –

Woman (*to the* **Girl**)   Forgive me! I 'ave t' tell 'em yer a child. (*Looks back at the soldiers.*) Their faces 'aven't changed.

Girl   Do the sails!

Woman (*holds out her coat flaps as sails*)   When yer kill 'er yer'd 'ave t' make 'er cry t' save yer self-respect – be cruel –

Girl   Mum-ma's a ship!

Woman   – it wouldn't work – yer tired – it's late – it's afternoon – yer'd 'ang 'er with the rope 'n still be bored. She'd laugh in yer face – 'er laugh would cut yer deep. Yer'd never forget 'er laugh. She'd turn yer in t' beasts. Yer'd take all that trouble for nothin. I'm sorry for yer. Kill me. I know 'ow t' suffer. I know all the ways. I'll put all that sufferin in the little time it takes t' kill me. I'm old 'n starved 'n 'ardly left alive. My sufferin's pure. Yer've never see the like before. Yer'll see it in my face. In every bit a' it. No need t' use a rope. Just kill me quietly in yer simple way. One old woman in this dirt. I'll show yer all the sadness in the world. I won't cheat. My rags show yer I'll keep me word.

Girl   Make the sails higher Mum-ma! Higher!

Woman (*lifts her coat flaps higher*)   Let me do this for yer an yer can go in peace. The mystery won't trouble yer again.

Girl   Look! Look! Mum-ma's sails!

Woman (*stumbles*)   I'm sorry – my leg can't take my – (*Stumbles a few steps. Stops.*) I wanted t' stand (*Forces herself to stand.*) t' show my gratitude before yer kill me . . . Yer still want more? Shall I scream? Listen – come closer, I won't 'urt yer – when yer shouted at us on the ledge yer voices went on mutterin backwards 'n forwards – backwards 'n forwards – on the rocks – I thought the rocks was crackin. I'll scream. Once. It'll echo on the cliffs – yer'll 'ear me screamin at yer when I'm dead – what more can I do? Listen – there is somethin – somethin yer can't imagine. I don't know what it is. When yer point yer gun at me, just as yer fire: I'll do it. Not till then. My sufferin's taught me that. Yer only 'ave this chance. If yer miss it yer'll regret it – always – regret it regret it regret it always – because yer wasted yer life t'day.

Girl (*delight*)   Mum-ma's a ship!

Woman (*sits*)   'N even when yer lose this war – yer'll be 'appy at the gift I gave yer.

Gregory   It must be the ciggie case! There's nothin else!

Simon *stands and starts to go.*

Gregory   Come back! (*Shouts.*) I order yer!

Simon *goes on walking. He laughs, comes back, goes to the* **Woman**, *puts his hand on her shoulder and laughs at her in genuine amusement.*

Simon (*laughing*)   She's good! (*He holds out the* **Woman**'s *coat – twirls – the* **Girl** *laughs.*) A ship with sails!

Woman (*to* **Simon**)   Will yer let me die for yer?

Simon (*laughs. To* **Gregory**)   Order? Yer couldn't order a corpse t' forget its name! Yer'd send me t' the front without a gun if it'd 'elp t' get yer ciggie case t' its fat owner! Gold gold the good ol' gold! Order 'im! (*To* **Nold**.) 'E's right! It all breaks when it starts! Goes t' pieces! I ain takin orders from 'im now – never never from 'im! (*Lethally low.*) She said be a ship. She was. 'E says be a soldier: yer scratch yer crutch! I seen yer strip t' yer teeth!

Simon *goes out.*

Gregory (*calls*)   Get back! Thass an order!

The **Girl** *drapes the rope on the* **Woman**.

Girl   Mum-ma's ship 'as ropes now! The sailors climb the top!

Woman (*to* **Girl**)   'Ush – we must wait – 'n decide.

Gregory   All right. Yer 'ave t' know when t' stop. When the string comes t' the end don't keep tyin knots. No one wins. I'll make a bargain. Shoot one. I'll settle for a gesture. I can make yer excuses: the ammo – accused a' theft – arrested. One. Good. (*Breathes out.*) We're back t' normal. This is where we should 'a started. It's good t' breathe even in this stink. One – agreed?

Nold   I knew 'ow it'd end. Knew all along. T'morra – 'Do this lad', 'Yes sarge'. Yer'll keep it balanced. Not too easy, not too rough.

Gregory   One. Yes?

Nold *nods.*

Gregory   I knew yer'd see it in the end.

Nold *takes the* **Girl** *from the* **Woman**.

Woman   Bless yer. Bless yer. Yer mustn't shoot 'er after! Yer mustn't cheat! Yer'd desecrate my death! It wouldn't work. Yer wouldn't see the sufferin. Yer'd asked too much. All yer'd see is stones.

Nold *aims his rifle at the ground at the* **Woman**'s *feet.*

Nold. One.

Nold *lifts his aim to the* **Woman**'s *head.*

Gregory   Yes – but it must be the girl. (**Nold** *looks at him.*) Kill the old bitch later – she's optional – but kill the girlie first.

Woman (*she doesn't hear the soldiers*)   Why're we waitin? . . . while I look at 'er – at 'er 'ands – there's so much love 'ere yer'd think the rocks'd opened like the seams of 'n ol' coat 'n took us in –

Nold   Why 'er?

Gregory   I must 'ave order.

Woman   This is the end a' the world. These men aren't born yet. They'll live with them 'oo're born later. The world'll be 'ell then. (*The* **Girl** *has come to her. The* **Woman** *holds her.*) There – there – stay close –

Nold   Why?

Gregory   It's wounds. Savages cut themselves 'n rub the blood t'gether. The wounds 'eal outside – 'n the inside's well. We could be father 'n son. When I rage at yer, this place gives me the right. 'S our privilege t' be 'ere. We bin where it's forbidden. Keep out. At all costs. When yer shoot 'er yer'll jump so high yer'll come down in another world. Yer'll roll about in it laughin. My sacred promise. I wish I was young 'n at the start again.

Nold   What'll I learn?

Gregory   Yer can't be told. Y'ave t' do it. Yer mate couldn't. I said turn yer back – 'e whip round. I knew yer could kill us – yer finger 'ad the itch. I didn't turn. Yer learn all sorts 'ere.

Nold   I don't 'ave t' go t' yer 'ouse. I bin there. It's where yer 'ide in comfort. Yer frightened a' the dead – a' what yer done t' them! I wouldn't let yer share my *kennel*! Yer want me t' climb in t' yer coffin with yer 'n 'old yer 'and. Thass the invite! Yer frightened a' the –

Gregory. *Shun!*

Nold *jumps to attention.*

Gregory   Ha! 'E moved! Look at 'im stood! Yer don't take orders? Yer take orders all the time! Yer my issue! – yer boots – yer uniform – yer eat out a' my tin! Yer turn in yer front door – my mail's on the mat! Yer breathe on my orders! Shun! – 'E shot up so fast 'e left 'is skin be'ind 'n took 'is shit up with 'im!

Girl   There's one. There's one.

Gregory   No no I didn't want it. Didn't want t' say all that! . . . Son son don't insult me. Don't make me angry. (*Pleading.*) If yer'd let me I'd send all this away. Make it vanish for yer.

Nold   Could yer get me a transfer?

Gregory   Don't say that yet.

Nold   'Temperamentally unsuited.'

Gregory   If yer pass this with me t'day yer the top. Yer special – I always knew it. Thass why I'm fightin yer.

Nold   Speak t' the CO t'morra.

Gregory   If yer want. Listen. I'll bring yer down 'ere early. If the ol' tart's still alive she'll be nursin 'er dead kid. Then yer'll see it from the inside. Let the fire see the stoker – eh? Or later – if yer don't – yer life won't be worth the time it takes t' pass – which ain long. There'll be un'appiness a woman kids 'n job can't take away. Look at 'er face t'morra. Everyone's face is a map a' death 'n we look for our own 'ouse in it. 'Ave to. I studied people in this war. All what I could tell you . . .

The brass run round with their map cases: they should look at the plastic sheet that covers 'em, where nothin's writ. No use t' tell yer now. T'morra. Then you tell me what yer future is. (*Slight hesitation.*) Though t' be 'onest I'm not sure what yer'll say. Not any more. Not yet.

Nold *pulls the* **Girl** *away from the* **Woman**.

Woman   Don't take 'er away! Yer can't kill 'er! She's not born yet!

Girl   There's one. There's one.

Nold (*to* **Gregory**)   'Elp me!

Gregory   Control it – measured time –

Nold   I want t' see 'er face when I do it! Not wait till t'morra! See it now!

Gregory   O good I 'adn't thought a' now – good good I'll get 'er for yer –

Woman (*trying to pass* **Nold**)   No no – (*Falls.*) I suffered for yer! – (*Crawls.*) it's in my face – look I can see it in the dust! – it wants t' be a mirror!

Gregory (*pushing the* **Girl** *down*)   Girlie girlie down – down –

Girl (*frightened*)   I stole the ol' man's coat! 'E'll punish me!

Gregory (*mechanical like a machine-gun, low*)   Yeh I'm dead 'n yer stole my bread but take it (*Still talking he picks up the crust he threw at the* **Woman** *and gives it to the* **Girl**.) 'n eat like a good little girl 'n don't move or the ol' man'll come –

Girl (*takes the crust. Conspiratorial*)   Mine! I'll eat it like a little mouse! (*Hunches her shoulders in glee.*) Stay till 'e says! (*Wail.*) My rope my rope my rope 'e took my rope –

Gregory (*throws the rope to the* **Girl**)   'Old it tight!

Woman   What do the soldiers want?

Girl   Sh!

Woman (*kneels, gestures round*)   All these dead – they've got enough. Stand up! Stand up! – Breathe on them! Yer're full a'

plagues! Breathe! Breathe! Turn their uniforms black! . . . My
lungs're crumpled up – a burnt map in my chest . . . The dead
can't breathe but they can cry: look their tears on my fingers –
full of light. (*Looks at the soldiers.*) Or I'll take all that back – if
yer take me t' my daughter – let me touch 'er for one moment
– the dead would bless yer – if I could reach 'er with this 'and
– this finger – (*Her hand stretches out.*) – look this finger's pointing
– if I could reach 'er with this finger – with the tip – 'n feel 'er
– run my finger on 'er 'ands – (*The finger reaches further.*) – feel 'er
– this finger would be in paradise 'n the rest a' the world in
'ell. Why am I content?: this space is mine – the space
between my finger and my daughter is mine. There's so much
pain in this space – so much sorrow – the dead can feel it. But
I'm content. The dead are ashamed t' be 'ere. I think they'll
stand up 'n walk away from you. I think they will.

Girl   Sh!

Woman   Quickly! Quickly! With me! They can't shoot yer
'ere! This space is mine!

The **Girl** *stands.*

Girl (*bewildered*)   The man said stay.

Gregory (*unshouldering his rifle*)   Now – or I'll end it – 'n yer
never be forgiven –

Woman (*stares down at her outstretched hand*)   My finger's
pointing –

Nold *stands behind the* **Woman**. *Forces her head up.*

Nold   Watch!

The **Woman**'s *head drops. She stares at her finger.*

Woman (*awe*)   Pointing –

Nold *jerks the* **Woman**'s *head back.*

Nold   Watch! Watch! Watch! Yer bitch!

Gregory   Measured time –

Nold *aims above the* **Woman**'s *head and shoots* **Gregory**.

Gregory   'E's mad. (*Feels pain.*) Ah. (*Half faints. Uses his rifle as a prop, spins round on it.*) Ahhhh-aaahhhhhh . . .

Nold *goes to* **Gregory** *and prods his rifle away with his foot. The* **Girl** *lies beside the* **Woman**.

Gregory (*laughs metallically*)   Yer don' it now . . . tell 'em 'n accident –

Nold   I shot t' wound. Stay on the ledge a while. (*Slight pause.*) I don't feel anythin.

Woman (*nursing the* **Girl**)   My finger pointed 'n – yer 'ere. My arm – my body – 'olds yer. So beautiful, so 'appy. No one'll take yer for a little while. It'll seem ever. (*To* **Nold**.) Tell us what t' do. They'll come. Don't let my daughter die now. Yer can't be so cruel!

Nold   Shut up! Shut up! Think – think –

Woman   'Ush – yer'll wake 'er – a little soldier's tantrum – I'm used t' that –

Nold   The soldier'll come back – 'e 'eard the shot – I 'ave t' shoot 'im –

Woman   Tell us what t' do! What d'yer want? Gratitude? In this place? It's a skull! – it tore at us when we fell down! Shoot us! It's what yer good at!

Girl (*sleeping*)   I 'ave food for days 'n days.

Woman   'Ush precious, sleep. I was so proud when I 'ad nothin. I was better than the dead – I 'ad clothes: *they* promised me I'd live. The lorries were our 'earse. The dead stink a' poison. It comes out a' their mouths. Out a' the bullet 'oles. Out a' their rectums. (*Rocks the* **Girl**.) Sleep. – Yer shot them full a' little arses. Weren't they 'uman enough for yer? Did more arses make them 'uman? What could I 'ope from a man 'oo puts extra arses in t' the dead?

Nold *goes to the* **Woman**. *She flinches away almost formally.*

Woman   No I didn't mean any insult on yer . . .

Nold *takes the coats from the* **Woman** *and the* **Girl**. *The* **Girl** *twists in her sleep.*

Girl I'm not dead, don't strip me yet.

Nold *covers* **Gregory** *with the coats.*

Nold (*to the* **Woman**) If she kep quiet I could tell 'im yer dead. – I could 'ide yer in the bushes. Yer'd spend the night t'gether. When yer rested get away. Find someone 'oo 'as pity. – One night's somethin. P'raps t'morra a flood'll wash this filth away.

Simon *comes on.*

Simon Finished?

Nold Yeh.

Simon Can't go back with no rifle. Would put the lid on. (*Half sigh.*) 'Ell. – Where's sergeant?

Nold Sloped off. In a paddy. Sorry I brought yer in t' this.

Simon Yeh well.

Nold 'Ow the 'ell it –

Simon None a' that! I tol' yer! Up t' '*ere*!

Girl (*sleeping*) I give the ol' man bread t' pay 'im for 'is coat . . .

Nold Somethin for yer t' see.

Simon Seen all the 'orrors a' this place.

Nold *goes to* **Gregory**. **Simon** *follows him halfway.* **Nold** *removes the coats.*

Gregory Ggrrhhhhhh . . .

Nold *shoots* **Gregory** *in the head.*

Simon I come back for me rifle. Yer 'ad a row. Never saw none a' this. Yer said the partisans'd – . Then *you* tell the rest. (*He turns and starts to go.*) Less I know a' this the –

Simon *suddenly remembers – spins round.* **Nold** *is aiming his rifle at him.*

Simon   No thass – I'll never tell –

Nold *pulls the trigger. The rifle is empty.*

Simon (*short shocked laugh*)   Heah! – it's – pull the trigger for a joke –

Nold   Empty. (*Slight shrug.*) Sorry. 'S like that.

Simon   Yippeeee! (*Holds out his hand to shake.*) – t' give me warnin not t' –

Nold *goes to* **Gregory**'*s rifle. Casually, quickly,* **Simon** *tries to get to it first.* **Nold** *picks it up.*

Simon   I'm not armed. Yer can't. Yer mate.

Nold *shoots and kills* **Simon***. The* **Girl** *wakes.*

Girl   Mum-ma.

The **Woman** *tries to stand.* **Nold** *supports her.*

Woman   Get t' the bushes –

Girl   The coat –

The **Girl** *goes to the coat.*

Nold (*to the* **Girl**)   'Elp me – take that side –

The **Woman** *falls. The* **Girl** *is putting on the black coat.*

Woman   Yer must leave me. Stay with 'er. If yer 'ave t' die with 'er what does it matter in this place? (*Delirious.*) Yer'll find room on the ledge . . . the people are comin up the 'ill . . . goin t' their graves . . . liftin their crosses above their 'eads . . . the sky after the rain . . .

Girl (*in the coat*)   I 'ad three meals t'day.

Woman (*conscious. To the* **Girl**)   Go with 'im. I'll catch yer up. Be good. – Tell 'er yer fetchin food. She'll go. (*Exasperated.*) Don't stand there – with yer shadow – torturin me.

Nold   When the soldiers come this'll be a bad place.

Woman   Bad? 'E says a bad place. 'E's still a child . . . If yer get 'er away nowhere's bad, the 'ole world's good.

Nold   Crawl as far as yer can. Take all yer clothes off. They won't see yer in the dead. If yer live for a few days – 'ope – 'ope – for 'er.

Nold *starts to take the* **Girl** *out.*

Girl   The rope!

Nold   Quiet for 'er sake.

Nold *gives the* **Girl** *the rope. As they go she ties it round her waist. The* **Woman** *is alone.*

Woman (*delirious*)   I'm with yer now . . . poor naked people . . . I was on the ledge with yer . . . I 'ave a right t' be 'ere . . . (*She makes a slight effort to take off her clothes. Can't.*) All you good people in 'ell . . . your poor empty bodies . . . the blood ran out a' the 'oles . . . t' find a 'ome as if the stones'd shelter it . . . the dry dust in yer eyes . . . the wind tears yer 'air all ways . . . a mad'ouse for the wind . . . poor naked bodies . . . if I could reach 'n touch yer . . .

The Fourth House

A corner of a room with a table and three chairs. A door. A blackout curtain half covers a window.

Daylight.

*A **Young Woman** has just let **Nold** into the room. She wears indoor clothes and has been cleaning. He is in old civvies sprinkled with masonry dust.*

Young Woman   Sit.

Nold *sits at the table with his fists on the table top.*

Nold   I thought yer was older.

Young Woman   I'm their daughter. (*She waits for **Nold** to speak.*) The 'ouse was bombed. They couldn't find Mum. Vanished. They said she must 'a bin out when it dropped. Killed in the street. I went back every day t' salvage things. I was downstairs – a week later. All the ceilin's 'ad fallen in. I looked up. She was lyin in the rafters. 'Er arm was pointin down. She tried t' get out or fell like that when she died.

Off, a child starts to cry.

Nold   Yer little brother?

Young Woman   A form came. (*She waits for **Nold** to speak.*) I can't feed yer. They cook soup once a day in a cauldron in the street. We stand in line.

Nold   I was with a girl. We 'id in some – . I overslept. When I woke up she was gone. The soldiers found 'er dancin on a ledge. She thought that was a place t' dance. They shot 'er.

Young Woman   The form said the partisans –

Nold   No I shot 'im.

Silence except for the crying.

Young Woman (*apologetically*)   I can't stop 'im cryin. I'm sorry. 'E ain little – it's the raids. (*Waits as before.*) The 'ouse was . . . the post didn't know where t' leave the form. (*Slight shrug.*) What did yer do?

Nold (*eyes clenched, fists clenched on the table, through his teeth*) I survived, I survived.

The child cries. The **Young Woman** *stares.* **Nold** *does not move.*

The Crime of the Twenty-First Century

There is no such thing as society.
– M. Thatcher

The Crime of the Twenty-First Century was first staged on 9 January 2001 at Le Théâtre National de la Colline (Paris). The cast was as follows:

Hoxton	Anne Alvaro
Grig	Carlo Brandt
Sweden	Éric Caravaca
Grace	Cécile Garcia Fogel

Directed by Alain Françon
Designed by Jacques Gabel
Costumes by Patrice Cauchetier
Lighting by Jöel Hourbeigt
Dramaturg Guillaume Levêque
Movement Adviser Caroline Marcadé

One

The site is an open space that was once a yard or two or three ground-floor rooms. It is in the 'clearance', a vast desert of ruins that stretch for hundreds of miles and have been flattened to discourage resettlement. The low remains of a wall enclose the site along the back and the two adjoining sides. The back wall is the horizon – the ruins beyond it cannot be seen. In places the wall is still man-high. To the audience's right is the cell – the remains of a room or cellar. It is roofed. Its front wall stretches across the corner between the walls to the back and the right. There is a wooden door in it. When it is open the cell inside cannot be seen. Towards the left a ramp of rubble leads up to a slight dip in the back wall. A smooth path has been trodden along the length of the ramp. The top of the ramp is a threshold on the horizon.

The site is littered with rubble and dust. Some of the rubble is gathered in heaps. To the right there is a sort of outdoor kitchen – an open grate and grid on a brick stand, a table, a chair, a few boxes used as chairs and for storage, pots, pans, tins, crockery, cutlery, a bowl, a large yellowish-white plastic water carrier and other bits and pieces. These things have been scavenged from the ruins.

Hoxton *bends over a large plastic container of washing as she puts it on the ground by the wall. She is in her mid-fifties. Her skin is weathered and her hair floats in strays. Her clothes are patched and dirty but not filthy. She wears black tracksuit slacks, a dark-blue jerkin, an old loose brown linen housecoat with slop pockets and thick grey socks rolled down to the top of workmen's boots laced with string and wrapped with rags to save wear.*

Hoxton *goes to the table, picks up a tin box and takes it into the cell.*

Grig *appears at the threshold on the ramp. He stops, looks at the cell and then at the table. He is in his early sixties. He is thin and tired and dusty from the ruins. His energy is shut in him. His clothes are different shades of grey-brown – an old worn jacket and slacks, scuffed dark boots, an outdoor coat and a cloth bag on a string on his shoulder. The string is threaded through the neck of the bag to fasten it. The bag holds all he has except what he is wearing.*

Grig *hears a sound in the cell. He goes back out of sight into the ruins.* **Hoxton** *comes from the cell and goes to the washing. She takes out a* *dark-grey shirt, gives it a final hand-wring and hangs it to dry on the wall. She picks up a pair of dark-brown trainer slacks, wrings them and hangs them on the wall. She stoops to pick up more washing – stops – she has heard a noise. Quickly she picks up the washing container and hides it under the table. She goes towards the cell, turns back and snatches the washing from the wall, looks at the table to see if there is anything she can hide, hesitates a moment and then goes into the cell with the washing in her hand. She shuts the door behind her.*

Grig *comes onto the threshold of the ramp. He looks at the cell door and listens. He creeps down the ramp and hides in the rubble.*

Hoxton *carefully opens the door. In her hand she grasps an iron rod a little larger than a poker. She looks round, goes to the side of the ramp and peers over the wall into the ruins. No one. She is frightened.* **Grig** *stands and* **Hoxton** *turns to see him.*

Grig   Ain a criminal!

Hoxton   My people 'ere!

Grig   Ain a criminal. 'S all right.

Hoxton   Gone lookin. Come back –

Grig   Give us some water.

Hoxton   – now.

Grig   Water. That's all.

Hoxton   Expect 'em.

Grig   What yer wash with?

Hoxton   Wash? All gone. Fetch it – the man – my boys. Won't 'ave yer 'ere. Got no –

Grig   Water. (*He takes a plastic bottle from his bag.*) Empty.

Hoxton   Gone. All gone.

They stare at each other in silence.

Grig   Water. Git food in the ruins. It's the water . . .

Hoxton   Men back. Any minute.

Hoxton *raises the rod and moves quickly but cautiously towards* **Grig**.

Grig (*with menace*) No violence. (*Tries to negotiate.*) Get water. Rest. Then go.

Hoxton *goes to the top of the ramp and shouts into the ruins.*

Hoxton Criminal 'ere! (*Turns to* **Grig**.) 'E don't believe me! My man – the boys – comin! (*Shouts into the ruins.*) Criminal escape! (*To* **Grig**.) They kill yer!

Grig (*still negotiating*) Don't make me search 'n smash . . .

Hoxton Escape! – seen 'em before.

Grig A drop of water! – is it too much?

Grig *goes to the table.* **Hoxton** *runs, snatches up the water container and clutches it to her.*

Hoxton (*too angry to cry*) My things! Ain be rob!

Grig *goes towards* **Hoxton**. *She turns the container upside down – it empties on the ground.*

Grig Yer got so much yer can waste it! – where's the rest?

Hoxton Tap in the wall – down there – 'arf a day – see the dogs in the puddle.

Grig *takes another plastic bottle from his bag. He stands the two bottles on the table.*

Grig I don't drink? – you don't. Stay wake longer 'n you. Must drink. Dust's brick-up me throat. That rod – yer come at me with that, yer might as well put it in me 'and. I'll kill yer. I slog this far, ain give in now. Good weight is it? – I'll put it in yer 'ead.

Hoxton (*points to the spilt water*) All I 'ad. Give yer water yer'd never go.

Grig Can't pay. (*Bag.*) Bits 'n pieces. Nothin. (*Gestures to table.*) Yer better provided.

Hoxton Escape. One come years ago. 'Id in the ruins. 'Elicopters come. Noise fetch the dogs. They stay up there 'n watch till the dogs flush 'im out. Then they come down 'n took 'im off. Remember it – dogs millin round – 'owlin – dust – propellers. No one get away.

Grig   Ain escape. Bin walkin in the ruins. People say it's bad. They don't know! – they ain seen it. Nothin's like this. Dust. Bricks. Go for weeks – empty – then yer meet some lunatic cryin 'n singin. If I was escape I wouldn't get this far. They tag yer ankle – track yer by that. I know where I was goin, but when I saw it I felt lost. Ain a prison, it's a city. No wall, no wire. Open track round it. Took me a week t' skirt a bit on the rim before I could turn off in t' the ruins.

Hoxton *angrily snatches up a mug and takes it into the cell.* **Grig** *goes to the table and searches in the pans. Finds food and moves away as he eats it.* **Hoxton** *comes from the cell with a mug of water. She puts it on the table and backs off. She still carries the rod.* **Grig** *goes to the table, takes the mug and gulps a mouthful. He gasps and falls back onto a box.*

Grig   Burn. Throat crack.

The mug shakes violently. He tries to steady it with both hands. Water splashes onto his clothes. He quickly gulps the mug empty. He licks the rim.

More. Lost 'arf the mug.

Hoxton *takes the mug and goes into the cell.* **Grig** *forces himself off the box and falls across the table. He steals more food and puts it in his pocket. He falls back and sits bent over on the box.*

Hoxton *comes from the cell with the mug of water. She puts it on the table.* **Grig** *doesn't move. She puts it on the ground beside him. He takes it and drinks.*

Hoxton   Now yer go.

Grig   Let the drink settle.

Hoxton   Yer said yer'd go.

Grig   I will. (*Looks round.*) Cook on that. Do yer washin. Kip under a roof. All set up. Why they let yer stay? No entry zone.

Hoxton   Fill yer bottles 'n go.

Grig   Let the effect a' the water wear off. Why's the road so straight? Army made it when they flat all this. White makes yer eyes run. Left me place – no permit. Wife was dyin. Scream – yer could count the interval, regular as a siren. Built up inside 'er then let itself out. Knew she weren't dead when she drop off, even if I was out the room – the interval 'd 'a slowed. Death takes its time to tell its tale: 'ers was cancer. When it reach 'er mouth she scream as if it's arguin with 'er in 'er throat. Next-doors bang on the wall: 'er scream upset the kids. No medical – that's all gone now. Neighbours brung 'er pills they kep back from before. Packets a' 'erbal cure. I come away. Do no good there. The street'll feed 'er – or let 'er go: best in the end. Crep downstairs – 'er scream at me t' come back or go. Whichever it was, it'd bin waitin in 'er for years. Still 'ear it blocks away. Then I cotton on it ain 'er scream. I'm in another bit a' suburb – it's screams from other people's 'ouses. Next morning the same. Everywhere.

Grig *takes a blouse from the washing container.*

Hoxton   Don't touch it!

Grig   'Ang it up. Odd job for the water.

Hoxton   Don't want it!

She snatches the blouse and puts it into the container. She takes the container into the cell. **Grig** *goes to the table and picks up the two plastic bottles. He takes a few steps towards the cell and waits.* **Hoxton** *comes out.*

Grig   Said I could fill these. (*He gestures to the cell.*) Tap in there.

Grig *goes into the cell.* **Hoxton** *follows him to the door and stands there. Then she goes inside.*

Two

The empty site. The door is closed.

Sweden *comes onto the threshold of the ramp. He is about twenty. Unshaven and white-faced. A shock of thick black hair crowns his forehead but is not long at the back. Dark eyes. His trousers and jacket are black but from different suits. There are narrow dark-grey stripes on his jacket. Black boots. His jacket and dirty white shirt are unbuttoned. A wide swathe of dirty bandage binds his chest from under his arms to his lower ribs. He carries nothing.*

Sweden *looks at the cell door. He sits on the ramp and falls asleep. Pause.* **Grig** *comes from the cell. He is in shirtsleeves and carries two sets of dirty plates and mugs. He takes them to the table and puts them in a bowl which aleady has other crockery in it. He pours water into it from the carrier and washes up.*

Grig (*calls to cell*)   Go out foragin in a bit.

The crockery clatters slightly as **Grig** *washes it. He sees* **Sweden** – *stops and puts down the plate in his hand. He goes to the cell and shuts the door. He turns to look at* **Sweden**, *then goes back to the table and continues washing and drying.* **Sweden** *wakes.*

Sweden   Give us some water. Mouth like a 'ole with a burial in it. (**Grig** *works.*) Less 'ave some. (*No response.* **Grig** *dries a mug.*) Bin 'ere weeks ago. Saw you 'n the skirt. Didn't want t' be a nuisance – went on. Couldn't find no water. Come all the way back. Legs shaky – 'ad a sit-down. Give us some water.

Grig *finishes drying the mug and pours water into it.* **Hoxton** *comes from the cell.*

Sweden (*pointing at* **Hoxton**)   Yeh – 's 'er 'n you I saw.

Grig (*takes the mug to* **Sweden**)   Drink that then on yer way.

Sweden *takes the mug with both hands, raises it to his mouth and drinks. The mug shakes violently. Water splashes onto his bandage. He half-whines and dabs the bandage. He gulps the rest of the water and slumps on his side.*

Sweden   Rest a bit more.

He sleeps. The mug lies on the ground with his finger looped in the handle.
Hoxton *searches through his pockets.*

Hoxton   Nothin, nothin. Useless. Escape! Why's 'e come
'ere? Why? Why? 'E'll bring the army!

Grig *has gone to the table to finish washing and drying. Silence except
for the small sounds of crockery.*

Grig   'Im or us. No alternative. Kill 'im. 'Ave to. Never
done it before. Must be easy. Use a brick. Yer allowed.
Escapes – law ain cover 'em.

Hoxton (*takes the mug from* **Sweden***'s hand*) Army still come.
Tag'll bring 'em even when 'e's dead.

Grig *holds out his hand.* **Hoxton** *takes him the mug. He washes it
carefully.*

Grig   Drag 'im out a couple a' days – on a plank.

Hoxton   No need for that. Drop the tag out there. Smash 'is
leg 'n git it off.

She goes into the cell. **Grig** *finishes drying up.* **Hoxton** *comes from the
cell with a blanket.*

Sleep – put a blanket on 'is face. Wash the puke off after.

Grig *folds the drying-up cloth. He goes to* **Sweden** *and lifts his
trouser legs.*

Grig   No tag.

Hozion   Took it off

Grig   Permanent fix. 'Ave t' take 'is leg off.

Hoxton   Escape – must be! That's why 'e's bandage – 'urt
gettin out. 'Oo tied it? – someone did!

Grig *kicks* **Sweden***'s leg. No response.*

Grig   Saw 'im when I come 'ere.

Hoxton Yer never said.

Grig   Kip in the ruins. Reason I stay.

Sweden *wakes.*

Sweden Where's me mug? I drop off?

Grig Where's yer tag?

Sweden Get blackouts since I bin walkin. Wake up – signs 'n drawins all round me in the dirt. Don't know what they mean. Writ 'em with a stick when I was out.

Grig Tag ain on yer ankle.

Sweden Ankle? Yer in the past! Don't tag no ankles. Tag inside, internal. Under yer rib.

Grig Yer got a medic t' cut –

Sweden Medic – no! They'd be in mega-terror – scare the army find out. Good stuff that water. Not the piddle yer get in puddles. Got a tap – must 'ave. (*He opens his shirt to show the bandage.*) Internal there. Cut it out meself. 'Ad t' get the preparations right. Orderlies come round once a week. Standin orders. Sanitary. Disinfectant. Nick a little every time. Just a drop – they monitor the usage. 'Id it in a bottle under the floorboards. One night check I 'ad enough. Walk out. Cross the cordon sanitaire. Kep goin t' the river. Pontoon army bridge – planks 'n girders. Cross that. Well, no point in 'angin round: sit down – feel for the target – scar where they put it – one two three – knife in. Point down not up. Poke me finger inside. Little plastic disc be'ind the rib. Stuck. Cement made a' animal bone. That's the easy bit. Didn't like the next. 'Ad t' saw it off. No teeth on the blade – straight edge. Sat there. Blood drop out the 'ole: black snake – there was moonlight. River slappin the pontoons sounded like kids shoutin. Couldn't do it. ''Ave to mate.' Couldn't. ''Ave to. Yer kill yerself – least it ain the army!' Don't know 'ow long it took. Last bit come off with a click. Slosh the disinfectant in. Wad it. Bandage. Tight – 'ardly breathe. (*He sees the mug on the table.*) Me mug.

He goes to the table, fills the mug and drinks.

Out a tap – definite. Bit a' wire ready in me pocket. Wire the

tag t' a bit of wood. Tight as nails – me life's on that wood.
Stood up. Totter down the bank like a drunken plank. Chuck
it in the river. Ain 'ear no splash! Must 'ave a fever. Turn t'
go. It's as if a 'and press on me shoulder 'n turn me back. I'd
throw it t' the other side! Throw it so 'ard it – !

*He stamps up and down the ramp waving his arms – it turns into a
dance.*

Cut me 'eart out! Rupture me gut! Slice me liver! An threw it
over the river! Over the other side! The other side! I should 'a
bin dead 'n I felt immortal! Run back on the bridge! Lights
ahead – the prison city – rows a' yeller teeth across the sky!
Jump down the bank – jungle – nettles – branches lash me
face – mud drag me boot off – rip the brambles with me raw
'ands! See it! – shine in the puddle – still tied t' the wood. Run
back on the bridge. Drop it from the middle. Watch it float.
That's 'ow I died – drown meself 'n floated out t' sea. (*Stops.*)
Moonlight catch it once – glints: me dead body winks at me.
Tag'll keep 'em 'appy. Go on bleepin the rest a' me life tellin
'em I'm dead. (*He is suddenly tired. He drapes himself in the blanket.*)
Water went t' me 'ead.

Hoxton   What yer doin?

Sweden   Need a nap.

Grig   Can't sleep 'ere!

Sweden *goes to the table and fills the mug with water.*

Sweden   Ain 'ere. Tol' yer – I'm dead. Yer safe with me.
(*Points to the cell.*) Loan yer bed in there?

Sweden *takes the mug into the cell. He leaves the door open.* **Grig**
moves closer to see inside.

Hoxton   Army ain come if 'e's got rid a' the tag.

Grig   Yer believe all that? 'Oo is 'e?

Hoxton   If 'e was lyin 'e'd a' made up somethin simple – 'is
mate 'elp 'im –

Grig   They make it up as they go along. Play the 'ero t' convince themselves. No – 'e wouldn't, 'e's more cunnin. (*He goes to the cell and looks in. He closes the door.*) Drop off again – or pretend to.

Hoxton   'E won't stay.

Grig   Why not? Get all 'e wants 'ere. – Could be anyone. Could be army. Or some gang.

Grig *goes up the ramp.*

Hoxton   What yer doin?

Grig   Could 'ave mates 'idin.

Grig *goes out into the ruins.* **Hoxton** *goes to the table and throws away the dirty washing-up water. She goes into the cell and leaves the door open behind her.*

Three

Morning. The door is open.

Sweden *is alone. He is stripped to the waist and washes himself at the table. The bandage still binds his chest.*

Sweden   Come on, say yes. (*No answer.*) All me life – army, law, prison breathin down me neck. Now – got away – they never bin closer! Don't notice the animal in the cage – notice it when the cage's empty. Stand 'ere in the wilderness drawin attention t' meself. Could pick me up by *chance*. Soon's they saw the scar that's it! Got a' get right away. (*Silence as he dries himself.*) *You* can't stay 'ere. They done the clearance – now they'll clean up the stragglers. Blow the ruins up. Shoot the dogs. Begrudge the rats their 'oles.

Hoxton *comes from the cell. She wears a pink slip and laceless plimsolls.*

Sweden   Won't put *you* in the suburb. Prison. Spend yer life watchin yerself die. Come on.

Hoxton (*shakes her head*)   I tol' yer.

Sweden   Ain leave yer with 'im. Prison's chock-a-block with 'is sort. Another reason I got out – stayed I'd a' end up like them. Dead bodies puttin their clothes on every mornin. They catch yer up t' somethin – sneak be'ind yer back: next thing yer on punishment squad. 'E'll grass yer t' the army. Come with me.

Hoxton   Nowhere t' go.

Sweden   There is if yer go far enough! Army don't go there – too far out, frontier too big t' watch. Got enough t' look after with the suburb 'n the prison.

Hoxton   It ain there.

Sweden   It is! Even the prison stiffs know. When they sleep their mouths blubber as if they're saying prayers 'n their eyes open in little slits – yer can tell they're lookin at it. Still in their eyes when they wake up – only they don't see through 'em then. Prisoners see what they're told to. (*He finishes drying and puts down the towel.*) What do I 'ave t' say?

Hoxton   Bin 'ere too long.

Sweden   Try it! Give it a few days – if it don't work come back.

Hoxton   This is my place.

Sweden   Anywhere's better 'n 'ere. Why yer come 'ere?

Hoxton That's all in the past.

Sweden   Why? Tell me.

Hoxton   Too far back.

Sweden (*placing the chair*) Sit down 'n tell me. Sit. I tol' yer my story. *Sit.*

Hoxton *sits in the chair.*

Hoxton   Town where I was – . I forget. Only women. Before the clearin – but all the men 'd bin draft on reconstruction. (*Stops.*) That's all I remember.

Sweden   Tell me.

Hoxton   They used t' – . If a woman fancy a 'ouse – some 'ouse that's better 'n 'er own – all the women gang up 'n drive out the woman 'oo owns it. Then the new one move in . . . Suppose the gang 'ad t' go there first thing in the mornin's. March down the street – arm in arm – shoutin – singin – bangin lids. Stop outside the 'ouse. 'Out! Out!' Chuck things. Yes – they never broke the winders so it was nice for the woman movin in. Usual, the woman inside run out the back. If she put up a fight – we drag 'er out by the 'air – swing 'er round on it so the pavement nigh on scrape 'er face off. She ain no bother after that – went off t' live in the mobile 'omes further out.

Hoxton *thinks in silence.*

Sweden   That's what they did t' yer?

Hoxton   My 'ouse was nice. They wouldn't touch me, I was in the gang. One mornin I 'eard 'em in the street. Knew it was me. Else they'd a' tol' me the day before.

Sweden   Why didn't yer go in a mobile?

Silence.

Hoxton What?

Sweden   Why d'yer come 'ere?

Silence.

Hoxton   Waited on me doorstep. Kid in me arms. We was rough when we chase the others out – but we 'ad a party, 'ad a laugh. Not when they come for me. Ain seen that sort a' rage before. Chuck stones. Saw 'em bendin down t' pick 'em up 'n put 'em in the 'ands a' anyone standin empty-'anded. All 'ad t' be in it. They'd 'a kill me on me own doorstep. Couldn't stay after that. Walk till I come 'ere.

Sweden   Ain like that where we're goin.

Hoxton   Like that everywhere. When it went wrong yer'd get rid a' me – chuck yer stones. Yer want someone t' nurse yer side when it go bad.

Sweden *jumps onto the wall and balances along it.*

Sweden   It won't go bad! Watch me! Look! Ain ill! Fit as a string orchestra! If me side play up – nurse it right! Start! – the rest 'appens by itself! We'll get there! I always get it right! I cut the tag – yer wouldn't 'a believe that! (*He sees something in the ruins and sits on the wall with his legs dangling.*) When I cut the tag I put me finger in. Push it up inside. Right up – where the 'eart is. Touch it with me finger. Felt it – tramp – tramp – tramp – tramp. Wouldn't think *that* could be done! It was just the once – yer don't do that again – so I kep it there! (*He drums the backs of his heels on the wall.*) This finger 'll wriggle when I'm dead!

Grig *comes onto the threshold of the ramp. He wears his coat and carries his bag in his hand. He has been scavenging from the remains of gardens in the ruins. He goes to the table and takes the food from his bag.*
Hoxton *puts it away.* **Sweden** *sits on the wall, casually swinging his heels against it.*

Grig   Cut the brambles back. Takin over.

Hoxton   'Ope yer ain took too much.

Sweden   Chriss chriss chriss . . . (*Playfully tosses a stone at* **Hoxton***'s feet.*) Come with me.

Grig   'As 'e took it off?

Sweden (*food*) Look at it! – muck.

Hoxton (*to* **Grig**)   Take too much local, 'ave t' go right out t' get anythin.

Sweden   Can't even feed yer.

Grig   Ask 'im why 'e don't go.

Sweden   Get yer share. 'E'd rob a baby of its spittle.

Grig   Can't go till 'e's got someone t' 'old 'is 'and.

Sweden   Ain leave yer with 'im.

Grig   Someone t' blame when 'e git lost.

Sweden   Don't listen t' 'im. I know places. Learn 'em in prison. Soldiers tell the trusties. Even let them what done 'em a big favour go there.

Grig   'E believe that! If they paint a pretty picture on the wall a' the execution shed 'e'd think they was takin 'im on 'oliday.

Sweden *jumps down from the wall and goes to the table for his shirt.*

Sweden   Yer comin or what?

Grig   Take that bandage off.

Sweden   Which is it – 'im or me?

Grig   What yer got t' 'ide?

Sweden   'E'll keep yer 'ere for the army!

Grig   Wrong again. I ain stayin. Yer the only reason I stay 'ere. (*Shakes the loose soil from his bag.*) Soon's she's rid a' yer I'm off.

Sweden   Where to? Yer said there ain nowhere.

Grig   Not yer sort there ain – somewhere yer dreamt up! I know where I'm goin. Bin there – born 'n brought up there. Army ain clear that – too small.

Sweden   They clear everythin! Is that it? – that's all 'e's bin rabbitin about?

Grig   If it's clear, I'll still find somewhere there. Live quiet. Army won't even know.

Sweden   'E wants t' live in the past! There ain no past, never was. It's in 'is 'ead! Met 'is sort out there. 'Goin back'! Pilgrims travellin up their own arse! If they found it they're too decrepit t' notice. Can't tell what their age is – if they got grey 'air or the dust's in it. Can't tell if they're men or women. Don't know themselves even when they piss! – all they got's a scar like a dry-up bit a' rock – which don't piss, it weeps! They forgot 'ow t' speak, forgot what a word *is*! Some of 'em even think they got there, found it – bundles done up in sacks sittin on a dung-'eap.

Sweden *starts to fill water bottles.*

Grig   Take it off. I don't want t' see. I'll come back when it's over.

Sweden   If yer go with 'im yer'll end up like two sets a' bones turn in t' Siamese twins.

Grig   Yer ain leave till it's off!

Sweden   I ain what?

Grig   Yer roll up 'n think yer got us at yer mercy! Lucky I ain break yer neck yer little twister! Yer a wrecker! What was yer in prison for? – if yer was! 'E ain escape – 'e's so low they ain let 'im in!

Sweden   Ho-ho! Look at 'im with his rag up! Tag – ain it? Can't get over it. Really riled! 'E 'as t' say 'is prayers before 'e cuts 'is toenails!

Grig   Take it off!

Sweden   Keep off!

Grig *grapples with* **Sweden**.

Grig   See it! See it!

Sweden *breaks from* **Grig**.

Sweden   Keep off! I got a wound! Yer ain takin risks with my life!

Grig   Yer tol' us 'oo we was! – now I'll see 'oo you are!

Sweden   Keep off!

Grig   Yer goin t' show!

Sweden   O no!

Grig   Why can't yer? All this make it worse! What's 'e 'idin?

Sweden   Nothin!

Grig   Then show me!

Sweden   Is 'e me executioner – I come 'ere t' meet 'im? The mates yer sleep with in the prison – yer never know which one – the army tell 'em: do it t'night – or in the daylight on the street where we can see!

Grig   'E's mad!

Grig *grapples with* **Sweden.**

Sweden   Bastard! My wound! Get off it – !

Grig *holds* **Sweden** *with his back against his chest. He forces his hand under the bandage and holds it away from* **Sweden***'s side.*

Grig (*to* **Hoxton**)   Look! Look!

Sweden   No! No!

Hoxton *starts to move slowly and calmly towards* **Sweden***.*

Grig   Still! – yer little twister!

Sweden   Keep off –

Grig   Quick – can't 'old –

Sweden (*wails*)   'E's tearin me wound!

Hoxton (*going slowly to* **Sweden**)   Soon be over – all over –

Grig   Keep still!

Hoxton *reaches* **Sweden***. He lashes at her with his feet.*

Grig   The little – !

Hoxton *steps aside from* **Sweden***'s kicks.*

Hoxton   Soon be over – all done –

Hoxton *looks under the bandage and walks back to the table.* **Grig** *lets* **Sweden** *go and walks away.* **Sweden** *sits on the ground, cries for a moment and then quietens himself. He puts his hand under the bandage and takes it out. It is red.*

Sweden   Bleedin.

Grig   'As 'e got a 'ole?

Hoxton *picks up the shirt and takes it to* **Sweden***.*

Sweden What do I 'ave t' do? Put me in prison – get out – cut the tag – walk. When's it enough? Why'm I always kick? – in the guts – in me 'ead. Now 'im – 'e 'as t' kick. (*He tries to tug the bandage down into shape.*) When I cut it out it ain 'urt. 'E touches it 'n it bleed.

Sweden *jerks the shirt from* **Hoxton**'s *hands and stands.*

Sweden Yer ain done it if I ain wore out. Touch me again – I'll open yer veins 'n pour the piss in 'em down yer throat.

Hoxton Wash it.

Sweden (*going towards the cell*) Go in there. (*To* **Hoxton**.) Keep 'im out.

Sweden *goes into the cell.*

Grig Was there a 'ole?

Hoxton Saw the blood.

Grig Could a' bin done by a knife or bullet. Weren't no tag – that's for sure. 'E cry like a kid.

The door is slammed shut from inside.

Can't leave yer with 'im. Come with me.

Hoxton Too changed – couldn't live with it.

Grig Yer should 'a look when yer took 'im t' bed.

Hoxton Kep 'is bandage on.

Grig 'E's dangerous. 'E could 'ang out there till I left. Begin t' think there's no way t' get away from 'im. What d'yer want me t' do? Come – it'd all be over.

Hoxton *takes a basin from the table and goes to the door. She knocks. Waits. The door is opened and she goes in. She closes the door behind her.*

Grig *stands alone for a moment. He goes to the table and takes the water bottles filled by* **Sweden** – *he checks the caps and puts the bottles into his bag. He puts on his coat and the bag over his shoulder. He goes out up the ramp without looking back.*

Four

Morning. The door is open.

Sweden *sits on the ramp looking into the ruins. He is in shirtsleeves.*
Hoxton *comes from the cell. She wears slacks and a jersey.*

Hoxton   Thought yer was gone.

Sweden   Army found the tag. Or soon will. Wash up the
bank. Stuck in the muck. Obvious – see it out 'ere. Even if I'm
dead they want their tag back. 'As t' be accounted for. Go out
t' sea if they 'ave to. Ships. 'Elicopters. – Got 'a move fast.
This is the last this 'ole sees a' me. (*He comes down the ramp.*) Yer
could still come.

Hoxton (*nods to the table*) Take somethin with yer.

Sweden   Don't wait for 'im. 'E won't come back. Bin gone
too long.

He goes to the table and packs food and water into a bag.

Know what I was done for? Not that it makes no difference –
get life for everythin. Cars. Ain allowed in the suburbs. Cars in
the rich ghetto. Everythin there – if it's made they got it. Gang
used t' raid it at night. Nick the cars. Drive fast. No one notice
– 's all fast there. Lit fires. Run through the flames. Lads stand
round in a circle – push yer back. Jacket singe! 'Air singe!
Jump! Stay in! 'Ow long can yer stick it? Jump! 'Igher!
Buggers push yer back! Grab a bit a' burnin wood! Chase 'em!
(*He picks up a piece of wood and pretends to jab it at bystanders.*) Jab!
Jab! Jab! Run! Run! (*He dances round* **Hoxton** *jabbing at her.*)
Run! Run! Yoweeee! Yer scorch! On fire! Burn yer witch!
(**Hoxton** *doesn't respond. He drags her into the fire.*) Jump! Yer in
the fire now!

Hoxton   Let go a' me!

Sweden   Jump! Jump! Jump! Fire! Fire! Flames splash up
like water! Up yer nose! Snuff it up! Lick yer face! Stamp it!
Stamp it! Stamp it! Kick the fire at the lads! Make 'em run!
Chuck the burnin wood! Red 'ot cinders! – grab 'em up! Hoo-

hoo! Chuck it at 'em! Coat on fire! – get it off! Chase 'em with it! Chase the lads! Chase the girls! Make 'em scatter! Make 'em scream! When they're spread out round yer in a circle – lit up by the flames – I walk back 'n stood in the fire – 'n whistle like the burnin wood.

He puts two fingers of each hand in his mouth and blows a shrill high whistle. He goes back to the table and finishes packing.

I 'ate the patch a' black earth when the fire's out. Yer won't change yer mind?

Hoxton   Shouldn't jump. (*No response.*) Did the fight open yer cut?

Sweden   Never look.

Hoxton   O? Should 'ave – now yer don't know what yer got in front a' yer.

Sweden   No point. It's open? – stay 'ere 'n get it better for the army t' shoot me?

Hoxton   I say goodbye then.

Hoxton *goes into the cell.* **Sweden** *finishes packing. He hesitates for a moment – leans with arms taut and palms flat on the table-top and bows his head. Then he takes off his shirt and unwinds the bandage. He shivers. His elbows and forearms cover his chest and sides. He raises his right elbow and gazes at the dully livid wound.*

Hoxton *comes from the cell. She picks up the wood* **Sweden** *jabbed at her and throws it aside. He winds the bandage round his chest and puts on his shirt and coat. They do not look at each other.* **Hoxton** *goes into the cell and* **Sweden** *goes out up the ramp.*

Five

The empty site. The door is closed.

Grace *comes onto the threshold of the ramp. She is in her late teens and thin. She is tired and dirty from walking. Her longish dress is faded green with a pale pattern of large red roses and blue leaves. Her mid-length coat* *is imitation hide. She wears brown ankle boots and thick bottle-green socks. Her fairish hair is medium-long, unwashed and straggly and bound with a blue band round her head. She carries a stong, heavy plastic carrier bag and two lighter ones.*

Grace *looks at the door and round the site. She puts down her carriers and takes a piece of brick from the heavy one. She stares at the door and then goes to it. She stands there a moment, opens it and goes in. Pause.*

Grace (*in the cell*)   Found yer!

Pause. **Hoxton** *runs from the cell, looking behind her. The piece of brick is thrown at her through the doorway.* **Grace** *comes from the cell.*

Grace (*pointing at* **Hoxton**)   Look at 'er!

The two stare at each other. **Grace** *runs to the heavy carrier, takes out a piece of brick and throws it at* **Hoxton.**

Hoxton   'Oo are yer? What yer want? (*Sudden idea.*) 'Im! – yer want 'im! 'E's gone – days ago! (**Grace** *stares at* **Hoxton**.) Ain come back.

Grace *takes another piece of brick from the carrier and throws it at* **Hoxton.**

Hoxton   O-god-o-god they empty the mad'ouses! (*She goes to the table and picks up the iron rod.*) Get out! 'Ad enough! One after the other! No more a' it! Get out!

Grace   Look at 'er! (*She takes another piece of brick from the carrier – is going to throw it but stops.*) No – ain waste 'em. Tell 'er first – then chuck 'em!

Hoxton (*bewildered*)   'Oo is she? What she want?

Grace   I found the bones!

Hoxton   She's mad!

Grace   In the wall!

Hoxton   Get out! Get out!

Grace   Can't 'ide from me!

Hoxton *stares at* **Grace**, *then goes into the cell and shuts the door.*

Grace   Thought yer got away with it! Bin caught out! (*She throws the piece of brick in her hand at the door.*) Army knock the walls down!

Hoxton (*in the cell*)   Madwoman! Get out a' my place!

Grace   Ain go! (*She sits on the ramp and clasps the carrier to her.*) Sit 'ere! All these years! Thought yer could 'ide! (*Pause. She goes to the door and hammers on it.*) Get yer when yer come out! (*She turns to the kitchen.*) There's 'er table. There's 'er chair where she sits! All the comforts! Proper 'ome! (*Bursts into tears. Stops. To herself*). Ain 'ide from me . . . (*She walks away from the table, sits on the ground and cries.*) That's 'er.

The door opens slightly. **Hoxton** *comes out and stares at* **Grace**. **Grace** *does not see her.* **Hoxton** *goes cautiously to the two carriers on the ramp and stoops to pick them up.* **Grace** *sees her.*

Grace   Leave that! Leave that!

Hoxton (*moves away from the carriers*)   Yer come t' my place. Got a right t' know 'oo yer are.

Grace   Yer know! (*She goes to the two carriers and picks them up.*)

Hoxton   Some tormented madwoman wanderin round with ideas in 'er 'ead.

Grace (*through her teeth*)   Said bones: yer face went like a stone – never forget that – can't lie t' me now I seen it.

Hoxton   Yer'll get nothin 'ere.

Grace   Army knock the street down. Knock our 'ouse. Bits a' bone in the walls. Trucks run over the rubble, level it with chains. I still saw! Thought it was bits a' wood. Kids' bones – smash! All my life I arst 'oo yer were, why yer run. Knew when I saw the bones. Murderer! Yer kill my little sisters 'n brothers! Took three years t' find yer. Arst every woman I met – ain know 'ow old they was, could a' bin my age – arst 'em all. They ain know – crep back in their ditch. (*Gestures.*) They ain got all this, they live where it's worst. Cripple – blind – done up in rags. I said 'At least yer spared my sorrow.'

Hoxton   Sorry I pry in yer bags. Spend yer life scavagin 'ere. Scavage everyin.

Grace   Yer 'ouse. Yer ran away. Must 'a bin you. Why yer kill 'em?

Hoxton (*shrugs*)   Woman I cleaned for. She 'ad money.

Silence.

Grace   Yes?

Hoxton   Took me kid t' work with me. She ain got one. Stare at mine. Scare me – well-off get what they want. (*She starts to tidy the pans on the table.*) 'Ad a woman friend I went round with. She 'ad a kid. Couldn't afford t' keep it. She let me give it where I clean. The woman paid me – she was loaded. I kep the money.

Grace   All the years in that 'ouse. No photos – no voices – not even their names.

Hoxton (*pauses for a moment*)   Things was bad 'n they got worse. No one still ain learnt 'ow t' cope in them days. Women pile their 'omes on the street. Stood by 'em t' sell 'em. Then some stranger I 'ardly met bring me 'er kid. 'O yer can give it where yer work, plenty there can take it.' I said yer'll 'ave t' pay me. (*She sits.*) The rest was bound t' 'appen. More women come. If I'd said no there'd 'a bin trouble: I weren't 'elpin when I could. The money went on things in the 'ouse 'n food – *one* kid was fed. Then they left 'em on the doorstep. I couldn't stop it.

Grace   They weren't my sisters 'n brothers?

Silence. **Hoxton** *doesn't hear the question.*

Hoxton   Roll 'em in a blanket till it was still. Done it that way.

Grace   They weren't my sisters 'n brothers?

Hoxton (*to herself*)   Only 'ad the one. (*Realises* **Grace** *has asked a question – raises her head.*) That must be you.

Grace   'Ow many?

Hoxton Didn't want t' know. Weren't many. (*Silence.*) They give theirs away. Kep mine.

Grace Call the woman I grew up with mum. One day she says 'No yer the skivvy – we chase yer mother out.'

Hoxton Yellin 'n cursin. Stood on the doorstep. Kid in me arms. Thought that'd remind 'em they owe me. Made it worse. Chase me. Chuck stones. 'It me back. Ain like a fist or a push. Like a thud inside yer 'ole body. Drop the kid. Scrabble t' pick it up. Run through a doorway in a wall. In a garden. Green. Put yer down in the doorway. Thought yer was dead. Look back – women all tryin t' get through at once – like a cloud bulgin through the door. Fancy! – yer weren't trample. Yer a lucky girl. Must 'a bin kick aside 'n the woman pick yer up. What'll yer do? I can't keep yer. They'll let yer in the suburb. Tell 'em yer miss the truck when the army left. Got lost. Sorry yer 'ad a wasted journey. A long way t' come for nothin.

Grace *gathers up her carriers.*

Grace Where's somewhere t' sleep?

Hoxton (*gestures to the cell*)   There's some water if yer want. Won't charge yer. (*Stares at the carriers.*) Thought yer might a' brought somethin in yer carriers.

Hoxton *watches* **Grace** *as she takes the carriers into the cell. Then she sits alone.*

Six

The empty site. The door is closed.

In the ruins, a shout. It is desperate but monotonous and hoarse as if it had been repeated at the same interval for a long time.

Silence. The shout.

Grace *runs in from the ruins. She stops at the ramp, looks back and then runs into the cell.*

The shout.

Grace *runs from the cell, putting on her coat and carrying the two light carriers. She runs up the ramp and looks into the ruins – no one. She runs to the table, fills water bottles and puts them in her carrier. She runs out at the ramp.*

The shout.

Pause. **Grace** *runs back in, runs into the cell and shuts the door.*

Silence.

Sweden *stumbles and falls onto the top of the ramp. He is in the clothes he left in but they are dirtier and more ragged. His boots are fastened with string. There is dry blood on the front of his jacket and on the lap of his trousers and his filthy white shirt. His hands are filthy, the palms and backs cut and scratched. His hair is wilder and his face livid under the dirt. He gets awkwardly to his feet. He has no eyes. The two enormous cavities have been painted with matt black paint. He opens his mouth to shout but stops and it shuts slowly: he has felt the threshold of the ramp under his feet.*

Sweden   'S it. 'Ere. 'S it. (*He feels a few steps down the ramp. Stops. Calls.*) Yer there? (*No answer. To himself.*) Is this . . . 'ave I found . . . ? (*He feels down the ramp with his foot, points directions to himself.*) Slope – this is – slep *there* – water *there*. (*Calls.*) Yer there? (*No answer.*) 'Elp me. Don't run if it scare yer – won't 'urt. Soldiers put me on the road – this way – straight. Need water. Bad.

Silence. **Sweden** *shouts once, as before.* **Grace** *comes from the cell.* **Sweden** *hears her.*

Sweden   Yer there. Why didn't yer come? Thought it was deserted. Army took me eyes. Left me in the ruins t' scare the stragglers – anyone 'idin. Easier t' kill 'em when they come. Give me some water. They paint me eyes. Permanent, won't come out ever. T' make the panic worse. – Seat. (*No response.*) Seat.

Grace *fetches a box and puts it against the back of* **Sweden**'s *legs. He sits.*

Sweden   Water.

Grace *goes to the table and pours water into a mug.*

Sweden   Thank chriss yer 'ere. Thought yer'd gone with 'im. Why don't yer speak?

Grace *touches his arm with the mug. He takes it and splashes water into his empty sockets.*

Sweden   Ohh.

He drinks the drops left in the mug and holds it out.

Water.

Grace *reaches to take the mug.* **Sweden** *grips her wrist. His head sinks, he talks almost to himself.*

Sweden   When they caught me – first five minutes – they took one eye out. Left me like that for days. Ain believe I cut the tag. "Oo done it? 'Oo done it?' Askin 'n askin. Each mornin I said t' meself 'Look at the light. Look at the light mate. Look at the light.' Water.

Sweden *lets* **Grace***'s wrist go. She goes to the table and fills the mug with water.* **Hoxton** *comes to the threshold of the ramp. She has been scavenging and has a sack on her shoulder.*

Sweden (*to himself*)   When the truck drove off – they didn't shout back – didn't laugh – that's what we are now.

Grace *gives the mug to* **Sweden**. *He drinks.*

Sweden   "Oo done it? 'Oo done it?' Plenty I could name. What for? – they'd 'a done this anyway. Could a' name you for revenge. If we gone when I said – wouldn't 'a bin caught. This wouldn't 'a bin done. Even when I left, went slow so's yer catch up. Can't make that mistake twice. Army'll clear all this – 'eard 'em say. Can't manage on me own. Yer 'ave t' come. Yer owe it t' me. Ain just lead me, eat 'n sleep till we get there. We're like a couple, what we bin through. I'm still a man. More than before. Ain afraid now – can't see on their faces what they're doin next – I let it 'appen. Same for you – yer stand there 'n it's started but yer don't know yet. Yer need me.

I'll take care a' yer. I think all the time now. I know the place is there. *This* ends. – Let's go t' bed.

Hoxton   Take the mug 'e'll break it.

Sweden   Yer – ! 'Oo I bin talkin to? (*Stumbles to his feet, knocks over the box.*) 'Oo else is there?

Hoxton   Me daughter.

Sweden   You? Yer daughter? Yer 'ave a daughter? (*To* **Grace**.) Speak! (*To* **Hoxton**.) Make 'er speak so I can know!

Hoxton   Let 'im touch yer.

Grace *doesn't move.*

Sweden (*points to the ground at his feet*) 'Ere – 'ere!

Hoxton *puts down the sack and goes to* **Sweden**. *He holds her.*

Sweden   Yes. Yes. If I could see – . Did yer 'ear? – army took me eyes. I never said 'bout yer 'n this place. We 'ave t' go – they'll come. – Where is she?

Hoxton   Touch 'im.

Grace *touches* **Sweden** – *he grips her arm. The three are held together.*

Sweden   Let me feel. Let me. (*He feels* **Grace**'s *face. She shies away.*) Yer give me water – why ain yer said? – 'Ow old's yer daughter? (*He feels* **Grace**'s *body.*) She's stiff. She's scare a' me. I stink. Me clothes stink. Me mouth wrench when they took me eye. It stay like that – I feel it with me tongue. Yer mother'll tell yer 'ow I used t' be – jump 'n laugh 'n always larkin 'avin fun. It'll come back – in time. (*He touches her dress.*) What's – ? (*Grabs it.*) A dress? She wear a dress? Talk t' me.

Grace   I brung yer the box t' sit on.

Sweden   Yer voice is like yer mother's as a child. (*He lets* **Grace** *go.*) Let's go t' bed. We'll get up early 'n leave this 'ole for ever.

Hoxton *picks up the sack on the ramp and leads* **Sweden** *towards the cell.*

Sweden   'E ain bin back. Tol' yer yer wouldn't see 'im again.

Hoxton *leaves* **Sweden** *to put the sack on the table. She comes back to him and takes his arm to lead him to the cell. He knocks against the side of the door.*

Sweden   Door.

Hoxton *takes* **Sweden** *into the cell. She closes the door.* **Grace** *goes towards the ramp and stares at the ruins. She goes to a heap of rubble and takes out the heavy carrier hidden there. She clasps it to herself and begins to walk up and down between the ramp and the cell to make a little path.*

Seven

Early morning. The door is closed.

Grace *carries a container of her washed clothes. She puts it down by the wall. She hand-wrings a yellow dress and hangs it on the wall to dry. She does the same with a pink blouse.* **Sweden** *comes from the cell. He is in shirtsleeves and trousers and carries his coat. He closes the door and leans against the wall.*

Sweden   Bin light long? (*No response.*) Yer was up early. 'Eard yer washin. (*No response.*) 'Ow long yer bin with 'er.

Grace (*shrugs*)   Few days.

Sweden   Yer wearin yer dress? (*No response.*) Think I'll 'ave a sit at the table.

He wanders trying to find the table. **Grace** *hangs her washing.*

Ain waste meself no more. People spend their life crawlin round their shadow in the backyard 'n think they're world explorers. I did the same. Runnin 'n jumpin 'n got nowhere. Now only stupid things'll stop me – bumpin in t' walls – not the big things. I know what they are. I never bin so strong. Feel I got two bodies in the dark. Two lots a' arms 'n legs. Learn 'ow t' use 'em – stretch 'n see 'ow they work. Come with me. I'll take yer out a' this. Ain take that ol' bitch. She'd get sick 'n 'old me back. She's dirty – got that stink yer can't wash off. Let 'er rot! Ain got a dress like you. She 'ad 'er chance. She done this t' me! . . . We could go now before she's up. Put yer washin in a bag 'n go!

Grace Yer want a skivvy t' nurse yer. I grew up with that. Yer couldn't even get the grub. I'd 'ave t' feed both of us.

Sweden (*stands still*) Yer got yer dress on? Let me feel it. (*No response.*) Army'll flatten all this. Machines. Pulverise it t' powder. Wind spread it out like a white sheet. Yer can't stay 'ere. Yer couldn't live in the suburb. Grey streets – grey bread 'n water – kids born with grey 'air. (*He searches for the table again.*) I kill a dog. Am I near? Day after *this* – face still wet. Crep in a corner t' sleep – out a' pain. Dog come in. Felt its breath on me face. Stank a' some dead meal. Snufflin, wanted t' lick the wet. 'It it with a brick. Yell went straight up through the sky – no roof. Trap it 'gainst the wall. Must 'a bin a window 'igher up. 'Eard it jumpin up t' reach the light – yappin – slither down the wall – kep brickin it on the ground.

Hoxton *comes from the cell and stands in the doorway.*

Sweden Yeh – ain no silence like the dead. Sacrifice the dog so I could live – show I 'ad the strength. If they come t' bury me now I'd grab the sides a' the grave 'n drag the world in with me – I got a right. Don't want these things t' appen, want t' get away.

He reaches the table and drops his coat on the ground. He sits at the table and stretches out his arms with his palms flat on the table-top.

There's a land spread out like the top a' this table – where yer ain 'urt 'n 'ungry – there's no prison 'n army – 'n yer eat 'n drink 'n sleep t'gether. I'll lead yer there.

Grace Can't go.

Sweden Ain got no choice. This time we won't leave it late.

Grace I can't go out.

Hoxton Yer can't stay 'ere. Weren't no suburb when I come – nowhere else t' go. Army find me, I'm a 'armless ol' woman soft in the 'ead. They find you two – I'm shelterin yer! What'll they do t' me? I forgot I 'ad a daughter, forgot where I was. If the army'd took me away I wouldn't 'a notice. Now I got t' forget it again. Take 'im with yer – it's 'is choice. If 'e turns out a burden, leave 'im 'n go t' the suburb. 'E'll 'ave t' put up with it. 'E'll manage. In a few weeks we'll forget we met.

Grace   I can't go outside.

Hoxton   Why not?

Grace   It starts when I go near the edge.

Sweden   What does?

Grace (*to* **Hoxton**)   Let me stay. When I walk up 'n down the path I'm all right.

Grace *goes to a pile of rubble and takes out the heavy carrier hidden there.*

Grace   Look! (*She takes a tin-opener from the carrier.*) Yer tin-opener from the 'ouse. Remember? Yer turn the 'andle. (**Hoxton** *is blank.*) Take it! (*She demonstrates the handle.*) Turn it like this. It's yer tin-opener! (*She takes a child's feeding bowl from the carrier.*) Look what else I brung yer. My feedin bowl! Yer got me that before yer left – remember? Take it!

Hoxton   Not mine – never seen 'em –

Grace (*tries to give* **Hoxton** *the things*)   Take 'em! Yer must! I brought 'em! It was your surprise!

Hoxton   Nothin from there! Nothin!

She throws the bowl and tin-opener into the rubble. She takes a piece of brick from the carrier.

What's this?

She empties the carrier onto the table: a pile of broken bricks.

Look at it! Bricks from the 'ouse! She brung 'em t' throw at me!

Grace   No no –

Hoxton   She come 'ere t' kill me!

Grace   No no – I 'ad t' 'ave somethin –

Hoxton   She carried it for three years! The little bitch!

Grace   – somethin t' keep me walkin – so far t' come – so I set out t' punish yer for me sisters 'n brothers – throw bits a' their graves at yer – it was just an excuse – I never thought I'd find yer – 'ow could I? I'll do all the work! Anythin! Let me stay! I'll work 'n yer'll live in comfort!

Sweden   There's nothin out there!

Grace   There is! – the sky – why's the dust white? – Take yer things! Take yer things! Let me stay.

Grace *searches for the tin-opener and the pieces of broken bowl.*

Hoxton *and* **Sweden** *sit at the table. Silence.*

Sweden   What they do to us ain enough – we make it worse. The three of us could go. I could take yer even like this. Nothin's change – we sit 'ere. One a' yer should 'elp me.

Grace *finds pieces of broken bowl and tries to put them together.*

Grace   Broken. I'll mend it.

Sweden   "Oo done it? 'Oo done it?' Wouldn't believe me. Travelled me round with one eye. Watch 'em eat. Shake the dust out their kit. Order t' move on come. Packed up ready. Soldier come up t' me 'n said "Oo done it?' Took out 'is knife. Flic the blade. Told me 'Take it. Cut it out. Yer done the tag. Prove it.' Saw 'is face bent down, look at me curious. 'As t' know t' satisfy 'isself so 'e can tell authority. Says 'Else.' 'E orders the trucks t' start. Knew what 'e'd do if 'e took the knife back – 'n still do the eye. (*Crying without tears.*) 'S 'umiliation. 'Umiliation. 'Ope – 'ope no one 'as t' be like I was – there. Knife – this 'and – I stuck it in, I stuck it in, I stuck it in. Told me 'Twist – sharp' – this 'and – twist – the 'umiliation. When 'e got back t' the truck I 'eard 'em murmur murmur murmur murmur: they ain believe me, I done the tag. Waste. I couldn't die – out there a week – crawl – things growin in the rubbish brush me face – I ate – I couldn't stop meself – I ate.

Sweden *stands for a moment. Crashes to the wall and lurches along it grabbing the washing.*

Grace   Stop 'im – what's 'e doin? (*Drops the pieces of bowl, tries to pick them up.*) 'E's broken the – . Stop 'im!

Grace *tries to stop* **Sweden** *tearing the washing from the wall.*

Sweden   Where's yer bag! Get it! We're goin –

Grace   Don't! Don't!

Sweden   There's nothin there! Put it in yer bag! Nothin!

Sweden *throws washing into the ruins.*

Sweden   Get it! There's nothin! Go 'n get it!

Grace   Give me – !

Sweden *crashes up the ramp with a slip in his hands.* **Grace** *struggles to get it.* **Sweden** *pushes her into the ruins.*

Sweden   There's nothin! See!

Grace *tries to get back. She is too shocked to scream.* **Sweden** *half-carries and half-drags her away into the ruins out of sight.* **Hoxton** *sits at the table with the broken bricks. She stands and picks up the scattered washing. She puts it into the container.* **Grace** *runs in down the ramp. She walks up and down her path, trying to calm herself.*

Hoxton   Yer'll 'ave t' go out for food. I shan't feed yer.

Grace *covers her ears with her hands and tries to go on walking the path. She runs into the cell and slams the door behind her.* **Hoxton** *goes to the table and sits.*

Hoxton   They brought the kids – I never arst. Chase me. Yell. Chuck stones. I must've 'eld yer over me 'ead t' protect it. I didn't know. I found I was 'olding yer up – a stone 'it yer 'ead 'n yer said yer first word: mum-ma. 'Eard yer voice close t' me ear like a whisper in the yellin. I drop yer. Was sure yer was dead. So I left yer in the doorway. Since then yer life's been misery, yer tell me. 'Oo's t' blame? I don't build cities 'n put people in armies 'n prisons. If this is penance, I paid it. (*She brushes the broken bricks from the table with a movement of her forearm.*) Muck where I eat.

Sweden *comes on the horizon at the ramp. He is breathless.*

Sweden   Fetch me coat.

Hoxton   Why?

Sweden   Lost 'er. Worst could a' 'appen. Stand out there. She might come if she see me. Fetch me coat.

Hoxton *picks up* **Sweden**'s *coat and takes it to him.*

Sweden   'Er trouble ain out there. 'S you. She come all that way – all that time – follow yer apron strings through the ruins. Now she panic if yer ain there. Funny yer ain come with me, now yer stop 'er. I'm in a trap inside a trap. Yer bigger'n the army – yer occupy the world.

Hoxton   Don't come back. This place is bad for yer. Yer'll find someone.

Sweden   'Oo? Where shall I go?

Hoxton *lifts* **Sweden**'s *arm and puts it in the sleeve.*

Hoxton   Someone'll 'elp. (*She pulls the front of his coat together.*) I'll pack yer some fresh water 'n somethin t' eat.

She steps back. **Sweden** *reaches for her.*

Hoxton   The buttons.

She fastens the buttons. **Sweden** *puts an arm round her.*

None a' that – no time for –

Sweden (*grips her with one hand*)   Yer do me buttons – 'n send me out!

Hoxton Ow!

Sweden   Where to? Where'll I go? Bitch! Crawl through the bricks! Meet someone! Waitin! Didn't before! Na na na na! Bitch! Bitch! Bitch!

With his free hand he takes a knife from his pocket.

Hoxton No – no – I – (*Tries to calm him.*) Said yer couldn't stay – yer said –

Sweden   Soil me knife on yer! 'S too good! Bitch!

Hoxton Yes – yes – don't – (*They struggle. She calls to* **Grace***.*) 'Elp me! 'Elp me!

Sweden   Don't call 'er! She's gone! (*Shows the knife.*) Don't 'ave t' – with this! Tell me 'ow I live! Out there! No eyes! No face! Tell me! Suggest it! Suggest somethin I – I can take 'old of 'n – suggest 'ow I can live!

Hoxton   Me – me – I'll come – me – me –

Sweden   Liar! Ain you speak! – the knife! – little voice bounce off the knife 'n echo in yer gob! 'Lie t' 'im – lie all sorts – 'e 'as t' believe – 'e's blind!'

Hoxton   Me – me –

Sweden   Tell me! Always manage – cope – 'ave to! Now you do it! 'Elp me! I want t' live – not die there like 'n animal – a dog with no eyes! 'Elp me t' be 'uman! All I arst was 'elp! Yer could 'a led me! If I let go I'll never catch yer – get 'old a' –

Hoxton   Me – me – me – me –

Sweden   Liar! She must do better!

Hoxton   I'll come –

Sweden   Not that! Somethin else! I arst before! Yer didn't! Yer never never come! I don't know what t' do! If I kill 'er 'ow'd I live? What'd become a' me?

Hoxton   Me – me – me –

Sweden   No! (*Making pawing gestures in the air with the knife.*) That's pass! Gone! Finish!

Hoxton   Let me – (*Calls.*) 'Elp! 'Elp! Don't! Don't! I ain want t' urt – I'll 'elp! Let me – time t' think t' –

Sweden   No time! It's finish! Finish! Finish! They said yer eye – stick it, stick it – no time, no time – I did, I did –

Hoxton   No no I tol' yer – *me* – it's solve! –

Sweden (*groping*)   Where's the – where's the –

Sweden *makes random stabbing gestures with the knife. Rips* **Hoxton***'s clothes.*

Hoxton Me – me –

Sweden   Where's the – I tol' yer – if yer suggest – I wouldn't 'ave t' –

Hoxton (*clawing*)   'Elp! 'Elp!

Sweden   Tearin me eyes! Too late! They're out! 'Er breasts! Where's 'er breasts?

Sweden *holds* **Hoxton** *with one hand and searches for her breasts with the back of the other hand holding the knife.*

Hoxton   Me – me –

Sweden   Give me 'er breasts! Where's 'er breasts! Can't find 'er –

Sweden *slashes* **Hoxton***'s arm.*

Hoxton   No no no – please – give water –

Sweden *stabs* **Hoxton** *in the back.*

Sweden   What's that? What's – ? Arm? Arm? (*One hand holds the knife in* **Hoxton***'s back – the other hand gropes to find it.*) Back! In 'er back!

Hoxton   Ah. Ah. Ah.

Sweden *takes out the knife with one hand and puts it into his other hand – holds it over their heads. His free hand gropes.*

Sweden   Can't find the – must be – where's the – ? Breasts! Breasts! My eyes saw it – couldn't 'ide it then – yer breasts – yer breasts – where's yer breasts?

The back of **Hoxton***'s head has slipped into the crook of* **Sweden***'s* *arm. His knife is still over their heads. His free hand gropes for her breasts.*

Sweden Breasts! Breasts! That!

Sweden's *free hand reaches up and takes the knife from his other hand. He holds it a moment – then stabs* **Hoxton**'s *breast once.*

Hoxton Ah!

Sweden *That!*

Hoxton *slumps against* **Sweden**. *He struggles to hold her weight.*

Sweden Don't fall! Don't fall! 'Old 'er! Not fall!

Hoxton *drags* **Sweden** *to the ground. He falls on her. He drops the knife on the floor.*

Sweden Bitch! She took – knock me knife – (*He feels* **Hoxton** *with one hand.*) Face. Neck. Breast. Wet. Well, I 'it 'er. Blood. (*Licks his hand.*) Bitter, bitter.

Sweden *gropes for the knife with one hand.*

Hoxton Me – me –

Sweden (*patting the ground*) Patter – patter – 'baker man'. (*He finds the knife.*) Knife. 'Baker man bake me a cake.' (*Stops. He draws breath.*) Can't see. Pity. Pity. Is that death? – she weigh 'eavy. (*He shakes* **Hoxton** *once.*) 'As fast as yer can. If yer ain got a penny.'

Hoxton Me –

Sweden She say a word? Or did a sound come out 'er mouth? A ventriloquist for the dead. It's 'im. 'E's come back, come 'ere. Speak in 'er mouth. Let 'er tell me if she's dead? (*Listens a moment.*) I 'eard a little peep a' pain. Alive. Tell 'er t' say goodbye. (*Silence.*) 'E's gone. I'm alone again . . . Better dead than dyin – 'ave done with it. 'Old me 'and. Squeeze if yer – ? (*He holds* **Hoxton**'s *hand. Slight pause.*) Don't know – don't know is that a tremor when there's no life in the – ? Terrible not t' see what yer done, sit by it 'n not know. Shall I 'ave t' sit 'ere 'n cut it up like dead meat? (*He holds* **Hoxton**'s

jaw.) Tell me if yer dead. Yer said before. 'Me – me.' Lies.
Now tell the truth. I put yer in a condition where what's true
come out yer mouth even when yer open it t' lie. Where's 'er
tongue? Lick the knife. Lick it.

He holds the knife to **Hoxton**'s *teeth. She licks it. He stands.*

She lick it. Blade move in me 'and.

He walks away from **Hoxton** *as naturally as if he could see.*

Put the washin out. I made it dirty.

Hoxton   Me.

Sweden (*turns to face* **Hoxton**)   Not dead. (*He gropes back to her
and stamps on her.*) Dead? 'Ang the washin – come back 'n see.

He searches for the washing. He trips over the container. Sits on it.

When they took me eye me face twitch: sprinkle blood on me
arm. Saw the drops drop on the white shirt. Ran in me
mouth, breathe up me nose. 'Er blood is bitter, mine tasted
more a' sorrow.

*He stands and picks up the container. He crashes with it to the wall,
drops it and treads in the washing. He hangs pieces of it on the wall, the
ramp and the rubble – chaotically, upside down. He stops to throw a piece
of brick at* **Hoxton**. *Listens.*

No. Ain easy t' die. Show 'er the knife mate. If she see it she
shudders.

He raises the knife and stands in an archetypal image of threat.

Hoxton   Me.

Sweden *sits on the ground and cries tearlessly.*

Sweden   I try – but it's not done.

He crawls searching for **Hoxton**. *He stops – mechanically stabs the
ground five times.*

No use, no use.

He gropes and finds **Hoxton**'s *body. He turns his head on one side to
listen but does not lower it to her face. He lifts her to her feet.*

She can't 'ear the music.

He dances with **Hoxton** – *her body sways, her feet drag on the ground.*
Grig *comes onto the horizon at the ramp and stops. He wears his coat,*
his bag is on his shoulder.

Sweden Tra-ra. Tra-ra. Tra-ra. Why did I make 'er lick the
knife?

Hoxton *is dead.* **Sweden** *lets her body slide to the ground. He*
crashes to the table, lurches into it, sloshes water into a bowl and washes
the knife. **Grig** *puts down his bag on the ramp and walks towards the*
body. He stops. He picks up a wet slip lying near it and stands with it
hanging in his hand. **Sweden** *hears a noise and turns to it.*

Sweden . . . Not dirty it again . . .

He puts the knife in his coat pocket. He gropes towards the body. When he
is near he crouches to search with his hands – crawls a few paces –
reaches out and touches the slip in **Grig**'s *hand. He feels the resistance.*

Sweden Yer come back.

Grig *lets the slip go.* **Sweden** *makes a vague gesture with the slip and*
drops it on the body.

Sweden Is she dead – somewhere . . . ? I tol' yer, nothin t'
scare yer out there. Was '*er* – scare t' lose 'er. Yer'd 'a clung t'
'er till yer was dead. Why I kill 'er. Yer can't stay 'ere: this is
'er restin place . . . where she won't rest. She'll fill it with 'er
terror. All 'oo stay 'ere she'll turn in t' 'er ghost. She draws
people to 'er. Sits by 'er tap 'n waits. 'Ow many she bury in
the ruins? Talk t' me. 'Ad a man 'ere when I come. 'E was an
evil man. 'Er mate. 'E try t' screw 'er before me. 'E couldn't
screw the lid on a coffin. Jealous when I join in. Out-classed. I
seen 'im off. She still waited for 'im. 'E was 'er skivvy. Wash
the pans, get the grub. "Ave t' cut the brambles back – takin
over.' This place reeks of itself but 'e was at 'ome in it. When I
kill 'er I 'eard 'is voice. 'E ain 'ere – 'e's dead. She brung 'im
back as a ghost. Ghosts make the best ventriloquists. Talk t'
me, don't punish me. Let me feel yer dress. Yer ain 'ad a life.
Ain grab yer share. Yer 'eard me in 'er bed. Knew yer was
listenin. I rammed in 'arder t' make yer wet. Yer 'eard 'er

holla – yer was listenin t' yerself come. Never see yer. Learn yer bit by bit. Yer breasts. The crinkly 'airs. When I 'ad blackouts I drew signs in the dirt with a stick. I'll draw 'em on yer with me tongue. Draw in the 'ole between yer legs – in the wet. We'll rattle the stars. Talk t' me. I know what it is – yer still scare I can't manage. Watch me get yer water.

He tries to find the table. He gropes in the wrong direction. **Grig** *takes off his coat and puts it down with his bag. He puts the body over his shoulder and carries it into the cell. He shuts the door.*

Sweden (*groping*)   Watch me . . . Yer watchin? (*He bumps into the wall.*) Don't 'elp, let me find it. (*He shuffles towards the table. He knocks over a box. He sets it upright, sits on it and puts his head in his hands.*) Must get away . . . go, go . . . Why did I make 'er lick the knife? (*He stands. Gropes and finds the table. He leans bent over it.*) Won't knock things in our place – know where it is. (*He finds the water container and a mug, fills it and holds it out.*) Drink. (*Pause.*) Yer still can't make up yer mind. I can feel it: a little doubt.

Grig *comes from the cell. He leaves the door open. He walks halfway to the table and stops.*

Sweden   I couldn't stay 'ere from the start. Ain tol' no one why: they knew 'n anythin went wrong – then the worst would 've 'appen. I nick cars – with the gang, then on me jack. I needed t' burn. Fire. Showrooms full a' cars. Nothin else. Splash petrol on the walls. Pour it on the office furniture. The stink a' wet petrol – yer don't know 'ow it feels. Go outside. All 'ave these big windows. Light a rag – chuck it – big sigh 'n the 'ole place roars up in flames. Yer don't know till yer done it.

Grace *stands in the doorway.* **Grig** *gestures her to be quiet.*

Sweden   Driv off – see the burn in the drivin mirror – 'ole car lit up inside. Driv up a 'ill – anywhere 'igh – sit 'n watch in the quiet. Still. Little red pimple in the night – cars inside it – white-'ot frames – sheets a' glass drop on the concrete – seethin rubber – cremation. One night the army nick me sittin there. Ain know I done the fire – that's miles away. But it 'as t' follow. Every showroom burnt goes in the computers. Every

showroom – one nick car. One night I'm sittin in it. The
computers never stop day 'n night. Churn through the facts t'
sort the patterns, find the pictures. They'd sort out a desert 'n
make a picture a' the sand. Yer walk in the ruins, set a'
footprints in the dust, wind blew 'em out years ago – the
computer 'll tell 'em where yer walked. That's 'ow we live.
Old lag in prison – they work out some little thing 'e'd done as
a kid – 'e cry when they kill 'im cause 'e couldn't remember
what it was – 'is beard was soppin wet. I wish there weren't no
stories, I wish we weren't in 'em – don't you? Only time
before they work out I done all the fires – in the *ghetto*: what's
the tariff for that? They'd make up a new one. That's why I
'ad t' get out a' prison – 'ave t' get out a' 'ere. (*Mug.*) Take it. I
pour it for yer.

Grig *takes the mug and puts it on the table.*

Sweden   Ain drink.

Grig *paddles his finger in the water.*

Sweden   Good. Finish? More?

Grig *puts on his coat and puts his bag on his shoulder.* **Sweden** *pours
himself a mug of water and drinks.* **Grig** *goes up the ramp. He turns –
he and* **Grace** *look at each other. He gestures to her to go in the cell. She
goes in and shuts the door.* **Grig** *goes out into the ruins.* **Sweden** *puts
down the mug and wanders to find the body.*

Grace (*in the cell*)   We'll wait before we leave.

Sweden (*stops*)   Wait? I tol' yer – 'ave t' go – army know
where I am –

Grace (*in the cell*)   A few days.

Sweden   – come straight 'ere – 'n you say wait!

Grace (*in the cell*)   Get yer eyes right before we go.

Sweden   My eyes ain change.

Grace (*in the cell*)   Dust get in 'em.

Sweden   'Elp me!

Grace (*in the cell*)   Ain go till yer eyes 're right. I 'ave t' cope when they go wrong.

Sweden *finds the slip he took from* **Grig**. *He runs it through his fingers. He drops it.*

Sweden (*to himself*)   Why did I make 'er lick the knife?

He goes to the door and leans on it.

(*To himself.*) The three of us should 'a go.

Grace (*in the cell*)   What yer doin?

Sweden (*to himself*)   That would 'a bin best . . . We couldn't.

Grace (*in the cell*)   Open the door.

Sweden   Where's the body?

Grace (*in the cell*)   Open the door.

Sweden   Where's the body?

Grace (*in the cell*)   There.

Sweden (*to himself*)   Why? Why? Why? . . . (*To* **Grace**.) I looked.

Grace (*in the cell*)   Open it.

Sweden   Ain there.

Grace (*in the cell*)   The washin's trod on.

Sweden   Where is it?

Grace (*in the cell*)   I want t' wash it.

Sweden   Where's the body?

Grace (*in the cell*)   Open it!

Sweden *opens the door. He catches* **Grace** *as she comes out.*

Grace   Look at it trod in the dirt!

Sweden   Where is it?

Grace (*turns* **Sweden**)   There.

Sweden No I looked.

Grace If yer can't trust me –

Sweden Don't punish me!

Grace Let go!

Sweden They treat yer like a child – tell yer what they like! Come with me!

Grace Stop it!

Sweden Yer promise!

Grace Yer trust me first!

Sweden Take me to it!

Grace Ain go with yer if yer like this! All the time 'Don't go that way – go the other way – I want that way!' Never get nowhere!

Sweden It ain there! 'As she walk? Is she alive?

Grace Stop it!

Sweden What's she look like?

Grace Let go! Yer seen the dead!

Sweden '*Er*! – what's she look like?

Grace Like all the dead!

Sweden What's it like t' look at yer dead mother?

Grace Let go a' me!

Sweden 'Oo's bin 'ere?

Grace No one.

Sweden Someone's bin!

Grace I tol' yer –

Sweden The body's move.

Grace I 'ad enough a' –

Sweden   Yer ain move it.

Grace   Why not?

Sweden   Yer drag it?

Grace   Ain answer no –

Sweden   I'd a' 'eard!

Grace   Let go!

Sweden   Why didn't yer arst –

Grace   Let me go!

Sweden   – me t' 'elp?

Grace   Wouldn't let yer touch 'er! Put yer 'ands on –

Sweden   Then she's move?

Grace   No!

Sweden   Yer said she –

Grace   Stop it! Stop it! Yer need me! Yer a blind man – blind cripple! Yer can't live out there without me! If I go I ain be bully – push around –

Sweden   It's 'im – it's 'im! 'E's the only one 'oo'd come! 'E knows she's 'ere! – She won't tell me! 'Oo can I trust? All I could 'a done – the laughin, jokes, the promise – ! They should 'a kill me! They blind me – send me out t' wander – scare 'armless people! – why should I be used like this?

Grace   Let go a' me. I ain say 'oo come 'n go – ain my fault.

Sweden *takes out his knife.*

Grace   Yer can't. Yer can't get away without me.

Sweden   'Ow long was 'e 'ere? Did 'e 'ear 'bout the fires? (*Panic.*) 'E's 'ere now! 'E's 'ere! There! There! Grinnin by the wall! It's 'im (*He drags* **Grace** *forwards a few steps, makes sweeping gestures with the knife at the wall.*) Come on! Come 'ere! I'll kill 'er! Slow while yer watch! Look at 'is eyes poppin! 'Elp 'er! – 'E won't! Stand 'n watch it! – She's dead a' fright! Ain last like that ol' one! . . . I saw 'im. I swear I saw 'is shadow move

along the wall . . . No, worse than that, I saw 'im in me 'ead.
(*He pauses.*) We're alone? (*No answer.*) Alone.

Grace Yes.

Sweden 'Ow long was 'e 'ere? Y'ain blind, ain got the
privilege a' ignorance.

Grace Don't know.

Sweden *lets* **Grace** *go. She goes to the ramp – goes up and down on
it trying to get out but can't.*

Sweden 'E knows I done the fires. Tol' 'im to 'is face. Gone
t' the army t' tell 'em. After 'is little ceremonials: carry the
body t' show respect. Expect 'e put a blanket on 'er. I kill 'er,
'e's worse: 'e pretends we're still 'uman this late, in this place.
It was 'im the first time. 'E tol' the army 'bout the tag. Thass
'ow they pick me up so quick. They knew where t' look. 'Ow
can 'e walk round with all that 'ate in 'im? Yer'd think 'e'd
burn a 'ole in the ground 'n sink in it. 'E did this t' me: I've
track it down t' 'im. This time the army'll let 'im choose the
tariff. Or will they make 'im beg for it?: 'Me – me – me.'

*He stamps to the cell – crashes into the wall – slithers along it – falls
through the doorway.* **Grace** *goes to her path and walks up and down on
it. The sound of breaking in the cell.* **Sweden** *comes out soaking wet.
He holds out his left hand – it is bright red.*

Trip on the body.

*He lurches to the table. He finds the water carrier and knocks it over. It
empties.*

Rid a' that. (*Hears* **Grace** *on the path.*) Can't take yer with me.
Yer could lead me t' the army. Can't leave yer. Yer could
follow me 'n tell. This 'can't, can't' could be a trick.

He lunges at **Grace**. *She runs up the ramp and crouches at the top.*
Sweden *scrambles after her and catches her.*

Bird flutterin in the window – up 'n down till it sits 'n shakes in
the corner. All yer body'll be a bruise – knockin 'gainst nothin.
They'll say I done it.

Grace   Let me go t' your place – live there like yer said.

Sweden   Yer'd see! Everywhere's the same for you – like this place.

Grace   Tie me eyes. Bind 'em with a cloth.

Sweden   She's forgot! – *I'm blind*! We'd be two kids lost in the ruins!

Grace   Don't kill me! – we'll live where yer said!

Sweden   Yes live with yer dress. Give it t' me, let me 'old it. (*He wipes his face in her dress.*) Yes . . . 'Ave t' be angry now. 'As t' be done in anger! (*He rips her dress.*)

Grace   No I done nothin – she 'urt yer – not me – 'urt no one –

Sweden   Make me angry! Can't do it else! 'E tol' yer! 'Keep 'im for the army! Put 'im in bed!' – yer poor bitch! – 'Give 'im water! – keep 'im till they come!'

Grace   No no nothin –

Sweden Look at me face! (*He presses her hands to his face.*) Feel it! Black! Me eyes on fire! 'Ot! 'Ot! 'Ot! 'E tol' yer! Now yer'll be punish!

Grace   Nothin – nothin –

Sweden   When yer dead I'll throw yer in the ruins!

Grace   No no – don't want the light t' see me!

Sweden   Tell me it's wrong! Wrong! (*He stabs her.*) Wrong! (*He stabs her.*) Wrong! (*He stabs her.*) Is she dead? A trick? Knife still. Dead. It was wrong.

He touches the dress with his right hand – lifts his hand, it is as red as his left hand. He rubs the tips of the fingers of his right hand against the thumb and nods. He points to **Grace** *with his right hand.*

'Ers.

He points vagnely at the cell with his left hand.

'Ers.

He stands.

Scorch earth now. When it's empty I'll be safe. What time is it? Army everywhere. Trucks breed like ants.

He gropes his way up the ramp. **Grace**'s *arms slither feebly over the ground gathering dust. She lifts her hands – the dust sifts onto her.* **Sweden** *gropes his way into the ruins.*

Eight

Grace *lies on the ground.* **Grig** *comes onto the ramp threshold. He is in his travelling coat with his bag on his shoulder. He sees* **Grace** *and sits on the ramp.*

Grig   Winded. Took it sensible but it wore me out. 'Ad t' do it. Army got 'im or soon will.

He comes down the ramp towards **Grace**. *He stops before he reaches her.*

Ah chriss ah chriss.

He goes into the cell. Pause. He comes out. **Grace** *turns her head towards him and grins.*

Grig   Yer awake! I thought – . Why yer lying there? Why yer grin? The pipe's tore off the wall. We 'ave t' go. Army owe me but they don't pay their debts. We'll go a few steps each day. When yer ready we'll walk t' the place 'e said of 'n live there. If we can't find it we'll go t' the suburb 'n live as we're directed. We'll be t'gether. I didn't know it could be so simple. In there. I took yer 'ands from yer ears – a few words 'n I knew we'd live t'gether. (*Crouches to touch* **Grace**'s *dress.*) O god that black's blood. (*He supports* **Grace** *on his arm.*) It's all right. Yer'll live. Yer'll live. I'm 'ere. Move. It'll be all right. Move – yer'll live. Water.

He goes towards the cell, remembers, goes to the table and searches.

Must be, must be. (*He finds the empty container. Goes on searching.*) Let it, let it. (*He finds the bowl in which* **Sweden** *washed his knife.*) Filthy! (*He brushes flies from the bowl.*) Filthy! Vile! (*He throws away the water.*) Water in me bag – if there's still a drop . . . !

He goes to the ramp and takes a bottle from his bag. It is empty.

Hn.

He goes to **Grace** *and rubs her wrists and arms.*

Don't die, don't die. Not now. (*He stands and shows* **Grace** *the empty bottle.*) Fetch water – see? Come back, ain leave yer. If she thinks I'll leave she'll die a' despair. Make a sign t' me! (*No response. He goes to* **Grace** *and nurses her, rubs her neck and shoulders.*) Don't die. 'Ow long is it that – ? Blood flakes on me 'and. 'E done it when I left. Bin 'ere so long . . . ! 'Arf a day t' the tap – yer'd be dead when I got back. An 'our ago there was water. Swill it t' get 'ere quick – n' see this! A cup a' water – 'n all the past – the wrongs – be wash away! I rinse me mouth 'n spat it in the dust! Why did I leave 'er with 'im? Why? Why? I could 'a kill 'im! (*Feels her breast.*) 'Er 'eart! Faint – feel it! Don't die! Fool – yer 'and tremble – yer felt that! 'Er breast's cold. Still beautiful under the crack blood. Why'd she grin? The dyin grin when it's the end. She 'eard a sound, tried t' move – 'n died. I come 'n kill 'er.

He stands.

Walked. Always walked. Walked t' where I was a boy. Gone. The 'ouses buried with the furniture still in 'em. Yer should 'a died a while ago – yer lived. P'raps my wife's alive. I'll go t' see. If she won't share the room with me – I'll try t' make it work. Be patient. Be what I am.

He goes to the ramp. He picks up his bag and puts the bottle in it. He sees a few stones on the ramp.

Two – three – four. (*He stops counting.*) Threw stones t' scare the dogs off while she die.

He goes to **Grace***, kneels and raises her arm from the elbow. He props it up and puts a stone in her hand.*

Grip. If I can get yer fingers – . Dogs see it. Remember.

He scrapes a few stones into a heap beside her. Her arm is propped, her hand holds a stone. **Grig** *goes out up the ramp.*

Nine

Grace's *body has gone. Where the dogs dragged it a few scraps of her dress caught on debris.* **Sweden** *half-sits and half-lies on his side facing the cell. His legs are drawn up under his coat-flaps. Patches of grey show through the dirt on his face. His eyes are deeper sunk. Filth and droppings matt his mop of hair. His hands are scraped raw.*

Grig *comes to the ramp threshold. His clothes are dirtier and more torn. He is covered in a day's dust.*

Sweden   'Oo is it? Ain army boots? What yer want?

Grig   Thought it was empty.

Sweden   I'll kill yer. (*One hand feebly claws at the dust.*) Why did yer go t' em? Twice! (*No response.*) Didn't yer!

Grig   Yes.

Grig *sits on the ramp.*

Sweden   Kill ain enough! (*His hands move in the air as if he's searching. His legs jerk.*) If I can't find a spade I'll scrape the ground with me spoon 'n bury yer. Come back each day 'n dig yer up 'n play with yer bones like a dog.

Sweden *straightens his coat-flaps and falls asleep.*

Grig   Walked t' find me wife. Weren't there. Took away. No record, no one could tell me. She's dead. Why they let us walk? They must get tired a' killin. Make us wait. Lost without us. When they've kill us they'll look for us. Walk through the ruins callin our names – then sit 'ere 'n wait.

(*He sees* **Sweden** *is asleep.*) Sleep.

He takes a bottle of water from his bag and moves towards **Sweden**. **Sweden** *wakes.*

Grig (*water*)   'Ere.

Sweden   Won't kill yer, army do a better job. They got yer tariff! Yer 'elp 'em – they won't forgive that!

Grig (*removes bottle cap*)   Drink this water.

Sweden   Go away! Go away! Choke on yer water! Choke on it!

Grig   I put it on the ground.

Sweden   Why did yer go t' – ? No, no point in arstin yer t' – . Twice! Twice! Why did yer go?

Grig   T' save the girl.

Sweden   I kill 'er cause a' you! It was wrong! Wrong! Wrong! I shouldn't 'a kill 'er! Should 'a let 'er live – 'n blind 'er –

Grig   Blind?

Sweden   – walk with 'er in 'n out a' hell 'n not be 'urt any more.

Grig   Get up. Yer ain draw lines in the dirt when yer was asleep. None a' all that ain true. Get on yer feet. I'll take yer t' yer place – the place yer said –

Sweden   There ain no place! No place there! Just this place I come to!

Grig   We'll find it. Get up.

Sweden   Keep off!

Grig *goes to* **Sweden** *to lift him.*

Grig   We'll walk there – I'll lead yer – take yer –

Sweden   Yer can't! Yer can't! Yer can't!

Sweden *pulls back his coat-flaps. His legs have been severed at the ankles and the ends bound in thick rags.*

Sweden   Mutilated. Army.

Grig *stares in silence.*

Sweden   Stumps.

Grig   They cut – ?

Sweden   It's dark. Went dark when they took me eyes. Keeps gettin darker.

Sweden *falls asleep.* **Grig** *walks away.*

Grig (*shock, flat*)   Don't leave 'im. Don't leave 'im. Stay 'ere.

Sweden (*asleep*)   Wanted t' 'ide – shamed a' what people do. Driv a truck over 'em. Easier t' 'ack off. Driv me 'ere – push me off the back – fell – that's when I learnt 'ow I 'ave t' live now.

Sweden *wakes.*

Grig   I won't leave yer.

Sweden   Get out! Yer done this!

Grig   No – !

Sweden   Yer done this t' me! Get out! Get out!

Grig   No! No! I can't! Can't walk away! Let me stay! Please! I'll 'elp yer – feed yer – carry yer – wash yer legs! I can't walk away 'n leave yer sat in the dark! I can't live if yer crawlin in the dirt – ! Let me carry yer – (*He tries to lift* **Sweden**.) – take yer t' yer place yer – !

Sweden   No! No!

He pulls away – tries to stand – totters on his stumps – two or three steps – a grotesque dance. He screams at each step. Falls.

Ah. Ah. Ah.

Grig   Innocent! Innocent! Innocent! Innocent! Innocent! This can't be – ! Yer can't be treated like a – ! This can't be done t' no one! No! No! No! Such – such – this can't be done! Let me carry yer! Share it!

Sweden (*dragging*)   No!

Grig   Share it!

Sweden   No!

Grig   Carry yer! Let me!

Sweden   No!

Grig   Let me! Let me!

Sweden   No! No! Never! It's done!

He drags himself away from **Grig**. *He stops for breath.*

'Ead clear now. Know what t' do. Live like a dog. Scraps,
sleep by the wall. Follow the other dogs. Can't keep up, don't
matter – 'ear their voices in the distance, they'll guide me.
Won't chase me off, I'll smell like a dog. Forget what I was
born. If I can't, if I 'ave t' remember I'm 'uman – I'll drown in
a puddle.

He crawls towards the ruins, away from the ramp. He stops for breath.

If I can't find a puddle I'll dig a 'ole with me spoon 'n piss in it
'n drown.

He crawls a little further.

Grig   I'll follow yer. In the distance.

Sweden *stops for breath. His head is bowed.*

Sweden   I could drown in a spoon.

Grig   Never let yer out a' me sight. Yer won't know. Come
when yer can't go no more.

Sweden   Army'll take yer away. Yer won't be there.

Sweden *crawls into the ruins.* **Grig** *stands and round him the site
changes into the grey room.*

Ten

*The grey room encloses the whole site. The floor is smooth and bare. The
walls are light grey and faintly luminous. The same pale luminosity fills
the room. It is empty except for* **Grig** *and a stone block in the middle.*

The stone block is like an empty pedestal. The top is about a foot higher than the seat of an ordinary chair. It is almost a cube but a little higher than it is wide.

Grig *wears an institutional smock. It is almost the colour of the stone. His legs and feet are bare.*

Grig *stands behind the stone and a little to the left of it. The distance between him and the stone is about one-and-a-half times the length of his body. He has stood there a long time. He stares across the stone at nothing. He moves a few steps to his right – all his movements are slow. He stops. His face turns to his right and he stares at nothing. His head lowers a little. Pause. His head lifts. Pause. He moves back to where he was. His face turns to his left and he stares at nothing. His face turns to stare across the stone at nothing. He takes a few more steps to his right. He stops. He seems to stare down at his body for a moment. He stares across the stone again at nothing.*

Silence.

He howls. He howls. He howls. He howls. He howls. He howls. He howls.

Silence.

He stares sightlessly over the top of the stone. His stare shifts a little to his left.

He stops.

Silence.

This is the scene of the seven howls.

The Site

It was said feed the people and they will be just
The age of peace will begin
It is not so
It is just that we should eat but eating will not make us just
We will starve for justice
Without justice our hunger to eat grows till we devour the
  earth
Look there is the man who sits on the ground and devours his
  own grave
But there is no justice
There is the machine
It meets our needs so there are no needs
Our hunger grew and to feed it the machine devoured the
  earth
The rivers dried – the seas became sewers where rats swam
    and ate fish – storms blew away mountains – uprooted the
      forests – the trees clutched the earth with their claws –
        cities were crushed into trenches of rubble where
          cannibals bred their children to eat – and the storm
            swept the human dust into columns and howled
              with the hunger that was in them
The machine said let them eat food
The machine was our hunger for food
The machine feeds us
Those it does not feed are hungry for food and justice
But the fed do not seek justice
The fed are hungrier than the unfed – that is the law of the
  machine
The fed steal from the unfed – that is also the law of the
  machine
And as they steal from another's plate they are afraid the other
  will steal from their plate
You cannot have your freedom at the cost of another's
  repression or create justice by rage
Once tyrants recast history but now there were no tyrants – no
  history – no need – no origin
There was nowhere

Nowhere is the site of the machine

The machine is our hunger

When people came to be fed the machine ate them

The machine worked as before but ate its own product

The machine took away need

On that day every mind in the world was emptied – made
    blank

The emptiness lasted a second or hours or ever

Who can tell how long it lasted when there is no past –
    nowhere – no origin?

What is the moment when the mind is emptied?

When fear locks the mind into a moment and food falls from
    the gaping mouth and hunger grows?

The more they ate the hungrier they grew and the more afraid

There was no past – no future – nowhere – no origin

The dead do not need their skeleton and in the moment of
    emptiness the living did not need their flesh

Humankind died

So the prisons were built

Then the houses were knocked down – not in rage but
    because they were an impediment to running prisons

The administration administered nowhere and people were an
    encumbrance to the administration – an inconvenience to
    the army

The dead were shut in a vast megasuburb that had no centre –
    they howled as their way of talking to themselves

The hungry were shut in a vast prison city called Priscit – as
    punishment they were made to laugh

The rich shut themselves in a ghetto – they played with toys
    that taught them to hate – they were mandarins of
    hooliganism

Imagination is more logical than reason

Reason clones facts and accumulates know-how so that
    science may make our ignorance useful

When reason destroys imagination we go mad

Imagination creates madness or humanness

It creates humanness when it desires reason

While there was still a past – and future and origin –

imagination created the Devil and God to help us to be
   human
The Devil came first and created God
Imagine the terrible loneliness of the Devil – he created God
   to comfort him as he sat in his prison
Prison is the House of God and a God can have no other
   house
In the past we needed madness to help us to be sane
But when the machine took away need and created the
   hunger that is greater than any greed taught by the Devil –
      too great to be sated by God – there was no reason for
         God and the Devil and they became icons of the
            insane
Now the desert mirage is not an oasis of brooks and date-
   palms
It is the gallows – the pit – the shadows chained to the wall
The man sits on the ground and vomits into his grave
I will record it as simply as I can
Reason and imagination are two practices
Together they are the paradox which we live
Learn a skill and practise it to make what is beautiful and seek
   what is just – that is what the wise do
But with our life it is otherwise: when we have learnt to live we
   die
We set out in one direction and travel in another
It is as if we pass our life backwards
We climb an abyss and know we must fall
Our children are our death
We work to build a just house but our children must destroy it
   to search the ruins for justice
How can we live in this paradox?
How can we turn catastrophy into freedom?
How can we turn the crime into justice?
How can we reverse all laws in this way?
It is easy: the reverse of all laws is justice
The just man reverses all laws so that he may be himself
The fall is a stage in the journey – part of the tragic drama
In your life there is a day in which you meet yourself coming
   towards you in the street

It is the messenger you sent ahead to enquire how you should
    live
The messenger will greet you and say you must die
But it is the messenger who will die – you will attend and weep
    but can do no more
Only remember this: do not kill the messenger
If you do your imagination will die
A reactionary lives in a coffin with a mirror set in the lid
Most people pass their lives as prisoners laying siege to their
    prison
If you kill yourself when you meet yourself in the street it will
    be as it was in the past – your children will fetch your body
    and wash it but will not take it for burial
They will set it at the head of your table and bang their hands
    together and say we are hungry let us eat
And your children will be served as meat and drink at your
    table
You will eat and drink and die of your hunger
One day humankind died
There was no future – nowhere – no origin
No one could meet themselves coming towards them on the
    street
The machine sounded a siren for the day of resurrection
The coffins were sprung open and from each there stepped a
    stranger who had not been buried in it
Water had no reflection
The universe is a mistake we must learn to live with
The young need not murder the elders because they are born
    or the elders imprison the young for murder
Each generation deceives itself in its own way but learns the
    same truths
It is the logic of reason that when two and two are added
    together they are four
We learn this and prosper
But the unjust are driven to fear by hunger and in anger they
    call the four five and then the machine is mad
Do not give God machines to play with – he kills us with toys
Each grain of sand is the universe because without the
    universe there could be no grain of sand

If the grain vanished it would take the universe with it
Eternity is in a second because without eternity there could be
  no second
That is also the logic of reason
Then how many naked bodies are in the heap at the camp
  gates?
Twenty? Fifty? One hundred?
All humankind are in the heap – that is the logic of
  imagination
All who are or have been or will be lie in the gateway
They are in you and you in them – the naked and broken and
  whole
Their hunger is your hunger and your hunger is theirs
If you do not seek justice those who come after you will bear
  your pain and die of your wounds
And then you must bear their pain or die of hunger
The hunger for justice makes us human
Justice is the reverse of all laws

The Swing

A Documentary

Author's Note

The end of Scene Two of *The Swing* should be played as a
farce. The farce begins when Skinner says 'Not till the day I
die'. Because the scene begins quietly and realistically the
actors may find it difficult, in earlier rehearsals, to play the end
as farce. Nevertheless they must, with all the stylised speaking
and mechanical movements that go with farce. Why? Because
I want to show that the white characters are not passive
victims of tragic fate. They may not fully understand who they
are and what they do, but they are still responsible for both
these things. They murder on one special day because every
day they are greedy, arrogant, exploitative and – as all such
people must be – afraid. They commit their final great
injustice because even when they sit quietly on their porches
and watch the sun go down their lives are rooted in injustice.
In this way they create their own fate, turning themselves into
monsters.

Like many people in the twentieth century – like whole
nations and classes – they may one day stand in bewilderment
before what they have done. But at least they can understand
and be responsible for the injustice of their daily life and their
city: not to say when they oppress and exploit that 'that is
human nature' but that 'that is what *I* do' . If they enjoy the
benefits of an unjust society, and seek their security in
maintaining it, then they are responsible for the great
injustices that always follow from little injustices. Those who
sniggered at the broken windows of a Jewish shop in 1933 are
responsible for Auschwitz. They made the building of
Auschwitz possible – just as they did the destruction of their
own homes. We, too, are responsible for the injustice of our
daily life – and therefore for the nuclear bomb sites that our
leaders build. Those bombs will be used to destroy our
enemies and ourselves unless we change our society so that we
may live justly.

In the end injustice always leads to catastrophe. That is the
lesson of history. Our species has no other alternative: either
we live justly or we destroy ourselves. The world no longer

provides a secure refuge for the unjust, we have made our
weapons too strong and our societies too interrelated for that.

Why do people passively accept Auschwitz and nuclear
death camps? How can our judgements be made so warped
and our sensibilities so deadened? It's partly because the
injustice, aggression and exploitation that we accept in small
things blinds us to the nature of the great injustices that they
lead to. The great catastrophies of history are the products of
people's ordinary lives, of the way they earn a living and
maintain their societies: *products* of that ordinariness, not
terrible aberrations that occur when things go wrong. That's
why 'ordinary decent people' do on occasions such terrible
things. They can only avoid responsibility for these by
changing their daily lives – and that means changing the
society in which they live: whatever anyone does to himself he
hasn't changed his life till he's changed his society.

So the killers in *The Swing* are responsible for what they do
and we won't help anyone to understand how they could do it
by trying to give their lives the dignity of tragedy.

The formal farce ends with the end of Scene Two. The play
then returns to realism. True, what happens then is a sort of
farce – but it is not farce used, as at the end of Scene Two, to
explain and analyse what is shown. The events in Scene Three
happened, in essentials, in life, and are neither tragedy nor
farce. They are the farcical-tragedy of the ordinary and must
be played as realism.

An actress who based her performance on a character's
psychology might try to find the meaning of Greta's madness
in the imagery she uses when she goes mad. This wouldn't
help the actress to understand Greta. Most acting is still based
on the idea of the soul, or psyche, as being like a white rabbit
a magician pulls out of a hat; or on the idea that a person can
be compared to a mysterious house out of the door of which
people are always coming but into which no one ever goes.
But I write on the premise that people don't live in a certain
way because they have a certain psychology but that they
develop a psychology that enables them to live in the way they
do. Character is the subjective habits we develop to enable us
to live according to the ideas we accept as useful and true. You

don't change people by changing their characters but their ideas.

Americans don't go to psychoanalysts because they have psychologies that prompt them to. They go because they think their problems are less pressing and fundamentally different from that of a man dying of starvation. They are wrong. Men don't live by bread alone and whatever else it is they live by – Americans are starving to death for lack of that. A man dying of lack of bread will tell you that he doesn't have a personal problem but a social one. He has no food because his society cannot (or will not) feed him. Thus those who starve for lack of bread know their situation better than the affluent know theirs: Americans still think their psychological problems are personal and not social. They go to church to be 'born again' not because they have a psyche, still less a soul, that prompts them to. They go because they don't want to change their way of life ('the American way') and are born into a 'new life' so that they can go on living the old one in the same old, American way. A sort of cultural schizophrenia which can never be the basis of justice.

Greta's imagery shows she's mad but not, except in a very superficial way, why she's mad. To understand why she's mad you must return to what I said earlier. She's driven mad by the ordinary, daily life of her town. If we watch Skinner behind his counter, if we watch him writing in his ledgers and locking-up his shop to go to church, we can tell there will be mad people in his town. Greta becomes mad because she has no economic power and this makes her vulnerable. It means that she has less social activity to disguise her madness in – in the way that Skinner does so well. She is neither a worker nor an employer and so there are few people it pays to share her views of the world. This means that they have little chance of being accepted as ordinary, normal views. So she is vulnerable and insecure and when in time the injustice of her town produces – as it must – catastrophe, she goes certifiably mad. But Skinner's madness is greater: he is politically mad, he suffers from the farcical-tragic madness of the ordinary in an unjust society. He is socially mad. All the other white people in the play share this madness. Fred as much as the others – as

Paul could easily point out. I don't know whether Greta was raped in the yard. I know the good, honest, decent, ordinary white citizens of her town destroyed her mind.

(1976)

The Swing was first presented by the Ambiance Lunch-Hour Theatre Club at Inter-Action's Almost Free Theatre, London, on 22 November 1976. The cast was as follows:

Paul (28)	Don Warrington
Skinner (53)	Glyn Owen
Ralph Skinner (17)	Kevin Elyot
Stagehand 1 (42)	Ron Travis
Stagehand 2 (19)	Garry Whelan
Stagehand 3 (26)	Kenneth Ryan
Fred (26)	Roddie Smith
Photographer	Gilbert Vernon
Clown	Henry Woolf
Helen Kroll (54)	Liz Smith
Greta Kroll (32)	Illona Linthwaite

Directed by Jack Emery
Designed by Norman Coates
Lighting by Suresa Galbraith
Sound by Pete Mount
Wardrobe by Monica Strauss

The action takes place in Livermore, Kentucky, USA, in 1911.

Scene One

A theatre. A simple swing of wood and rope hangs motionless from the flies. It has been decorated with bright paper flowers and bunting. There is a pile of props – cut-out trees and birds, folded hangings and so on.

Paul *comes on from the wings. He is black.*

Paul   In the fall of nineteen eleven in Livermore Kentucky a blackman was charged with murder. He was taken to the local theatre and tied to a stake on stage. The box office sold tickets accordin to the usual custom: the more you paid the better you sat. The performance was this: people in the pricey seats got to empty their revolvers into the man. People in the gallery got one shot. An pro rata in between. Course he died very easy compared t' the style of some lynchin's. What you're gonna see is substantially true. We thought it right t' give the plot away. Obvious, if there's gonna be a lynchin you'll sit more comfortable if you know exactly what seat history's sat you on.

Paul *starts to pack up props. He works silently and efficiently at his own pace.* **Mrs Kroll** *comes on. She's in a bad mood, but she doesn't let much of it show. She stands in silence for a moment. Paul works as if she wasn't there. She sits on the swing but doesn't move it.*

Mrs Kroll   Home, profession – gone. Vamoosh. (*Sings.*) 'Life is a milliner's show . . . ' (*To* **Paul**.) That's a wonder: know something?

Paul (*going on working*)   No Mrs Kroll.

Mrs Kroll   I didn't fall off this swing last night and have the doctor saw my leg off. Really bring the last curtain down. (**Paul** *works in silence.*) Go tell her make coffee.

Paul (*puts some props down*)   You could send some of the bits and pieces to the school.

Paul *goes out,* **Mrs Kroll** *looks at the props.* **Skinner** *comes in. He has a bunch of flowers.* **Paul** *goes in and out with the props while* **Skinner** *and* **Mrs Kroll** *talk.*

Mrs Kroll   Why hello! O flowers! How divine of you. You shouldn't have.

Skinner   Drove by the churchyard an nip cross the wall an found a fresh one.

Mrs Kroll   Now they're lovely and don't you tell lies. O dear! I'm going to cry. You've been to Beaumont and Wains and I do believe you were a real beau and asked Lillian for my favourites. (*Smells the flowers.*) Heavenly. (*Sighs.*)

Skinner   It's a new life Helen. All the things you ever wanted to do – now's your chance.

Mrs Kroll   What things?

Skinner   All the things woman – I don't know! Mrs Skinner's always sayin if she only had the time . . . Travel!

Mrs Kroll   Too old to travel.

Skinner   Ain true.

Mrs Kroll   Paul put these lovely flowers in water would you? I'd go out of my mind if they withered before their time. (**Paul** *takes the flowers with him next time he goes out.*) O I'm not complaining. I'm too old for vaudeville. Some of the boys out there could be my grandsons.

Skinner   Accordin t' my book they look up t' you.

Mrs Kroll (*shrugs*)   That's not what boys buy tickets for. Nice of you to think of flowers. If you're going go fast. Soon's we're out of this place I'll be fine. Never have sat in the corner and wept.

Paul *comes on with a ladder. He unfastens the swing and drops it to the ground.*

Mrs Kroll   She fixing coffee?

Paul   Told her agin.

Mrs Kroll   Nothing more dead than an empty theatre in the morning, is there? (*Stares out front.*) Worn patches in the plush. Soiled seats. (*Grimace.*)

Skinner   I'm takin over. They tell you?

Mrs Kroll   This place?

Skinner   That's right.

Mrs Kroll (*confused*)   They didn't tell me.

Skinner   This town's gonna boom. If they only find half the coal they're talkin about – we're still gonna boom. The company's stipulatin for three hundred more miners next year. An families. They're plannin t' pave the sidewalks in the centre. Now's the time to expand. I'm openin up a new store right here. Fine frontage. Best part of town. I'll have my warehouse here in the back.

Mrs Kroll   Got the freehold?

Skinner   Two year lease. Go cautious first.

Mrs Kroll (*looks out front*)   Well it could have been an abbatoir.

Skinner   Haw haw. (*Stamps on the stage.*) Make a fine cellar down there.

Greta (*comes on with a tray of coffee things.*)

Greta (*cold but polite*)   Good day Mr Skinner.

Skinner   Good day Miss Kroll.

Greta   I brought you a cup. Paul told me you were here.

Skinner   Real kind. (**Greta** *pours.*) Did you see the cut flowers I brought your mother?

Mrs Kroll   Heavenly.

Skinner   Let on I'd been robbin the churchyard. Haw haw.

Greta   Milk?

Skinner   Always say the corpses can kick up their own. Haw haw.

Greta   Sugar?

Skinner Jist the three.

Greta (*hands him a coffee*) There.

Skinner Thank you, thank you.

Greta (*pouring coffee*) How is Mrs Skinner?

Skinner Fine, fine. I'll tell her you ask. She'll sure –

Greta Coffee mother? That's nice Mr Skinner (*Hands a coffee to* **Mrs Kroll**.)

Skinner My your coffee sure is a cup-an-a-half.

Greta Pocohontas. I have it mailed in.

Skinner Real good stuff. Think I might try stockin some. Pricey I suppose?

Greta I really wouldn't know Mr Skinner.

Skinner Ah no, no.

Greta (*finishing*) There.

Mrs Kroll Don't leave all the packing to Paul. Have you packed your books yet?

Greta All except the two or three I'm reading.

Skinner You read more'n one book at a time?

Greta That's called studying Mr Skinner.

Skinner My my!

Greta There's more Pocohontas when you're ready for it.

Skinner Much obliged Miss Kroll. (**Greta** *nods and smiles.*) Suppose you'll have time on your hands.

Greta Now I wonder why you should suppose that?

Skinner You won't be helpin your ma t' run the theatre.

Greta O I've never helped her –

Mrs Kroll That's true.

Greta   – much in the theatre. My work keeps me busy.

Mrs Kroll   If you're counting on living off Sitting Bull coffee you'd better forget your work and get a job.

Greta   Don't you think mother made a fine light commedienne Mr Skinner? People never knew the effort it cost. Mother has quite exhausted herself for years. (*To* **Mrs Kroll**.) Thank heaven you're going to get the long rest you deserve.

Skinner   Yup, stock up a few packets an see if they move.

Greta (*turning to go*)   I'll leave it there for you to serve yourselves.

Skinner (*stopping her*)   Ralph – my son Miss Kroll.

Greta   Yes?

Skinner   A good lad. Helps fine in the shop. Ralph's mother never have t' tell him anythin twice.

Mrs Kroll   Sounds a model kid.

Skinner   School ain done him much harm but it ain done him much good. He hardly know more'n me an Mrs Skinner. Speakin to an educated person, it won't be out of place if I say that ain enough.

Greta   Come now.

Skinner   Thank you Miss Kroll. I knew you'd understand. Now I know your time's precious – only I was hopin you might spare a bit of it t' git Ralph educated up.

Greta (*refusal*)   O I'm sorry Mr Skinner.

Mrs Kroll   What a heavenly idea! I've always told her she was a school-ma'm.

Greta   I'd like fine to help. Knowledge has no meaning 'less it's passed on to the young. But . . .

Skinner   Yup – I want him t' talk jist like that.

Greta   My work . . . Our situation is unique. We live on the border between civilisation and barbarism. Which way shall we go? Do we know the answer? I see it as my duty – to posterity – to record our lives – in all their colour and shades. The chiaroscuro of history. I keep a diary Mr Skinner. Even the words we're exchanging now will be touched on in it.

Skinner   Well I'm honoured. I shall sure tell Mrs Skinner that I'm goin in a diary. And you're gonna change your mind for Ralph's sake.

Greta   Why Mr Skinner I really think I've made my decision very –

Skinner   This town's gettin a new class of citizen. Educated people like yourself. Their needs have t' be catered for. I intend t' open a new store – an run the old one for the miners. The two class of folk don't wanna mix. I'll run the miner's store myself – I'm rough enough for them. But Ralph – he's kinda clean an lean. I'd like him taught so's he can carry on like you did jist now – 'bout civilisation an so on. He came out with that he could sell a real classy line of goods.

Greta   We must not despise the practical benefits of education.

Skinner   I envisage the sort of store that pulls in the money end of the market. Chairs for people t' sit on while they're bein served. A pot plant on the counter maybe. Y'know the sort of store Miss Kroll. Course with people like that you don't sell the bulk. But you git the turnover on the higher prices.

Greta (*refusing apologetically*)   My work . . .

Skinner   I know the best don't come cheap. I'll invest money in my son. An you'll choose your own time. Ralph's no trouble. We brought him up t' believe in manners. He know how t' treat a lady.

Greta (*takes his cup*)   I'd like to help. Our young people so desperately need guidance. There's so much low in their backgrounds – they're pulled down by – . (*Stops short.*) I'm tempted. One couldn't do much. A little Latin and Greek. Was it milk?

Skinner   O please.

Greta (*pouring*)   And some Hebrew would be possible. Three I believe?

Skinner   Er –

Greta (*puts in sugar*)   Hebrew is a much neglected language. Wrongly in my opinion. Those without it miss so much. I would like Ralph to have access to the original texts at Bible classes. No translation can give that Mr Skinner. The original offers – well, the heart. O there are so many things I can do for Ralph. (*Hands the coffee to Skinner.*) I wouldn't have suspected you could realise that! He shall have the best. Light light light!

Skinner (*taking the coffee*)   Thank you kindly. Now I –

Greta   To think! (*Walks away from them.*) Here in this quiet town, hidden behind the counter of a general provisions merchant, is a young soul yearning to be touched, opened, freed. I went in every week with my shopping list – and never saw! How blind we intellectuals can be! Of course I had noticed the sensitive white face, so shy and yearning. Not unlike the dying Keats. What do you think mother? (*Walks away again.*) And those delicate white hands. The long tapering fingers on the scales. I'm sure he writes verse! (*Turns to them.*) Yes – I will help! I must!

Skinner   That's mighty handsome. Now the money can be –

Greta   Arranged arranged arranged! The harmonium too. Is he musical?

Skinner   You should jist hear him whistle when he git mad!

Greta   I'll plan a whole course. No more time must be wasted. Books! He'll need grammars, primers, dictionaries –

Skinner.   Well – if it's necessary it's fine by me. Learn him t' talk good an I'll be happy. We'll skip the Latin an Greek. I aim for him t' talk t' customers better'n I can. Now he start spoutin Latin an Greek – they ain gonna understand him at all!

Greta   But surely! The classical languages give a gentleman such a –

Skinner   English'll do. An not *too* fancy. Jist fancy enough so's he sound real mean when he talk, like educated folk. So's it makes you feel hot an kinda embarrassed. If he talks t' the hands like that – he ain have no bother in keepin 'em in their place: they'll know they're in it.

Mrs Kroll   It's a heavenly idea. And the money will be useful won't it Greta?

Skinner   An you can help him catch up on his numbers. He give ol' Miss Leggit thirty cent short last Friday. Come back squarkin like a turkey-cock laid a square egg. I sub his money thirty cent. *That's* the sort of lesson he want taught. Sweat roll off me by the time I got shot of Miss Leggit. Thirty cent! Least that's the right way. How many times he give too *much*? They don't come hollerin back then. Couldn't sleep that night with the idea runnin through my head. Mrs Skinner got quite fiery!

Mrs Kroll   That poor dear.

Skinner   Always tell him it's your store one day, you'll *have* t' take care then.

Greta   Ah, I've remembered. I'd decided to start a new series of papers on the effect of local geological structure on character. I shall have to disappoint Ralph after all.

Mrs Kroll   Harry's an old friend, and you'll help him out.

Skinner   I'll send him round t'morra an – (*Turns to* **Greta**.) – you can decide.

Mrs Kroll   She's decided. Send him today.

Skinner   Well that's a weight off my mind. I mean, t' think he's got – (*Forgets.*) – culture. Move with the times! Remember the old days? Rustlin, gun feudin, when a man got drunk he shot the town up's though that's as natural as spewin. We formed the Citizens Committee of Justice Riders. Soon stamp it out. Time was a man didn't know if he cussed he wouldn't be strung up on the pole. Soon had law an order. Hope that

go in your diary Miss Kroll. Now I'm the last t' complain
'bout all the new developments hittin town. But new industry
mean new folks, strangers who ain familiar with the ol' ways
an can't respect 'em. That means hooliganism. Law breakin.
Who rob the bank last year? We git thievin out the store.
White boys too. (*To* **Paul**.) Ain jist Blacks, White, who had
advantage. Funny: good always bring the bad. Paint the wall
an someone'll write dirty on it. Ain bin no justice ridin round
these parts for fifteen years. Bit of colour trouble but that's
somethin else. Look at him – (*Indicates* **Paul**.) – tryin t' look
innocent. But we never broke up the Justice Riders. (*To*
Greta.) If there's any taint of the hooligan hid up in Ralph
you're gonna chase it out of him. That matters t' me an I'm
grateful. If he don't do his lesson right, I'll back you up. Still
hang the harness strap up in the kitchen dresser. I've larrupt
him till he salute the flag an step off the sidewalk for a lady.

Greta   Good manners are next to –

Skinner   Right on. An numbers an the art of speakin
rhetorical t' customers. But no Latin an Greek. We're a
general stores an we don't git no call for that. Good day ladies.
Mrs Skinner's mindin the shop.

Mrs Kroll *goes with* **Skinner** *to show him out.*

Paul (*indicates the tray*)   Finished?

Greta   I wonder if mother knows she's a bad actress? I'm
not a holy Anna. You can't study the classics without knowing
what men are for. But to expose her little routines up here! It's
the betrayal of my father I mind. Night after night. He'd never
let her go on stage when he was alive: knew too much about
talent. He never wanted to go on himself. It was all he could
do. But his *mind* – I know something of *that*. That was on
better things.

Paul (*puts cups on tray*)   I'm takin these through.

Greta   The moment he died up she hops, dancing – well,
tripping – and singing, and she never thinks she's dancing on
his grave. And so badly. He must be turning – and the only
one of them in time with the music.

Paul *goes out with the tray.* **Greta** *goes upstage, turns and comes down reciting.*

Greta
O lord Apollo
Come come come and speak the truth at last!
How often I, Electra, asked
Offering my cheap offerings, all that I could buy.
Now I come with all I have:
Veneration and longing!
To ask, to beg, for aid.
Help us to show men
How well the gods reward their crimes.
Show war and blood-lust running side by side
To the fixed end.
Let the hunters into the murderer's house!
None shall escape!
Wake dreamers to the sound of ropes!
See! the spokesman of death
Creeps in the rich old mansion
Armed with –

Greta *stops. A young man has come through the audience. He is tall and thin, with short crinkly fair hair. He wears a blue denim suit, a white T-shirt and a floppy white denim hat. He carries a tray covered with a cloth. He supports the tray with one hand, takes off his hat with the other and puts it on top of the tray.*

Fred   Gee I'm sorry ma'm. Didn't know you were rehearsin.

Greta   The theatre's closed.

Fred   That's what I thought. 'S why I didn't –

Greta   I'm not rehearsing. What is it you want?

Fred   See Paul.

Greta (*calls*)   Paul. (*To* **Fred**.) Why?

Fred (*lifts tray slightly*)   Show him this.

Greta (*calls*)   Paul!

Slight pause.

Fred   Sorry t' butt in . . . (*Pause. Suddenly.*) Great guy Paul! Teached me a lot.

Greta   Teached?

Fred   Electricity.

Greta (*confused*)   O. Lights.

Fred (*whipping his index finger through the air*)   You're there.

Silence. **Greta** *turns and walks off.* **Fred** *comes up on stage. He carefully sets the tray on the ground, kneels by it, gives a little clap of excitement and rubs his hands together.*

Fred (*quietly*)   Yow-eeee . . .

Paul *comes on.* **Fred** *whips the cover from the tray.*

Fred   Ta ruummmm!

It is a large plain white-icing cake, covered with very large candles.

Paul   . . . Your birthday?

Fred   Naw stupid! *Diploma* Day!

Fred *presses a switch on the cake stand. The candles light up with flashing coloured lights.*

Fred (*quietly*)   Yow-eeee! Will yer look at that!

Paul (*honestly*)   Great man.

Fred   My gall bake the cake an I fix the wirin. Hell man ain you notice yet?

Paul   What?

Fred   The lights! They go zing-zing-zing-zing-boom! (*Stares at* **Paul**. *No response.* **Fred** *makes a deprecating gesture.*) Aaaahhh! I'm a graduate of the Ernest Webster Correspondence College of Electric Science. With honours!

Fred *and* **Paul** *shake hands.*

Paul   Congratulations Fred.

Fred (*pumping* **Paul**'s *hand*)   I owe the honours to you.

Paul No man you're just plain smart.

Fred Right on! – but you sure helped me a lot. Guy says – I have a letter signed by the President of Ernest Webster College – I'm the sort of pupil give electricity a good name. He says: go forth young man an prosper!

Paul When do we git t' eat it?

Fred We don't git. I'm preservin that for posterity. Know what them lights are sayin?

Paul No.

Fred Y' don't know everythin. Them lights is codified lights. Morse – least I learnt somethin useful at the Band of Hope. You'd've learnt too if they let blacks in. Them lights is flashin out a message to the United States! That cake is announcin to the world: FRED OSPENSKY IS CUTER THAN THE WIZARD OF OZ!

Paul *laughs*.

Fred Yow-eeee! I'd stand on my head if I didn't have t' act respectable like a son of Ernest Webster College!

Paul You're a fool man.

Fred Say that agin.

Mrs Kroll (*off*) Paul!

Fred Hell why d'you stick them two ol' maids? Me? – quit! Now you listen Paul. Me an the gall's puttin by every cent we git. Couple of years we're gonna start a little shop. Electric installation. Repairs. Apparatus. This town's growin so fast y'have t' run t' keep up with the suburbs. Come in with us.

Paul You crazy?

Fred What you don't know 'bout electricity belong t' the age of the candle. Hell I can't *risk* leavin you out!

Paul Ospensky blacks don't git t' jobs like that.

Fred I worked it out. Course you don't go out installin an

Dorothy keep the counter. You stay out the back an do all the real work – them bad, bad repairs make my head ache. Hell folks'll think you jist mind the babies – which we'll have by then.

Paul (*unpersuaded*)   So you encourage uppity niggers. What Dorothy say?

Fred   Hell you know women on anythin like that. I'm boss. (*Brightens up.*) Right on! I'm boss! Leave it t' Big Fixer!

Mrs Kroll (*off*)   Seen Paul Greta?

Paul (*smiles*)   You're so stupid one day Dorothy'll give you the push.

Fred   Don't be like that Paul. Black ain what it was. Things change.

Mrs Kroll (*off*)   Greta?

Paul   They don't change that easy. Not for anyone. You git fixed on the past like you pumped it into your arms. It's a terrible habit t' shake. One day your people are gonna lynch each other in the gutter over a drop dime.

Fred   It's Diploma Day. Ain rowin.

Paul   You'd better go out the back.

They go off. The stage is empty.

Scene Two

Greta's *room. A round table. Books.* **Greta** *sits at one side of the table.* **Ralph** *at the other.*

Ralph   The one who's all hassle. This ain right, that ain right.

Greta   Isn't.

Ralph   Yeh. Nothin's right. Two minutes later his girl follows him in. They don't know each other. One hassles an kicks up a stink an the other drops half the store in her coat linin.

Greta　You have to keep your eyes open.

Ralph　Sure do have to.

Greta　And what d'you read?

Ralph　No time t' read. Pa says read. Soon's I sit down with a book he say git up you lazy – do this, do that.

Greta　But you can read?

Ralph　Sure I can read! I read *Forty Thousand Leagues Under the Sea* by Jules Verne. That's a good book. You ever git t' read that? I read that at school.

Greta　Today you're going onto Virgil.

Ralph　Wow! . . . Virgil, isn't he some sort of Greek?

Greta　Latin.

Ralph　Only Pa said for me not t' –

Greta　In English translation.

Ralph　Well Pa said for me –

Greta　Now Ralph. There's no need for your father to know what we study. Frankly your father is a – well never mind. I don't want you to discuss our work with anyone. You're a young man. You must start making your own decisions.

Ralph　Okay, okay. If you say so Miss Kroll.

Greta (*looks at the time on her fob watch. Opens the book*)　A very extraordinary thing happens in Book Two of the *Aeneid*. Troy is burning. Aeneas the Trojan hero addresses his father. (*Reads.*)
　　The fire-ball comes raging through the town
　　The rolling blast of furnace heat.
　　'Up on my back, dear father – '
(*Explains.*) He was old.
　　– 'I'll carry you on my shoulders.

The burdens we love are light! We must chance our luck
And run through the burning city.' So I lifted my father
Onto my back with hands still –

What are you looking at Ralph?

Ralph (*nods*)   That.

Greta   My fob? You have good taste Ralph. My father
Reinhart gave it me. He brought it with him from Germany.
It was my grandmother's. Fine isn't it?

Ralph   Yeh.

Greta (*holds out the watch. The chain is still fastened to her dress*)
The engraving will interest you. Mountain gentian. We will be
doing botany. The silver's so fine and delicate. Touch it. Feel:
soft, burnished with touching.

Ralph (*touches the fob with his finger*)   Yeh.

Greta   It's my proudest possession perhaps. Well – shall we
get on? (*Reads.*)
    'The burdens we love are light! We must chance our luck
    And run through the burning city – '
(*Explains.*) To escape the Greeks.
    – So I lifted my father
    Onto my back with hands still red from war.
    My son twined his fingers in mine and ran at my side
    With his short steps. My wife came behind.
    We kept to the –

She stops. **Ralph** *is still staring at her. Slight pause.*

Ralph   Never heard such a quiet tick.

Greta   Almost silent. It was made in Chamonix high up in
the European Alps. Ruskin mentions it in *Praeterita*. The air up
there is so clear and the craftsmen sit in their windows. They
need light for their delicate work. Centuries of craftsmanship
and history and struggle ticking by in a little watch. Don't you
like the story?

Ralph   O it's fine.

Greta　Please like it. Try. If there was one person I could
share these things with – (*She stops. Puts the book down. She speaks
with a light voice.*) The ancients were dry? They were passionate,
angry, questing! Our lives on the frontier are so like theirs –
and so different. We have the violence and killing – my own
father was killed – but what else? They had the lyre – we have
the banjo. Wine – the four-ale bar. Attic drama – vaudeville.
Aeneas' son saw men killed – so have you. But what else have
you seen? You haven't even seen the naked body! Because
everything else is ugly, that's ugly! Aeneas' son saw the naked
body. We cover ours – like you put blemished fruit at the back
of the store. Don't some of them wash? Ralph have you – as
your teacher – tell me – did you ever see a woman's breast?

Ralph　Well –

Greta　No.

Ralph　Er – kinda – the lads – once –

Greta. I'm not ashamed to ask a young man that question.
What is education? For god's sake! – how to read invoices and
weigh up soup powder? Can't you see this strong man with his
father on his back, tears streaming down his old beard, the
little boy running to keep up, his wife hurrying behind. The
trackless waste. Their city burning. Murderers foraging for
refugees in the long grass. Doesn't that say *anything* about the
human condition? Ralph! (*As she reads she slowly uncovers one of
her breasts and takes it out.*)
　We reached the gates of the city,
　An arch of fire and through it a world on fire.
　My father said 'Faster! Run! See their shining armour!
　The flashing bronze!' In the panic and haste
　I lost my wits! We ran from the city streets
　Out in the open fields. Then – O terrible!
　My wife was gone.
　Did she stop running because fate meant to rob me?
　Fall with weariness – and not shout for my help
　Because she wanted me to save my father and son?
　Or lose her way in the smoke? It is not known.
　We never saw her again. If I had looked behind –

Ralph   It's beautiful.

Greta   You think that?

Ralph   Let me touch it.

Greta   No.

Ralph   Miss.

Greta (*gently*)   How firm the nipple is. It glows. It means I like you Ralph. When the lady's breasts are firm it means she likes the man. Always remember. The sign of fondness. (**Ralph** *stands*.) Now you've seen what Aeneas and his son saw. Sit down. (**Ralph** *sits*.) Now. Your turn. (*Hands him the book*.) Seventy-two. It's marked.

Ralph (*reads*)
  Did she stop running because fate meant to rob me?
  Fall with weariness – and not shout for my help
  Because she wanted me to save my father and son?
  Or lose her way in the –

Ralph *stands*.

Greta   I shock you.

Ralph   No, no –

Greta   It's wrong?

Ralph   No! It's – I want to – let me –

Ralph *crosses to her. She stands.*

Greta   Ralph. No. Sit.

Ralph *walks away across the room. She covers herself. She sits.*

Ralph   I – think I'd better go home.

Greta (*stands*)   Your parents – father – you mustn't – don't say –

Ralph (*alarmed*)   God no no no! Hell. Jesus. No.

Greta   No. (*Sits*.) We must understand our lives and then act as if we didn't. There are women Ralph – men go to. I

understand them too. But we can't speak of them. We must be
as silent as this book –

A tap on the door.

Greta   Come.

Paul *comes in with a lighted oil lamp. He puts it on the table.*

Greta   That's very good Ralph. Go on. Thank you Paul.

Ralph (*reads*)
    If I had looked behind
    To see she was keeping up!
    I had not even thought of her till we came to the grassy hill
    Holy to –

Greta. Ceres.

Ralph (*reads*)
    – where all the survivors assembled.
    She alone was not there. Without knowing it, I her husband,
    Her son and friends, lost her forever.

They both look up at **Paul**. *He stands some way from the table waiting
and watching them.*

Paul   Was there anything else?

Greta   No thank you.

Paul *goes.*

Greta   D'you like my oil lamp Ralph? I try to keep up the
old ways in my room. I love this soft light at dusk. And the
quietness. Strange evening. You mustn't think I've ever –

Ralph. No, no, no.

Greta   How kind and good you are. I wonder if any other
women will feel your presence as I do. Talk about yourself.

Ralph   O. (*Slight pause.*) I'm jist part of the store. Dad's had
our name put right cross the big windows. Big gilt letters. And
son.

Greta   That's nice.

Ralph   Yeh . . . The fellas out the mine grin at me through the letters. Wet their fingers in their mouths an wiggle 'em in the air.

Greta   We have to live with the sordid.

Ralph   That store's so dark –

Skinner (*off*)   Ralph! Ralph!

Greta *and* **Ralph** *stand.*

Ralph   That nigger! He's told!

Greta   What? No! How could he?

Skinner (*off*)   Ralph!

Greta   Sit! Books!

Paul (*off*)   Sir!

Greta   Books. (*They sit and frantically open books.*) We must look as – . He couldn't have told. He couldn't. There's no time! Seventy-four!

Ralph   Seventy –

Greta (*angrily*)   Four!

A moment's silence.

Paul (*off*)   Miss Kroll's room.

Ralph (*stands*)   That nigger saw!

Greta (*pulls him down*)   *Sit!*

Silence. **Skinner** *comes in.*

Greta (*rising.*) Why Mr Skinner have you come for a lesson as –

She stops: she has noticed **Skinner**'s *torn clothes, bruised face, and his right hand and forearm crudely bundled into a blood-stained splint-bandage.*

Ralph   What in . . . ?

Paul *comes in behind* **Skinner.**

Ralph   Pa! Sit down!

Skinner (*stands. Gasps*)   Son!

Ralph (*to* **Paul**)   Whiskey!

Paul *goes.*

Ralph   Pa – for god's sake – ?

Skinner   Store. Broke in. Hoodlums.

Ralph   Ma?

Skinner   Next door. Riders out. Called 'em out. Went for me. Smashed. Lootin hoodlums. The store. Cut. Look. (*Gasps.*) Aw god!

Greta (*calls*)   Mother!

Skinner   Smashed windows. Spillin sacks. Tea chests. I'd better – big window's smashed –

Greta   How terrible! My god that blood!

Skinner (*to* **Ralph**)   – git back. Guard the store. God *I'd* better come!

Ralph (*pushing him down*)   Stay there.

Skinner   They'll burn the store!

Ralph   They won't. I'm goin.

Greta (*calls*)   Mother!

Paul *comes in with whiskey and glasses.*

Ralph (*impatiently to* **Paul**)   Here!

Ralph *pours a drink, gives it to* **Skinner** *and goes out.*

Greta (*to* **Paul**)   Where's my mother?

Skinner (*calls at door*)   Mrs Kroll!

Greta (*looking after* **Ralph**)   Will he be safe?

Paul (*to* **Greta**)   She's comin.

Skinner (*gasps and splutters as he reaches for the bottle. Knocks his arm on the bottle. Half spills it. Shouts, then winces*)   Aw! Ah!

Greta   Spilt. O god. (*She mops up the whiskey.*)

Paul   Let me do the –

Greta   I can manage!

Mrs Kroll *comes in.*

Mrs Kroll   What in god's name is – (*Sees* **Skinner**.) Harry!

Greta (*angrily indicating* **Paul**)   Does he think I'm an idiot?

Mrs Kroll (*to* **Skinner**)   What is it?

Greta   Does he think I can't –

Mrs Kroll (*to* **Greta**)   Shut up!

Skinner   My store.

Mrs Kroll   What?

Skinner   Hoodlums.

Mrs Kroll   On the streets? Paul put the front shutters up. (*She has taken the bandage off, she controls her shock.*) Then get Dr Load. How did they do this?

Skinner   Hatchet.

Paul *goes out.*

Greta (*fascinated by the wound*)   How awful! They could have killed him.

Mrs Kroll (*to* **Greta**)   Hot water. (*Calls.*) Paul fetch the first aid from the box office.

Greta *rushes out.* **Mrs Kroll** *pours* **Skinner** *a drink. She prepares the wound.*

Skinner   My store, my store.

Mrs Kroll   It's going to hurt.

Skinner   Heard this gigglin. Knew Mrs Skinner wasn't back. Crep down in the dark. My little spyhole back of the shelves. Looked. Light from the street lamp. Saw some shapes. (*Drinks.*) Gigglin: thought – kids. Went in. Men! Come for me. Drag me on the floor. Held my head down. This guy stood on my hair. Can't move. Nailed there.

Mrs Kroll Still.

Skinner My store. Slashed the sacks an the insides ran out. Broke my bottles. Bringin things an smashin 'em by my head so's I saw – in the light from the street. Rip up rolls of calico. Thought they'd see the meat slicer. (*Suddenly bursts into tears.*) Aw god! thank chriss there's insurance.

Mrs Kroll (*calls*) Greta! Quick! (*To* **Skinner**.) Your wife?

Skinner Next door. Wednesday: plays cards. Run round when they left. Saw me – screamed. Aw god. (*Touches his scalp.*) It's bad . . .

Mrs Kroll A bit.

Skinner My store.

Paul *comes back. He brings a first aid box.*

Paul Barricaded the front. Locked the doors. I'll git Dr Load.

Mrs Kroll Send that girl up! I need water!

Paul *goes.*

Skinner Didn't see their faces. Strangers. Got their voices.

Mrs Kroll *pours two drinks. They drink in silence.*

Skinner Someone has t' spoil it. Gets goin – then 'long they come smash smash smash.

Paul *comes in with a bowl of water.*

Paul (*quietly*) She ain in the house.

Mrs Kroll What? You sure?

Paul Street coat's gone. An her hat.

Mrs Kroll (*subdued exasperation*) God almighty.

Skinner   She go after Ralph?

Mrs Kroll   I've no idea. (*Takes the water from* **Paul**.)   Get the doctor.

Paul   You all right on your own?

Mrs Kroll   Yes, yes. Go on.

Paul *goes.* **Mrs Kroll** *talks as she cleans and dresses* **Skinner**'s *wound – almost as if she were talking to it.*

Mrs Kroll   I hate this town. And I'll be buried in it. Didn't choose it. Just a stop on the vaudeville circuit. The lease going cheap – Reinhart said we couldn't afford to miss it. Only get the chance once. We put in all we had. A year later he was shot. Stupid. A bar brawl. He wasn't even involved.

Skinner (*shaking his head in his hands*)   My store.

Mrs Kroll   Wouldn't let me see him in the bar. Waited at the police house till they brought him. I went in the bar on my way home. The huge mirror had fallen out of its frame. Smashed. Blood on it. Must have been his.

Skinner   We strung up the guy that shot him. Still think of Reinhart when I pass the telegraph pole. Wish he'd had the satisfaction of knowin.

Mrs Kroll   He never saw me act. He'd hate it. I'm not good. (*Shrugs.*) No money. Theatre lease I couldn't sell. What could I do? Now they don't come. Tired of the same old –

Off, a scream. They both hear it.

Mrs Kroll   Her!

Skinner (*stands*)   The yard!

Mrs Kroll   Quick!

Skinner   Listen! Listen!

A moment's silence.

Skinner   Nothin.

Mrs Kroll   It is! You heard!

Skinner   Listen!

Mrs Kroll (*not stopping*)   She screamed. The lane out the
back.

Skinner   We're on edge. It was a horse. An automobile.

Mrs Kroll (*going*)   All right.

Skinner   Stay here!

Mrs Kroll   You go!

Skinner   The window! (*Opens the window off right. Pokes his
head out.*) O hell there's a fire! Not near the store. Thank god.
(*Calls.*) Miss Kroll!

Mrs Kroll   Harry we must go to –

Skinner (*head still out*)   Will yer listen! (*Calls.*) Hello?

Mrs Kroll *goes out.*

Skinner (*Head still out.*)   She's round the store with Ralph.
He'll see she's okay. What the hell she go out for any-road?
Wants her bottom smack. You let her do what she like. She
put on any more airs the whole town'll laugh. (*Calls.*) Miss
Kroll? (*Suddenly realising.*) Hell someone could be out there with
a gun –

He has turned back quickly. Sees **Mrs Kroll** *has gone. Curses silently.
Pours himself a drink at the table. Picks up a book, leafs over a few pages.*

Skinner   My store . . .

He shuts the book and tops up his glass. **Greta** *comes in. She carries a
bowl of water, a clean towel and some medical dressings.*

Greta   Now Mr Skinner where is that wound?

Skinner   Where you been?

Greta   It must be washed. Every speck of dust must come
out. That causes the trouble. Where's mother?

Skinner   Out lookin for you.

Greta   O.

Skinner   Ain you bin out? We heard somethin out back.

Greta (*goes a few steps towards the window and glances out*)   I hope she's all right. Should I go and see?

Skinner   Goddam it no! The whole town'll be runnin round lookin for each other.

Greta (*touches her forehead*)   It's so silly. (*Looks at his arm.*) She saw to your arm . . .

Skinner   Are *you* all right?

Greta   The – . I'm worried for Mrs Skinner.

Skinner (*pours a drink and hands it to* **Greta**)   Drink this.

Greta (*shakes her head*)   It fuddles my brain. (*Takes the glass.*)
Perhaps . . . tonight . . . (*Drinks in silence.*) How very silly.
(*Starts to fuss at the table.*) Books everywhere. Such disorder.
(*She picks up some books and holds them futilely.*) Ralph.
Such a promising – . I have high hopes. A natural talent for – .
Of course undeveloped, but –

Mrs Kroll *comes in.*

Greta   I was telling Ralph's father. We must be proud – yes,
I was most –

Mrs Kroll   Where've you been?

Greta   I'm sorry I took so long. (*Points vaguely.*) The water.
Anything like this – I find so upsetting. Mr Skinner's been kind
enough to –

Mrs Kroll   Your coat was gone.

Greta (*puts the books back on the table*)   The whiskey. (*Starts to
cry.*) How silly.

Skinner (*reaches out to pat her*)   Now you mustn't let –

Greta (*big flinch*)   Don't!

Skinner (*mumbled apologies*)   O I jist – you seemed –

Mrs Kroll   What is it?

Greta   I want to tear the skin off my hands! I want to tear my skin away!

Mrs Kroll (*motions to* **Skinner**)   Outside.

Greta   Filthy. Horrible. Dirty. (*Pounds the table.*) Unclean.

Skinner (*going, bewildered*)   What is it?

Mrs Kroll (*to* **Greta**. *Quietly firm*)   Stop it.

Skinner *goes out.*

Greta   You don't know. You don't know.

Mrs Kroll   I'm trying to find out. (*Pours whiskey and gives it to her.*) Drink it.

Greta   No, no.

Mrs Kroll *puts the glass in* **Greta***'s hands and tilts it against her teeth.*

Greta (*dribbles and drinks*)   Oooo.

Mrs Kroll   Well – out in the yard –

Greta   Yes. Yes. Yes.

Mrs Kroll   And?

Greta (*face down across the table*)   Nothing.

Mrs Kroll   A man?

Greta   What's the use –

Mrs Kroll   A man was –

Greta   Yes, yes, yes! (*Spits the words in her mother's face.*) A man! A man! Does it satisfy you!

Mrs Kroll   Don't talk to me like that! What happened?

Greta   I'm going to gag! (*She bends over a basin but only dribbles.*) Ah . . .

Mrs Kroll   The man hurt you? Greta!

Greta   What?

Mrs Kroll   He assaulted you?

Greta   It was dark. He put his hand on my mouth. Mother he ripped – (*Touches her breast.*) Here.

Mrs Kroll   He pushed you on the ground.

Greta   What?

Mrs Kroll   The wall?

Greta   My dress was torn. When I got in I found my watch was gone.

Mrs Kroll   Greta you're not a child. I'm asking you: were you assaulted? Sexually.

Greta   The wall? . . . He showed me his wound and I wanted to go out. Out, out. There was a fire out there! I went down the yard – through the gate – in the lane. I turned to the fire. Someone shut the gate behind me. I heard a noise. A hand came out of the dark and – (*Lies face down across the table again.*)

Mrs Kroll   You *were* assaulted? (*Gestures to her own body.*) Here.

Greta   I came indoors and my watch was gone. Ripped off.

Skinner *comes back. He looks enquiringly at* **Mrs Kroll**.

Mrs Kroll (*quietly*)   I'm not sure. I think she's . . .

Skinner (*quietly to* **Mrs Kroll**)   A man?

Greta   I won't go out any more. Never. People will look at me like a dog running with its nose from ditch to ditch! An old maid who – . I won't go out!

Skinner   We'll git the beast. (*To* **Greta**.) Did you see anythin? (*To* **Mrs Kroll**.) You? (**Mrs Kroll** *shakes her head. To* **Greta**.) Would you know his voice?

Greta   Who?

Skinner   He didn't say nothin? No, the swine knew what he was up to. Done it before. Some lad spur of the moment, he'd've blurted out. 'Please.' 'Shut up.' This lad know what he's at.

Greta   I suddenly saw my father in the dark. (*Picks up a book.*) I thought I was being murdered. Then it was all over. (*Looks at the table.*) So disorganised . . .

Paul *comes in.*

Paul (*slightly out of breath. Quietly*)   No doctor. No one. They've gone into town. A gang started a fire.

Mrs Kroll *takes* **Greta** *out.* **Paul** *starts to follow.*

Skinner   Hey.

Paul (*stops*)   Whiskey Mr Skinner?

Skinner   What you called now?

Paul   Paul sir.

Skinner   Right. (*Holds the bottle.*) Drop left. How long you worked for the Krolls?

Paul   Fourteen year.

Skinner   My how faithful you black race are. Must've seed you around but . . . (*Drinks.*) Some git sweet when they drink, rest sour. Right?

Paul   Yes Mr Skinner.

Skinner   Took your time.

Paul   Don't follow your drift sir.

Skinner   Dr Load.

Paul   Knocked. Went round the back. Made sure his horse was gone. Then I waited a while. Knew that cut was bad. Doctor ought t' see that.

Skinner   If niggers had blue eyes yours'd be blue. (*No answer.*) Follow my drift?

Paul   Yes sir.

Skinner   Step in the light boy. Wanna make sure I'll know you when the next fourteen years gone by.

Paul   I'd better see if Mrs Kroll –

Skinner   You ain shy?

Paul *comes close enough for the light to shine on him.*

Paul   What's wrong Mr Skinner.

Skinner   Aw – you tell me boy.

Paul   I weren't round your store Mr Skinner. You know I was here when you come –

Skinner.   Who see you round the doctor's?

Paul   No one. I don't think.

Skinner   When you git back?

Paul   I come straight up here.

Skinner   Blue eyes an a smart tongue. They sure knock out a fancy brand of nigger round here.

Paul   Mr Skinner it ain right for you t' –

Skinner   Shut up! Shut up! Shut up! Listen nigger I've had the privilege of chasin niggers out that swamp – O I know where they hide up! – an' the pleasure of bouncin 'em on the end of their braces strung round their neck. Up an down. In the good ol' days. Which ain passed yet!

Silence.

Paul (*quietly*)   I'm sorry they broke your store Mr Skinner an –

Skinner.   You make excuses for me? Shut up! Shut up! Shut up! You make excuses for *you*! You need excuses. What excuses you got? (*Silence.*) Now what you do when you come back 'fore you come straight up here?

Paul   Nothin.

Skinner　No detour?

Mrs Kroll *comes in.*

No. None. Cause you never even went! You'd never have time t' go an then do what you done!

Paul　What have I done?

Skinner　Don't use words t' me.

Paul　Could I go now Mrs Kroll.

Skinner　Stay right there. At the wall.

Mrs Kroll (*quietly to* **Skinner**)　Harry the funny thing is I'm –

Skinner　Get her t' bed?

Mrs Kroll　Yes. I'm not sure anything happened.

Skinner　She ain said? (**Mrs Kroll** *shakes her head.*) Next best thing t' caught in the act. Young gall – she wouldn't know the words.

Mrs Kroll　O you can't live over a theatre and not –

Skinner　If she did she'd never bring herself t' use 'em. I wouldn't embarrass the lady by askin. Listen Helen: a man in the dark? – a gall? Of course he did! What could *she* do? Knowin your daughter – she's been brought up a lady, which does you credit – she jist fainted. Probably don't even know what happened.

Mrs Kroll (*impatiently*)　O! – (*Tries to keep calm.*) Perhaps it was just – she lost her watch.

Skinner　Robbery make it worse.

Mrs Kroll (*becomes aware of* **Paul**, *vaguely wonders why he's standing at the wall*)　Paul?

Skinner　He ever give trouble before?

Mrs Kroll　Trouble?

Skinner　What is he? Some sorta saint?

Ralph *comes in with* **Fred**. **Fred** *carries his hat in both hands*.

Ralph   Pick him up in the yard. Prowler.

Fred   I was not prowlin any! Hell what is this?

Skinner (*to* **Fred**)   You in the yard?

Ralph   Yeh.

Skinner   Where you from?

Fred   Oak Street.

Skinner   Miner?

Fred   Look I don't know you mister –

Skinner   Why you prowlin in someone's private back yard?

Fred   I was visitin.

Mrs Kroll   Here?

Fred   See Paul ma'm.

Skinner   Why?

Fred (*shrugs*)   Social call.

Ralph   Social?

Skinner   Funny world where white man pays social calls on the nigger community.

Paul   He don't mean it that way. I been teachin him bout electricity.

Skinner   You sure are an unorthodox nigger. This nigger's teacher now. Don't teach niggers like bona fide niggers teach. He teach white. Not readin an writin an anythin good an wholesome like that. He teach the wonders of science! Nigger, this white man don't need you t' talk for him. He can talk for hisself. (*To* **Fred**.) So you pay a social call on the nigger with a little electric demonstratin throwed in on the side. What sort of a freak are you?

Ralph   Yeh.

Skinner   Empty his pockets.

Fred   Now hold on.

Ralph goes *to search* **Fred**. **Fred** *pushes him off.*

Fred   Git off! (*To* **Skinner**.)You ain got no right t' –

Skinner   I'm a foundin officer of the Justice Ridin Committee. In my book that's *right*. You think before you reply: you tellin the citizens of this town you don't co-operate with them?

Fred   Hell no – I . . . ! (*Empties his pockets.*) Billfold. Handkerchief – (*Honestly.*) sorry the handkerchief's dirty ma'm. Smokes. My knife – wipe the blood off 'fore I come in . . . Come to tell Paul bout the fire.

Skinner *picks up the handkerchief, stares at it a moment and puts it down without uncrumpling it. Nods.*

Skinner   Son you got into bad company with this here nigger. Thank your lucky stars I step in an stop it 'fore you was mixed up in somethin real bad.

Ralph   Pa – ?

Skinner   Miss Kroll was raped by a dirty man t'night. Back up the yard.

Ralph   Jesus!

Mrs Kroll   Well we don't know that Harry. I'd rather we hoped –

Skinner   Helen why don't you go and look after your little girl?

Mrs Kroll   We don't know. Not for sure.

Skinner   Dr Load will confirm.

Fred   Hey! You didn't think I – ?

Greta *comes in. She wears a long nightgown and behaves like a child.*

Greta   Could anyone tell me the right time? (*To* **Ralph**.)

Have you the exact time on you please? Mother my watch has gone. I've lost my watch. Who took my watch? (*To* **Ralph**.) Why you staring? (*Cries*.) Father will be cross! Where did I put it down! (*To* **Paul**.) Lean and clean doesn't wash. (*To* **Skinner**.) Could you oblige me with the correct time? (*To* **Paul**.) It's late! It's late!

Mrs Kroll   Greta come to bed.

Greta   Where-o-where is my little watch gone? (*Cries on her mother*.) Mother my beautiful silver watch.

Skinner   What a terrible sight. I'll never let myself forget this.

Greta   Look at your watches! Are they there? The watch thief is coming! (*Calm*.) Could you oblige me with the right time?

Skinner   Not till the day I die!

The farce begins. **Mrs Kroll** *pours herself a drink*.

Ralph (*weeps*)   O god it's terrible.

Mrs Kroll (*drinks*)   She's my only child!

Greta   It's late! Late! Late! Father will be cross! A clock tower striking!

Mrs Kroll (*drinks*)   I'm her mother!

Greta   Where's the clock tower?

Ralph (*sobbing*)   Gee god! Jesus Mary.

Greta   The yard! That's where I lost my watch!

Skinner   That poor kid!

Greta   In the dark! At the gate! The yard! The yard!

Mrs Kroll   Honey baby!

Greta *runs out*. **Mrs Kroll** *runs out after her*.

Skinner (*violently*)   Now I'll have my say!

Ralph   I'll git Dr Load.

Paul   There's no need. He'll come as soon's he git –

Skinner   You said no one was there!

Paul   So I left a note.

Skinner   A note?

Skinner
Ralph } He left a note?

Paul. In his door.

Skinner
Ralph } In his door!

Ralph   If he left a note –

Skinner   – in his door –

Skinner
Ralph } He ain done it t' Miss Greta!

Ralph   It was someone else!

Skinner (*to* **Ralph**)   Get to Dr Load's. Find if that note's there! Knock the door down but find out if it's there!

Greta (*off*)   My watch!

Paul (*looking through the window*)   They're in the yard. Her mother's chasin her round.

Mrs Kroll (*off*)   Greta!

Off, a chicken squawks as it flies out of the way. **Ralph** *pours himself a quick drink.*

Greta (*off*)   My watch! If I don't wind it up it'll die! I know it'll die!

Ralph (*to* **Skinner**)   Sure you can manage while I –

Skinner   Go! Go!

Ralph   Got it at home. (*Gives a pistol to* **Skinner**.)

Skinner   That-a-boy! Your pa's proud of you! (*They shake hands.*)

Ralph *goes.* **Skinner** *pours a drink and empties his glass.*

Mrs Kroll (*off*)   Greta I'm hurt too! Can't you understand! (*A chicken squawks.*) I carried her. Fed her at this breast. It's all gone. Sold up. Theatre closed. Life finished. O Reinhart thank god you never lived to see me old!

Skinner (*shouts through the window*)   We won't forget Helen. You're hurt too. (*Goes to* **Fred** *and hits him with his unwounded hand.*) The mother's hurt too okay?

Fred   He's mad!

Skinner   My son'll never be the same again. (*Calls.*) Drink! (**Paul** *fills his glass.*) Look what you done to this family! (*Cries, pistol in one hand and glass in the other.*) An me a strong man weepin. (*Drinks and cries.*)

Greta (*off, fading into the distance*)   My watch is dead! Will no one help me to bury my dead? Ashes! Ashes!

Mrs Kroll (*off, fading into the distance*)   Not in the street! Not in your night dress!

Paul *is backing away. The bottle hangs from his hand. He stares at* **Skinner**.

Skinner   An my store too! Animal! (*Hits* **Fred**.)

Fred (*white*)   He's mad!

Skinner   Beast!

Scene Three

A theatre. The vaudeville orchestra plays the orchestral version of 'I Wore a Little Grey Bonnet' (The Quaker Girl. Monckton) Three **Stagehands** *dressed in white overalls set the swing.* **Mrs Kroll** *comes on in theatrical Edwardian dress. She carries a parasol. As the* **Stagehands** *finish she sits for a moment on the swing and gracefully* *thanks them with a smile and and a bow of the head. Then she promenades as she sings.*

Mrs Kroll (*sings*)

Life is a milliner's show
Every young lady confesses
Even the quaker you know
Has to take care how she dresses
So when at home I went out for a walk
I had to mind that the folks didn't talk

I wore a little grey bonnet
Not a flower or feather upon it
Always hidden my face would be
Cause it was under my bonnet you see

I wore etc.

So I was very demure
Folly and flattery scorning
All the young fellows I'm sure
Liked just to bid me good morning
They would come up as I went on my way
Saying it's really a very fine day

I wore a little grey bonnet
Lots of eyes were fastened upon it
Though they wanted to look at me
They couldn't peep under my bonnet you see

I wore etc.

Once on a Sunday in June
Such a nice gentleman met me
Talked for the whole afternoon
Told me he'd never forget me
He couldn't see I was blushing so pink
I didn't know what to say or to think

I wore a little grey bonnet
All the time his eyes were upon it
Then I found he was kissing me

His face had slipped under my bonnet you see

I wore etc.

Applause. **Mrs Kroll** *goes off. She returns for a bow.* **Skinner** *comes on clapping. He is dressed rather formally: black jacket, white shirt, spotted bow tie.*

Mrs Kroll   You heavenly audience! It's been divine!

Skinner   This really is the last appearance of Mrs Helen Kroll on her own stage. Give her a big hand. (**Skinner** *leads the applause.*) Okay lads.

Skinner *gestures offstage. The three* **Stagehands** *come on. They lay protective sheets over the stage. They are nervous and this makes them brash. They grin at the audience while* **Skinner** *talks. One waves to a girl.*

Skinner   Brothers an sisters. Citizens of this town. I'm glad t' see such a full house t'night. (*Spreads his hands.*) These hands serve you good people in the store. Wrap your bread, weigh your beans, measure your coffee. (*To the* **Stagehands**.) I git in your way fellas tell me t'move. (*To the audience.*) These hands have held a whip an a gun. They've held men's legs while the noose was drop over their head.

Audience   Ya-haaaa! Wheeeeee!

Stagehand 1   Right on Mr Skinner!

Skinner   Fellow Americans. How we run the law's the same how we live our lives. The store, street, law: one. Let the law slip: you git bad measure in the store an' the sidewalk end up death-row for the good citizen. That's how it is!

Audience applause.

Skinner   Law ain somethin above. We make it with these hands every day of our lives.

Stagehand   Jist a foot Mr Skinner.

Skinner (*moves slightly*)   T'night we ain ridin for justice in the dark.

Whistles and applause.

Skinner   We're ridin in the footlights. There's nothin t'
hide. We ain ashamed of doin what's right. I declare this stage
t' be a hall of justice!

Applause. **Stagehands 1** *and* **3** *go.* **Stagehand 2** *stays on stage,
folds his arms and listens.*

Skinner   The good ol' Justice Riders – they were a group of
brave, public-spirited men. Half the manhood of this town
stayed at home in bed. Now I'm glad t' see most the whole
town here! Barrin a few ol' maids who ain quick on the draw!
I'm honoured t' see our venerable ol' gran'pappies. I'm proud
of you young fellas ain yet out of school. I see many of you've
got your wives an sweethearts an mothers along! Let's say a
special hello to our ladies.

Skinner *leads the audience in applause.* **Stagehands 1** *and* **3**
return with **Fred**. *He has been dressed in a grey suit and pale shirt (no
tie). He is roped. He is white with terror. The* **Stagehands** *are
nervous. They try to tie* **Fred** *onto the swing. He falls on the ground.
Audience whistles, cheers, hoots.*

Fred   Fellas. Please.

Stagehand 1   Hell.

Stagehand 2   Hold him, hold him.

Stagehand 1   Git the seat.

Stagehand 3   Billy.

Fred   Please. Please.

Audience   Hold his head up. He's shy.

Laughter, hoots.

Skinner   Like men we do our own work. Like honourable
men we git pleasure doin it. We know the sort of man don't git
his pleasure doin right. *He* git his pleasure doin bad.

Audience   Right on!

Skinner   Friends. If this is wrong – it ain, but if – we done it t'gether. We act and speak united. You're all in this. No one man t' blame. The guilt's on all. No man can point out his brother or pour scorn on his neighbour. Git your hands off your butts – I know you're itchin t' go – an study your palms. No lady I ain askin you t' tell fortunes. What's there?

Heckler   Dirt!

Skinner   Lines! Everyman's hand's much the same – an everyman's hand's different.

Stagehand 2   Ought 'a hoist him up a bit.

Stagehands 1 and **3**   Wha' for?

Stagehand 2   Git his feet off the ground.

Stagehand 1 (*shrugs*)   Okay.

*The **Stagehands** raise the swing so that **Fred**'s feet clear the ground.*

Skinner (*hands spread*)   Yes brothers! The same but different. God put it on our hands for a purpose. When we work, play, pat our off-spring on the head, help the oldfolk, give the hand of friendship, wave farewell t' the departed – (*Applause grows.*) god put it right there before our eyes. The same – members of one community: we owe it service an duty – but different – each man has his own place an rank: with his own tasks an ability t' carry them out. Law an order writ on the palm of your hands as sure as Cain's curse was writ on his head. (*Applause.*) Step out of line: you take on tasks for which you ain got abilities. In my book that's anarchy: you cut off your hands!

Applause.

Fred   You gotta stop him. You gotta stop him. He's mad.

Skinner   Hey fellas stuff his mouth so's I can finish.

Stagehand 1 *gags* **Fred**. **Fred** *makes noises from time to time and tries to shake the swing.*

Skinner   This is how I've organised this do. Every ticket-buyin member of this audience is entitled t' one shot. Them that paid the higher prices git first shot.

Audience applause and boos. Cries of 'Shame'.

Skinner   Pit, gallery, gods. Anyone step out of line, the usherette ladies 've been told t' git their names. They'll hear from the Committee. T' show this ain based on favouritism, I give up my go.

Audience applause, 'Shame'.

Skinner   Was happy t' do so.

Woman in Audience   Can't shoot straight.

Skinner   Git her name. Don't none of you red-necks complain. You work harder you could afford first go. (*Applause, boos.*) I'll tell you what I'm gonna do. Every gun-carryin man woman an child in this audience is gonna git themselves a voucher. That voucher is exchangeable for goods on the day I open my new store – in the new one *or* the old one! That voucher's worth fifty cents. Can't do fairer than that! (*Applause, cheers.*) Now you won't often see prayin on stage. I'm gonna ask you to join in an act of prayer. (*Bows his head.*) Lord god guide our aim. We ain numbered 'mongst them mugger-lover folk who think of the criminal all the time. We remember the victims an their loved ones lord. Amen.

Audience   Amen. Right on. Yow-eee. Born again.

Clown *comes on. Long white face, bulbous nose, black hunting cap with long peak, black tail-coat, baggy trousers, long black shoes.*

Clown   Er Mr Skinner. Mr Skinner sir. Er beg your pardon Mr Skinner.

Skinner   I'm busy here.

Clown   Did you say – er – did you say jist a while back –

Skinner.   Speak out son. I won't eat you. (*Aside to audience.*) Ain never be that hungry! (*Laughs.*) My new store go bust I'll git a job on stage. Haw haw. O indeed!

Clown   Pardon me Mr Skinner. Mr Skinner sir.

Skinner   Well son?

Clown   O . . . (*Mock modesty: slots his two hands together at the fingers, turns the palms down, straightens his arms and rocks his hands from side to side in front of his crutch.*) Could I have your go?

Skinner   Could you have my . . . ?

Clown   Let me, let me, let me. (*Produces an old pistol.*) Look what I got.

Skinner   What is that?

Clown   My brother's weapon.

Skinner   What is your brother – deformed? Runs in the family.

Clown   This was used at the Boston Tea Party.

Skinner   T' stir the tea? (**Clown** *cries quietly.*) I'm sorry.

Clown   I wanted t' help. No one lets me help. I know why.

Skinner   Why?

Clown   There's something wrong with me. Something horrible, twisted, ugly, unnatural –

Skinner   I wouldn't put it as bad as that!

Clown   O yes it is! I bite my nails! (*Bursts into tears.*) Mother always told me t' git my own lunch, Mr Doctor-sir.

Skinner   Dry your eyes an have my go.

Clown   Thank you, thankyou Mr Skinner. (*Bobbing and bowing.*) Thankyou sir. Thankyou. Thank –

Skinner   All right, all right.

Clown (*inspects the pistol*)   Where d'you wind it up?

Skinner   You don't wind it up! (*To the audience.*) Wind it up! (*Points at* **Fred**.) Hey take that man's gag out. Guess he's dyin t' laugh at our funny friend here.

Stagehand 3 *ungags* **Fred**. *The* **Stagehands** *go, pointing to the* **Clown**, *making derisive gestures about him and miming laughs to each other.*

Skinner   Don't blame you guys quittin while he's around.

Fred   Please. Please.

Clown   What a polite man!

Skinner   Okay let's see you have first go.

Clown *aims at* **Skinner**.

Skinner   Other way! Other way!

Clown *aims at himself.*

Skinner   O fine! Much better!

Audience   Lights! Lights! Lights!

Skinner   My son's on the lights.

Audience *groans.*

Skinner   All right Mrs Leggit Ralph'll fix it okay! (*He shouts off.*) How's things Ralph? Give us all there is.

The lights don't change.

Fred   I didn't do it. I didn't do it.

Audience   Why not? He's a pansy!

Fred   I keep tellin yer! Please!

Audience   Please!

Skinner (*to* **Clown**)   Look at the sights.

Clown (*running round stage*)   Where? Where? Where?

Skinner   On the end of your gun!

Clown   Sights? I thought you meant show-girls – an show-girls – an show-girls – an – (*Starts running round the stage again.*) Where? – where? – where? – where? (*Stops. Raises his arm and aims the pistol at his armpit.*) If I press this little trigger fellas do I get a little spray? (*The audience screams.*) Whassamatter don't you want me to smell nice? (*Looks down the barrel.*) Hello can Alice come out t' play with me – I mean play? (*Puts the pistol to his ear.*) Huha operator. Huha. Huha. Huha – (*Suddenly.*) O mother! I didn't recognise your voice. I thought it was the answerin service. Yes mother. Yes mother. (*Bored. Scratches his crutch and his behind with the pistol. Quickly speaks into the phone.*) No mother I didn't say a word. Must be a bad line. (*Smacks the pistol.*) You bad bad line. Naughty.

Fred   Please!

Audience   Please!

Fred   I didn't. Didn't. Didn't. Didn't. I told yer. O please! Please!

Clown   Is he tryin t' say somethin?

Skinner   Look down the sights!

Clown (*running round the stage*)   Show-girls – show-girls – show-girls –

Skinner   My last warnin!

Clown *peers down the sights. He slowly leans forward till he's almost horizontal.*

Clown   Show-girls . . . show-girls . . . show-girls – show-girls – show-girls –

Clown *starts running round the stage again.*

Skinner   That does it!

Skinner *goes after the* **Clown**. **Clown** *rushes round the stage. He gives the swing a push. It rises very high. The audience screams and sings 'The Daring Young Man on the Flying Trapeze!'* **Clown** *stares in fascination at the swing. Tries to aim at it from the side. The swing keeps swinging out of aim.* **Clown** *exasperated. Suddenly becomes very cunning. Slowly creeps round to the front of the swing where it's easier to aim.*

Clown (*foxy*)   Ha-haaaaaa!

Audience   Ha-haaaaaaaaaaaaaa!

Clown   One. Two.

Fred   O no!

Clown   Eleven. Eight. Seventy-two. (*Counts fingers.*) Six.

Fred   Please.

Clown   What comes after six?

Audience   Three!

Clown   Can't hear!

Audience   Three!!

Clown (*to* **Fred**)   What they say?

Audience   Three!!!

Clown   Seven!

Clown *shoots* **Fred** – *with a jet of water. He squirts water under his arms. Under his crutch. Behind his ears. In his mouth. Gargles. Runs round stage shouting 'Show-girls'.* **Fred** *laughs with hysterical relief.*

Fred   O fellas. Fellas. I thought it was real. I thought you were goin – (*Laughing weakly.*) I thought it was real. I thought it was real.

Clown (*still running*)   Where? Where? Where?

Clown *pulls out the front of his trousers.*

Clown   Down boy! Down boy! Down! Down!

Clown *squirts water into the front of his trousers. A stream comes back in retaliation. The audience roar.* **Skinner** *pushes the swing to keep up momentum.* **Clown** *runs round the stage screaming with a hand over his eye.*

Clown   Blind! Blind! Blind! Blind! (*Shoots* **Fred** *in rage.* **Fred** *jerks violently. Screams.*) Foot!

Audience   Me! Me next! My turn!

The first isolated shots escalate almost immediately into a disorderly volley.

Knee! Foot! Arm! Leg! Gut! Chest! Head! Side! Front! Patsy! Dick!

Skinner *(waving his arms from the side of the stage)*   Order! Order!

Ralph *rushes on, crouches at the side, shoots repeatedly.*

Clown *shoots once from the other side.*

Audience *(screams)*   Lights! Lights! Lights! Lights! Lights!

Fred *spins, twists, jerks, screams. After screams, blood spurts. Lights snap to half, flicker out, come on immediately at full, fade, come back to full, cut out for a second, flash, come back to half, snap up to full.*
Ralph *runs out, back, crouches, shoots.*

Skinner   Hold it! Hold it! Hold it! Hold it!

Shooting stops. The audience noise seethes in a crescendo. **Skinner** *runs to the swing, pushes it, runs back shaking blood from his hands.* **Ralph** *and* **Clown** *open fire.*

Skinner   One more time!

Last volley. Audience noise explodes. **Fred** *has keeled over. He swings slowly and silently upside down. Blood falls and swishes over the stage.*

Skinner   Hold it! Hold it!

Skinner *marches authoritatively to the centre of the stage. He carries a hat. He holds it over his heart.*

Skinner   Up! Up! Up!

Skinner *starts to sing the American national anthem. The vaudeville orchestra joins in, in full, sonorous orchestration, and then the audience.* **Skinner** *raises his hat and waves it like a venerable senator. The lights go. The music ends.*

Scene Four

The same.

The lights come up. It is morning. The body is still on the swing but a sheet has been thrown over it. A **Photographer** *is crouching in front of it.* **Ralph** *and* **Stagehands 1** *and 3 watch.* **Stagehand 2** *removes the cover. He pushes the swing once.* **Paul** *comes through the audience and goes up on stage.*

Photographer (*flash*)   Fine. Fine. Dandy. Great.

The **Stagehands** *start to take* **Fred** *down from the swing.* **Ralph** *supervises.*

Ralph (*sees* **Paul**)   Wait there Sambo.

Paul *stands on the edge of the stage.*

Stagehand 1. We gonna paste him up outside town Mr Skinner?

Ralph   Dad says.

Stagehand 1   On a tree?

Ralph (*nods*)   Better git a box. He's a mess. Cartons outside. We're movin goods in.

Ralph *goes out.* **Stagehand 3** *helps the* **Photographer**: *he holds* **Fred** *in a sitting pose.* **Stagehands 1** *and 2 watch.*

Stagehand 2   I was goin that way I'd expect more'n a poke off Miss Diary Kroll.

Stagehand 3   Heard she was so wide the doctor could've got both arms in.

Stagehand 2   That where she keep her diary?

The **Stagehands** *laugh.*

Stagehand 1   My kids told the wife she took t' goin down the river. Make out she's took short. Hitch up her skirt an squat. (*Flash.*) The long yeller grass tickle her tail. (**Stagehands** *laugh.*) Regular habit.

Ralph *comes back.*

Stagehand 1   Kids got t' know. Followed her down. I clip their ears. Know what they get up to down there.

Ralph *carries a large cardboard carton. It's taller than it's long. Stencilled on its side in black is a brand sign and the number and weight of the tins it contained. The* **Stagehands** *start to lift* **Fred** *into the carton. His body remains doubled up.* **Ralph** *goes to* **Paul**.

Ralph   Where was you?

Paul   Come for my things.

Ralph   Your job was on lights. That's disobeyin orders.

Stagehand 2   Shoe catchin.

Photographer   Hold it. (*Flash.*)

Ralph   Don't disobey orders.

Stagehand 1   'S luck have it he set double.

Ralph   Orders is good for the health.

Ralph *goes back to the others.* **Paul** *goes off into the wings.*

Photographer   I do two regular sizes. Twelve by eight for mountin an wallet size t' carry round an show folks. I'll send a list round. You fill in your name an requirements.

Ralph   Okay.

The **Stagehands** *drop the sheet into the top of the carton.*

Photographer   Sorry – cash in advance.

Ralph   Okay.

Paul *comes on stage. He carries a medium size suitcase. He walks over the stage.*

Photographer   Been caught too often. Weddin's. Sunday school outin's. Masonics. You'd be surprised.

Ralph   Okay, okay.

Mrs Kroll *comes on.*

Mrs Kroll   Paul your case . . .

*The **Stagehands** lift the carton by the bottom corners. They carry it out slowly and carefully.*

Paul (*stops*)   I quit Mrs Kroll.

Mrs Kroll   Paul!

Ralph   You makin some sort of protest over last night?

Paul   Applied for my job a month back. Check with the mine office.

Mrs Kroll   Greta's ill. I can't cope. She knows you.

Paul (*refusing*)   Sorry.

Mrs Kroll (*crying*)   It's too bad. On top of everything.

Ralph (*goes to her*)   Mrs Kroll you can't cry for a nigger. (*Puts his arm round her shoulder.*) That's gonna upset folks. You can't cope with Miss Kroll? She'll go in a good institution. The best. I'm sure folks of this town'd git up a subscription. Why I guess the Justice Riders start it off with part of last night's proceeds. They always support a good cause.

*The **Stagehands** wander back. **Stagehand 3** has a bottle of beer. They watch **Ralph** take **Mrs Kroll** out.*

Stagehand 2 (*to **Paul***)   Mrs Kroll sure is sore at you.

Stagehand 3 *sits on the swing. He opens the bottle and drinks.*

Stagehand 1 (*little laugh. Nods at the swing*)   Mostly *black* folk die so spectacular.

Stagehand 3 (*giggles*)   One time you could've stayed for the fun Paul. (*Stands suddenly.*) Have a peep!

Stagehand 2   No sir! That make Paul nervous!

*The **Stagehands** laugh quietly and easily for a moment. **Paul** drops a dime on the stage. The **Stagehands** laugh and scramble for it.*

Stagehand 2 (*laughing*)   Mine!

Stagehand 3 (*laughing*)   Get off!

Stagehand 1 (*laughing*)   Got it first!

Stagehand 2 (*laughing*)   Will you shove off!

The **Stagehands** *scrap playfully for the coin. They laugh and mug each other a little.*

Stagehand 3 (*rolling on the ground*)   I got Paul's dime! Hey Paul why you throw your dime away?

Stagehand 2   Paul always was a show off.

Stagehand 3   Bye Paul. Keep good!

Stagehand 2 *has knocked the dime from* **Stagehand 3**'s *hand. They roll, cuff, laugh, and ruffle each other's hair. In the fight the swing is knocked. It zooms from side to side – not in the direction of the normal swing – over their rolling bodies.* **Paul** *has gone.*

Stagehand 1   It's mine anyway!

They giggle and tussle. They get up, snatch at each other and wander away.

Derek

Author's Note

The play is set in the present.

In the first production realistic scenery was not used. Props were reduced to a few objects such as a newspaper, a broom and a chair which was used in several scenes. The sacks and money in Scene Three were mimed. Performances lasted approximately fifty minutes.

The characters in the play should not be played as the caricatures they sometimes appear to be. A caricature is abstracted from reality. Its energy comes from its freedom from reality. This is what gives its comment on reality such force. But in this play caricature is not abstracted from character. It is produced from character.

The play is a farce. In conventional farce reality is not allowed to interfere with the energy of the play. But in this play energy is produced from the reality of the farce. So the play should be performed with farcical energy. But to produce this energy the director and performers must base their work on the realism – social realism – of the play's actions and characters.

(1982)

Derek was first performed at the Royal Shakespeare Company's Youth Festival at The Other Place, Stratford Upon Avon, on 19 October 1982, with the following cast:

Derek	Michael Maloney
Julie	Katy Behean
Mother	Brenda Peters
Biff	Christopher Bowen
Doctor	Ian Talbot
Foreman	Peter Postlethwaite

Directed by Nick Hamm
Music by David Shaw-Parker
Lighting and sound by Leo Leibovici

Derek was subsequently presented by the Royal Shakespeare Company in October 1983 as part of its 1983 autumn touring programme. The cast was as follows:

Derek	Jimmy Yuill
Julie	Sue Jane Tanner
Mother	Sheila Hancock
Biff	Simon Templeman
Doctor	George Raistrick
Foreman	Don McKillop

Directed by Sarah Pia Anderson
Music by Ilona Seckacz

One

Kitchen.
Mother, **Julie**, **Derek**.
Mother *and* **Derek** *wear indoor clothes.* **Julie** *wears outdoor clothes. She has a newspaper in one pocket.*

Mother *sits and talks without expecting to be listened to. She is satisfied with not being interrupted.* **Julie** *and* **Derek** *are 'vacant'.*

Mother Thank god 'is dad's dead. Killed in the army while I was carryin 'im. Break 'is 'eart t' see 'ow 'e's turned out. I didn't give in. Struggled t' bring 'im up. Wasn't easy. I don't complain. 'E's no 'elp t' me. 'Ad t' do it all on me own.
Yer'd've thought when I was a bit older I'd've got me reward. Find 'isself a nice steady job. Look after me for a change.

Julie (*to* **Derek**) Fancy a cuppa tea?

Mother Let me put me feet up for once.

Derek (*to* **Julie**) Nah.

Mother 'Ave a few of the comforts other women get.

Julie Fancy a walk?

Mother Don't know what yer see in 'im unless it's pity.

Derek Where to?

Mother If 'e did get a job 'e wouldn't know what t' do with it.

Julie Up the park.

Mother All 'e knows about is sittin down till 'e's worn out an then lyin down.

Derek Might rain.

Mother Pass me me paper Julie.

Julie (*gives paper to* **Mother**) I like walkin in the rain.

Mother   Ta dear.

Derek   Me mac leaks.

Mother (*paper*)   Still there: join the army. Be a man in a
man's world. Free clothin. Bed and board all found. Free
recreation. Just suit 'im: sounds like 'ome. An they learn you a
trade. Electricity. Drive a car. Foreign travel thrown in.
Better'n a 'oliday. Julie tell 'im t' join the army.

Julie   Yer know 'e won't Mrs Jones.

Mother   Why won't 'e?

Julie   'E doesn't like killin people.

Mother   'E wouldn't 'ave t' kill people if they didn't come
over 'ere an take our things.

Julie   'E says 'e asn't got anythin t' take.

Mother   Well 'e would 'ave if 'e joined the army. It was
good enough for 'is father. (*Paper.*) Look there's a job in a
factory for a reliable cleaner. Yer could manage that if yer
made the effort. 'Ad enough practice watchin me.

Mother, **Julie** *and* **Derek** *go.*

Two

Harley Street consulting room.
Biff *and* **Doctor**.
Biff *wears a neat grey suit. The* **Doctor** *wears a black jacket and pin-stripe trousers.*

Biff Doctor the eldest son in our family has been MP for the county town since there was a House of Commons. I am the present eldest son. Naturally when the old fella felt he'd earned the right to be let out to grass he took me along to the selection committee to wag paws. Pure formality as I thought. But dammee they turned me down! Never been so surprised. They weren't being bolshy. S'matter of fact the chairman was most humble. Sort of knelt and tried to polish the old boot with the elbow of his jacket. Poor fella in tears. Grocer the name of Rodgers. (Keeps a brilliant line in biscuits.) 'Look here Rodgers,' I said, 'dab those eyes' – and extended him the pocket handkerchief. Mumbled something about medical grounds. Then his tears choked him and not another syllable could he utter. Naturally I hot-footed it to Harley Street.

Doctor (*sings* 'Doctor's Song')

You ask me why I cure the rich instead of the poor
Surely the pains of the poor are as sharp and their wounds
    are just as sore?
The truth is the rich can pay me more.

You ask me why I teach the pupils in private schools
Not only the poor are dunces – the rich can also be fools
The reason I have an upper class job is that I'm an elitist
    mindless snob

And why do I say the trouble today is too much equality?
The reason – which even the poor can see – is that more
    inequality benefits me

Why d'you want to be an MP? You could be plenty of other things. Why be anything with your money?

Biff   Tradition. And in any case I want to know what the
League of Grocers was getting at. I felt as if I was something
unfit for human consumption that had turned up on his
display counter.

Doctor   You've a good heart, good liver – but watch the
drinking – good lungs. Sound in wind and limb. There's only
one point on which you are not – quite A1.

Biff   What's that?

Doctor   You have a mental age of ten.

Biff   Years?

Doctor   Yes.

Biff   Good lor.

Doctor   Don't lose a moment's sleep over it. It gives you the
mental tunnel vision that gets you to the top. Between
ourselves, I doubt if the mental ages of most cabinets would
add up to the calendar years of one moderately elderly
statesman. I have seen in this room the same bewildered
expression on the faces of men destined to become field
marshals, admirals, captains of industry, telly pundits, bishops,
national editors. In our society the ranks of leadership are
filled by the upper classes. That is a fact. But how could those
classes always produce those most eligible for leadership? It
would not be possible. And so the customs and institutions of
society must be designed to conceal the truth. You may leave
this consulting room happy in the knowledge that although
your mental age is ten, your voice, clothes, education,
manners, attitude and money will hide it from others as well as
till now they have hidden it from you. For those born into
your situation the ladder is already there with the lower classes
firmly holding its foot: you have only to climb, like a toddler
climbing out of its cot.

Biff   Switched off halfway through that. Never was any
good at political philosophy. But as long as you're
satisfied . . . ? Ten? I'll be blowed! – if it was nine there'd be
no stopping me!

Biff *goes. The* **Doctor** *happily hums the opening of his song.* **Biff** *returns. He looks confused.*

Then what's the grocer getting so uppity about?

Doctor (*shrug*)   Someone must have decided that in order to be an MP you can no longer be as stupid as most of the people who would be prepared to vote for you.

Biff   But that's anarchy! Doesn't it mean that any Tom, Dick or Harry could run the country regardless of their background . . . ? Sir Harry I may not be bright but I am resolute! I avoided swatting at Eton because I didn't want to foul the brain – and they didn't expect it of one at Sandhurst. But if it's for the country's good, I'll swat! Recommend me a list of books – but not too long.

Doctor   Useless. A transplant would be necessary.

Biff   What of?

Doctor   The brain.

Biff   That's much better: I'm spared the swatting! We wait till some ancient don is knocked down on a crossing and scoop up the grey matter before anyone else gets to it. I must say I find all of it a bit daunting. I don't want to turn into some bloody bore. The know-all is a most depressing type.

Doctor   I'm afraid the donor would have to be living.

Biff   Better still! I can chat to the chap first and see what I'm taking on. If I don't like him I'll turn him down. All we need is a genius who's broke.

Doctor   I don't know any.

Biff   The garrets must be full of them. The old man would cough up a penny or two.

Doctor   Unfortunately the donor would have to be prepared to accept your brain. That might not be easy to arrange.

Biff   Good lor! This is getting beyond me. I'd have thought

– the economic situation being what it is – people would be queuing up to sell their brains. A bit of cash would give the fella a leg up – and he gets the Eton education thrown in. I certainly wouldn't swap my brain if it wasn't for the damned League of Grocers. My brain may be a bit low on amperage but it's never done me any harm. You've got to admit doctor I'm a sunny, outward-going, likeable sort of chap. When I've got this damned super brain I'll have all the miseries of the world on my shoulders. Swapping a state of bliss for a permanent depression. However, I shall do my duty. We'll get some poor fella so totally brilliant he's on the verge of suicide, wait till he climbs the parapet, nab him, offer him a cheque and a signed photograph of me – smiling – and the brain's in the bag. (*Imitates shooting a pheasant.*) Ping!

Biff *and the* **Doctor** *go.*

Three

Factory.

Derek *and the* **Foreman**.
Derek *carries a broom.*

Foreman   Derek this is your first day with the company. I look back over the forty years – crowded with history – that have passed since *my* first day and share with you the fruits of my experience. You may think that sweeping floors is one of life's humbler stations –

Derek   Yes Mr Swatherly.

Foreman   You would like to start at the top. Wrong Derek. Floors are foundations. Get them right and you're ready for the spires.

Foreman (*sings* 'Foreman's Song')

As long as you live you've got something you can give
You can give your breath to a tin whistle
Or your boot to a mangy cur

When times were good I gave them my labour
They paid me what they said was fair
Now times are bad they don't need my labour
Their machines do my job faster
But they want to be boss so they still need my mind
They take it and give me what they can spare
And I give thanks to my master

As long as you live you've got something you can give
You can give three cheers for those who lead
And spare a tear for the ones who bleed

This is the safe. Be careful when you sweep this spot. The director stands here when he opens the safe. The company likes you to know what goes on on the floors you sweep. Then you sweep better and enjoy it more. Upstairs in the director's suite is one computer. Built into the door of this safe is another computer. Both computers have the same programme. Now, each time the safe is opened a new code is needed. To get that code the last five codes are fed into the computer upstairs. Quick as a flash – you can hear it humming with satisfaction – the computer goes through nine hundred thousand calculations: and pronounces a new code. Now suppose – don't be alarmed – a wrong code was to be recorded in the code book? Next time the last five codes were fed into the computer upstairs it would come up with a code that didn't match the code programmed into this door . . . !

Derek   Nasty, Mr Swatherly.

Foreman   We wouldn't get paid at the end of the week. Have no fear. When the code is pronounced upstairs it's written into the code book – and then read out (clever!) for the director to dial. So the code as written is proved correct by the opening of the door! In this company the director and the broom boy, the might of science and the simple brain of the working lad, all work together for the common good. Well now you have something to meditate on while you sweep the floor.

Foreman *goes.* **Derek** *reads the codes from the code book.*

Derek   65291X – 00751P – 78927W – 89016M – 45857H. (*He points a finger at his forehead, shuts his eyes, smiles and says:*) Click click. (*Immediately he begins to dial the new code, speaking the figures as he dials them.*) 44201K.

The safe door opens and **Derek** *looks into the strong room.*

Bloody 'ell.

Foreman *comes in.* **Derek** *shuts the door.*

Foreman   Derek I forgot to give you your allocation of plastic bags. (*Gives him a pack.*) Five: your first week's supply. And five malleable, plastic-covered wires for fastening the bags when full. Don't lose any. You don't want to get into bad habits.

Derek   Thanks, Mr Swatherly.(*Sings quietly to himself.*)
00751P78927 –

Foreman   That's right Derek. I like to hear a lad singing at
his work.

Derek   Yes Mr Swatherly. (*Sings.*) W89016M –

Foreman *goes.*

– 45857H44201K. (*He points a finger at his forehead, shuts his eyes,
smiles and says:*) Click click. (*Immediately he begins to dial the new
code, speaking the figures as he dials them.*) 71256C.

The door swings open.

Bloody 'eck. Bloody double 'eck.

Quickly and excitedly **Derek** *goes into the strong room, fills the five
plastic bags with paper money, ties the tops with the plastic-covered wires,
drops the bags outside the safe door – and shuts it just as the* **Foreman**
comes back.

Foreman   Good heavens Derek you have been busy.

Derek (*excited and jolly*)   Yes Mr Swatherly.

Foreman   A good clean sweep! I knew you weren't a slacker
when I chose you from the three hundred and seventy
applicants for the job. I know a reliable man when I see one.

Derek (*as before*)   Mr Swatherly can I borrow the trolley to
take this lot to the incinerator?

Foreman   Certainly Derek.

Foreman *helps* **Derek** *to load the sacks onto the trolley.*

We shall get on well lad. You've found your role in life. What
d'you do in your spare time?

Derek   I used to do the space invaders.

Foreman   I'm sorry to hear that Derek. A waste of hard-
earned money.

Derek   I used to win Mr Swatherly – till the pubs barred me.

Foreman   The whole thing sounds very unsavoury. Fortunately all that's behind you and you won't have to waste your talents in the future.

Foreman and **Derek** *wheel out the trolley.*

Four

Cell.

Derek. **Biff** *comes in.*

Derek You my lawyer?

Biff My old man owns the company you robbed. Congratulations. You got away with two millions. When you worked out the code your brain went through nine hundred thousand calculations. You're an Einstein. What school did you go to?

Derek Didn't. Played truant.

Biff Ah one of the underprivileged. At last your luck has changed. I shall inherit five hundred thousand acres and six houses. I've got seven cars and a seat on the company board – and as you can see I'm dripping with charm and panache. Not bad for one chappie eh?

Derek Seen worse.

Biff From now on you shall be like me.

Derek What's the catch?

Biff Sell me your brain.

Derek My brain?

Biff A painless operation – and you get my brain in exchange.

Derek You must be joking.

Biff (*sings* Owner's Song')

I had a dancing table
It jigged about in joy
And whistled like an errand boy
But when the hour struck to eat

I shot my table dead
And covered it with a snow-white sheet
And laid a plate of blood-red meat
And sat at my table and started to eat
And the table stood still on its wooden feet
As still as a box deep deep in the ground
Under a little green green mound

There's something you ought to know. My old man owns a
newspaper – well fifteen actually. They're running a series on
master criminals that will happen to coincide with your trial.
Rotten luck. You know the sort of headline: 'Men too
Dangerous to be at Large.' 'Crime is Big Business.' Ninety per
cent of jury members read the old man's rags. And there's
something else: my old man belongs to the same club as the
beak who'll try your case. The beak's told him he's going to
hand you down thirty years with a recommendation to serve
the lot. That means when you come out you'll be – half a mo.
(*He tries to calculate it on his fingers. Gives up.*) Well a lot older than
when you went in. What use is *any* brain in the jug? Worse if
it's bright. Keep reminding you it's rotting away. Now, what
we'll do is this. I say I gave you the code, told you to get the
money out of the safe so that I could buy some shares or pay
my bookmaker – but forgot to mention it to the old man. Well
it was Ascot week so it could have happened to anyone.
Damned busy time for us all. Then you took the money home
because – wait, it's coming: I'd footed it off to the races and
you being a conscientious employee didn't want to leave it
lying around. My lawyer explains it all to the beak and you're
a free man. You get the best lawyer, best doctor – and a
million pounds.

Derek   You'll give me a million?

Biff   Well it's a bit steep but under the circumstances, yes.

Derek   No.

Biff   Half a mo (*takes a letter from his pocket*) while I go through
my lines. (*Reads letter.*)

Derek   What's that?

Biff My lawyer's letter. (*Reads.*) Yes, it says you'd say no. (*Reads.*) Dum-di-dum-di – really? (*Reads to* **Derek**.) What use is intelligence to you? You don't need a brain to play truant or be unemployed or sit on your bottom all day or push a broom. You'll never control anything – you know nothing about management. You'll never build anything – you aren't trained as an engineer or an architect. If you joined the army you would be a private – so you need to know nothing about strategy. True, from time to time you vote in an election – but the newspapers – (*He looks up at* **Derek**.) the old man's. Fifteen! – (*Reads.*) tell you what to think then. Worse – (*Looks up at* **Derek**.) it says – (*Reads.*) for someone in your situation intelligence is a *liability*. When you use it you end up in a cell. (*Looks up at* **Derek**.) Well, he hit the bull's-eye there! (*Reads.*) Society runs only because – (*Looks up.*) – now this is interesting – (*Reads.*) people in your class are content to believe they are stupid. Look statesman-like and raise finger. (**Biff** *does this and reads on.*) What would happen if the criminal were more intelligent than the judge, –

Derek But I am!

Biff – the factory worker more intelligent than the director, –

Derek *takes the paper from* **Biff** *and reads it aloud.* **Biff** *lip-reads over* **Derek***'s shoulder.*

Derek – the comprehensive schoolboy more intelligent than the public schoolboy? All the advantages would go to those least able to use them. Thus society would waste its best efforts on the incompetent. Lower voice and exude compassionate understanding. (**Biff** *adopts a compassionate pose and expression.* **Derek** *reads on.*) Derek you are a social misfit, a danger to yourself and others –

Biff I say old man what rotten luck! I'm really cut up about this!

Derek (*gives the letter to* **Biff**) 'Op it!

Biff Half a mo. This is interesting. (*Reads.*) I on the other hand am your leader, whether you are –

Derek (*reads*)   – in or out of prison. Clasp hands, raise head proudly but adopt humble tone –

Biff (*clasps his hands, proudly raises his head and adopts a humble expression*)   You see the contortions we have to put up with for you chaps. I sometimes think the rewards of being in the upper class are not worth the efforts needed to stay in it.

Derek (*reads*)   Even if I do not become an MP I shall, with my Eton education, Sandhurst training and business connections, enter the House of Lords, head royal commissions and advise the CBI and the government –

Biff   And there's the newspapers! Fifteen!

Derek (*reads*)   I am born to power. Like it or not –

Biff (*pointing his finger at a line in the letter*)   This is a nifty phrase!

Derek (*reads*)   – your destiny is in my hands. Begin to crescendo. Is it not better that I should have the best brain? (**Biff** *nods.*) While that brain is in your head society will not allow you to use it –

Biff (*taking the letter and reading*)   When it's in mine, I can use it for you!

Derek   Scram!

Biff (*reads*)   I've always felt sorry for the underdog – huh-ha – lower paper and strike chummy pose. (**Biff** *does this and holds the paper so that he can surreptitiously read it.*) This is a personal off-the-cuff confession. Those born to my privileges should help those less fortunate. Give me your brain and I will protect your grey-haired old mother.

Derek   Drop dead.

Biff   No no! You're supposed to say yes now! Look it's in the letter!

Derek   Stuff your letter!

Biff Two million! Not a penny more!

Derek No!

Biff I'll give you my address book. It's full of crumpet!

Derek No!

Biff O dear back to the lawyer!

Biff *goes and* **Julie** *comes in.*

Derek Know what 'e wants?

Julie 'E asked me t' talk you into it.

Derek We'd be millionaires! What a life! All the things in the ads 'd jump out an grab us! If you're rich yer don't need a brain! Yer pay people t' think for yer. What's the alternative? Shut up in the jug till I'm gaga. See you once a week, sittin over a cup of cold coffee with a screw starin. An once a fortnight yer'd visit me mum in 'er cell – that's all 'er kitchen is. Then someone'd smile at yer, – probably when yer was on yer way 'ome from seein me – that's when yer'd feel loneliest – and yer'd shack up with 'im. Then visit me and stare at the coffee.

Julie No.

Derek O come on! Two years, three at the most.

Julie No!

Derek Then what?

Julie I don't know.

Derek I wouldn't blame yer. If my life's wasted it don't mean yours 'as t' be.

Julie It wouldn't 'appen like that.

Derek Yer see, you're lying already. Yer can't love someone for thirty years if yer don't see 'em – unless they're dead. That's our problem Julie: I love you. Thirty years? I'd knock me brains out on the wall.

Julie   No Derek. I don't want the money. I want you as you are.

Derek   Yer can't: that's the one sure thing about our life. Everything you say makes it worse. Tell me t' grab the money an fly off t' Bermuda. Then I could say yer ain't worth it: she's a 'ard-faced grabbin bitch! I don't need a brain t' love you. They'd 'ave t' skin me t' change that. It'll be like a street accident. The car's spinnin an yer think christ this is it! Then yer wake up in 'ospital with a busted leg. But you're alive. So yer get a stick an learn t' walk. My life's like a car crash in slow motion. You're the only good thing I've got. Let me sell my brain.

Derek *goes out in the direction taken by* **Biff**.

Julie (*sings* 'Girlfriend's Song')
  They said you died for your country
  But you didn't own one tile on a house
  You didn't own one small plot of land
  Or the shirt on your back
  Or the gun in your hand

  You didn't own the papers you read
  That put the ideas you had in your head
  You didn't own your life
  That's why you're dead

  And those who cry don't own the tears they shed
  Any more than the floating clouds own the sky
  Unless they own the thoughts in their head.

Julie *goes*.

Five

Kitchen.

Mother.
Biff *comes in.*

Biff Whacher me ol' darlin! 'Ere's yer favourite ray of sunshine come t' shine on 'is favourite flower! I 'ear your boy's comin on a treat!

Mother I'm sure 'e's tryin 'is best t' do what –

Biff Congratulate me ma! I'm now a member of the 'ouse. Doubled me old man's majority. Stand for a democracy that can speak t' the people in their own voice – accordin t' the old man's papers: No doubt yer'd like t' 'ear me maiden speech.

Mother O I couldn't follow all that high-fallutin' –

Biff "Onourable mates and matesses! We all know the types who speak against the fluff. Next minute they're in yer livin room fillin their pockets. The louts who mug ol' dears for their pensions. People say the criminal's bin misunderstood. When someone kicks me in the privates an snatches me wallet I know what I understand. "Mummy 'it me when I was little!" Not 'ard enough mate! I'd flog 'em till the skin peeled. 'Onourable members laugh. If yer want the benefit of a free society, then protect it by treatin a thug like a thug. One fine mornin I want t' switch on the radio an 'ear the disc jockey say "This mornin two were dropped at the Scrubs – an 'ere by popular request is a number for the 'angman! Swing it fellas!'"

Julie *wheels* **Derek** *in in a wheelchair. His face is white and he is three-quarters paralysed. A blanket covers his knees, and a skullcap of bandages covers his head. He speaks with a fake gentility.* **Mother** *points at* **Derek** *– repeatedly poking her finger towards him – and nods and smiles at* **Biff** *for his approval.*

Well if it ain me ol' mucker Derek boy!

Derek   Yes sir. Thank you very much, sir. Well sir –

Julie   Why you walkin round an' 'e's in a wheelchair?

Biff   I 'ad private treatment after the op. Can't fix anythin like that for Derek juss yet. Don't want it t' look like there's bin a bit of hankypanky, know what I mean? (*Pinches* **Julie***'s bottom.*) Goes a bit limp after teatime does 'e darlin? 'E'll soon be chasin yer up them apples an pears. I know me ol' Derek. Now would you ladies take the air for a bit? It's time for a little man t' man chat.

Julie   Yell if yer need me.

Julie *and* **Mother** *go* – **Mother** *poking her finger at* **Derek** *and nodding and smiling at* **Biff** *for his approval.*

Derek (*hand out*)   Yes sir. Have you got my money sir? Thank you sir.

Biff   That's what I wanted t' talk t' yer about Derek. I could give yer the money. An if it was up t' me own personal inclination I would give it t' yer. But the matter ain as simple as –

Derek (*hand out*)   Yes sir. The money sir. As you promised sir.

Biff   I did, I did. I 'ope yer don't expect me t' go back on me word?

Derek   O no sir. Sir wouldn't do that sir. Didn't mean to speak out of turn sir.

Biff   But when I gave it I 'ad your brain, so I was – well t' speak frank, stupid. Now I've got me own brain.

Derek   Yes sir. So sir won't let me down sir.

Biff   I shan't do anythin you don't agree to Derek. That's what I told me voters an that's what I'm tellin you. Suppose I give yer the two million?

Derek (*hand out*)   Thank you sir.

Biff   Don't interrupt there's a good lad. Your brain ain worth two million. It's worth twenty. But Derek did yer or did yer not rob me ol' man's safe?

Derek (*smiles*)   Yes sir. Thank you sir.

Biff   Now I've been elected t' parliament. Of course me natural charm was an asset an the gift of the gab didn't 'urt. But what swep me in was the law an order ticket. Nah what would you say – as a private citizen – if I was t' pay you – as a crook – for breakin the law? As a private citizen yer'd be outraged. With your brain yer ain smart but even you know right from wrong when its spelt out t' yer.

Derek   No sir. If you don't pay sir. Sir stole my brain.

Biff   Derek, Derek, yer *give* me yer brain – for yer own good, remember? If it was a matter of my wishes I'd give yer the money, leave parliament, beg in the gutter, work for Oxfam. But I couldn't pass an ol' lady on the street without blushin for shame if I'd done anythin t' encourage the criminal classes. I've 'ad a change of 'eart Derek. That's thanks t' your brain an the good, kind nature that went with it. I want us all t' live t'gether like brothers and sisters. Of course I'm tempted t' give yer the money just t' see your face light up with gratitude. But it would be wrong. I'd rather 'ave me own brain back.

Derek   But sir promised.

Biff   Derek I assure you that when I say no – nine hundred thousand calculations went into that decision.

Derek   No sir. Can't accept it sir. With respect sir. Sir's cheating me.

Biff   I'm sorry you said that. (*Grabs* **Derek** *by the front of his collar, jerks him halfway out of the wheelchair and sticks his face into his face.*) Now listen shrink 'ead – I'm your MP, so try t' get this into that bandaged nut! For a start, if this comes out – an whatever 'appens I swear yer won't get a penny out of me – you're back on trial! An me? I'm blamed for 'elpin yer with the cover-up, the ol' man's papers – nineteen: he's bought four more! – run a few leaders on the danger of kidglove methods – treat 'em decent an they kick yer in the crutch – I apologise t' the public an call for the return of the rope – an next election I treble me majority. It's the way of the world, Derek. (*Lets go of* **Derek**'s *collar*.) As it is, you're a free man with a roof over your 'ead an two lovely ladies t' wait on yer every whim. Leave it where it is eh? Frankly I'd like t' close the matter in a gentlemanly way but if yer want a fight –

Derek   O no sir. Sorry sir. No disrespect sir. Very grateful for all sir's done. Sir knows I didn't mean t' –

Biff   I know yer didn't Derek. You're just confused. People in your class can't think for themselves. Thass why I do it for them. I'll send in the ladies.

Biff *goes and* **Julie** *comes in.*

Derek   What is it? You've changed.

Julie   I don't think so.

Derek   Yes Julie. More than me. In the hospital. When you collected me. I thought it would be the old times. I knew before we got to the street it was different.

Julie   All right. I've changed.

Derek   Don't tell me. I can't deal with any more trouble.

Julie   I'm leavin you.

Derek   No Julie. Give it time. You can't decide anythin while I'm in a wheel –

Julie   It's over.

Derek   For god's sake Julie you didn't love me because I was good at sums!

Julie   I don't love you now.

Derek   You do.

Julie   You know I don't. Let's face it before we ruin the rest of our lives.

Derek   Don't leave me. You're afraid. It'll be all right when I –

Julie   I warned you, but you wouldn't listen.

Derek   I had no choice.

Julie   Even if I'd've married someone else I'd've still loved you. I wouldn't 'ave minded bein un'appy if I could've seen you. Now you're not even dead. Yer've vanished! There's nothin there! 'Ow can I love that?

Derek   Please Julie.

Julie   Don't grovel. Yer never grovelled before. Now yer grovel t' everyone.

Derek   Please Julie! What if he's outside? He'll hear!

Julie   Let 'im! Yer're like a kid! Yes sir no sir three bags full sir.

Derek   Be quiet woman! He could turn us out of the flat. Stop me getting another job. He came to help us. People like him know what's best. That's why we have to respect them. He understands us better than we –

Julie   You creep!

Derek   Julie I need his help. It's – it's not my world any more! Julie I – (*He reaches towards her and falls from the wheelchair onto the floor. She looks at him.*) He won't give me the money.

Julie   None of it?

Derek   No.

Julie   (*laughs*)   Not a penny? The dirty little sod! I thought 'e'd give yer a few thousand t' shut yer up!

Derek   (*lying still, doubled up on the floor*)   You can't leave me now. Give me six months. A week. You've got to stay. Someone's got to give me somethin.

Julie   (*she goes to him, picks him up from the floor as if he were a child, puts him in the wheelchair and tucks the blanket round his legs*)   I can't. You give too much away. Yer 'ave t' fight for every little thing or yer lose the lot.

Julie *goes and* **Mother** *comes in.*

Mother   Showed 'im t' the lift. I was afraid those little buggers would've done their business in the corner – or messed 'is new car. Thank god they'd be'aved theirselves.

Mother *wheels* **Derek** *out.*

Six

Kitchen.

Mother (*sings* 'Mother's Song')

How foolish a work is man!
He kills his children in wars
And burns down his stone cities
Yet condemns what he does and fights to be free
Who can explain this riddle to me?

If we ran the world so that we were free
To own our heads and our hands and our feet
The place where we work and the streets where we meet
The papers we read and the films we see
Then we would find
That the human race
Is the race of human kind

(*Worried.*) Why? . . . Why did I let 'im out? 'E's still not isself.
(*Suddenly very angry.*) That 'eartless little 'ussy! (*Suddenly very quiet.*)
No, I mustn't say such things. If it wasn't for me 'e wouldn't
'ave been arrested. When I saw those sacks of money I don't
know what came over me. (*Smiles.*) I felt as excited as a little
girl with a skippin rope. (*Suddenly begins to laugh.*) If it 'd've bin
one I'd've bin all right. It was the – (*Her laughter becomes
uncontrollable. She can't say the number.*) – five! I opened the
window and threw 'andfuls of notes down t' the street an
shouted – (*Her laughter increases.*) – I'm rich! I'm rich! (*Quietens
down.*) Then the law came. I – (*Her laughter explodes uncontrollably
again.*) tried t' 'ide 'em under the sofa but the – the – inspector
sat on it! – an they – (*She hears a noise outside.*). It's 'im. (*Controls
her laughter. Shouts angrily.*) Where've you bin you wicked boy?
Frightenin yer mother! No consideration! (*She turns her back to
the door, trying to calm herself.*) All self an no –

Derek *marches in. The military automaton in army uniform. He
crashes to attention.*

(*Stunned.*) What've you bin up to?

Derek (*as if shouting a reply to an officer. Still at attention*)   Joined the army. Can't sit round here all day!

Mother (*throws her arms round her shoulders and hugs herself*)   You good boy! Your dad'd be proud of you! Look just like 'im! Give me a turn when yer come through the door.

Derek (*as before*)   Paid active service bonus. Send money home.

Mother (*angry again*)   And that little madam won't see a penny! I know why she walked out. All they care about is money! When I see 'er on the street I'll give 'er a piece of my –

Derek (*moving one hand to gesture. Otherwise still at attention*) Mum don't. I'm tired.

Mother   Of course you are. (*Goes closer to him.*) Sit down. (*She is about to touch his uniform but stops herself.*) I'll go an cook yer a soldier's dinner.

Mother *goes out.* **Derek** *looks down at himself. He is quiet and bewildered. He begins to talk to himself.*

Derek (*Derek 2.*)   (Big boots. Clump clump. Horse's hoofs. Tunic. Thick. Hard. Comb with a wire brush. Scrape scrape. A long time ago . . . it was different . . . I was someone else. (*Little pause.*) If I could remember.

(*Derek 1. Quietly, temptingly.*) Come on, yer remember. We 'ad all the laughs. Walkin down the windy street with yer 'ands dug in yer pockets. Whistlin.

(*Derek 2.*) Long time ago.

(*Derek 1. More confident, reassuring.*) Rough ol' days but at least yer knew 'oo yer was an where yer was goin even if yer didn't always 'ave the fare t' get there.

(*Derek 2.*) I – I'm afraid. Don't know what'll 'appen. They're sendin me t' war. Don't know the name of the place. Sounds like the name of a disease.

(*Derek 1. Angry.*) Derek ol' son yer don't think. Not even when yer 'ad the right equipment.

(*Derek 2.*) I'm sorry.

(*Derek 1.*) Don't give me that yer thick bastard! Yer're killin me – well, doin yer best! Let me give yer a piece of advice.

(*Derek 2.*) Who are you?

(*Derek 1.*) Yer best friend. Now get me out of this bloody clown's gear. Yer only put me in it because they took yer 'ead. First you put me in a uniform! Next they'll put me in a wooden box! Derek, I'm a peaceful bloke but I'll kick the bloody daylights out of yer! Yer don't deserve someone like me.

(*Derek 2.*) It's too late. The military cops would arrest you.

(*Derek 1. Shrugs.*) Fair enough. Then they'd put me in a cell. I'd be a bloody sight safer there than where you're takin me!

(*Derek 2.*) Too late!

(*Derek 1.*) It's never too late till they pick up yer pieces!

(*Derek 2.*) They've done something to my brain, Derek! With a knife. I can't think any more.

(*Derek 1.*) Too bloody true Derek! At last: (*Quietly.*) a pearl of wisdom . . . ! Look yer don't 'ave t' be a genius t' see what's starin yer in the face. Suppose yer got the sharpest eyes in the world but yer skulkin in a ditch afraid t' look out? What d'yer see? Mud two inches in front of yer face. Yer got one eye but yer're stood on top of the mountain. What d'yer see? The world. Derek, yer can be smarter now than yer've ever bin. A rat ain got much brain but it knows what the cat eats. If you was a rat yer'd ask it what it fancied for dinner. I'll tell you what yer want mate. Not brains. Guts. The guts t' open your eyes and see you're on top of the mountain. See who yer are. See what they done to yer. Then yer'll know yer enemy. If yer don't 'e'll creep up be'ind yer an push you off the top.

(*Derek 2.*) I'd like t' remember . . . somethin . . . what I used t' be. I'm *afraid*. I could do it if you stayed with me.

(*Derek 1*.) Through thick and thin.

(*Derek 2*.) Till I learnt t' think it out.

(*Derek 1*.) Who you are. Where you are. What you doin.

(*Derek 2 reaches forwards for Derek 1*.) 'Elp me when I was goin t' fall. Talk t' me when I was confused. Show me 'ow t' –

Derek *hears a noise and stops.* **Mother** *comes in.*

Mother   Why aren't you sittin down? Yer'll overdo it an get discharged! (*Sees he is disturbed.*) I'm glad we never got the money. It'd've made a difference. Could've done this room up. Bought a reliable 'eater. But I'd've always bin listenin for a knock on the door. It's better like this. Evil gains bring evil losses. At least this way we can look ourselves in the face.

Mother *goes.*

Derek (*sings* 'Soldier's Song')

I worked at their factory bench
And now my arms are gone
I marched in their khaki ranks
And now I've lost my legs
I sailed in their ships
Now I'm under the sea
I lived in their city
And now it's on fire
I gave them my head
And now I'm dead
And these are the last words I said
Why should these things be?
And they don't answer me

Derek *goes.*

Seven

Kitchen.

Mother.

Biff *comes in in staff officer's uniform.*

Biff   Mrs Jones I've come t' tell yer 'ow your boy died.

Mother (*flatly, not looking up*)   Very obliged sir.

Biff   Imagine. Side of the 'ill. Nasties dug in up front. We bomb an shell an rocket an gas an grenade an defoliate the little savages for 'ours. But never trust a nasty. Shot one once. Lay down dead. Went up t' give 'im the terminal boot in the crutch. The little bleeder sits up an tosses a grenade at me! Fortunately me batman threw isself across it an I was saved. (Rumour 'as it 'e was tryin t' scarper an I tripped 'im up – but that ain true) 'Owever it's the story of your boy that must be told. I surveyed the field of battle through me ultra-long-distance binoculars. Suddenly Derek jumps up an starts t' run – would yer believe it? – t' the rear. Sergeant major next t' me says the little bleeder's done a bunk. Some people's faith in 'uman nature takes a toss. Yer see, Derek'd started t' talk to 'isself. The MO said shell shock. But I never doubted 'im: 'e was swearin at the nasties under 'is breath. Anyway what should 'appen next but the nasties jump up out of the ground right in front of 'im! The bastards'd bin creepin up our rear. Derek must've sensed this – 'e was a sensitive lad – an threw 'isself into the thick of 'em t' save the command post. I ordered the artillery t' open up an they flattened the lot. Your son died a 'ero.

Biff *gives* **Mother** *a small transparent plastic bag with mud in it. The bag is tied with a plastic-covered wire.*

Mother (*flatly*)   Is this Derek?

Biff   Fraid 'e went up with the barrage. We found 'is boots an interred 'em. A volley bein fired over the open grave an the

padre sayin a prayer for Derek's sole – 'umour means a lot t'
the British army. Thass a sod from the top. Thought yer'd
appreciate a fond remembrance.

Mother (*flatly*)   It's muddy.

Biff   Weather out there ain very clement. Funny thing Mrs
Jones, Derek died but lives on in me. It's my duty to look after
all 'e left be'ind in this tattered world in the way 'e'd've
wished.

Mother (*quiet bitterness*)   Thank you sir.

Mother *goes.* **Julie** *and* **Derek** *come on.*

Julie, **Derek**, **Biff** (*sing* 'Last Song')

> I walked along the street
> And sucked my ice lolly
> When somebody dropped the bomb
> My lolly was yellow and green
> It melted and marked the spot
> Where my two feet had been
>
> I walked along the street
> And chewed my fried chicken-leg
> When somebody dropped the bomb
> The hell-fire picked it clean
> And burnt it up to ashes
> That fell and marked the spot
> Where my two feet had been
>
> I walked along the street
> Whistlin a happy song
> That had no reason or rhyme
> And the tempest when the bomb was dropped
> Blew my whistle to the edge of the world
> Where it will shriek till the end of time

Fables and Stories

Author's Note

Service records the author's own experience. *A Man in Ruins* is
from the preparatory Notebook for *The Crime of the Twenty-First
Century*.

(1997)

Certain Stories

A man was walking alone on a street at night in Morocco. He did not know the city. There were groups of young men about but because he did not know the city he called the groups gangs. A man overtook him. He wore a dark suit. He stopped in front of him, turned to face him and blocked his way. The man in the dark suit said 'Would you like me to kill you?' He did not speak in anger or violence. He sounded as if he wished to help. Of course the other man sidestepped and hurried on. The man in the black suit followed him. Again he overtook him, stopped and turned to block his way and without any apparent offence he asked 'Would you like me to kill you?' Again the other man hurried on. He didn't run because he was afraid of attracting attention. Perhaps some of the men would come from the gangs to help the man in the black suit. A third time the man followed him, overtook him, stopped, turned, blocked his way and asked the question and the man hurried on. This time the man in the black suit did not follow him and he got safely back to his hotel.

When I was told this story I was with friends. They began to explain the story. Perhaps 'to kill' was a code. Perhaps it meant 'Would you like some drugs?' Perhaps the man in the black suit was homosexual and had said kiss not kill and the other man had misheard because he was tense. Perhaps it was a special local invitation. Perhaps it meant a visit to certain brothels. Perhaps the killing was symbolic. Or a fantasy. Perhaps the other man had misunderstood altogether. And so on. These explanations spoilt the story for me. They explained it but gave it no meaning.

Suppose the word had been misheard or misunderstood — what follows from that? The point is that the man could walk on the street and believe he heard such a word. Perhaps this tells us more not about Morocco but about Manchester or Chicago. What is interesting is that the mystery of the story throws so much light on reality. We should avoid confusion and mystification but that does not mean that stories should not be left to make their own points.

The Dragon

There was once a dragon who breathed fire. Everyone chased him through the streets because they said that breathing fire was bad. He tried to hide in a shop. It was a linen shop. The dragon set fire to all the sheets and curtains. The shop assistants chased him out of the shop and down the road. He tried to hide in a doorway but set light to a very big mansion. The man who owned the mansion was very rich. He had a lot of dogs. They were angry because their kennels were burnt. They joined in the chase. By now a large mob was chasing the dragon. He was very tired. The harder he ran the more he panted and the more fire he breathed. He hid in a copse in a beautiful park. That caught fire of course. The park-keepers joined in the chase waving pitchforks and rakes. He tried to hide behind an ice-cream van and melted all the ice-cream. The ice-cream man also joined in the chase. He blared out his chimes as loudly as they would go.

The dragon ran into the countryside. He found a huge pond. He said 'I must put out this fire in my throat.' He drank and drank but the fire still burnt. The water started to get hot and to steam and to sizzle. The ducks quacked at him. They were afraid.

The dragon turned away and walked down a stony road. It was very cold. He came to some poor people living by the roadside. Their children were shivering and trying to sleep. Suddenly they woke up. What was this lovely warmth filling their hut? They went outside. The dragon was sitting in the road breathing fire. The poor people were very pleased to see him. They didn't chase him away and so he didn't bump into anything or hide inside anything and so he didn't set fire to anything. He toasted their sandwiches. And they named the dragon Summer because he brought them good times.

The people came from the city. It was a fortified city, by the way. Round it there was a high grey wall. The gate was made of iron spikes. They looked like rusty teeth. The people from the city said the dragon was dangerous. He would set fire to all the fields. The poor people said he wouldn't as long as no one chased him into the fields. The people from the city said the poor people were as dangerous as the dragon and they would all be chased away. So the poor people sighed and set Dragon Summer onto the people from the city and he burnt them all up.

The Boy Who Threw Bread on the Water

A young boy read in a big book 'Cast your bread upon the waters and it shall be returned to you after many days.' So he went to the Serpentine in Hyde Park. He threw his bread upon the waters and sat down to wait. He knew he would have to wait many days but he didn't know how many. This meant he couldn't go away and come back. It might happen that his bread would be returned while he was away and someone else would get it. He waited three days. Then a policeman came to arrest him for loitering with suspicious intent. The boy said 'I'm waiting for my loaf.' The policeman asked him where it would come from. The boy pointed to the lake. The policeman arrested him. In court the magistrate sent him to a madhouse to have his head examined.

A priest visited the boy in the madhouse. He bought the boy a present. It was a copy of the same big book. The boy said he thought the book was misleading. He said he had cast his bread upon the waters but it had not been returned to him. The priest explained to him that the book did not mean what it said. It had to be interpreted. The boy said 'Who is to interpret it?' The priest said 'The priests'. The boy said 'Well, what does the line about casting your bread on the waters mean?' The priest said 'Well, there is much disagreement about that.' The boy said – and you must remember that he was very angry because he was sitting in a madhouse – that god must be a great fool to have all that power and still not be able to write clearly. The priest was shocked. He told the magistrate the boy was wicked. The magistrate sent him to prison.

I'm sorry to say the boy behaved badly in prison. The first morning he was sentenced to solitary confinement. They took him down to the punishment cells. They locked him in. After

a while the door opened. The warden handed him his dinner.
It was bread and water. He ate the bread and drank the water.
Here you see the wisdom of man contrasted with the wisdom
of god.

The Boy Who Tried to Reform the Thief

A boy was playing in the playground. A big boy came up to
him and stole his apple. Before the big boy had taken two
mouthfuls of the apple the little boy kicked him in the shins.
A master was looking from an upstairs window. He hurried
down to the playground. He grabbed the little boy by the
collar and pulled him away from the big boy. The little boy
said 'He stole my apple'. The teacher said 'I saw him steal it.
That was a very bad thing. But two wrongs don't make a
right. When someone injures us we must appeal to their
reason. We must explain that it's wrong to steal and then we
must ask for our property back. That is what civilised people
do.' The little boy said, 'But he wouldn't have given me my
apple. He'd have eaten it.' 'No doubt' said the teacher,
'nevertheless, where is your apple now? Look, it fell to the
ground and was trodden on in the fight. Now no one can eat
it. And your collar is torn and your face is bleeding. It is true
that by doing the right thing you would not have got your
apple back. But then you wouldn't have been cut and your
clothes wouldn't have been torn. And what is more: you
would have had the satisfaction of doing right. For virtue is its
own reward. And the reward of virtue is better than a pound
of apples.' The teacher was very pleased. There was the
crushed apple lying on the ground and it almost seemed as
if it was agreeing with him.

Next day the boy was walking past the staff room. He
looked in the window and saw the teacher tied to the chair
and with a gag in his mouth. And there in a corner was a thief
in front of the open safe. He was stealing the wages of the
masters. The teacher was very pleased when he saw the boy
peering in. When the boy disappeared from the window he
sighed (secretly, because he didn't want the thief to hear) with

relief. He said to himself 'The boy has gone to telephone the police. Soon I shall be rescued.' Imagine his surprise when the door opened and the boy walked in. The thief was also surprised. The boy carefully closed the door behind him. The boy knew that good boys do not leave doors open.

The teacher said to himself – he couldn't say it aloud because he was gagged – 'What a brave boy. He's come to tackle the thief single-handed. Soon I shall see him kick the thief in the shins. Of course it's very foolish of him to tackle the thief alone. But at least the thief will be disturbed and will run away without our wages.'

The boy said to the thief 'This is a school in which we are taught to do the right thing. It is wrong to steal. So I must ask you to put the money back. I assure you that the satisfaction you will receive from returning the money to its rightful owners will far outweigh the satisfaction you will get from spending it on ice-cream and racing cars,' which are the sort of things the boy imagined the thief would spend it on. The boy continued 'Of course I know that you may very well not return the money. In fact I'd be very surprised if you did. Nevertheless my teacher is wiser than me and I must try to do what he would do in these circumstances. Fortunately he has already told me what that would be. And so I will say what he would have said if he were not gagged.' And while the thief carefully bundled up the ten pound notes and put them in his bag the boy told him of all the delights that are the reward of virtue. From time to time the master made gurgling noises behind the gag. The boy was pleased because the noises sounded very enthusiastic and he was glad to see how eagerly the master responded to the way he repeated his lesson. The thief said 'Thank you for talking to me young man. I'm glad to see that the standards of education are not slipping. It's obvious you're being taught all a gentleman should know. I must go now.' The boy said, 'Thank you for allowing me to address you.' The thief and the boy shook hands and just in time the boy remembered that it would be the polite thing to do to see the thief to the school gate. There he found a large car waiting and he opened and shut the door for the thief and waved goodbye as he drove away. He went back to the staff room. He cut the ropes tying the teacher to the chair. The teacher pulled the gag from his mouth. I regret to tell you – and we must understand that it is very uncomfortable to be tied up for an hour – that the teacher kicked the boy in the shins. Then he rushed out shouting 'Stop thief' and telephoned the police. Later the headmaster severely reprimanded the boy and he was almost expelled. He could not understand why.

When the teacher came home without his wages his wife was angry. She wouldn't talk to him for a week and fed him only on bread and butter for a month. He tried to explain to her the rewards she would receive from behaving in a civilised way. She wouldn't listen.

The Good Traveller

Hear the story of the good traveller and what followed from his great kindness.

A poor man lay at the roadside. He had been beaten up by soldiers. His head bled. He came to and reached a decision. The soldiers were hired by the Marquis. He lived in a great fortress. He sent out the soldiers to rob the countryside and cower the people. He didn't care what the soldiers did as long as they brought him back money and goods when they returned from their raids and as long as the people continued to bow to the ground when he was carried about in his palanquin. As the poor man came to he decided he had nothing left to live for. He would steal into the fortress and murder the Marquis. He knew he would not get out and that the soldiers would kill him. But at least he was sure he would get in. He was thin enough to get through a tiny crack in the wall. To seal his resolution he dashed his begging bowl to the ground. It broke into tiny pieces.

It was at this moment that the good traveller came along the road. He saw the poor man dash his begging bowl to pieces. He said to himself 'This man's despair is so great that he breaks his begging bowl that he might die more quickly.' It happened that the traveller was a merchant. It was the evening of market day. At the market he had cheated a silly old man by giving him a few coppers for a fine silver candlestick. He had told the silly old man that the silver candlestick wasn't worth much because it was only one of a pair. Next he took a table back from a young woman who had already paid half its price. Her husband had suddenly fallen ill. She asked for more time to pay what she owed. The merchant said it was against the rules of the Market Committee. This wasn't true but it made it seem to the young woman that nothing could be gained by arguing with him because she knew (so he thought) that he would not break the law. Instead the young woman cursed him. This upset him. He happened to have become more superstitious since he had started to pay the priests to pray for the security of the great chests in his cellars.

He took the table from her house and sold it to someone else. He had been troubled in mind ever since he left the market. When he saw the destitute man he said to himself, 'It would be as well to do a good deed and thus remove the curse.' He gave the man a coin. It was quite a large coin because the day's business had been good.

What starving man would not think of meat and bread and wine when he is suddenly given a large coin? The idea of killing the Marquis went completely out of his head. He ran to town and feasted and drank. Nor did he forget to take his wife and children to share his table at the tavern. And there was some money left over. The poor man said to his wife 'Think, wife. If I had gone off to kill the Marquis I would not have been at the roadside when the good traveller passed.' His wife said 'And I and our child would never have seen you again.' If the unaccustomed presence of food in her stomach had not made her so happy she would have cried. The poor man said 'I shall never lose patience again.'

Now god had watched all this from his window. He thought of all the other poor men who begged at the roadside. Then he thought of the silly old man who had been cheated and of the young woman who had lost her table. Her husband had just died so she had another reason to need comfort. God decided to send an angel to them all with a message of hope. The angel came down and whenever he saw the people suffering he told them the story of the good traveller. They were, he told them, to live in hope. It might happen that on any day someone would give them a large coin. Who could say? What's more, god had seen into the heart of the poor man. So the angel was able to tell them that the good traveller had even saved him from committing the mortal crime of murder. 'Yes' said the angel 'but for this good deed the Marquis would have been murdered that very night.'

When the poor people heard this they ran after the angel and threw stones at him. The angel had to fly back to heaven with some of his feathers missing.

The good traveller went smiling on his way and the cries of the poor, the widowed and orphaned, the beaten and imprisoned, rose to heaven. But god had turned away when he saw how the wicked had stoned his ministering angel.

The Cheat

One day Billy sat his examinations. The questions were hard. He couldn't answer all of them. He looked over his friend's arm. He saw the answers neatly written down on his friend's sheet of paper. He copied them onto his own sheet of paper. The master saw him spying and copying. Billy didn't pass the exam and what's more he was punished.

That night he was too upset to sleep. He went downstairs for a glass of water. Passing the sitting-room door he heard his father plotting with his mates to burn down the house on the corner of the street. They didn't like the man who lived in it. His skin was a different colour to Billy's and his Dad's. Billy said to himself 'Spying again! Shall I tell my teacher what I've heard? It would make the man who lives in the corner house happy if I told my teacher. But I cheated at the exam because I wanted to pass and make my father happy. My father says he can't get a good job because he didn't pass any exams. But if it's wrong to cheat to make even your father happy it *must* be wrong to cheat to make the man in the corner house happy. I will say nothing.' But he was very unhappy when the corner house burnt down. The man who lived in it was also burnt. He had to go to hospital.

Now the man's son was Billy's classmate. They often played together. But Billy didn't enjoy their games any more. He felt sad. He decided to ask the master about it. He went to him and said 'I knew my father was going to burn the house down. I didn't tell because that would be cheating. Now I don't like to play any more.'

The master beat Billy. His Dad and his mates were sent to prison. And of course Billy's classmate wouldn't sit by him any more. Everyone looked at Billy and said 'What d'you expect? Comes from a criminal background.'

In time Billy grew up. He went to work in a government office. He found lots of plans in a cabinet. One plan showed a town in the next country. It showed where his country was going to drop bombs on it. The plan said that the town and everything in it would be burnt to cinders. Billy thought back over his education. He decided to tell the people in the next country that they were going to be burnt. He took the plan from the cabinet and put it in an envelope. He was seen posting the envelope by a suspicious superior. The superior was suspicious because he knew about Billy's criminal background. A special order was issued instructing the postman to open the postbox and hand the envelope to a high official. The high official read the address on the envelope and then opened it. The plan was inside. Billy was shot.

The Fly

There was a poor man who could not pay the rent for his house. The landlord said he must pay it the next day or be thrown out of it. The poor man was in despair. His neighbours were too poor to lend him money.

The poor man said, 'I will walk through the town. Perhaps I will find a coin in the street.' He couldn't think of a more likely way of getting money. He walked through the town but did not find a coin or a brooch or anything of value. The dogs had even run off with the bones.

He was returning home down a narrow street. He did not know the street very well. He looked up at the houses on either side. In the upper window of one sat a man. He was very like the poor man only he smiled. The poor man looked in at the open door. Inside he saw a clean table and three chairs. The table had been carefully laid with plates and knives and spoons. There was even a piece of carpet on the floor. A child played on it with some sticks and stones. In the hearth there was a small fire. The housewife cooked a meal in a black pot. The food smelt good.

The poor man called up to the man in the window.

'You are my age. As it happens you look like me. Our hair is the same colour. I too have a wife and child. We live in the same quarter of our town. I live in a house much like this in the same sort of street. But I have no money.'

The man in the window looked down at the poor man and listened carefully to him.

The poor man went on 'Tomorrow when I can't pay my rent the landlord will throw us out on the street. The winter in these parts is cold. Already the first snow has fallen. We cannot live through winter on the streets!'

A fly settled on the cheek of the man in the window. His face twitched. The poor man saw this and said to himself 'He is moved. Whether by anger or pity I cannot tell.'

The poor man called up.

'We have sold our furniture. We have sold our clothes except for a few rags we dare not sell. We must wear something for decency's sake. Would you have us run through the streets as naked as the dogs? For my work I have a knife, a hammer and a dowel. If I sold these I would not be able to work even if someone wished to hire me. My situation would be without hope. I would never again earn another penny. Have pity on me, townsman.'

The man in the window leant forward. He wanted to hear all that the poor man said. The fly buzzed round his head. He whisked it away angrily with his hand.

The poor man's heart sank. But he went on.

'Perhaps one day your child will not be able to play on the carpet. The fire will not burn in your hearth. Your wife will have nothing to cook in the pot. Your house will not fill with the good smell of food. Misery may come to any man in these hard times. Perhaps you will have to seek for a friend among strangers.

The man in the window craned forward to hear the poor man. The fly settled on his nose. He shook his head angrily to be rid of it.

When the poor man saw this he gave a cry of despair. He turned and ran away down the street.

The man in the window was troubled by the poor man's strange behaviour. Next morning he set out to find him. He asked for a poor man who looked like himself and was that day to be thrown out of his house by the landlord.

Someone soon pointed out the house he was seeking. He knocked at the door. It was opened by a child. He looked into the room. He saw the poor man stretched on the floor. Beside him a woman sat quietly weeping. The man said, 'What is the matter?' The woman answered, 'Last night my husband came home late. In despair he gave me his work tools to sell. Then he killed himself.'

The Tree

When the gods got tired of men they sent an angel to cut down the tree of the world. This tree is called Yggdrasil. When it is cut down the world will die.

The angel was pleased to be of service to the gods. He reached the world and began to walk through the town. Towards evening he felt tired. He saw an old woman watching him from her doorway. She said 'What are you doing?' The angel said 'I am looking for the tree of the world. The gods have sent me to cut it down.'

Now the old woman was ambitious. She said to the angel 'My son is a woodman. He will find the tree and cut it down.'

The angel said 'If your son is a woodman he will be able to cut down the tree more quickly than I can. The gods will be pleased. But the gods told me to bring a piece of the tree to them so that they could know the tree was down.'

The old woman said 'My son will bring a piece of the tree to heaven.'

The angel thanked her. The old woman woke her son early next morning and said to him 'Go quickly and cut down the tree of the world. And don't forget to bring me some of the wood.' She hoped for a great reward when she took it to heaven.

But the gods changed their mind and decided to let men live. When the angel came back and told them the tree was not yet cut down they were glad. They sent him back to the old woman to tell her the tree was not to be cut down.

The old woman was angry when she heard this. She said to herself 'The angel is lying. He wants to take the piece of tree to the gods and get the reward.' She said to the angel 'Hurry along that path. You will reach my son in time to stop him cutting down the tree.' The old woman sent him on the wrong path.

When the son reached Yggdrasil he cut it down. He chopped off some of the tree. The old woman and her son took it to heaven. The gods saw what had been done and were angry. They said to them 'We will not take the wood. But men and women will carry it forever.' That is how death came to the world.

A Dream

(for David Dapra)

A boy walking on the shore saw a grey thread. It ran into the sea. He picked up the end and began to pull. There was a weight on the other end. All the same he managed to pull it fairly easily. After pulling for half an hour there was so much thread on the shore that he decided to roll it into a ball. Otherwise it would have become tangled. He pulled all day. In the evening he went home.

Next day he came back. There was the ball of thread with the end disappearing into the sea. He began to pull and wind. He did this day after day. One day he realised that the thread he was winding was the sea itself. This excited him because it made him ask what was on the end of the thread.

His eyes became skilful. He was able to see that the sea was a thread twisting and winding round itself. Sometimes as he wound the thread snagged. Then he had to tug. Sometimes whole seas or oceans turned over as he tugged on the thread to release it.

The ball became very big. Soon it took up a large part of the world. It was so heavy that the land on which it rested began to dip. Soon the world was shaped like a valley holding the ball of thread and what was left of the sea.

After a time the ball was so big that the sea was only a lake on a little flat shore. The boy worried that if the ball got much larger then one day there might be no more space to hold it left in the world. He went on winding and there was just enough space. One day the boy came to the end of the sea. Fixed to the end there was a hook and on the hook a fish.

The boy was silent when he saw the fish writhing on the dry shore. He picked it up and climbed to the top of the ball of thread. The ball was as big as the world had once been. He sat on top of the world and looked down at the fish. He began to cry. A salty pool formed round the fish and it began to swim. The boy smiled.

The Rotten Apple Tree

An apple tree grew in a garden. This tree bore rotten fruit. From the moment the blossoms withered and the tiny apples began to grow they were rotten. As they grew the rottenness grew with them. They were bruised and soft and had a rank smell. Patches of skin were brown or black and mildew and white fur grew on the patches. The crows loved this rotten fruit. They cawed and tore at it with their beaks. You would think that the man who owned the tree would have cut it down after first having had it examined to see what caused the fruit to rot and to find out how to prevent it infecting other trees. But it was not so. The people of the village heard of the tree and came to see it. Its fame spread. Soon people travelled

to it from far away. At the crossroads signs were erected so
that pilgrims should not lose their way. People prayed to the
tree to punish their enemies and kill their rivals. They brought
the sick to it: crippled children, old blind people and people
who were carried in litters and had not taken one step on the
earth since they were born in it. Stories began to be told. A
blind woman who had touched the bark saw – though a
school of thought held that she had touched a root where it
stuck out of the ground. A barrier was built round the tree so
that the soil in which it grew should not be trampled to dust or
mud. Guardians were appointed to stop worshippers
removing twigs and pieces of bark. Relics were cut from the
tree but these were sold at high prices to potentates, rich
merchants and the intendants of cathedrals. The king sent
pieces of bark to his allies as a special pledge of fidelity. Near
The Garden of The Tree that Bore Rotten Fruit there was an
orchard of apple, plum and pear trees. These were cut down
and burnt and the place where they had stood cemented over
and used as a car park. Hotels were built and trade prospered.
The village grew into a town. Pictures and models of the
sacred tree were sold in the shops, even in breadshops and
greengrocers. Cuttings were taken from the tree and planted
in special places where there were temples for worshippers
and houses in which the keepers of the trees could live. This
transplanting was carefully regulated. It was done so well that
in a few years many places boasted their own Rotten Fruit
Trees. Indeed one city boasted of a small orchard of such
trees. This caused consternation in the town where the first
tree had grown. But its owner was a wise man and he told his
fellow townsmen they had nothing to fear. The more Rotten
Fruit Trees there were the more the mind of the nation would
be turned on Rotten Fruit Trees. And the more the mind of
the nation was turned on Rotten Fruit Trees the more they
would venerate The First Rotten Fruit Tree. Even when it
died and was replaced by one of its saplings people would still
venerate the spot where it had grown. His fellow townsmen
saw the sense of this – especially as he added that there were,
after all, enough people to go round. People began to be
ashamed of apple trees on which good fruit grew. Wives

complained to their husbands about them. Schoolboys threw stones at the windows of houses that stood in gardens where they grew. Crowds of drunken youths swung on their branches to break them. Residents Associations sent letters to those who grew and protected them. All over the country you could hear the sound of the axe. When the people had cut down the good apple trees they cut down the good pear trees, good plum trees and good cherry trees. They tore up the raspberry canes and gooseberry bushes. No one wished to be accused of protecting any tree, bush or shrub that could be regarded as an insult to The Great Bearer of Rotten Apples and all The Lesser Bearers of Rotten Apples that had been grown from it. The day was made dark and the night was made bright by the fires which consumed them. Action Groups of Tree Fellers were trained in the expert use of axe and saw and hauling chain. They began to chop up furniture. First they chopped up furniture made of apple wood. Then because it could be difficult to tell the tree from which the wood had come they chopped up all wooden furniture. Next they chopped up wooden doors, wooden picture frames, wooden fences and every other wooden thing – except for Rotten Apple Trees and their Relics. A faker was arrested for sticking rotten chestnuts on a tree and claiming it to be the first Rotten Nut Tree. After a spectacular trial – during which many women fainted and one woman threw a box of sawdust in the faker's eyes – and which the judge summed up in a voice that quivered as he described the danger in which he saw youth standing – the faker was condemned and shot by bow and arrow on National Rotten Apple Day before a great crowd of people who as a sign of contempt for his heresy had stained their faces, hands, clothes and shoes with the pulp of rotten apples. They ended the day by dancing round a giant effigy of William Tell's Son with a replica of the historic rotten apple on his head – the fact that it was a rotten apple had been established by the researches of the country's leading university. Music for the dancing was provided by a chorus of children dressed as apple leaves. The country is now in a state of high readiness. The people are dedicated to the worship of Old Pippin – as The First Rotten Apple Tree has now

declared itself (through The Senior Oracle) to be named. All
Old Pippin's enemies dwell in fear. They are said to shake like
aspen leaves. The government has declared it an article of
religion and a fact of science that neither the leaves nor the
branches of Rotten Apple Trees shake. The arts of chopping
with the axe and cutting with the saw are zealously taught in
schools and Felling Institutions. Workers are required to
practise felling for the nation for one hour a day after the end
of their normal work. It is true that the nation has run out of
trees – except for rotten apple trees which of course may not
be touched. It has even run out of wood – since the coffins
were removed from churchyards in the Special Night Actions.
So there is nothing left to fell. But as the Leader of the Action
Groups said to a mass rally of Fellers drawn from all parts of
the country and with contingents from abroad 'We are loyal,
devoted, trained and eager for whatever our task may be. We
stand ready with axe in hand. We merely await the order of
our Leader.'

The Call

A woman heard a voice calling from time to time in the
mountains. She would take a short walk into the foothills to
see if she could find who it was that called. Sometimes she was
away whole days. But she did not find who called. She could
not even be sure where the calls came from. There were so
many rocks and slopes and paths. The calls seemed to come
along the paths. But to make it worse sometimes the rocks
seemed to be calling. Perhaps this was the echo. Soon the
woman listened for the call all the time. She would wake up
and lie in bed or go out in the yard and every hour or so hear
quite clearly single shouts coming from the mountains. At last
she decided she would find out who made them. She packed a
few things and went into the mountains. When she had eaten
her provisions she ate wild food. There was plenty of clear
water in the streams. On the lower slopes there were isolated
farms. She would go to the wooden farm houses and ask for
food. In return she was asked to do a little work. Higher up

she met a few goatherds. They gave her milk. When she asked
about the calls they shrugged their shoulders. They had heard
them for so many years that now they ignored them. Only at
first had they set out to search for someone trapped in the
mountains. Now they were certain it was the sound of the
wind or falling rocks amplified by the passes. The woman
thought they were afraid of the calls and went into their huts
and shut the door on the days when the voice called all the
time. The woman went higher, following the paths down
which the calls came. One day she sat on a rock and said 'My
life is now a bundle of sticks tied with a string. I have given up
everything to find the voice.' So she went on. Sometimes on
the higher ranges the sun shone brightly but often there was a
snow-storm or a silent mist that stretched for miles. At such
times she rested in a crevice. She was nearer the voice. Away
from all other noises except those of the wind, springs and
rocks, the call was very clear. She called to it but there was no
answer: there was only every hour or so the same brief, sharp
call. She followed the voice to the highest peak. She stood on
it and was confused. No one else was there. Then she looked
round and because it was the highest peak she could see the
whole world. There was a shout of protest at what she saw.
She realised that the shout came from her own mouth and
that it had always been her voice she had heard on the
mountain. She went down the mountain. It was easier than
climbing up. She did not go to her village. She went on new
travels. At first wherever she went she cried with the short
sharp calls she had heard. Later she learnt to talk to people.
But the sound of the mountain calls never left her voice. She
told those who still mocked her that they had not seen the
world.

On the Pride of Some Who Rule

A ruler sailed back from war to his country. By accident he
dropped his golden ring into the sea. This made him sad at his
homecoming.

A month later fishermen caught a large fish. They took it to the palace and it was cooked for the king. When it was cut open before him there in the stomach was the golden ring.

The king said 'See how the gods favour me!' This pleased him and he was very proud.

When he was a little older he needed to show the people that the gods still loved him. He went to the quay and threw his ring over the sea. A seagull flying in to land saw it glittering as it fell. It snatched it out of the air and flew with it towards the quay. When it found that the thing in its mouth was as hard as stone it dropped it. It landed on the quay at the king's feet. His courtiers marvelled.

The king boasted of his good standing with the gods. To prove it he often threw away his ring. Into crowded streets, dark forests, thickets, swamps, battlefields – it was always returned to him and his courtiers marvelled.

One day he saw a man ploughing a field. He shut his eyes and threw his ring into the field. But the ploughman couldn't plough it up: the ring was lost. The king had the ploughman disposed of and went home. He was not worried. He said 'The ring will be returned to me. I am a favourite of the gods.'

A year later the king was hunting. The huntsmen chased a deer through the forest. It escaped and vanished into the deepest part of the forest where the trees were thickest. The king chased it for a while and then stopped. He wasn't sad. His forests were full of game. He decided to step down from his horse and rest. A wild boar stepped out onto the path. The huntsmen blew their horns. The boar charged and caught the king just as he stepped down from his horse. It gored him fatally in the stomach. On the tusk of the boar that killed him the courtiers found the golden ring.

The Cliffs

The cliffs were proud of their height. They strained to hold their heads even higher. Because of this they could not see clearly what happened at their feet. But they were proud of the constant fawning of the sea. Often the sea would try to run away from them but it would never go far. Always it returned to the foot of the cliffs often more boisterous and fervent than before but sometimes quietened and humbled. The cliffs were stoic and brave as they faced the sky. They regarded with contempt – or compassion – the listless turmoil of the sea, so unstable, so inconstant. And at first they did not know what was happening when one day, their foundations having been burrowed into and eaten out, they fell down into the sea and it washed them away.

Not a Tragedy but an Error, Not an Absurdity but a Mistake

A man may be struck dumb on the day he has learnt a new language. But there are those people who are absurd and tragic in their own behaviour. It's wrong to criticise the world as if it resembled such people. I have in mind those, for example, who climb for the highest apple in the tree. They pick it and carelessly drop it as they look for a higher apple. Then they complain that they have lost the highest apple. Some of them have become so much creatures of habit that they even try to climb into the sky. They reach out on the slender branches and of course they over-reach themselves and fall through the tree. We find them lying dead in the grass beside the apple they had picked and dropped. But it would be ridiculous to call the *tree* tragic or absurd.

A Man Sat on a Gate

A man sat on a gate to watch the world go by. He sat there so long and grew so fat that the gate fell off its hinges. The man toppled over backwards and lay on the ground with his mouth open. From then on he lay there. No doubt he studied the great engine of the universe as it displayed itself to him in the sky but as he was unable to move his mouth to speak or his hands to write (the fall had paralysed him) he was unable to tell us. Eventually a bird nested in his open mouth. It would be pleasant to say that the birds who were hatched and reared so close to what might well have been the fountain of truth had the secrets of the engine whispered to them and carried it aloft on their wings. But it would never be true to say this.

The Wise Man Who Broke His Vow

A man vowed as a protest against the war of the rich on the poor that he would not open his eyes till the people had won justice. Many things happened that might have made him open his eyes in surprise. A car crashed. A door shut on his hand. A wasp stung him. A dog bit his leg. People shouted at him for being a fool. His wife and children pleaded with him. His dying mother asked him to look at her. Then there was the weariness of walking the streets like a blind man. Many of the things that had once been easy to do now became labours. In all this he kept his eyes closed.

One day as he passed an open doorway he heard a mother on the doorstep saying farewell to her son as he stepped into the street. The man learnt from their farewell that the son was a poorman going to fight for the rich against the poor. His mother told him he must obey his officers like a good boy and be brave. The man who had vowed to shut his eyes said 'The sight of some things is more terrible than blindness. And I must look at them.' He opened his eyes and watched the soldier in his smart uniform, with the buttons shining as brightly as his eyes, as he smartly marched away down the street to fight for the rich against the poor. The man said 'I was a fool to shut my eyes. I must see these things so that I will never stop fighting for the poor against the rich.'

Water

In a certain city there had been for many hundreds of years a shortage of water. This caused disease and other suffering to the citizens. Each spring there was a heavy rainfall and the silent people watched the precious life-stream running in gutters that would soon be as dry as bone. In time modern machines were constructed. There were new spinning factories and iron foundries in the city. These places needed more water and so did the new workers. The city's rulers were practical and philanthropic men. They used their new machines to build a dam in the hills over the city. The dam collected all the water the city needed. Unfortunately, when the spring rains fell, the lake behind the dam became too full. There was a danger that the pressure of water would explode and engulf the city in sudden destruction. The dam wall shook like the hand of a sick man. This terrified the workers and some of them ran away from the factories and lived in the hills. In the general panic there was rioting and looting. Priests held special services. Factory owners called on the government to enforce law and order.

As the rulers of the city had been clever enough to build the dam they ought to have been clever enough to make it safe. They might have built aqueducts to take the water safely round the city or through the parks and squares to make them beautiful with lakes and fountains. But understand that there was panic and fear of collapse. In such times rulers don't blame the machinery of society but its people. Indeed they look on disaster as a test of national spirit. So instead of reconstructing the dam the rulers called on the citizens to serve their city with greater efforts: they were to drink more water.

Water drinking festivals were organised. Drinking squads patrolled the streets. The good citizen was seen at all times sipping from a glass of water in his hand. Medals were given to those who consumed large quantities. It's surprising what well-intentioned and public-spirited individuals can do on such occasions. One man drank fifty gallons of water each week for three weeks running before he drowned internally. He asked to be buried in a bath. There was much washing of the person and of possessions. People whose curtains were not constantly dripping could expect to have their windows broken by groups of young pioneers who were called The Water Babies. As the whole city was damp and as people went about in clothes that had been laundered to shreds and slept in damp beds, there was a lot of influenza about. Newspapers published daily casualty lists. These showed great increases in the number of cases of pneumonia. People also suffered from water on the knee and on the brain. Because the door-steps and streets were washed so often, many people slipped and the casualty service had to deal with sprained ankles and broken legs and backs. Of course the wounded – who had already made the sacrifice – could no longer drink very much or wash very often. The burden fell more heavily on the rest.

About this time patriotic people began to set fire to their houses so that firemen could hose them down. Loyalists also burnt public buildings such as galleries, museums and schools. Nothing could be allowed to impede the city's efforts. National security was at stake. We can confidently say that the people's morale was never higher. And it worked. The level of water behind the dam fell. This overwhelming argument was used against those few disruptive elements who asked whether there might not be an easier way of controlling the dam. The dam wall no longer trembled. Dissenters were taken to their cell windows and made to stare up at it and declare that it stood as firm as a rock. Every day the media reminded the people of the days when the dam had been called Old Palsied and they had lived in fear of The Burst. Things were going well. All the more reason, then, for the massive outbreak of dropsy to come as such a severe blow to the regime. This blow was followed by another: people began to burst. The rulers even wondered if the people could hold out. As the governor looked from his window he saw passers-by fall over in the streets and roll to the side of houses and lie there for minutes at a time without drinking. Perhaps there were inherent weaknesses in the national character. How could such a nation survive?

The governor himself felt worn out by the struggle against water. He decided to address the people – perhaps, he told himself, for the last time. The Water Police rounded up the survivors and assembled them on the main square. The governor was surprised at the smallness of the crowd. If the people had not been so bloated he would have seen that it was even smaller than he thought. As the governor spoke one or two exploded. A new illness had broken out: a fever which heated the blood and so caused the water to boil. Sufferers

emitted large amounts of steam and a high whistling scream
from their ears, mouth, nose and anus till their bodies burst.
The governor spoke with great dignity, raising his voice over
the screaming, blurping, plopping, pissing and exploding.
'Fellow citizens! This morning the figures were delivered to
my desk. The level of water in the dam is now so low that –
should any of you survive – you will be assured of three whole
years without danger of a dam burst. What the future holds
beyond then we cannot tell, but these three years are safe – no
matter how much rain falls! Citizens I salute your great
victory! God bless us!' He then became over-heated with
patriotic fervour and began to boil. He screamed and emitted
a cloud of steam. The crowd had counted up to five before he
exploded. As spring rainclouds gathered on the hills water
police went among the crowd using the new-fangled hose-and-
pump contraptions that had recently been introduced to
enable them to pump water down the gullet of those who,
however willing, were unable to swallow any more.

There was a Cunning Wealthy Man

There was a cunning wealthy man who coveted a poorman's
house. The poorman did not wish to sell it. It was where he
and his wife and children lived. They would have great
trouble in finding another house. But the cunning rich man
was determined to get the house. He did not wish to give
money for it. Instead he waylaid the man. He did this himself
because although he was wealthy he did not like to pay others
to do work he could do himself. One evening he waited in a
shop doorway. He stepped out as the man passed and killed
him with a cudgel. He left his body in the street. The dead
man's wife saw this. She had been watching in a window of
the house for his return. Her neighbours pitied her but they
would do nothing against the murderer. He was too powerful.
He sent his bullies round to the house and they chased the
woman and her children into the street. He had to pay the
woman a little money or his title to the house would not have
been legal. But he paid her less than he would have paid her

husband because he said her story that he had killed him had given him a bad name.

Now the rich man wished to take up public office. His friends in the government were worried. They wished all officials to appear as men of honour. The woman's stories had blackened him. The cunning man said he would stand trial so that his name might be cleared. Then he would become the government's good servant. He was to be in charge of social services. So his friends charged him with the poorman's murder. He briefed a great lawyer who was as cunning and powerful as himself. In the meantime he heard that the poorman's widow had died of misery and exposure or something. This made the case against him even weaker. Now all the evidence would be hearsay. It is true that the dead man's children were also witnesses of the crime. They had been waiting in the doorway of their house for their father's return. But as yet they had not learnt to speak and could only cry when they saw the cunning man. And so the lawyer went into court with his fat brief under one arm and his cunning friend's arm under the other. And then happened one of those things that our experience of life does not lead us to expect. As the cunning man entered the court he looked up. There in the judge's chair for all to see was the ghost of the dead woman – pointing her finger at him.

Now this story is not true. People do not come back from the dead armed with a power to do those things they did not do, either from weakness or neglect, when they were alive. If justice was to be done to the memory of the dead man and woman, and the house restored to their children, this would have to be done by the neighbours.

Incident on the Island of Aigge

A fisherman on the island of Aigge was caught carrying the carcass of a sheep which was the property of the Laird of Aigge. He was hanged for sheep stealing. His body was left on a gibbet by the shore. As he was hanged on the afternoon of the day he was caught his wife did not know he had been hanged when a message reached her telling her to collect his body for burial.

The woman had a child of seven months. She had no neighbour to mind it and so she took it with her in the boat when she went to collect her husband's body. When she was three-quarters of the way across the bay she could see the body hanging on the gibbet on the shore. The child slept, nursed by the rocking of the boat.

She beached the boat and with his fisherman's knife she cut down her husband from the gibbet. There was no one on the beach to help her and so she partly lifted and partly hauled the body to the boat. Its feet dragged on the shingles.

She lay the body on the bottom of the boat and as there was little room she lay the child on its father's breast. The child felt the human body and mistook the rocking of the boat for being rocked in its arms and so it reached out to embrace it. It happened that the child's warmth warmed the man's throat and chest. It was this and perhaps also the rocking of the boat that stirred a glimmering of life in the man. The hardships he had lived through had made him strong and even on the rope he had clutched to himself a last draining of life. The woman saw the man's hand move on the child's back. She rested the oars on the bottom of the boat and chafed and rubbed his body. Soon she heard his faint breathing. When she got home she wrapped him in a blanket by the fire and in a few days he had recovered. In this way the child gave life to its father even before it could speak its father's name.

The Letter

One day just before she went to bed a woman looked through her bedroom window at the sky. It was covered with mist. There was a full moon and a patch of moonlight shone through the mist. It reminded the woman of the circle of churning water left by someone who had thrown themself from a bridge. Immediately she thought of her daughter. She had married and gone with her husband to live in a distant town. The woman said 'I have not heard from her for months.

I would like to know how she is. Tomorrow I will write to her.'
The next day the woman was busy. She worked in a factory
and cooked for her husband and ran their home. So she did
not write.

The day after she was shopping and saw in a shop window
the naked body of a dummy lying on the floor. Its arms were
awkwardly bent. A man knelt beside it. Immediately the
woman thought of her daughter and wondered how she was.
She said 'I will write to her this evening.' That evening she did
the washing and ironing.

The next day the woman heard that fifty of the newer girls
at the factory were to be sacked. She saw one of them leaving
the factory. She carried an empty shopping bag and her face
was white. She had lately moved into a new house. She and
her husband had both worked and so had been able to afford
the mortgage repayments. Again the woman thought of her
daughter. She said 'I wonder how she manages in these hard
times? Tomorrow is Saturday and I will write.' On Saturday
the woman finished her weekly cleaning before lunch. After
lunch she sat down for a short rest. She said 'Have I told her
her cousin has had a baby? I must think what to write to her.
She'll be as worried about me as I am about her. I must
reassure her. Perhaps there'll be no more sackings at the
factory . . .' The woman was tired and dozed till her husband
came in and woke her. She cooked their supper and after that
there was no time to write.

On Sunday she felt rested. She cleared a space on the
corner of the kitchen table. She looked in the shoe box where
she kept a writing pad and envelopes. It was empty. She went
next door to her neighbour Mrs Harrison to borrow some
paper and an envelope but Mrs Harrison didn't have any.

Fortunately when the woman got home from work on
Monday there was a letter from her daughter on the doormat.
She made herself a cup of tea and sat at the table to read the
letter. Her daughter was well and getting on with her husband. Both of them had work. She was friendly with her
neighbours. The weather in the North was colder than at
home but she was getting used to it.

The woman's tea was stronger than the canteen tea and she

enjoyed it. She picked up the newspaper and began to read. A fly settled on a photograph of an African family massacred in their village.

Service

The form came in the morning post. It was printed on better paper than most forms. There was also a brochure explaining the duties of jurors and their role in the administration of the law. Part of the form was to be sent back. He was asked to state on this part his willingness to serve or his reasons for asking to be excused. He didn't think very seriously about it. He wrote down his reasons for asking to be excused and sent the form back.

A week later another form came. It said the official who sent the forms couldn't accept his reasons and he would have to serve. But the form said there was an automatic reconsideration of the official's decision. This was made by a judge in chambers. He could attend and explain his reasons to the judge. But he did not have to attend. If he did not attend the judge would make his decision on the reasons written on the form. He decided to attend.

The new form said he should report to the court at 10.15. He got there on time. There were a few policemen in the corridor outside and two women reading a notice pinned to the wall by the court door. He looked through the glass panel of the court door. He could see along one side of the court. It was empty. It reminded him of a glass aquarium. He went out into the street and looked in the window of a record shop. One of the covers showed a pistol being fired straight at the spectator.

He went back. He was going to ask the policeman at the door where he should go but he didn't. His name wasn't on the list of names on the notice pinned by the door. He didn't know the other names. About thirty people were there now. A young man leant against a wall. He was wearing a brown wool shirt and blue jeans. He had a small empty push-pram in front of him. The hood and sides were bright blue. He was holding

the rail with both hands. He looked at the man and noticed
with quiet shock that the man was afraid. There were a few
women on a bench. They were wearing best clothes and
they'd done special things with their hair and this made them
look rather ugly. They were silent. A man with well creased
trousers was reading a *Daily Express*. There were two male
ushers in black gowns. They were old, retired men making a
little pocket money. They chatted in a quiet relaxed way like
discreet porters in a Pall Mall Club. There was also a woman
usher for the children's court. She was middle-aged and had
blonde hair and a nice efficient face. A door opened and some
barristers shot out and swept towards him. Most of them were
young. He supposed the older barristers usually went to bigger
courts. They wore black gowns and little wigs tightly curled
like the hair of the women on the bench. The wigs were grey
and this made the young men look strange. They didn't look
at the people waiting in the corridor. Perhaps they were going
to see clients in the cells. The young man with the pram still
leant against the wall and he looked up as the lawyers passed.
One of the women tugged at her skirt to smooth it.

Suddenly he walked out. He strolled round the market in
front of the court. It was sunny. He stayed there ten minutes.
Then he went home.

A few days later a registered letter came. He was summoned
to explain why he had failed to attend as a juror. 10.15 in a
week's time. Penalty £100.

So in a week's time he went back. He didn't bother to get
there till 10.30. There were about ten people waiting. He
recognised some of them. They'd been there on his first visit.
That had been on the opening day of the new sessions. Now
even the ordinary citizens seemed a bit more at home. They
had learnt some nonchalance. Perhaps from imitating the
lawyers. But their little smiles seemed awkward and their
relaxed poses still slightly uncomfortable. The glossy smiles of
people in hospital. He felt more at home too. He began
making little jokes to himself. Chin up, as the hangman said to
the victim.

A dark figure came into the light at the end of the corridor.
A tall man in a dark blue suit. The face was hidden against the

light but it was obviously round. He carried a heavy
briefcase and in the other hand a lumpily rolled umbrella.
He held the umbrella up in the air so that the ferrule was
about eighteen inches off the ground. But the odder thing
was his hat. It was an old-fashioned hat. A bit like a pork-pie
but formal and dark. He hadn't seen a hat like that before.
The man nodded to the policeman and went through a small
door that obviously led to the back of the court. There was
an air of caricature about the man – and he knew
immediately it was the judge. He didn't like that. He didn't
like people to look their role so exactly that they seemed to
be imitating themselves.

   He asked the usher where he should go. The usher already
knew about him and had been told his name. The usher was
very polite. He said the jury in waiting would soon be called
into court and he was to go in with them and sit on the bench
in front of them.

   During the week he'd phoned an organisation concerned
with civil liberties. They'd said there was no modern precedent. But if he served he could return whatever verdict he
liked. Even a verdict against the evidence. Even though you
had to take the juror's oath? There was a precedent for it. The
seventeenth century. Penn and another Quaker. A jury had
refused to convict them for refusing to serve on a jury. A judge
had locked the jury up without bread or water. But they still
refused to convict . . . It wasn't only a matter of £100. That
was for refusing to answer the summons to appear. If he now
appeared and still refused to serve that would be contempt of
court. Prison. Till you apologised. Or agreed to serve? And a
friend explained to him that if you said it was your busy time
at work or your grandmother was dying, they'd always excuse
you. But if you objected on principle, that was a challenge.
And the judge wouldn't ignore that. Dying grandmother – the
juror's Chiltern Hundreds. He was making these jokes to
himself because he was nervous.

   The usher said 'Let's go' and the jury hurried into court.
The space between the side of the dock and the benches was
small so they had to walk in single file. He walked at the end.
He hadn't walked in single file since he was in the army. The

judge came in. Everyone stood up. The judge wore a grey robe with red and blue sashes crossed on his chest. He had a small grey wig. He was plumpish and his round face was red. The man hated all these details. It seemed so threatening, almost malicious, to appear so true to type.

The judge, the lawyers, and some of the jurymen bowed to each other. Then they all sat down. Suddenly a door opened somewhere at the back behind the dock. Two policewomen came out. They wore navy blue skirts, pale blue shirts with metal buttons and badges, and smart white and navy blue bonnets. Two healthy-looking blondes. With them they had a thin woman with a bony face and dark eyes, narrow little shoulders and bony hands. About fifty. She was wearing a dark blue overall-dress with thin red piping round all the edges. It was quite smart and fitted fairly well. It might have been designed by an airline for the cleaning women to wear when they cleaned the empty planes between flights. He didn't realise before she went into the dock and stood between the two policewomen that she was the accused.

The clerk told him to stand. The judge looked up from his papers. The judge smiled at him and asked why he had failed to attend as a juror. His voice was puzzled and kind. As if he was talking to a child who'd trod on his toe.

The man took the forms from his pocket. He was surprised to see that his hand shook. He leant against the side of the dock to steady himself. He explained that he had been told he could attend a hearing of an appeal against the official's refusal to excuse him service. (He didn't say he had attended but had gone away – in despair at seeing the frightened man with the empty pram and the lonely women on the bench.) He read the details from the form. The judge started to hunt in his file for his copy. His voice trailed away and he waited for the judge's attention. He said 'If I could go on . . . ?' He was surprised to hear himself using this lawyer's phrase. The judge went on searching and the silence lasted. The judge found the form and looked up. Still shaking, he read out the new summons about the £100 and about failing to attend when summoned and said 'But I don't think I was summoned. The second summons was incorrect. I hadn't been summoned to appear as a juror – only to hear the appeal. And the form said I needn't attend if I didn't want to.' There was a silence. Of course all these details weren't important. They had nothing to do with his reason for refusing to serve. But he was indignant that a false summons could be issued so easily. Where was truth if even in little things it – ? The judge said, 'I see you were under a misunderstanding about this summons and I will take no further action on it' – he smiled kindly – 'but there is still the matter of your refusal to serve as a juror. I've read the reasons you give on the acknowledgement form and I must tell you I cannot excuse you on those grounds.' The judge smiled again.

No, he thought. He still doesn't say it right. I was not under a misunderstanding about the second summons. *He* was. It was falsely issued. He was indignant that even this small truth couldn't be seen and respected. He looked across at the woman in the dock. Her eyes with the little dark pupils were staring straight ahead at the judge. She had been brought up from the cells and made to stand and listen to all this. Was she relieved to have her case put off for ten minutes? Or angry at being made to stand there while he talked about the first summons and the second summons and the appeal and the reasons?

A group of schoolchildren were packed into one box. They were there as part of their civic studies. To see how the court worked and how everyone had a chance to speak.

The judge smiled gently and said, 'Would you like to add anything to the reasons you state on the form?'

He was confused. He wasn't prepared. The form said he would be heard by a judge in chambers. But they were in open court. And he couldn't understand why he was so agitated. What more could he say? The reasons given on the form were perfectly adequate. They were enough for him. Why not for the judge? He said. 'No – just the moral and political reasons I put on the form.'

The judge was speaking again. 'Many people of different political persuasions . . . differing moral outlooks serve on the . . . Perhaps the last civic duty the citizens of this country are

still called upon to . . . Freedom of our courts . . . The protec-
tion of the interests of the accused . . . '

He looked at the schoolchildren crammed in the box.
Everyone here had public, court expressions. How could he
tell what they were thinking? They might have been staring at
a film he couldn't see.

In another box on their own were a girl and a young man.
In Sunday best. Hair groomed. Staring at him and then at the
woman in the dock. He knew immediately they were her
children. Fair hair and blue eyes – and she was dark with tiny
black pupils. But there must still be some family likeness he
could sense. There was no man there. Perhaps she was a
widow.

'. . . so that perhaps you were unaware that you are not
required to decide on legal or moral matters but purely on
questions of fact – '.

'But I dealt with that in the reasons I put on the form. I said
I couldn't agree with you what facts would be relevant. You
want the record of a crime to begin at the time when the
criminal thought of it. I want to know more. I said – there on
the form – that when you desocialise people in schools – when
you take away their responsibility in their work – how can you
be surprised when they act anti-socially . . . ?'

The small court seemed to get larger. He could breathe in
it. And although it seemed larger he didn't feel so lost. The
judge and he started to argue.

Suddenly he remembered what had been in the back of his
mind since he read the first form weeks ago. Two furniture
vans were being driven across Germany. The windows had
been sealed up and the sides reinforced. They had been
requisitioned by the SS. They were driven through busy little
towns and along open country roads all day till it was dark.
Then they'd been parked in front of a row of little houses out
in the open. The houses were separated from the road by a
wide grass verge. The houses were dark because of the war.
The lorry drivers had a smoke and stretched themselves across
their seats to sleep. In the night the Jews in the vans had
started to scratch and beat on the sides. They called for water,
not even for something to eat. No light came on in the row of

houses, no door opened, no curtain was pulled aside. The Jews were too weak and afraid to make much noise. The lorry drivers didn't even bother to shout at them – the vans were sealed anyway so the lorry drivers couldn't have carried out any threats even if they'd made them except perhaps to jolt them and give them a rough ride the next day. And the grass verge between the vans and the houses was wide. But still, the people in the houses had heard the Jews. In the morning the lorry drivers smoked a cigarette, started their lorries and drove to the crematorium.

It wasn't a good argument with the judge. Saint Joan would have done better. It ended in a silly way. The judge said unsmilingly 'You will serve,' and he said 'I will not'. The judge looked away and began to count to ten. He waited like a sheep until the judge had got to three before he said 'So what are you going to do about it?'

From time to time during the argument the lawyers sitting below the judge's bench had slowly turned round to look at him. Now they all stared at the judge.

The judge said 'I strongly advise you to sit down and wait to see if your name is called. Then, should they so wish it will be open to either the prosecution or the defence to object to your being on the jury. Either side may object to seven jurors without even giving a reason for doing so.'

For a moment he was puzzled. Was it a game?

The judge said, 'Perhaps your name won't even be called.'

He said angrily 'I hope not!' He sat down. He was still bewildered. He was unsure of what was happening.

The clerk of the court stood up. He took an envelope from the desk. He took a slip of paper from it and read out the name on it. A juror-in-waiting stood up, crossed the court, and went into the witness box. He'd seen him several times in the streets. He was a van driver for the town's biggest multiple store – a friendly-looking man who wore good jackets and ties because he got them on discount. The clerk took another slip from the envelope.

When his name was called he would go quietly into the jury box. The judge would pretend that nothing unusual had happened but he would grunt to himself with satisfaction that the force of the law had been upheld. Or probably he would sigh and smile with genuine contentment that the difficult juror had finally been sensible – as most people were in the end. But when the Bible was put into his hand for the oath he would ask the judge 'What book is this?'

The judge: 'The Bible'.

'Unlike my fellow jurors I haven't read it. Or even held it in my hand recently till now. I am perfectly prepared to swear on it. But I must read it first.'

The judge: 'How long will you need?'

'It's a thick book on very thin paper and I see that it starts with the words "In the beginning God created the heaven and earth". It's obviously going to be a long story and I shall need at least two years.' And he would refuse to affirm instead of swearing because that would mark him off from the other jurors and put him at a disadvantage in their discussions. The judge would then threaten him with contempt of court and he would say 'If I were a judge, I would regard only one thing as contempt of my court: when someone didn't tell the truth in it. I have told the truth.' That would have done for Saint Joan.

The clerk put his hand into the envelope for the twelfth paper. Their eyes met. The judge was busy with his files. His name wasn't on it.

And so there was to be no confrontation. Instead the argument about truth had been disposed of by a game of administrative tiddly-winks. It seemed to have little to do with the dignity of the law. Just a piece of thieves' cunning. He sat on the bench and felt as crumpled as an empty sweet bag. Had his name even been in the envelope? It was so easy to avoid an unprofitable complication by a little official dexterity.

Each juror took the Bible and swore the oath. He'd expected starched collars but some of them were in shirt sleeves and without ties. A friend at work had said that he would have sat on the jury and refused to convict. But that had now been taken care of by more tiddly-winks: majority verdicts.

Everyone listened while the indictment and charges were read. The charges repeated the indictment but added more details. There were twenty-one charges. The woman answered

not guilty to all of them. She was an accountant accused of
taking her employers' money.

The judge dismissed the jurors who hadn't been called. He
apologised to them. He explained that it would be undemo-
cratic to call only the exact number of jurors needed. It was a
small town and some of them might have known the accused.
The judge smiled when he said that of course he understood
some of them were naturally disappointed at not being able to
have a go . . .

He was surprised at the judge's words. He might have used
an expression that didn't suggest the funfair.

A Man in Ruins

Afterwards most of the city was ruins. People lived in houses in
the narrow band of suburbs that ringed the ruins and beyond
that in camps of tents and huts. The centre of the city was a
great ruined world. In the few years that had passed the
weather had worn down the jagged edges. It had bleached the
rubble and the few bits of low-standing wall. Everything was
the dull grey of sea on a nondescript day. It was a landscape of
rubble dunes. Because the destruction had been evenly spread
out all the heaps were almost the same size. Fireweed, docks,
nettles and a few thistles grew in the brick dust and in cracks
in the walls and fallen concrete slabs.

The people living on the edge of the ruins did not go into
them. There was fear – that the ruins were contaminated, that
there were unexploded shells and bombs and grenades. And
there was fear of ghosts and of walking on human bones and
ash.

A man lived in the ruins. He looked as if he were made from
the ruins. His jacket and trousers were the same faded, dirty
blue-grey as the rubble. So were his face and hands. His boots
looked like clumps of clinker bleached by scorching. He moved
over the rubble dunes with the gawky agility of an old goat.

When the municipal council was reinstituted it posted no
entry signs round the ruins. SolPol patrols kept an eye on
them. At first whenever they saw him they shouted and blew

whistles. The man tottered rapidly away. The SolPols followed him. After running up and down the dunes they entered a corner of a house or part of an alley or yard. There was never anyone there or any sign of anyone having been there for a long while. So the SolPols went back to the perimeter patrol. After a few days they did not see the man any more. He had learnt where the SolPols patrolled. He knew their times. He kept away from them. He hid in the vast ruins. The SolPol major said the man must be a survivor or a deserter. Either way he had lived in the ruins for years. He was contaminated and a lunatic. He would die in the ruins.

The man had made a settlement for himself in the deepest part of the ruins. He had found a corner of a room. Three walls were more than man-high. The two side walls sloped. They were lower at the ends where the fourth wall would have been. It had been blown away. There were still windowsills and marks on the walls where cupboards had been fixed. They had been burnt as firewood. In one wall there was the gap of an empty doorway. The door lay in the rubble. The man set the door on two stacks of bricks. That was his table. He used a wooden crate as a chair. He slept on a scrap of carpet against a wall. He made fires. He struck flints into stalks of dry weeds and built up the flames with wooden slats and bits of posts. To one side the top of an arch stuck from the ground. It had been part of a cellar or vault which now was filled with rubble. In bad weather the man slept under the arch. He trapped water in buckets and sinks. The ruined gardens had survived and seeded. He lived on vegetables and fruit. He found bits of soap, razors, pages from books.

One day he sat in his settlement. He had found a screwdriver with a yellow handle. The shaft was bent. He banged it with a stone to straighten it. He looked up. A black dog stood in a clearing outside the rubble. It watched him through the empty doorway. The man and dog stared at one another. The man put down the screwdriver. He leant across the table to pick up an apple core. He threw it at the ground before the dog. The dog lurched – startled. Even before the core had landed the dog had vanished into the ruins. Ah yes said the man. He went out through the doorway and climbed a rubble dune. He could not see the dog.

Now the dog knew the man was there. The man did not see the dog when he went foraging. He thought at night the dog slept close to the settlement. He didn't find any marks. No paw-prints, no droppings. Sometimes in the morning he caught a faint smell of dog.

A few weeks later the man was looking in his mirror. It was a piece of mirror about twice as large as his face. It was a corner of a much larger mirror. The man recalled a story. You looked into a mirror and it showed you the answers to your questions. The man wondered who had lived here before him. He made up a family. Two parents and three children. He tried to hear their voices. All the mirror showed, though, was his face and the ruins behind him. If he moved the mirror sharply – jerked it – the bits of wall caught in it seemed to fall down again. Then he saw the dog in the mirror. It stood on a rubble dune opposite the side where there was no wall. The man put down the mirror. He turned. He stared at the dog. It stared at him. The man bent down to the ground and picked up a cabbage stalk. He threw it on the ground a few yards to the dog's side. The dog's eyes switched to it. They stared at the stalk. Now and then they flicked back to the man. After a long while – there were no clocks in the ruins – the dog stretched its front paws along the ground in front of it. It rested its jaw on the paws. Its brow wrinkled and twitched. Its tail was still. The man stood up. The dog lifted its head. It stiffened. The man went to the stalk. He picked it up. He tossed it to the foot of the mound – closer to the dog. The man went back into his settlement. He got on with tidying things. He did not look at the dog. After a while the dog stood. It came down the side of the mound. Its slither dislodged a few bits of brick and a rivulet of dust. It picked up the stalk in its mouth. It trotted to the side. It lay down. It held the stalk in its front paws. It licked and chewed it as if it were a bone. Its eyes stayed on the man. The man went on with his work. The dog swallowed what was left of the stalk. It tossed up its head as its jaws snapped at the last shreds. Beads of spittle were strung between its fangs. It stopped for a moment. Suddenly it leapt backwards and dashed into the ruins.

After that the dog came regularly for scraps. One day the man returned from foraging. He had an old carpenter's tool bag. He carried his booty in it. The dog was waiting on its dune. The man went into his settlement. The dog followed him. The man put his bag on the floor and sat by it. He took off his coat. The dog came up to him. It stuck its head into the bag and poked about with its snout. The man emptied the bag onto the ground. The dog helped itself to a potato.

These were hard times for the dog. Once there had been bodies in the ruins to dig out and eat. Then bones to crack to get at the marrow. Now there were only vegetables and trash. The dog was grateful to the man. But it did not come into the settlement to sleep. It slept outside by the empty doorway. The man wondered if the dog had been a puppy in the house before it had been ruined. Or it might have come here later. A stray from the suburbs.

In this way the old man and the black dog lived in the ruins for more than a year. There were new rumours in the suburbs. People were still afraid of the ruins. Of diseases and explosions. But people said money and other valuables were buried in the ruins. There had been a rich quarter. Even the servants had been better off than the people in the old slums. So gangs of young men started going into the ruins. That was a crime because it was still forbidden. But the young men were desperadoes. They carried spades and jemmies and knives. They always wore black. One day the man saw them. To him they seemed like a little mob of black crows pecking in the rubble. He kept out of sight. He hurried back to his settlement. He sat there in silence. The dog stared at him. It did not understand the man's stillness. Or why he came back with nothing to eat.

One morning the man was shaving. He dipped the razor in the mug of water and stared into the mirror. The dog lay at his side toothing through the hair on its paws. The man heard a call. It was answered from further away. The man realised that the men were close to his settlement. He put the razor in the mug. He threw away the water. He put a stone slab on the fire. He gestured to the dog: 'Leave – leave.' The dog stared at him. The man hurried out through the empty doorway. He looked back. The dog's head was raised. Its ears were pricked. The man hurried into the ruins.

He went further off. He thought he would not hide nearby. He would go a long way away and spend the day there. If they found his settlement nothing would come of it. They wouldn't waste time hunting for him. There was nothing worth stealing. If they stole anything he would replace it from the heaps of rubbish. But in the end he didn't go very far. He seemed to be circling backwards and forwards along the same few ruined streets and tracks. About an hour later he heard a shout. There was a moment's silence. Then a howl. Clear and unmistakable. It rose over the ruins. Like an aural star. A shooting star by day. The man stood still in the silence. He saw his unmoving shadow on the rubble. It seemed like a body floating underwater. He moved to the side and stood against a wall. He stared at his hand on the bricks. What should he do? He was empty. There was a great hollowness inside him. He told himself it was a man's howl. Perhaps one of the men was playing with the dog. The men had found the settlement. The tables and boxes. The warm fire stone. Probably in the suburbs there were stories about him. Perhaps the men had come looking for him. SolPol knew he was there – in the ruins where he ought not to be. There would be a reward for his capture. The captors would say they'd been outside the perimeter. Not scavenging in the ruins. Then they saw him. That's why they broke regulations and went in the ruins after him. And they caught him because they were fed and fit and ran faster than he did.

The man went deeper and deeper into the ruins. He stayed there till it was night. He started to go back in the dark. He wasn't used to the ruins in the dark. There wasn't much moon. He kept losing his way. He thought he might sleep out there. Go back in the morning. But if the men now knew where he lived, wouldn't they come back and – ? He went on. He came to the place where he'd first stopped in the morning. That was the wall. It seemed strange. He paused. He wondered what had been done there in the past. Had prisoners huddled against the wall to wait for transport? Or hostages been shot? At least now he knew where he was. He made his way towards his settlement. Perhaps the dog would come out of a shadow. He stopped. He listened. Nothing. Silently he went round and round the walls. He kept some distance off. He couldn't see or hear anything unusual. Perhaps the men were asleep inside. If he whistled low to the dog? But he had never whistled to the dog. He had never spoken to it. And the dog had made no sounds to him. If he whistled would the dog bark? Wake the men? Perhaps the dog was deaf and dumb? It managed because dogs lived by their nose.

It was dawn. He went into the settlement through the open side. The crate-chair had been stamped into matchwood. The table had been thrown over. The mirror had been shattered against a wall. In the low light the shards gleamed like silk. There was a snake-track of urine in the dust. By the arch lay the shape of the dog. The man sat on the floor with his back to the wall. There was no thought in his head. He did not regret the damage to his settlement. He did not wonder about the dog. He did not wonder about himself. Or the ruins or suburbs.

It was lighter. He saw the damage more clearly. But it told him nothing more. The urine track had dried. It looked like an old scar in the dust. The dog did not move. The man wondered if the men might be watching from the rubble. Why would they bother? They were gone. If there was a reward they'd have grabbed him as soon as they saw him. He picked up the glass shards and threw them aside. Out of the way where they wouldn't be trod on. He went to the dog. It was lying stretched out. Not moving. He bent down. He pushed his hand under the dark fur. Wet. Piss. The body was cold. Heavy. He turned it over. The neck was stiff – as the body turned it was as if the dog lifted its head. Its tongue stuck from the side of its jaws. It had bitten through it. He saw the sharp teeth. The eyes were open. The yellow plastic handle stuck from its temple. The screwdriver had been hammered into it.

The man went to a garden plot where he knew there was a rope. He tugged it to test for strength. It had not started to rot. He carried the rope back to the ruins. He did not look at the dog. He dragged the door over the rubble. He set it under a piece of joist that stuck out of the highest wall. He rebuilt the bricks in two stacks. He laid the door across them. He climbed onto it. He reached up and tied an end of the rope to the joist. He wound the other end round his neck. He knotted it. Out of the corner of his eye he could have seen the dog but he did not look. He stood on the edge of the door. He made a great leap straight up into the air. As he crashed down he kicked back at the edge of the door as he had planned. The crash sounded through the ruins. The door lurched back. Tilted up in the air and stopped. It was wedged on the ground. As the man fell his boots hit against it. Crash crash. The man swung. Knock knock. The swing became gentler. Tap tap. The boots went on tapping after the heart had stopped. The man turned. The boots scuffed against the door with a scratching sound. The scuffing and scratching stopped. The man was still. The dog lay in the corner. The yellow handle of the screwdriver stuck from its head.